RESIDENTIAL FRAMING

A HOMEBUILDER'S CONSTRUCTION GUIDE

William P. Spence

Sterling Publishing Co., Inc. New York

This book is set in Caledonia.

Library of Congress Cataloging-in-Publication Data

Spence, William Perkins, 1925–
    Residential framing : a homebuilder's construction guide / William
P. Spence.
        p.   cm.
    Includes index.
    ISBN 0-8069-8594-1
    1. House framing.   I. Title.
TH2301.S64   1993
694'.2—dc20   93-15960
                                                                          CIP

Edited by Rodman P. Neumann

10   9   8   7   6   5   4   3   2   1

Published in 1993 by Sterling Publishing Company, Inc.
387 Park Avenue South, New York, N.Y. 10016
© 1993 by William P. Spence
Distributed in Canada by Sterling Publishing
c/o Canadian Manda Group, P.O. Box 920, Station U
Toronto, Ontario, Canada M8Z 5P9
Distributed in Great Britain and Europe by Cassell PLC
Villiers House, 41/47 Strand, London WC2N 5JE, England
Distributed in Australia by Capricorn Link Ltd.
P.O. Box 665, Lane Cove, NSW 2066
Manufactured in the United States of America
All rights reserved.

Sterling ISBN 0-8069-8594-1

Contents

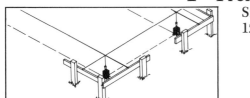
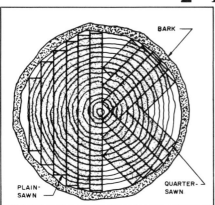
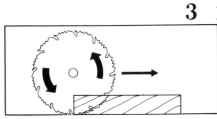
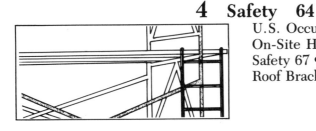

PART II Floor, Wall, and Ceiling Framing 77

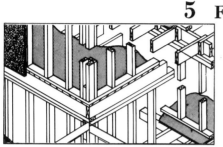

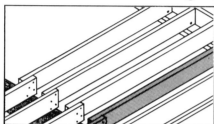

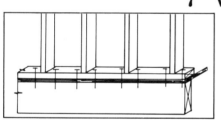

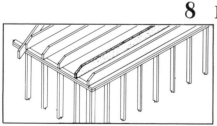

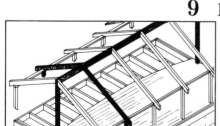

PART III   Roof Framing   161

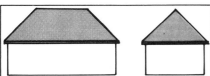
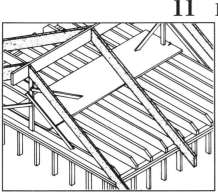

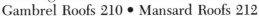

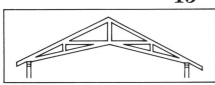

PART IV   Finishing the Building   227

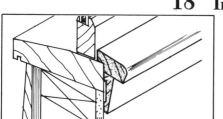
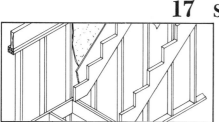
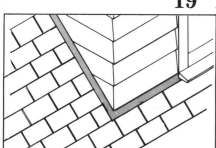

APPENDICES 289

Preface

Residential Framing is designed as a guide for the home craftsman who would like to begin a project that requires light wood-frame construction and as a reference for experienced framers. It details the basic framing processes and covers more difficult procedures such as laying out rafters.

An understanding of framing materials is important and is covered in Part I, General Considerations, in the second chapter. The major portion of the book, Parts II and III, is on the framing details. These are explained and illustrated with hundreds of drawings and photos. The organization is in a logical sequence beginning with a description of the commonly used framing systems and devoting individual chapters to each step of the framing process. Floor, wall, and ceiling framing, Part II, are covered in one or more chapters on each topic, along with a chapter on post-and-beam construction that follows different procedures. Part III, roof framing, being especially difficult, is divided into six chapters including roof designs, gable roofs, hip roofs, dormers, shed and flat roofs, and gambrel and mansard roofs. A separate chapter on roof framing with trusses is included.

Part IV of the book covers many separate and related topics concerned with finishing the building. Instructions on finishing the exterior are detailed, in-cluding sheathing, installing doors and windows, and installing various types of siding. Stair construction, a common framing task, is explained in a chapter on how to design and install stairs and platforms.

After the building is framed and the electrical and mechanical systems work is accomplished, the interior wall finish is applied. This is usually gypsum wallboard or plywood panelling. When this is complete the trim carpenter appears and installs the finish interior trim and specified mouldings. The techniques for measuring, cutting, and nailing are covered. Decks and wood-framed porches are common, and typical designs and installation details are shown in a well-illustrated chapter.

Throughout the book an emphasis on safety is stressed. Two chapters are included in Part I, General Considerations, to serve as a useful reference covering the safe use of power tools and safe use of ladders, scaffolding, and other types of elevated work platforms. Requirements of the U.S. Occupational Safety and Health Administration that pertain to the construction site and related tools are stressed.

This book will provide all the necessary framing information for both the novice and the professional who are involved with any of the aspects of light wood framing.

William P. Spence

PART I
General Considerations

1

Preliminary Work

Before the framing beings there is considerable work that must be performed by others. The building must be designed and plans checked to be certain they meet local **building codes**. Building codes establish minimum requirements for various aspects of the building such as structural, electrical, plumbing, mechanical design, light, ventilation, and fire safety.

The general contractor must get the plans approved by the local building official and get a **building permit**. A building permit is issued by the local government indicating that the plans meet building codes and local zoning ordinances. **Zoning ordinances** regulate the use of the land. The building official inspects the building as it is constructed to make certain it meets the building codes. The inspection begins by checking to see that the building is properly located on the site. Then inspections continue as the footings are dug, foundation is built, framing is constructed, and on through all the other phases of construction that are required.

Site Preparation

The site is cleared of unwanted trees and brush. The driveway is usually roughly located and serves as the main avenue for access to the building. Trees to be saved must be clearly marked and, if necessary, have fences built around them to protect them during construction.

A surveyor locates the corners of the building as shown on the site plan. These must allow for the setbacks required by local zoning ordinances. A **setback** is the minimum distance the building must be set in from the property line on all sides. Stakes are driven at each corner. An area for a septic tank and the location of a well should be staked if they are required. These must meet approval of local health department officials.

Preparing for Excavation

After the surveyor stakes the exact corners of the building, batter boards are set up and chalk lines are run locating the line of the foundation. Batter boards are usually made with 1×6 boards and are supported with 2×4 stakes set into the ground at least four feet away from the corner stake.

A chalk line is pulled tight across the batter boards and located so it is directly above the nail in the stake locating each corner (see 1-1). The string is set into a saw kerf or tied to a nail in the batter board. The corner can be checked for squareness by measuring 9 feet and 12 feet on two sides and measuring the hypotenuse of the triangle formed. If the corner is square the hypotenuse will measure 15 feet. Where two lines cross at a corner, a plumb bob can be dropped to verify that the cross point is directly above the nail in the stake. The completed layout can be checked for squareness by measuring the diagonals. They should be exactly the same length. The chalk line should be level because the depth of the footing to be dug is usually measured from it. This will produce a layout as shown in 1-2.

Excavation

Excavation can be accomplished with a backhoe or bulldozer. The backhoe disturbs the soil around the building less than a bulldozer. Often the topsoil is stripped off and saved. Foundations should be dug to the exact depth required, and, if dug too deep, they must not be filled back up with soil. The concrete footing must rest on undisturbed soil. The size of the footing is indicated on the working drawings. If soil is firm and the sides of the excavation will stand firmly, footings can be poured without forms. If the soil crumbles, wood forms must be used.

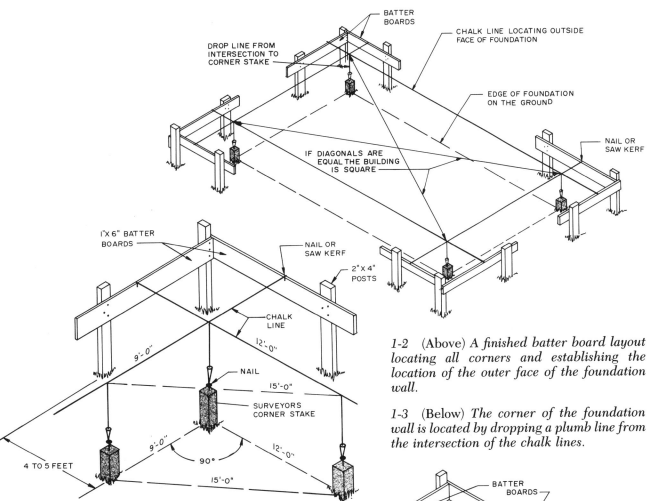

1-1 (Above) *The batter boards are set four feet from the corner stake and chalk lines are run so that they intersect over the nail in the corner stake.*

1-2 (Above) *A finished batter board layout locating all corners and establishing the location of the outer face of the foundation wall.*

1-3 (Below) *The corner of the foundation wall is located by dropping a plumb line from the intersection of the chalk lines.*

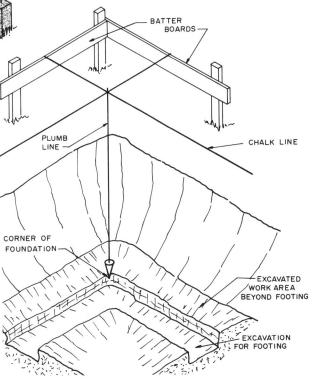

As the foundation is excavated the original corner stakes are dug away. The corners are located by the chalk line on the batter boards. The corner for the foundation wall in the excavation is located by dropping a plumb bob from the chalk line (see 1-3). This locates the exterior line of the foundation. The footing will extend several inches beyond this, as determined by its design. Notice that the excavation is dug far enough away from the footing to allow room for the workers and a place to locate drain tile and gravel.

Footings for piers, columns, and fireplaces are now located in the excavation. All footings are poured concrete. The size and reinforcing is specified on the working drawings.

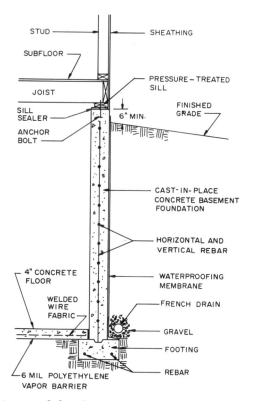

1-4 *A typical detail for basement construction using a cast-in-place concrete foundation wall.*

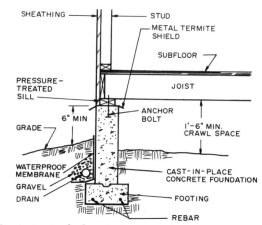

1-5 *A typical detail for crawl space construction using a cast-in-place foundation wall.*

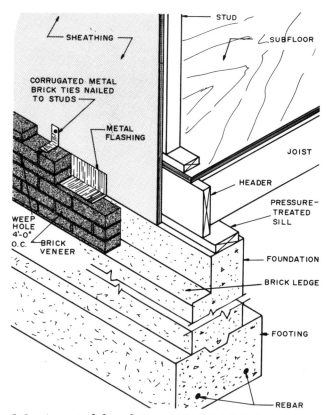

1-6 *A typical foundation with a brick ledge.*

Types of Foundations

Framers must be able to build upon any of the foundations used for light frame construction. Those most commonly used are concrete block, cast-in-place concrete, and pressure-treated wood. The foundation may form a basement, form a crawl space, or have a concrete slab on grade. The foundation will also vary depending upon the exterior finish material, such as wood siding or brick veneer.

Cast-in-Place Concrete Foundations

A cast-in-place concrete foundation for light construction will usually be 8 or 10 inches thick. Anchor bolts or straps are placed in the top surface before it sets. These are used to secure the wood sill to the foundation. A typical construction detail for a basement is shown in 1-4. Basements are usually dug so they provide a 7- or 8-foot ceiling height.

A detail for a cast-in-place foundation for a building with a crawl space is shown in 1-5. The minimum clear area in a crawl space is usually 1'6" in most codes, but a larger space is recommended. Anchor

bolts or strips set in the freshly poured concrete are used to hold the sill to the foundation.

If a building is to have brick veneer the foundation would have a brick ledge (see 1-6). The framer sets in the header so the sheathing is flush with the face of the brick ledge.

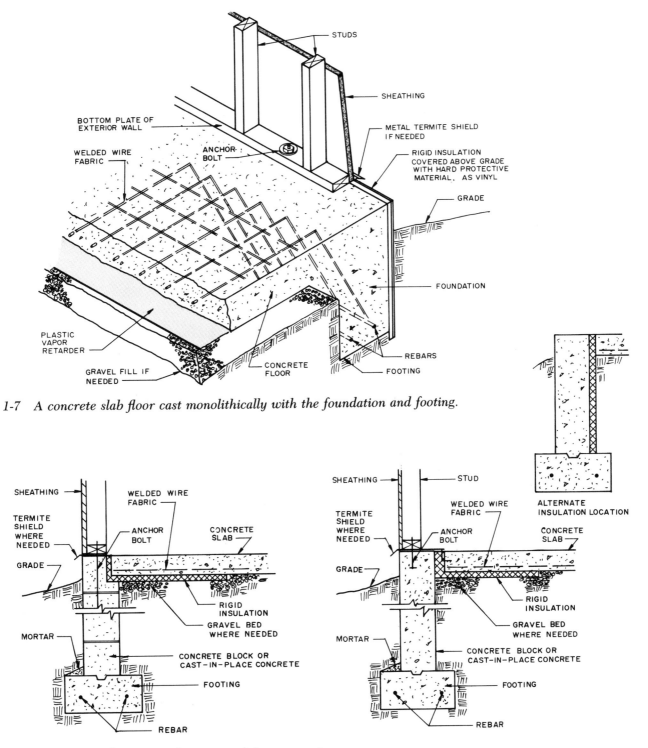

1-7   A concrete slab floor cast monolithically with the foundation and footing.

1-8   Typical earth-supported concrete slab construction.

A detail for a building with a concrete slab floor cast monolithically with the footing and foundation is shown in 1-7. Anchor bolts are set in the concrete to bolt the bottom plate of the frame wall to the foundation. Other foundation designs for concrete slab construction are shown in 1-8.

Masonry Foundations

Most masonry foundations are built using concrete blocks, though solid brick foundations are sometimes built. In either case the framer faces the same situation. A detail for a masonry basement foundation is shown in 1-9. It is much the same as that shown for cast-in-place concrete, except that the top course of blocks is solid or the cores in the top course are filled with concrete. Anchor bolts or straps are set in this concrete or in the mortar joints between the solid top blocks. Details for a masonry foundation for a building with a crawl space are shown in 1-10. Notice that these details show a pier supporting a beam.

A detail for a masonry foundation used with a concrete slab floor is shown in 1-8. Anchor bolts are placed in the mortar joints between the solid top

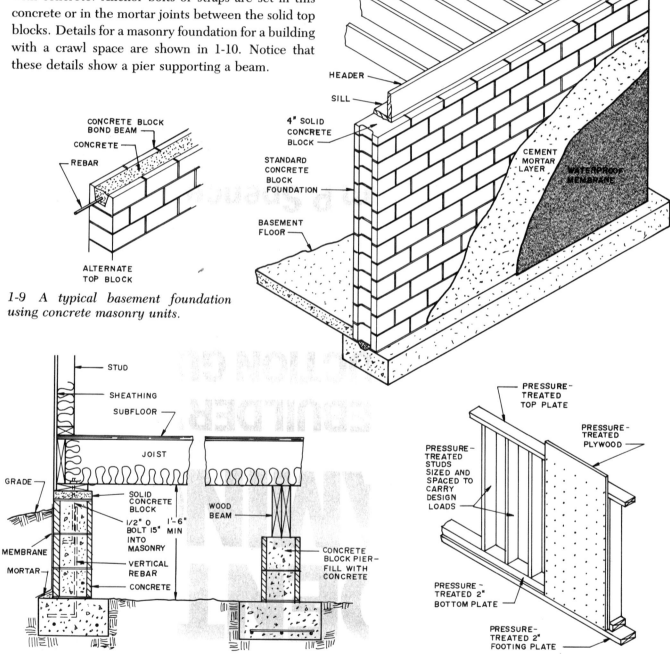

1-9 A typical basement foundation using concrete masonry units.

1-10 A typical detail for crawl space construction using concrete masonry units.

1-11 A typical wood foundation wall panel.

16

block. Notice how the L-shaped top block serves as a form to contain the concrete as the floor is poured.

Permanent Wood Foundation Systems

Foundations built of pressure-treated plywood and solid-wood members have been used in some areas. The lumber and plywood are stress-graded to withstand lateral soil and subsurface water pressures. The preservative treatment of the wood and plywood is specified in the American Wood Preservers Bureau (AWPB) Standard FDN. Lumber treated according to this standard will bear the AWPB stamp. This treatment produces a rot-resistant wood product.

The wood foundation has a number of advantages. It can be built in sections in a shop and rapidly erected on the site even in freezing weather. Since the panels are made with wood studs, the walls can be easily insulated, providing a warmer basement.

A typical panel is shown in 1-11. It must be carefully built using silicon, bronze, copper, or stainless steel nails, and following the design specifications established by the National Forest Products Association. The panels are set on a gravel bed instead of a concrete footing. They are used for basement and crawl space foundations. A sill plate is not required. Instead, the double top plate of the panel receives the joists. Construction details are shown in 1-12.

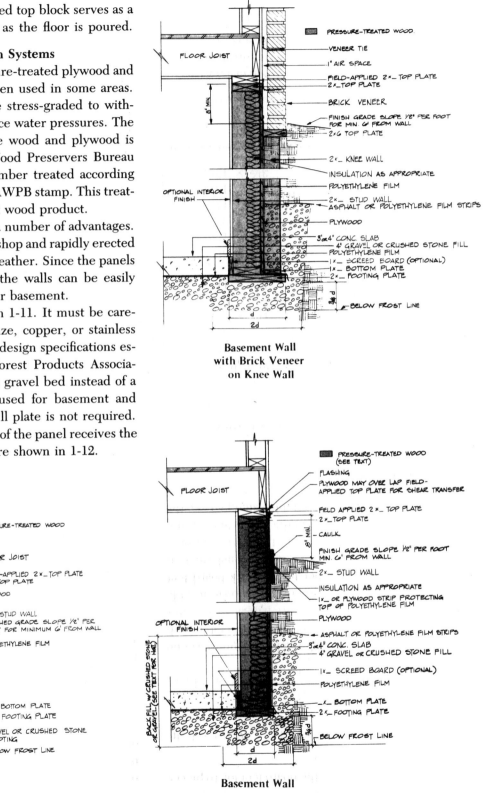

Basement Wall with Brick Veneer on Knee Wall

Crawl Space Wall

Basement Wall

1-12 Framing details for the construction of wood foundations. (Courtesy of the National Forest Products Association, Washington, D.C.)

Installation requires that the gravel footing be level. The panels are set on the gravel bed, braced, and fastened together (see 1-13). After all of the pan-

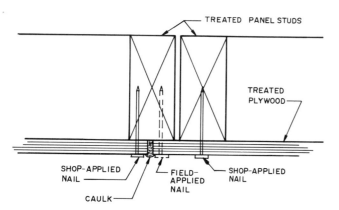

1-13 *Panels are joined by nailing the overlapping sheathing to the next panel and caulking the joint. (Courtesy of the National Forest Products Association, Washington, D.C.)*

els are in place, the joints are caulked and the exterior is covered with 6-mil polyethylene plastic sheets. In a basement the gravel bed is covered with 6-mil polyethylene plastic sheets and a four-inch concrete slab is poured over it.

Provisions to remove subsurface water are necessary. A sump pump in a pit in the basement is required in areas having high water tables.

After the Foundation

After the foundation is in place the framers arrive on the site to construct the floor (see 1-14). If the building has a crawl space, the open area around the foundation can be backfilled. If it has a basement, no backfilling should occur until the floor beams and joists are in place and the subfloor is glued and nailed to the joists. If backfilling occurs before this work, the pressure of the soil could cause the foundation to collapse. This is a special danger if it rains after backfilling, increasing the exterior pressure a great deal.

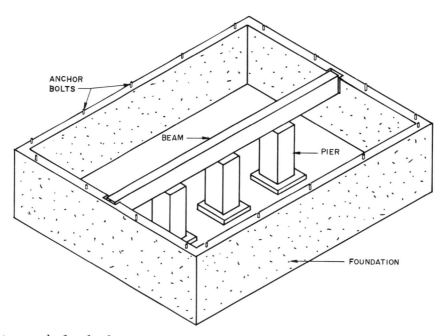

1-14 *A foundation ready for the framers to construct the floor.*

2

Framing Materials

The major use for wood in light frame construction is for structural framing and exposed, finished surfaces such as siding, trim, and flooring. Many factory-manufactured units, such as cabinets, doors, and windows, are of wood construction.

Wood is an excellent construction material because it is light in weight, strong, a good insulator, and is attractive. Some woods are stronger than others and some can withstand exposure to the weather or soil or insects. The selection of the best species of wood for a particular application is important to produce a satisfactory end result.

Species of Wood

While there are hundreds of species of trees, only a few are used extensively in construction. The species are divided into two major groups, softwoods and hardwoods (table 2-1). **Softwoods** have needle-like leaves and produce some form of cone. They retain the needles year round and so are green all the time. Typical examples are pine, fir, cedar, cypress, spruce, and redwood. **Hardwood** trees have broad fan-like leaves that drop off in the winter. Typical examples are walnut, oak, maple, poplar, and mahogany. The descriptors "hardwood" and "softwood" do not refer to the actual hardness, since some hardwoods are softer than some softwoods.

Construction framing and finishing lumber is primarily from softwood trees. Some commonly used softwoods harvested in the United States include Douglas fir, white fir, southern yellow pine, white pine, Ponderosa pine, sugar pine, western larch, western red cedar, spruce, cypress, and redwood.

Table 2–1 Common species of softwoods and hardwoods.

Softwoods		Hardwoods	
Alaska cedar	Western larch	Black walnut	Hickory
Incense cedar	Jack pine	Mahogany	Basswood
Port Orford cedar	Lodgepole pine	Philippine mahogany	
Eastern red cedar	Norway pine	Sugar maple	
Western red cedar	Ponderosa pine	Yellow birch	
Northern white cedar	Sugar pine	Black cherry	
Southern white cedar	Idaho white pine	White oak	
Cypress	Northern white pine	Red oak	
Balsam fir	Longleaf yellow pine	Yellow poplar	
Douglas fir	Shortleaf pine	Willow	
Noble fir	Eastern spruce	American elm	
White fir	Engelmann spruce	Sweet gum	
Eastern hemlock	Sitka spruce	White ash	
Mountain hemlock	Tamarack	American beech	
West coast hemlock	Pacific yew	Cottonwood	
Western juniper	Redwood	Rock elm	

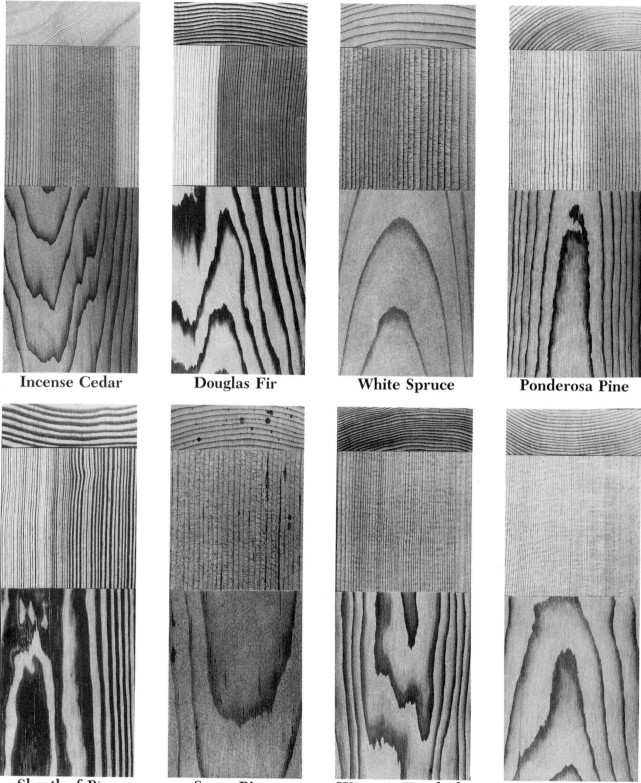

2-1 *Some of the commonly used softwoods.* (Courtesy U.S. Forest Products Laboratory, Forest Service, USDA)

Western White Pine

Western Red Cedar

Commonly harvested Canadian softwoods include spruce, larch, hemlock, red cedar, poplar, and several species of pine, fir, and aspen (see 2-1).

Hardwoods are used for cabinets, built-in furniture, floors, and sometimes interior trim that is left natural or stained to bring out the color and grain.

Properties of Wood

Wood has a number of desirable properties that make it excellent for light frame construction. These include:

1. It is easily cut and shaped.

2. It is a good thermal insulator.

3. It is a good electrical insulator.

4. It provides a barrier to sound transmission.

5. It can be glued to form large structural members and sheet products.

6. It will not rust or corrode.

7. It can be painted. (Continued.)

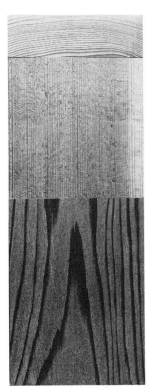

Redwood

Sitka Spruce

Bald Cypress

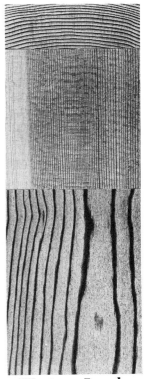

Western Larch

2-1 *Continued.*

8. It can be joined with mechanical fasteners, such as nails, screws, staples, bolts, and metal truss plates.

9. It absorbs chemicals, enabling it to resist rot and fire.

10. It is lightweight and has a good strength-to-weight ratio.

11. It has some resistance to alkalies and acids.

Likewise wood has limitations which must be considered as material choices are being made. These include:

1. It is readily combustible and special precautions must be taken if a potential fire danger exists. It can be impregnated with fire-retardant chemicals.

2. It is hygroscopic: It absorbs moisture and swells, and it dries, releasing moisture and shrinks. It must be protected from moisture.

3. When subjected to high moisture levels spores of wood-destroying fungi attack the wood, causing it to decay. Most species of wood in this situation must be protected with preservative chemicals.

4. Wood is attacked by a variety of insects, such as termites, beetles, and borers. Proper construction practices and insect-controlling chemicals are necessary to prevent damage to most species of wood.

5. Wood is a naturally occurring material. Therefore, it is not of uniform quality or strength as other materials such as steel. It will have defects such as knots, cracks, and checks that influence appearance and strength.

6. Many species of wood are used in light frame construction. Each has different physical and mechanical properties. The framer must consider the properties of the species being used so that the building is structurally sound.

7. If improperly installed, dried, or protected, wood will twist, cup, bow, and crook. Once this happens it cannot be restored to the original flat condition.

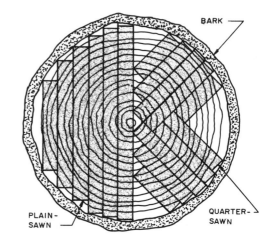

2-2   *Lumber can be plain-sawn or quarter-sawn.*

Cutting Softwood Lumber

Lumber used for framing purposes is plain-sawn. If used for finished floors, it might be quarter-sawn (see 2-2). **Plain-sawn** lumber is manufactured by first squaring a log and then cutting the boards tangent to the growth rings. Plain-sawn lumber is cheaper and produces wider boards than quarter-sawing. It does tend to warp and shrink more.

Quarter-sawn lumber is produced by cutting a log into quarters and cutting each of these into boards. The growth rings are cut so they form an angle of 45 to 90 degrees with the surface. This exposes the edges of the growth rings on the surface, and since they are very hard, they resist wear. This also reduces warping, shrinking, and twisting.

Two ways a sawyer could work a log to produce boards or larger-dimensional stock are shown in 2-3 and 2-4. Small logs are commonly cut as shown in 2-4, because they would not produce many wide boards. After the boards are cut from the log they are ready to be seasoned.

Seasoning Sawed Lumber

Before wood can be used for construction purposes the amount of moisture in it must be reduced. Often half the weight of a freshly sawed board is water. For general framing use, the lumber should have a moisture content of 12 to 15 percent. For furniture and cabinets it must only be 6 to 10 percent.

Lumber can be air dried or kiln dried. **Air drying** is done by stacking the lumber in piles with wood

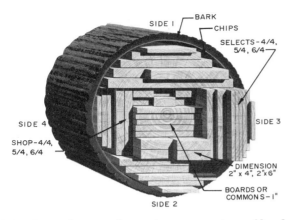

2-3 *Large logs can be cut into many sizes of lumber.* (Courtesy Western Wood Products Association)

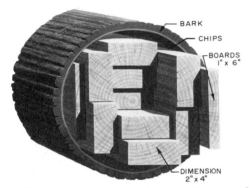

2-4 *Small logs are often cut into thicker members.* (Courtesy Western Wood Products Association)

2-5 *Lumber stacked and air-drying. Notice the cover boards on top.* (Courtesy Western Wood Products Association)

sticks between the layers so that air can circulate between the layers. The lumber is then let to sit out doors. It usually has a layer of protective boards on top. It takes several months to lower the moisture content to 15 to 20 percent by air drying. It is difficult to control moisture content by air drying. Therefore, quality lumber is usually kiln dried (see 2-5).

Kiln-dried lumber is stacked on carts with sticks between the layers. It is then run into long oven-like buildings called kilns (see 2-6). The moisture, temperature, and airflow are controlled. Steam is pumped in, saturating the wood. Then the steam is reduced, and heated air is passed over the wood, removing the moisture. Softwoods for construction purposes can be kiln dried to the required moisture content in three to five days. A wood preservative is applied to the ends to prevent splitting. Kiln-dried lumber should be covered with plastic sheets to protect it from rain.

2-6 *Typical dry kilns used to dry lumber.* (Courtesy Western Wood Products Association)

As wood is seasoned, some surface checks, cracks, and splits occur. Kiln drying reduces these defects to a minimum. It is important to remember that the moisture content of wood will vary with the environment in which it is used. Wood with a 15 percent moisture content used in an area with a natural 8 percent moisture content, as in a dry western U.S. state, will continue to lose moisture after it has been nailed in place. This causes the wood to shrink, which will produce, for instance, cracks in gypsum and plaster walls. Likewise, wood in a moist climate will swell, causing doors and windows to stick. It is important that the moisture content of the wood be in balance with the environment.

Checking Moisture Content

The moisture content of wood can be checked on the job with a moisture meter. One type has two

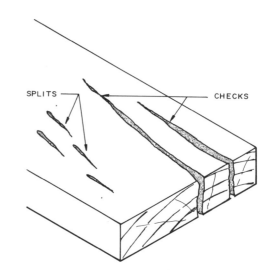

2-8 *Splits and checks are frequently found defects.*

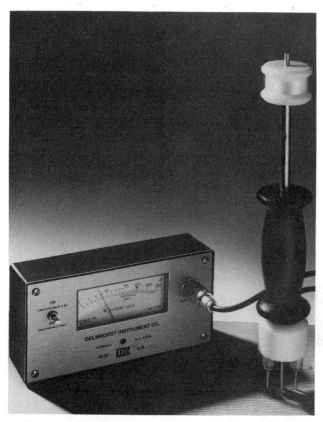

2-7 *Moisture meters are used on the job to check the moisture content of lumber.* (Courtesy Delmhorst Instrument Company)

needles that are pressed into the wood. It measures the electrical resistance of the current flow through the wood between the two needles (see 2-7). Another type uses metal plates that are pressed against the surface of the wood. It measures the relationship between the moisture content sensed and a fixed setting.

Moisture Content Designations

Most construction lumber is kiln dried to 15 to 19 percent. Generally the moisture content is included in the information found on the grade stamp placed on each piece. Typical designations include MC-15 (moisture content 15 percent), KD-15 or KD-19 (kiln dried 15 percent or 19 percent), S-DRY (surfaced at 15 percent), and DRY-19 (kiln dried to 19 percent). If the lumber is surfaced green (not dried) it will be stamped S-GRN. The moisture content will be somewhere above 19 percent. S-GRN lumber is surfaced larger than S-DRY, so that when it dries and shrinks, it will be the same size as the S-DRY lumber. It is not widely used.

The moisture content of wood is important because it influences the use of structural lumber and engineering designs, such as truss design. Wood becomes stronger and stiffer as the moisture content is **lowered**. Therefore, a member marked KD-15 is stronger than the same number at KD-19. Fasteners placed in wood at a high moisture content tend to loosen as the moisture content is lowered. This influences the strength of the structure.

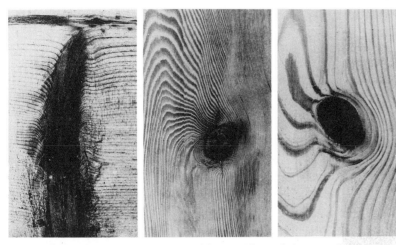

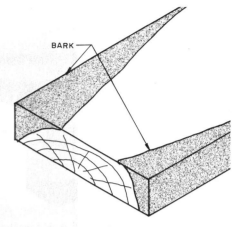

2-9   The most common types of knots (from left to right): spike, intergrown, and encased. (Courtesy U.S. Forest Products Laboratory, Forest Service, USDA)

2-10   Wane is the presence of bark on the edges of lumber.

Defects in Lumber

Defects in lumber reduce its strength and affect its appearance. Defects are considered as lumber is graded. The defects are described in rules used to grade lumber. Some frequently listed defects and descriptions follow:

Bow is curvature flatwise from a straight line from one end of the board to the other.

Checks are separations of the grain fibres running lengthwise. The cracks go into the board but not through it (see 2-8).

Crook is curvature edgewise from a straight line from one end of the board to the other.

Cup is curvature flatwise from a straight line across the width of the piece.

Decay is soft, crumbling wood caused by attack by fungi.

Knots are growth defects caused by branches. The branches embedded in the trunk are cut when the boards are sawed (see 2-9). When grading lumber, the size, location, and firmness of the knot are considered.

Pitch is a heavy concentration of resin in wood cells in a single location.

Pitch pockets are open cavities between growth rings which are filled with pitch.

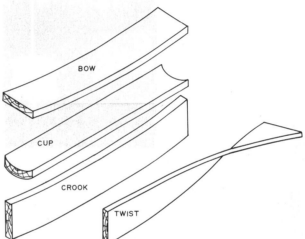

2-11   Wood can warp in various ways.

Shakes are lengthwise grain separation occurring between or through the annual rings.

Splits are separations of the grain fibres running lengthwise which go completely through the board (see 2-8).

Stains are discolorations of the board which damage the natural color but do not affect the strength.

Wane is the presence of bark or a lack of wood on the edge of a manufactured board. It causes the edge to be rounded (see 2-10).

Warp describes variations from a straight, true plane surface. It includes bow, crook, cup, twist, and combinations of these (see 2-11).

2-12 *Grade marks used by the manufacturers of southern pine lumber.* (Courtesy Southern Pine Inspection Bureau)

Softwood Lumber Grading

Grading specifications for lumber manufactured in the United States are recorded in the National Grading Rule for Softwood Dimension Lumber: Product Standard 20-70 (PS 20-70). This standard provides a common classification for sizes, grades, terminology, and moisture content for softwood dimension lumber. It provides standard rules for graded lumber regardless of the physical properties. National and regional agencies involved with the grading of lumber manufactured in their area are listed in Appendix R.

Canadian lumber grading rules are formulated and maintained by the National Lumber Grades Authority (NLGA). The NLGA rule is approved and enforced by the Canadian Lumber Standards Accreditation Board and by the American Lumber Standards Board of Review. This approval provides acceptance under all Canadian and U.S. building codes. Membership in the NLGA includes all the lumber manufacturers' associations in Canada that have approved grading agencies as well as independent grading agencies. Lumber manufactured according to NLGA rules meets the provision of the Canadian standard, CSA 0141, and the American standard, PS 20-70 (see Appendix R).

(Courtesy Alberta Forest Products Association)

MACHINE RATED

(Courtesy Southern Pine Inspection Bureau)

SPIB—Southern Pine Inspection Bureau, the grading authority

KD19—Kiln dried to 19% moisture

S-DRY—Surfaced after it was kiln dried

1950f—Extreme fibre stress in bending .

1.5E—Modulus of elasticity in millions of pounds per square foot

MACHINE RATED—Machine tested for strength properties

7—Number of mill manufacturing the lumber

2-13 *Machine stress-rated lumber grade marks.* (Courtesy Alberta Forest Products Association and Southern Pine Inspection Bureau)

Lumber is graded by two methods: visual inspection and machine evaluation. Most wood used for general construction is visually graded. The grading agency, grade classification, and moisture content are indicated on the grade stamp placed on each piece of lumber (see 2-12).

Machine-Evaluated Lumber

Machine-evaluated lumber is used where physical properties must be more accurately determined, such as in the manufacture of trusses, laminated beams and columns, and I-joists.

Machine-evaluated lumber is tested to ascertain the bending stress (F_b) and the modulus of elasticity (E), which is a measure of the stiffness. Engineers designing structural components, such as laminated beams or trusses, need this information so that they can select a satisfactory species and proper sizes to carry the design loads over the established spans.

Machine stress rating gives a more precise grade designation than visual stress rating. The process involves passing the piece of lumber through a machine that applies a load and measures the deflection. A computer records the average and minimum elasticity values, which are stamped on the lumber as it leaves the machine. The piece is then visually graded for any defects that may reduce its strength and a grade stamp is printed on the piece (see 2-13). Detailed information on lumber grades is available from lumber manufacturers' associations.

Table 2–2 Classification of dimension lumber.

Lumber	Grades
Structural light framing 2″ to 4″ thick 2″ to 4″ wide	Select Structural (Sel Str) No. 1 No. 2 No. 3
Light framing 2″ to 4″ thick 2″ to 4″ wide	Construction (Const) Standard (Stand) Utility (Util)
Studs 2″ to 4″ thick 2″ to 4″ wide 10′0″ and shorter	Stud
Structural joists and planks 2″ to 4″ thick 5″ and wider	Select Structural (Sel Str) No. 1 No. 2 No. 3

Use Classifications

Lumber is classified into five major areas related to its intended use. These are structural, industrial-and-shop, yard, select, and common lumber.

Structural lumber is two inches or more in thickness and width. It is machine stress rated for strength.

Industrial-and-shop lumber is used for the manufacture of various wood products such as doors and windows.

Yard lumber includes grades and sizes intended for construction and building purposes. It is classified as select and common.

Select lumber has good appearance and finishing qualities, and it is available in grades B & B, C, C & B, and D.

Common lumber is used for general construction and utility purposes. It is available in grades No. 1, No. 2, No. 3, and No. 4.

Size Classifications

Lumber is classified into three groups by the size of the members. These are boards, dimension lumber, and timbers.

Boards are under two inches in nominal thickness and one inch or more in width.

Dimension lumber is from two inches to, but not including, five inches thick and two inches or more in width, and it is identified as framing, joists, planks, rafters, studs, small timbers, etc.

Timbers are five inches or more in their least dimension, and they are identified as beams, stringers, posts, caps, girders, purling, sills, etc.

Dimension Lumber

Dimension lumber is used for framing members such as joists, studs, rafters, planks, and small timbers. It is classified into two categories by width, 2 × 4 inches wide, and 5 inches and wider. These are classified into four use categories: structural light framing, light framing, studs, and structural joists and planks (table 2-2).

Structural light framing grades are used for engineered applications where higher design values are needed. Light framing grades have good appearance but lower design values. Stud-grade lumber has design values making it suitable for stud uses including the construction of load-bearing walls. Structural joists and planks have qualities needed for engineered applications required of lumber five inches and wider.

Table 2–3 Classification of timbers.

Timbers	Grades
Stress Rated 5″ x 5″ and larger	Select Structural (Sel Str) No. 1 SR (Stress Rated) No. 2 SR (Stress Rated)
Non-Stress Rated 5″ x 5″ and larger	Square Edges and Sound (SE & S) timbers No. 1 No. 2 No. 3

Timbers

Timbers are wood members 5 × 5 inches and larger. There are two categories: stress rated and non-stress rated. Stress rated timbers are used where high strength and stiffness values and good appearance are needed. Non-stress rated timbers have not been tested and permit a number of defects to be present. Timber grades are shown in table 2-3. Lengths are available from 10 to 16 feet, 18 feet, and 20 feet.

Nominal Size

Boards and other lumber are typically designated by nominal size. Nominal means that the stated size approximately matches the size of the rough lumber before it is surfaced. The stated—nominal—size of the thickness and width of lumber differs from its actual size. Thus rough lumber 2 inches by 4 inches that is surfaced is actually closer to 1½ inches by 3½ inches, but it is still refered to as two-by-four lumber. In this book the nominal size "two-by-four" is written without units as 2 × 4. When a measurement is actual, the units are given. The same is true for one-by-six, four-by-four, etc. written as 1 × 6, 4 × 4, etc.

Table 2–4 Softwood lumber sizes for dressed dimensional and structural lumber.

Thickness[a] (inches)		
	Standard ALS Minimum Dressed	
Nominal	Dry	Green
2	1½	
2½	2[b]	2¹⁄₁₆
3	2½[b]	2⁹⁄₁₆
3½	3[b]	3¹⁄₁₆
4	3½[b]	3⁹⁄₁₆
5 and thicker	½ off nominal	½ off nominal

Width (inches)		
	Standard ALS Minimum Dressed	
Nominal	Dry	Green
2	1½	
3	2½	2⁹⁄₁₆[c]
4	3½	3⁹⁄₁₆[c]
5	4½	4⅝[c]
6	5½	5⅝[c]
8	7¼	7½
10	9¼	9½
12	11¼	11½
14	13¼	13½
16	15¼	15½
18	17¼	17½
20	19¼	19½
5 and wider	½ off nominal	½ off nominal

[a] *2″ dressed green thickness of 1⁹⁄₁₆ applies to widths of 14 inches and over.*
[b] *Not required to be dry unless specified.*
[c] *These green widths apply to thicknesses of 3 and 4 inches only, except as provided in footnote a.*

American Standard Lumber Sizes

The standard sizes of lumber used for light frame construction are shown in tables 2-4 and 2-5. Other sizes, such are for siding, are available from lumber manufacturers' associations. The sizes shown are for lumber surfaced on four sides (S4S). However, for

Table 2–5 Softwood lumber sizes for finish lumber and boards.

	Thickness (inches)		Width (inches)	
	Nominal	Dressed	Nominal	Dressed
Finish	⅜	⁵⁄₁₆	2	1½
	½	⁷⁄₁₆	3	2½
	⅝	⁹⁄₁₆	4	3½
	¾	⅝	5	4½
	1	¾	6	5½
	1¼	1	7	6½
	1½	1¼	8	7¼
	1¾	1⅜	9	8¼
	2	1½	10	9¼
	2½	2	11	10¼
	3	2½	12	11¼
	3½	3	14	13¼
	4	3½	16	15¼
Boards	1	¾	2	1½
	1¼	1	3	2½
	1½	1¼	4	3½
			5	4½
			6	5½
			7	6½
			8	7¼
			9	8¼
			10	9¼
			11	10¼
			12	11¼
			Over 12	Off ¾

2-14 *A grade stamp used by the Alberta Forest Products Association.* (Courtesy Alberta Forest Products Association)

some applications it may be surfaced on one side (S1S), two edges (S2E), or some combination of sides and edges (S1S2E, S2S1E, or S1S1E). The nominal size, as stated above, matches the rough size to which the material is first sawn. Generally when speaking about lumber sizes the nominal size is referred to rather than the actual size. Surfaced lumber is smaller than the nominal size because material is removed in the planing operation. Notice that the pieces lose ½ inch in thickness and width as they are surfaced. This applies to lumber up to and including six-inch-wide stock. After this the width loses ¾ inch.

Green lumber is dressed slightly larger than dry lumber so that when it air dries it is the same size as dressed dry lumber. Green wood shrinks about ¹⁄₃₂ inch per inch of width across the grain and in thickness. Length is basically not changed by shrinkage.

Softwood lumber is manufactured in lengths from 6 to 24 feet in two-foot increments.

Canadian Lumber

The species of Canadian lumber are about the same as those harvested in the United States. Canadian softwood species are combined into four main species groups: Spruce-Pine-Fir (S-P-F), Douglas fir-Larch (N), Hem-Fir (N), and Northern Species. The various species in each group are similar in strength and appearance. About three-fourths of the production of lumber is from the S-P-F group.

Grade stamps for the first three groups use the group name. Woods in the Northern Species group are identified by the actual name of the species, such as red pine. Grades of Canadian dimension lumber are identical to those in use in the United States and meet the requirements of the American Softwood Lumber Standards (ALS) PS 20-70 and are designated by Canadian lumber standards (CSA 0141). There are twelve Canadian lumber grading agencies. Each has its own grade stamp. One example is shown in 2-14. All grade stamps contain the same information. The only difference is the identification of the grading agency.

Span Design Values in the United States and Canada

New design values for lumber manufactured in the United States and Canada were published in 1991.

These were developed over a period of years by a project entitled the In-Grade Testing Program. (New span values for Southern Pine wre published in 1993, and are included in Appendices J, K, and L.)

The In-Grade Testing Program developed new design values for visually graded North American (U.S. and Canada) softwood species. These design values are based on actual experience from tests with full-size lumber specimens. This research effort was conducted by the Southern Pine Inspection Bureau, the West Coast Lumber Inspection Bureau, the Western Wood Products Association, the Canadian Wood Council, and other rule-writing lumber associations. The U.S. Forest Products Laboratory conducted the research in cooperation with the various lumber associations. The new design values for dimension lumber are available in the Supplement to the *1991 National Design Specifications® for Wood Construction* (NDS®), which is available from the National Forest Products Association, 1250 Connecticut Ave., Washington, D.C. 20036. The various lumber associations publish span tables for species available in their region. The NDS provides the basis for the design of wood structures adhering to United States building codes.

The new data are reported by the Southern Pine Inspection Bureau publications using a size-adjusted/repetitive member-adjusted format and named by them **empirical values**. The Western Wood Products Association, the Northeast Lumber Manufacturers Association, and the Canadian Wood Council present the new data as constants for particular species combinations that can be adjusted for the application to which the lumber is to be used. These new numbers are identified as **base values**. The base value is more accurate mathematically and fits into the design and engineering procedures as used for steel and concrete design.

The base values are the core of structural lumber safety. Design values for visually graded lumber are assigned to six basic properties of wood. The person ascertaining the performance of lumber can assign **conditions of use** to the base value to ascertain the strength of the member for the specified conditions. The six base values include (1) extreme fibre stress in bending (F_b), (2) tension parallel to grain (F_t), (3) horizontal shear (F_v), (4) compression parallel to grain ($F_c\!/\!/$), (5) compression perpendicular to grain ($F_{c\perp}$), and (6) modulus of elasticity (E or MOE). An example of base values is shown in table 2-6.

Table 2–6 Base values for western dimensional lumber, sizes 2 inches to 4 inches thick by 2 inches and wider.*

Species or Group	Grade	Extreme Fibre Stress in Bending "F_b" Single	Tension Parallel to Grain "F_t"	Horizontal Shear "F_v"	Compression Perpendicular "$F_{c\perp}$"	Compression Parallel to Grain "$F_{c\parallel}$"	Modulus of Elasticity "E"
Douglas Fir-Larch	Select Structural	1450	1000	95	625	1700	1,900,000
	No. 1 & Btr	1150	775	95	625	1500	1,800,000
	No. 1	1000	675	95	625	1450	1,700,000
	No. 2	875	575	95	625	1300	1,600,000
	No. 3	500	325	95	625	750	1,400,000
	Construction	1000	650	95	625	1600	1,500,000
	Standard	550	375	95	625	1350	1,400,000
	Utility	275	175	95	625	875	1,300,000
	Stud	675	450	95	625	825	1,400,000

* Use with appropriate adjustment factors. (*Courtesy Western Wood Products Association*)

To find the final design value of the member, the base value must first be adjusted for **size**, and then adjusted for conditions of use.

There are seven conditions of use which are applied to the various base values to get the **adjusted value**. These adjustment factors include:

Size Factor (C_f)—applied to dimension lumber Base Values

Repetitive Member Factor (C_r)—applied to size-adjusted F_b (bending stress)

Duration of Load Adjustment (C_d)—applied to size-adjusted values

Horizontal Shear Adjustment (C_h)—applied to F_v (horizontal shear) values

Flat Use Factors (C_{fu})—applied to size-adjusted F_b (bending stress)

Adjustments for Compression Perpendicular to Grain ($C_{c\perp}$)—applied to $F_{c\perp}$ (perpendicular compression) values

Wet Use Factors, (C_m)—applied to size-adjusted values

The value derived after applying the conditions of use is the **adjusted value**. This is the actual design value for the piece of lumber under the prescribed conditions. Adjustment factors and detailed instructions may be obtained from lumber associations, such as the Western Wood Products Association or the National Forest Products Association.

Following is an example of how to use base values. Assume the lumber is DF-S SS 2 × 4 inches (Douglas Fir-South, Select Structural grade, nominal 2 × 4 inches member). The designer selects a base value, for instance, the extreme fibre stress in bending, F_b, to be considered. The base value for the extreme fibre stress in bending for this specie and grade is found in the base value table to be 1300 psi. Multiply the base value by the **size factor** for 2 × 4 inch stock, which is found in the size factor table to be 1.5. Therefore, 1300 × 1.5 equals 1950 psi. If the member is to be used in repetitive loading applications, such as a floor joist, multiply 1950 psi by the **repetitive factor**, which is found in the repetitive factor table to be 1.15. Therefore, 1950 × 1.15 equals 2242.50 psi, which is **the adjusted bending stress** required for the member.

Lumber associations publish manuals giving span data for members, such as joists and rafters. The person using these data must read the section in the front that explains what these span data represent. This section tells what factors have been applied to the base values to get the span. For example, typically joists and rafter data will be adjusted for bending values, repetitive loads, duration of load, and deflection. Procedures are given in the manuals for calculating other factors such as shear, tension, and compression.

When the In-Grade Testing Program was designed, the various softwood species used for structural dimension lumber were grouped to assist in the specification of their properties. Canadian softwood species were combined into four species groups, Spruce-Pine-Fir (SPF), Douglas Fir-Larch (North), Hem-Fir (North), and Northern Species (cedars, aspen, poplar, and several species of pine). The Western Wood Products Association grouped their species into six groupings. These groupings include Douglas Fir-Larch, Douglas Fir-South, Hem-Fir, Spruce-Pine-Fir (South), Western Cedars, and Western Woods (all of the above plus others species of pine, fir, and hemlock). The Southern Pine Inspection Bureau has one group, Southern Pine. These groupings were used when the base values were developed. The base values are for all wood species in the specified group.

Metric Lumber Sizes

Lumber in the United States is still manufactured using feet and inches. In Canada some is manufactured in feet and inches because it is sold in the United States. Metric sizes used in Canada are shown in tables 2-7 and 2-8. Metric lumber dressed green is two millimetres larger than the dressed-dry size to allow for shrinkage.

Specifying Lumber Quantities

When lumber is ordered it is specified by giving the thickness, width, length, and the number of pieces of this size. Lumber is priced by the board foot. A **board foot** is equal to 144 cubic inches of wood. For example, a piece 12 × 12 inches that is one inch thick contains 144 cubic inches (see 2-15). Board feet are calculated by multiplying the nominal thickness in inches, width in inches, and length in feet and dividing this resultant by 12. Note the following example for finding the board feet for 10 pieces of 2×8 lumber 14 feet long:

$$\text{Board Feet} = \frac{\text{No. of Boards} \times T\,(\text{in}) \times W\,(\text{in}) \times L\,(\text{ft})}{12}$$

$$= \frac{10 \times 2 \times 8 \times 14}{12} = \frac{2240}{12} = 186.7 \text{ board feet}$$

Boards less than one inch thick are figured as one inch. If board feet are figured frequently, a table such as table 2.9 is used or the data are part of a computer estimating program. The proportions shown in table 2-10 are useful to remember to get quick board feet answers. These figures are for one-inch-thick stock. If thicker stock is to be figured, get the answer for one-inch stock and multiply by the thickness. Some framing squares have board feet tables stamped on the blade. The figures are based on one-inch-thick stock.

Table 2–7 Metric dimension lumber.

Surfaced dry* (actual size in millimetres)	Surfaced dry* (equivalent size in inches)
38 × 89	1½ × 3½
38 × 140	1½ × 5½
38 × 184	1½ × 7¼
38 × 235	1½ × 9¼
38 × 286	1½ × 11¼
89 × 140	3½ × 5½
89 × 184	3½ × 7¼
89 × 235	3½ × 9¼
89 × 286	3½ × 11¼
89 × 337	3½ × 13¼
89 × 387	3½ × 15¼

* Lumber dressed green—add 2 mm to dry thickness and width surfaced dimensions.

Table 2–8 Metric boards—thickness.*

Surfaced dry (actual size in millimetres)	Surfaced dry (equivalent size in inches)
17	43/64
19	¾

* Widths same as shown in Table 2–7 for dimension lumber.

The inch markings on the outer edge of the blade represent the width of the board in inches. The length is given in the vertical column under the figure "12" on the outer edge of the blade. The figures appearing where the two rows meet are board feet for a one-inch board. The number represents whole and fractional board feet (see 2-16). For example, assume a board 10 inches wide and 14 feet long. Where these two rows meet is the figure 11.8. This means the board contains 11.8 or 11⅘ board feet.

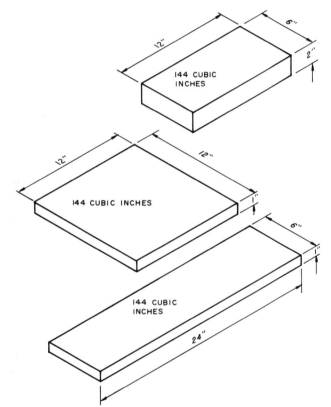

2-15 *Examples representing one board foot.*

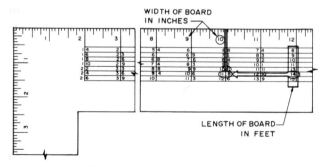

2-16 *Some framing squares have board feet tables on the blade.*

Table 2–9 Board feet for selected lumber sizes.

Nominal size (inches)	Length (feet)								
	8	10	12	14	16	18	20	22	24
1 × 2	1⅓	1⅔	2	2⅓	2⅔	3	3⅓	3⅔	4
1 × 3	2	2½	3	3½	4	4½	5	5½	6
1 × 4	2⅔	3⅓	4	4⅔	5⅓	6	6⅔	7⅓	8
1 × 5	3⅓	4⅙	5	5⅚	6⅔	7½	8⅓	9⅙	10
1 × 6	4	5	6	7	8	9	10	11	12
1 × 7	4⅔	5⅚	7	8⅙	9⅓	10½	11⅔	12⅚	14
1 × 8	5⅓	6⅔	8	9⅓	10⅔	12	13⅓	14⅔	16
1 × 10	6⅔	8⅓	10	11⅔	13⅓	15	16⅔	18⅓	20
1 × 12	8	10	12	14	16	18	20	22	24
1¼ × 4	3⅓	4⅙	5	5⅚	6⅔	7½	8⅓	9⅙	10
1¼ × 6	5	6¼	7½	8¾	10	11¼	12½	13¾	15
1¼ × 8	6⅔	8⅓	10	11⅔	13⅓	15	16⅔	18⅓	20
1¼ × 10	8⅓	10⁵⁄₁₂	12½	14⁷⁄₁₂	16⅔	18¾	20⅚	22¹¹⁄₁₂	25
1¼ × 12	10	12½	15	17½	20	22½	25	27½	30
1½ × 4	4	5	6	7	8	9	10	11	12
1½ × 6	6	7½	9	10½	12	13½	15	16½	18
1½ × 8	8	10	12	14	16	18	20	22	24
1½ × 10	10	12½	15	17½	20	22½	25	27½	30
1½ × 12	12	15	18	21	24	27	30	33	36
2 × 2	2⅔	3⅓	4	4⅔	5⅓	6	6⅔	7⅓	8
2 × 4	5⅓	6⅔	8	9⅓	10⅓	12	13⅓	14⅔	16
2 × 6	8	10	12	14	16	18	20	22	24
2 × 8	10⅔	13⅓	16	18⅔	21⅓	24	26⅔	29⅓	32
2 × 10	13⅓	16⅔	20	23⅓	26⅔	30	33⅓	36⅔	40
2 × 12	16	20	24	28	32	36	40	44	48
3 × 3	6	7½	9	10½	12	13½	15	16½	18
3 × 6	12	15	18	21	24	27	30	33	36
3 × 8	16	20	24	28	32	36	40	44	48
3 × 10	20	25	30	35	40	45	50	55	60
3 × 12	24	30	36	42	48	54	60	66	72
4 × 4	10⅔	13⅓	16	18⅔	21⅓	24	26⅔	29⅓	32
4 × 6	16	20	24	28	32	36	40	44	48
4 × 8	21⅓	26⅔	32	37⅓	42⅔	48	53⅓	58⅔	64
4 × 10	26⅔	33⅓	40	46⅔	53⅓	60	66⅔	73⅓	80
4 × 12	32	40	48	56	64	72	80	88	96

Table 2–10 Quick estimate for the number of board feet in a piece of lumber.

Width (inches)	Thickness* (inches)	Board feet equals	Width (inches)	Thickness* (inches)	Board feet equals
3	1 or less	¼ of the length	9	1 or less	¾ of the length
4	1 or less	⅓ of the length	12	1 or less	Same as the length
6	1 or less	½ of the length	15	1 or less	1¼ of the length

* For thicker stock, find board feet or 1 inch of thickness and multiply by the thickness.

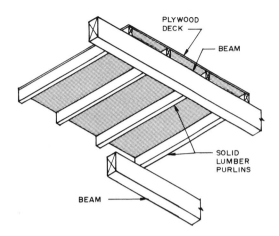

2-17 A typical plywood structural floor panel.

Structural Panels

There are a wide variety of wood panels manufactured that have no use in light frame construction. Examples include lumber-core panels veneered on the front and back with hardwood, particleboard core panels with exterior veneers that are used for cabinet construction, and many types of plywood including cabinet woods and panelling. Those used in framing are **Performance-Rated structural plywood** and **structural nonveneered reconstituted wood panels.** These are used along with the structural wood frame to enclose and strengthen the structure. Typical uses include subflooring and sheathing on walls and roofs. They are also used to form lumber-ribbed structural panels that will span widely spaced beams or trusses (see 2-17). These structural panels are designed to carry normal floor and roof loads over specified spans. Performance-Rated structural panels include plywood, oriented strand board, and Com-Ply®. They are manufactured following American Plywood Association (APA) Performance Standards. The standard specifications define how each product must *perform* in designated applications rather than how it should be manufactured.

Plywood is made by bonding thin sheets of veneer, called *plies*, in layers forming a panel. The plies are always in odd numbers of layers, giving balanced construction. By alternating the layers the grain runs perpendicular to the adjacent layer, producing a strong, stiff material that will not split like a solid wood board (see 2-18).

Oriented strand board (OSB) is a nonveneer APA Performance-Rated panel made of compressed wood strand plies. The strands in each ply run in the same direction. The board is made by bonding these plies at right angles to each other in odd numbers of layers as is done for plywood. Most panels are rather textured on the surface (see 2-19).

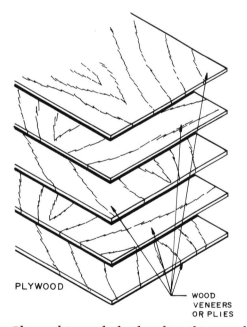

2-18 Plywood is made by bonding thin wood plies with the grain in each ply perpendicular to the plies on each side. There is always an odd number of plies in a panel.

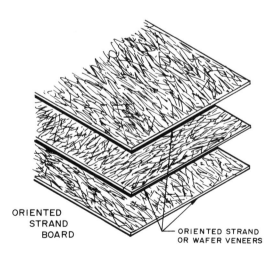

2-19 Oriented strand board panels are made from plies of bonded, compressed, wood strands.

Com-Ply® is another APA Performance-Rated panel made by bonding reconstituted wood cores between wood veneer plies. This gives a strong panel that has the wood grain appearance on the face and the back of the panel (see 2-20).

APA Performance-Rated panels are rated for use as single-layer flooring; sheathing for roofs, floors, and walls; and exterior siding. These are broken down into exposure-durability classifications indicating the resistance to moisture and a special sheathing rating, Structural 1, which indicates extra strength in the cross-panel direction and in racking.

Exposure Ratings

Performance-Rated panel exposure ratings for panels permanently exposed to weather or moisture are Exterior, Exposure 1, and Exposure 2.

Exterior panels are waterproof and can withstand permanent exposure to the weather or sources of moisture.

Exposure 1 panels are used when there will be a long delay in construction causing the panels to be exposed to the weather for some time before they are covered with finish materials. Most Performance-Rated panels are Exposure 1.

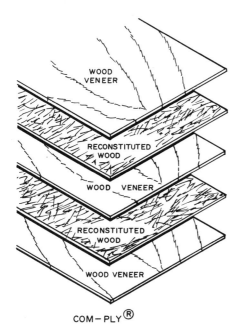

WOOD VENEER

RECONSTITUTED WOOD

WOOD VENEER

RECONSTITUTED WOOD

WOOD VENEER

COM—PLY®

2-20 Com-Ply® is a composition panel made by bonding wood and reconstituted wood strand plies.

Exposure 2 panels are used when there will be only a slight delay in construction before they are covered with finish materials.

APA Rated Products

APA Performance-Rated products include sheathing, Sturd-I-Floor, and siding.

APA-Rated Sheathing is used for wall and roof sheathing, subfloors, and other construction applications. It is available in the following thicknesses: $5/16$, $3/8$, $7/16$, $15/32$, $1/2$, $19/32$, $5/8$, $23/32$, and $3/4$ inch. It has the following span ratings: $16/0$, $20/0$, $24/0$, $24/16$, $32/16$, $40/20$, and $48/24$. The span rating indicates the maximum safe unsupported span when used as sheathing. The first number is for use as roof sheathing and the second number is the span when used as floor sheathing. It is available in square-edge panels. APA-Rated Sheathing is manufactured as plywood, oriented strand board, and Com-Ply®, and in Exposure 1, Exposure 2, and Exterior durability classifications.

APA Structural 1 Rated Sheathing is used where cross-panel strength and stiffness or shear properties are of maximum importance, such as the construction of shear walls and panellized roofs. All plies are special improved grades, and panels marked PS1 are limited to group 1 species (the strongest species). They are made with span ratings of 20/0, 24/0, 24/16, 32/16, 40/20, and 48/24 and in Exterior and Exposure 1 durability classification. Structure 1 panels are manufactured as plywood, oriented strand board, and Com-Ply®.

APA-Rated Sturd-I-Floor is a structural panel used as a combination subfloor and underlayment over which carpet can be directly laid. It has high resistance to concentrated and impact loads. Usually an underlayment is placed over it if vinyl floor covering is to be laid. It is available as square-edge and tongue-and-groove-edge panels. Square-edge panels require that wood blocking be installed below unsupported joints between panels. It has span ratings of 16, 20, 24, 32, and 48 inches and durability classifications of Exterior, Exposure 1, and Exposure 2. Standard thicknesses are $19/32$, $5/8$, $23/32$, $3/4$, and $1\frac{1}{8}$ inches.

APA-Rated Siding is available in panel and lap siding. It includes a variety of products such as plywood, overlaid oriented strand board, and composite materials.

Panel siding can be applied directly to the studs or over sheathing. It is available in a variety of surface textures and patterns. Panel thicknesses vary with the particular pattern but range from $^{11}/_{32}$ to $^5/_8$ inch. Panel sizes are 48 × 96 inches, 48 × 108 inches, and 48 × 120 inches (see 2-21).

Lap siding is available in rough sawed or smooth overlaid surfaces with square or bevel edges. It is available in thicknesses of $^{11}/_{32}$, $^3/_8$, $^{15}/_{32}$, $^1/_2$, $^{19}/_{32}$, and $^5/_8$ inches, widths up to 12 inches, and lengths to 16 feet (see 2-22).

Span Ratings

APA Performance-Rated panels have an identifying grade stamp. Span ratings are found on this stamp. The span rating is the maximum center-to-center spacing of supports, in inches, over which the panel is to be placed.

Sheathing and Sturd-I-Floor ratings are based on the placement of the long dimension of the panel being perpendicular to the supporting members. The span rating is shown as two numbers, such as $^{32}/_{16}$. The left-hand number, 32, is the span for the panel used as roof sheathing. The right-hand number, 16, is the span when it is used as subflooring. Panels with a roof span rating of 24 or more can be used vertically or horizontally as wall sheathing over studs spaced to a maximum of 24 inches on center. Those less than 24 can be used on studs spaced 16 inches on center.

Some sheathing is manufactured especially for wall sheathing. It is marked W-16 or W-24. Horizontal edges of wall sheathing must be blocked if the panels are used to brace the walls. Allowable spans for structural sheathing panels are given in table 2-11. Manufacturers' recommendations for panels available in various parts of the United States should be observed.

APA Rated Siding is available with span ratings of 16 and 24 inches. It may be used directly on the studs or over sheathing.

The design loads for APA sheathing and Sturd-I-Floor at maximum span is 85 psf live load for floors plus 25 psf for dead load. Other design loads can be achieved by placing supports closer together.

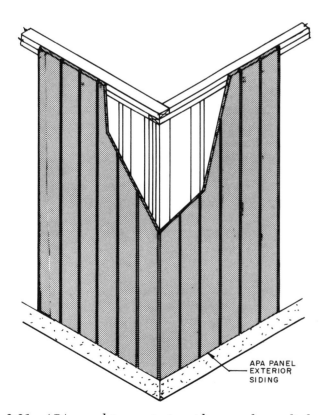

2-21   APA panel-type exterior siding can be applied over sheathing or directly to the studs.

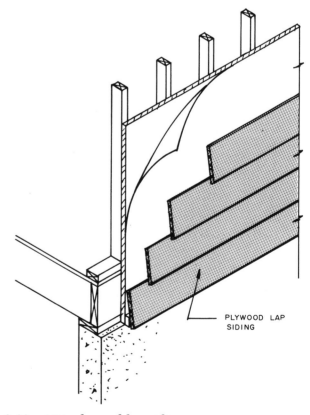

2-22   APA plywood lap siding.

Table 2–11 Typical Allowable Spans for Structural Panel Products.*

Material	Wall sheathing (studs 16″ O.C.)	Roof sheathing (framing 24″ O.C.) edge support	no edge support	Subfloor (joists 16″ O.C.)	Subfloor-underlayment (joists 24″ O.C.)
plywood	5/16″	3/8″	1/2″	1/2″	3/4″
Com-Ply®	3/8″	3/8″	1/2″	1/2″	3/4″
waferboard	3/8″	7/16″	9/16″	5/8″	3/4″
oriented strand board	3/8″	3/8″	7/16″	7/16″	3/4″
particleboard	3/8″	3/8″	9/16″	5/8″	3/4″

* These are general spans. Consult with manufacturer's data for panels available in your locality.

APA Grade Stamp

The APA grade stamp for Performance-Rated panels, Sturd-I-Floor, and siding are shown in 2-23. It gives the panel grade, siding face grade, span rating, thickness, species group number, exposure durability classification, mill number, product standard, FHA recognition, code recognition of APA as a quality assurance agency, and the APA Performance-Rated Standard. The APA grade stamp is placed on each piece of sheathing, siding, and Sturd-I-Floor.

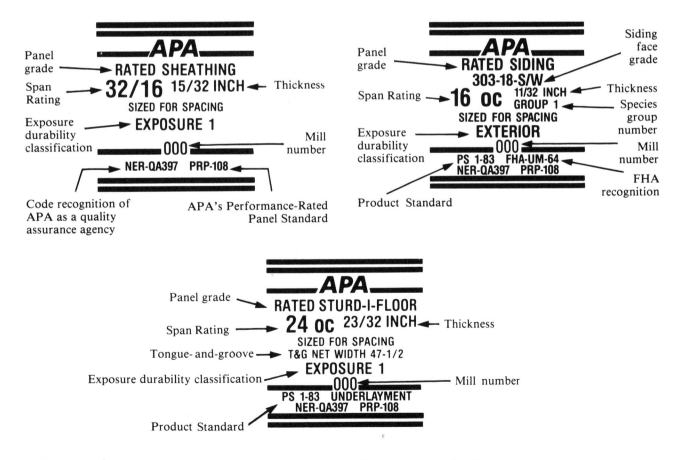

2-23 Examples of APA-grade stamps for sheathing, siding, and Sturd-I-Floor. (Courtesy American Plywood Association)

Treated Plywood

Plywood is an approved structural panel that can be pressure-treated to resist rot and decay or treated with fire-retardant chemicals. Panels that are treated must have Exterior or Exposure 1 adhesive. Panels treated with waterborne preservative must be dried to a maximum moisture content of 18 percent after treatment. Those treated with fire-retardant chemicals must be dried to a moisture content of 15 percent after treatment.

Fire-Retardant-Treated Wood and Plywood

There are situations where the local building code requires the framer to use fire-retardant-treated wood (FRTW). Fire-retardant treatments differ for interior and exterior use. There are two types of interior formulations in use. The oldest is classified as interior type B (AWPA-C20). (AWPA is the American Wood Preservers Association.) It is a formulation of mineral or organic water-soluble salts, such as zinc chloride, boric acid, ammonium sulfate, monobasic ammonium phosphate, dibasic ammonium phosphate, or sodium tetraborate (borax). Borax resists flaming but is not good at retarding glow. Ammonium phosphates will check flaming and glowing. Boric acid is not the best flame-resistant material but does check glowing. It is recommended that the manufacturer of the fire-retardant material be consulted before making a choice. Wood treated with one or more of these salts is more hygroscopic than untreated wood or than wood treated with an exterior-type retardant. When used in areas of high humidity, the moisture draws the salts in the wood to the surface, causing nails and other metal parts to corrode.

A newer interior formulation, type A (AWPA-C20), is no more corrosive than untreated wood, but is not intended for exterior use. Treated wood must be redried to the required moisture content.

Exterior types (EXT-FRTW) vary with the manufacturer but in general consist of water-soluble monomers or phenolic resins which, when polymerized, become insoluble in water.

The best way to apply fire-retardant chemicals is using some form of pressure treatment. This provides a deeper penetration of the soluble salts into the wood. Some situations require a partial penetration while others require penetration completely through the wood. After the wood has been pressure-treated it must be redried to the required moisture content and to set the chemicals.

Ordering APA Performance-Rated Plywood Products

When ordering APA-Rated Sheathing specify the APA trademark, span rating, thickness, exposure, dimensions, and number of pieces. Following is an example:

15/32″, APA-Rated Sheathing, 32/16, Exp 1, 48″ × 96″, 50 pcs.

When ordering APA-Rated Sturd-I-Floor specify the APA trademark, span rating, thickness, exposure, tongue-and-groove or square edge, dimensions, and number of pieces. Following is an example:

23/32″, APA Sturd-I-Floor, 24″ O.C., T and G, Exp 1, 48″ × 96″, 50 pcs.

When ordering APA-Rated Siding specify the thickness, APA trademark, span rating, face grade, texture, pattern, dimensions, and number of pieces. Following is an example:

5/8″, APA 303-16″ O.C., 6 S/W, rough-sawed Texture 1-11, grooves 4″ O.C., 48″ × 96″, 50 pcs.

Waferboard

Waferboard is sometimes used for sheathing, but is not under American Plywood Association jurisdiction. It is a panel that is made from open flakes ranging in size from 1½ to 3 inches that are, in general, rectan-

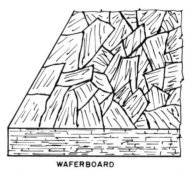

WAFERBOARD

2-24 Waferboard is made from wood flake chips bonded with a phenolic resin.

gular in shape. They are bonded in a heated press using a phenolic resin. The flakes fall in a random pattern in the panel. It can be made in sheets 8 to 24 feet long, 4 feet wide, and with square or tongue-and-groove edges. Panel thickness ranges from ¼ to ¾ inch (see 2-24).

Wood Preservatives

Wood exposed to the soil or exposed to, or immersed in, water requires treatment by some type of wood preservative.

Creosote is an oil-borne preservative used to treat wood to be in contact with the soil, such as railroad ties, or in water, such as pilings for piers. The most effective type is coal-tar creosote, but oil-tar, water-tar, and water-gas-tar creosotes are available. Creosote gives the wood a black to dark-brown appearance.

Pentachlorophenol is an oil-borne preservative that penetrates deeply into the wood and is long-lasting. It is used on many products, including pilings for use in land or water, glued laminated beams (glulams, *see* Chapter 6), and utility poles.

Waterborne preservatives are odorless and paintable. They are infused by a pressure-treatment process. Wood must be dried to the desired moisture content after treatment.

The types of inorganic arsenic waterborne preservative in common use include ammoniacal copper arsenate (ACA), chromated copper arsenate (CCA), and ammoniacal copper zinc arsenate (ACZA). These protect against insect attack and decay. They should never be used where they will come in contact with food or be burned. Those handling treated wood should wear gloves and wash their clothes separately from other clothes. When cutting treated wood, you must wear a mask.

Other Wood Products

There are a number of manufactured wood products used for structural purposes. These include parallel-strand lumber beams, glulam members, laminated-veneer lumber beams, and I-joists. These are discussed in detail in Chapter 6.

Nails

There are many different types of nails produced for use in specific applications. The nail recommended for a particular use should be used to provide satisfactory results.

Nails are made from a variety of metals including steel, aluminum, and copper. Aluminum and copper resist rust. Steel nails can be zinc-coated to resist rust and improve holding properties. Cement-coated nails are used when increased holding power is needed. High-carbon steel nails are very hard and are used to nail into concrete and masonry. Nails used in structural framing have large-diameter heads, while those for finishing purposes have very small heads, which permit them to be set below the surface of the wood and allow the hole made to be hidden with a filler. Some nails have smooth shanks, while others have threaded, barbed, grooved, twisted, or ring shanks that increase holding power.

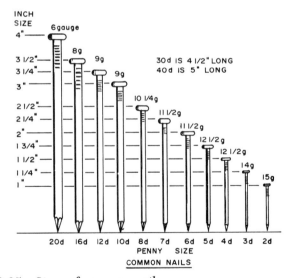

2-25 *Sizes of common nails.*

Nail sizes are indicated by the term *"penny,"* which is represented by the symbol "d". For example, a 10d nail is a 10-penny nail (see 2-25). When the size is specified this also establishes the wire diameter used to make the nail (tables 2-12 and 2-13). For example, a 10d common nail is made from No. 9 wire. The smaller the wire gauge number, the larger the wire diameter.

Nails are sold by the pound. A pound of 20d nails will contain fewer nails than a pound of 10d nails (table 2-14).

Nails commonly used for framing and general carpentry are shown in 2-26. The **common nail** has the thickest head and the largest wire diameter. The **box nail** has a large, but thinner head, and is made in smaller wire diameters than common nails. It is used when splitting may be a problem.

Finish and casing nails are used for securing interior trim, baseboards, and some types of cabinet work where the head is to be concealed. Casing nails have a larger head than finish nails, and they are used where greater holding power is needed.

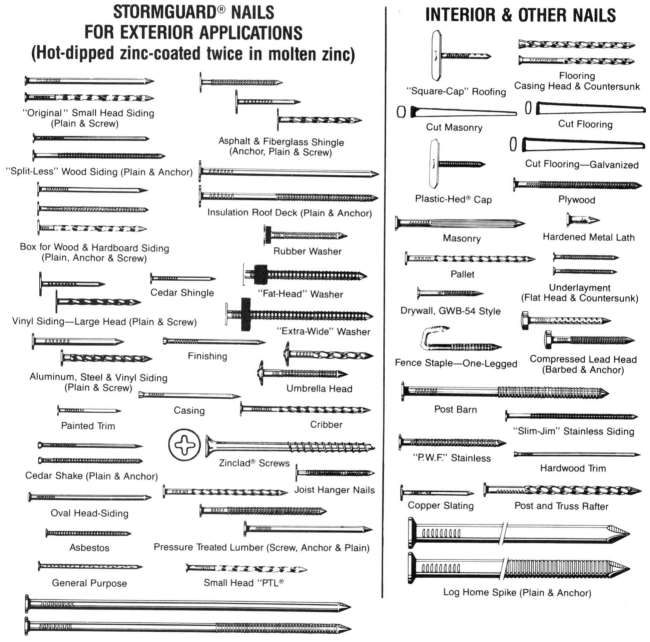

STORMGUARD® NAILS FOR EXTERIOR APPLICATIONS
(Hot-dipped zinc-coated twice in molten zinc)

"Original" Small Head Siding (Plain & Screw)

"Split-Less" Wood Siding (Plain & Anchor)

Box for Wood & Hardboard Siding (Plain, Anchor & Screw)

Vinyl Siding—Large Head (Plain & Screw)

Aluminum, Steel & Vinyl Siding (Plain & Screw)

Painted Trim

Cedar Shake (Plain & Anchor)

Oval Head-Siding

Asbestos

General Purpose

Gutter Spike (Plain & Anchor)

Asphalt & Fiberglass Shingle (Anchor, Plain & Screw)

Insulation Roof Deck (Plain & Anchor)

Rubber Washer

Cedar Shingle

"Fat-Head" Washer

"Extra-Wide" Washer

Finishing

Umbrella Head

Casing

Cribber

Zinclad® Screws

Joist Hanger Nails

Pressure Treated Lumber (Screw, Anchor & Plain)

Small Head "PTL®"

INTERIOR & OTHER NAILS

"Square-Cap" Roofing

Flooring
Casing Head & Countersunk

Cut Masonry

Cut Flooring

Plastic-Hed® Cap

Cut Flooring—Galvanized

Masonry

Plywood

Hardened Metal Lath

Pallet

Underlayment (Flat Head & Countersunk)

Drywall, GWB-54 Style

Fence Staple—One-Legged

Compressed Lead Head (Barbed & Anchor)

Post Barn

"Slim-Jim" Stainless Siding

"P.W.F." Stainless

Hardwood Trim

Copper Slating

Post and Truss Rafter

Log Home Spike (Plain & Anchor)

2-26 Nails used in light-frame construction. (Courtesy W.H. Maze Company)

Table 2–12 Finishing nails.

Size	Gauge
3d	15½
4d	15
6d	13
8d	12½
10d	11½

Table 2–13 Casing and box nails.

Size	Gauge
4d	14
6d	12½
8d	11½
10d	10½
12d	10½
16d	10
20d	9
30d	9
40d	8

Table 2–14 Approximate number of nails per pound.

Size	Common	Box	Finishing	Casing
2d	875	1010	135	1010
3d	585	635	805	635
4d	315	470	545	470
5d	270	405	500	405
6d	180	235	310	235
7d	160	210	235	210
8d	105	145	190	145
9d	95	130	170	130
10d	70	95	120	95
12d	65	86	110	85
16d	50	70	90	70
20d	30	50	60	50

Power staplers and nailing devices are used considerably by framing carpenters (see 2-28). These power-nailing tools operate on compressed air and are available in a wide range of nailers and staplers.

Duplex (also called double-head or scaffold) nails have two heads. They are used to hold parts together that will eventually have to be disassembled, such as carpenter-built wood scaffolding. They are driven in until the lower head hits the surface. The second head is used to pull out the nail (see 2-27). Other types of nails, such as underlayment, siding, and wood shingles, are also shown in 2-26.

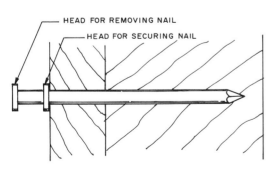

2-27   A duplex nail is used where it must eventually be removed.

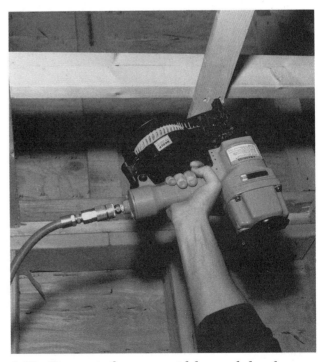

2-28   Power nailers are widely used by framers doing light-frame construction. (Courtesy Stanley-Bostitch)

Typical nailers use either coils or nested-head strips of nails (see 2-29). A wide variety of nails can be power-driven. These include small brads, finishing nails, trim and siding nails, sheathing and decking nails, roofing nails, concrete nails, and long heavy-duty spikes for timber construction. Nails are available with smooth, ring, and screw shanks.

Power staplers are sometimes used instead of nailers. They are especially useful when securing soft materials, such as foam insulation. Types of staples typically available include those for use on sheathing, decking, asphalt shingles, insulation, installing finish materials, and hardwood flooring.

There are power-driven tools using .22 caliber crimped loads that drive specially designed fasteners into concrete, steel, and masonry. Other pneumatic fasteners can join metal to metal, wood to metal, and gypsum board to metal.

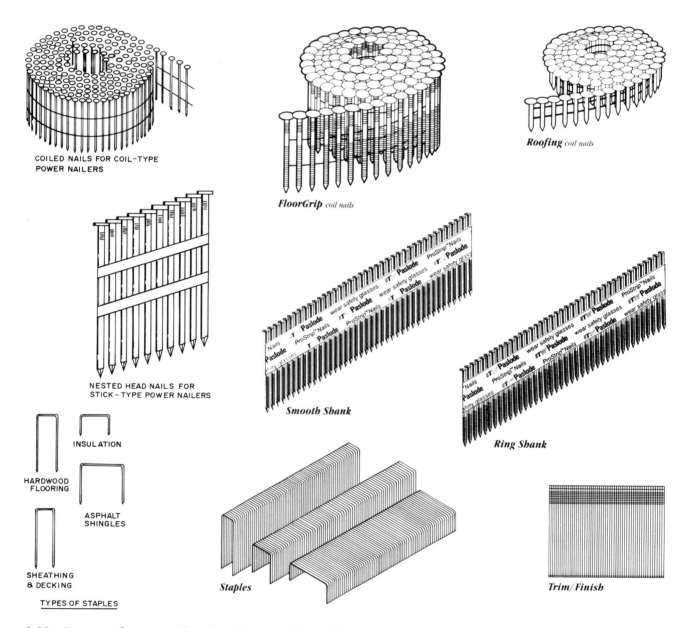

COILED NAILS FOR COIL-TYPE POWER NAILERS

FloorGrip coil nails

Roofing coil nails

NESTED HEAD NAILS FOR STICK-TYPE POWER NAILERS

Smooth Shank

Ring Shank

INSULATION

HARDWOOD FLOORING

ASPHALT SHINGLES

SHEATHING & DECKING

TYPES OF STAPLES

Staples

Trim/Finish

2-29   *Power nailers use coil- and stick-type nail cartridges. Power staplers can drive a wide variety of specialized staples. (Courtesy ITW Paslode Company)*

Wood Screws

Wood screws are used for many applications in construction. Most commonly they are used in cabinet construction and for installing hardware. Gypsum wall panels are also frequently installed with screws. Screws have greater holding power than nails and are used where this extra strength is needed. They take longer to install than nails but can be easily removed if necessary.

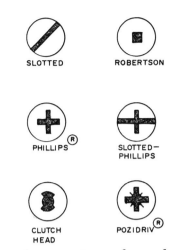

2-31 *Types of recesses in wood screwheads.*

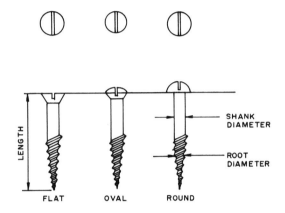

2-30 *Common types of wood screws.*

The most common head types are flat, round, and oval. Flathead screws are set flush with the surface and are used to install hinges and hardware. The head of roundhead screws remains above the surface. Oval heads are partially in the material and are used where an attractive exposed screw is required (see 2-30). Screwheads are made in a variety of head recesses (see 2-31). The slotted, Phillips, and slotted/Phillips recesses are most commonly found. The Phillips-type recess makes driving the screw easier and faster.

The sizes of commonly used wood screws are given in table 2-15. The length is the distance the screw will penetrate the wood, as shown in 2-30. The diameter of the screw shank is indicated by the gauge number of the wire used to make it. Each length of screw is available in inches for each gauge number of the wire

Table 2–15 Typical sizes of wood screws.

Length (inches)	Shank diameter (wire gauge number)
¼	2, 4
⅜	2, 3, 4, 5, 6
½ and ⅝	2, 3, 4, 5, 6, 7, 8
¾, ⅞, and 1	4, 5, 6, 7, 8, 9, 10, 11, 12
1¼	4, 5, 6, 7, 8, 9, 10, 11, 12, 14, 16
1½	6, 7, 8, 9, 10, 11, 12, 14, 16
1¾	6, 8, 9, 10, 12, 14, 16
2	8, 9, 10, 12, 14, 16
2¼	10, 12, 14
2½	8, 9, 10, 12, 14, 16
3	10, 12, 14, 16

used to make it. Each length of screw is available in several gauge sizes. The approximate diameter in inches for each group is listed in table 2-16.

A particleboard screw is designed for fastening into particleboard. It has widely spaced threads that are needed to set itself into the particleboard (see 2-32).

2-32   *A special screw designed for use in particleboard.*

Table 2–16 Wood screw diameters in inches and by gauge number.

Wire gauge number	Decimal size	Fractional size
0	0.060	1/16
1	0.073	5/64
2	0.086	3/32
3	0.099	7/64
4	0.112	1/8
5	0.125	1/8
6	0.138	9/64
7	0.151	5/32
8	0.164	11/64
9	0.177	3/16
10	0.190	13/64
11	0.203	13/64
12	0.216	7/32
14	0.242	1/4
16	0.268	9/32
18	0.294	19/64
20	0.320	21/64

3

Power Tools

Framers use a variety of power tools to saw, drill, shape, nail, staple, and set screws. Some are stationary and others are portable. **Stationary power tools** are mounted on a base which rests on the floor. **Portable power tools** are lightweight and are carried with the framer as the work progresses. Portable power tools are operated by electricity, batteries, or compressed air.

It is important to purchase only high-quality tools. Anything less will not produce the work expected and could be dangerous. Select only tools that have their electrical system insulated to assure that electrical shocks are not possible. All tools should have guards that provide good protection on the cutting edges. Be certain the manufacturer has a reliable service and repair system.

General Power Tool Safety Rules

The construction industry is one of the more dangerous of industries. Therefore, observance of safe working conditions is essential. Following are some general safety rules governing the use of power tools. The U.S. Occupational Safety and Health Administration (OSHA) requirements for power tools are detailed in the publication *Hand and Power Tools, OSHA 3080*. Order from OSHA Publication Office, 200 Constitution Ave., NW, Room N-3647, Washington, DC 20210.

1. Wear some form of approved eye protection.

2. Use only tools with guards in place.

3. Be certain the electric cord and extension cord are not worn or damaged.

4. If the tool has a third-wire plug, be certain the source of electricity has a third-wire ground.

5. Remove all rings, bracelets, necklaces, etc., that may become caught. Long hair can also be a problem and should be confined with a hair net.

6. Do not use a tool that is not in good condition.

7. Be certain the switch operates properly.

8. Use only sharp saws and cutters. Dull tools can cause accidents.

9. After changing a saw blade or other cutter, recheck before starting the tool to make certain it is properly seated and securely locked in place.

10. Work being cut must rest on a secure surface so that it will not slip while being cut.

11. Avoid working when you are excessively fatigued.

12. Let the tool cut at its normal pace. Do not force or overcrowd to speed up the cut. This can cause kickbacks.

13. After finishing a cut, let the saw or cutter stop rotating before laying the tool down.

Stationary Circular Saw

The stationary circular saw is used for a variety of cuts and produces more accurate results than the portable circular saw. The most common operations include ripping and crosscutting. When it has table extensions it will accurately cut large panels, such as plywood and particleboard. This tool can cause many accidents, so observing safety rules is very important. The saw in 3-1 has a 10-inch blade and will cut stock 3¼ inches thick at 90 degrees and 2⅛ inches thick at a 45-degree mitre. It is light enough that it can be easily moved around the construction site.

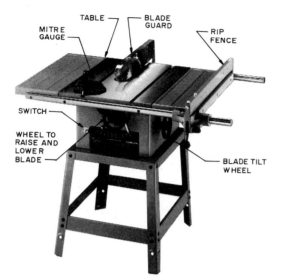

3-1 A lightweight 10-inch contractor's stationary circular saw. (Courtesy Delta International Machinery Corporation)

Circular Saw Safety

Following are safety recommendations for using a stationary circular saw.

1. Do not adjust saw while it is running.

2. Always wear safety goggles or safety glasses with side shields.

3. In some operations a dust mask should be used.

4. The saw table and the floor around the saw should be kept free from sawdust and debris.

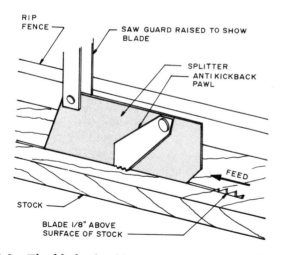

3-2 The blade should extend ⅛ inch above the surface of the board.

5. When cutting wide stock, such as a plywood panel, use an auxiliary support to keep the panel level.

6. Keep all guards in place. Repair them if they do not function properly.

7. The blade should project no more than ⅛ to ¼ inch above the work (see 3-2).

8. Never reach over the blade or place your hands within several inches of it.

9. Never cut a piece of stock freehand. Always use a mitre gauge or the rip fence.

10. Do not stand directly behind the blade. Kickbacks do occur and can cause serious injury.

11. When ripping narrow stock, use a push stick (see 3-3).

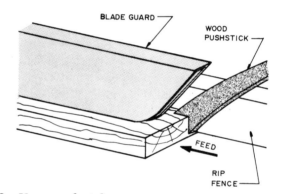

3-3 Use a pushstick to rip narrow pieces of stock on the circular saw. Always keep the blade guard in place.

12. Be certain the rip fence is parallel with the blade. This reduces binding and burning as well as possible kickbacks.

13. Do not use cracked or burned blades.

14. Blades that wobble or vibrate must be destroyed and discarded.

15. Be certain the blade is installed so that it rotates in the proper direction.

16. Have someone help tail off the end when cutting long boards.

17. Do not cut wet, cupped, or warped boards.

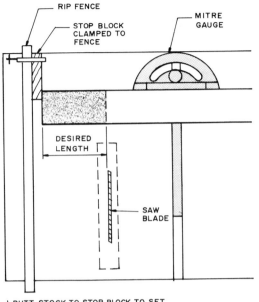

I. BUTT STOCK TO STOP BLOCK TO SET THE LENGTH.

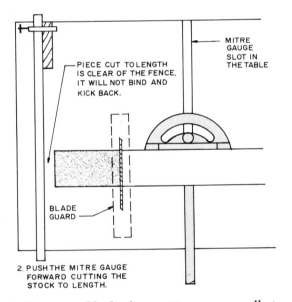

2. PUSH THE MITRE GAUGE FORWARD CUTTING THE STOCK TO LENGTH.

3-4   Use a stop block when cutting many small pieces to length.

18. Do not use the rip fence as a stop when cutting short pieces to length. Use a stop block instead (see 3-4).

19. Do not leave a running saw unattended. If you have to leave it, shut it off.

20. Use the proper blade for the job at hand.

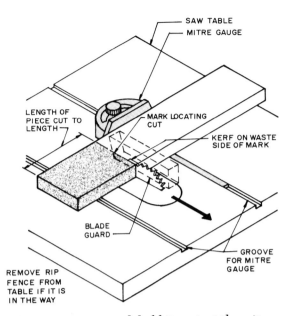

REMOVE RIP FENCE FROM TABLE IF IT IS IN THE WAY

3-5   To crosscut stock hold it against the mitre gauge and move them together towards the blade.

Blade Selection

There are many varieties of circular saw blades available. The hole in the blade must match the diameter of the shaft on the saw. Following are the common types of blades.

A **crosscut blade** is used to cut stock across the grain. A **hollow-ground blade** is used for fine, smooth cuts. The teeth have no set, so that it makes a very narrow kerf. A **ripsaw blade** has large, set, chisel-like teeth and removes wood rapidly. It is used to cut with the grain. The **combination saw blade** has a combination of crosscut and rip teeth and is used for both ripping and crosscutting. The **plywood saw blade** is designed to cut plywood with a minimum of chipping and leaves a smooth surface.

Circular Saw Parts

A typical saw is shown in 3-1. Before operating a saw, be certain you are familiar with the operating parts and adjustments. Usually the switch is located on the front within quick and easy reach. Two handles below the table are used to raise and lower the blade and to tilt it for cutting on angles.

Crosscutting

Following are steps for crosscutting stock (see 3-5).

1. Set the mitre gauge on the desired angle. Slide it in the groove in the table.

2. Crank the blade up so that it protrudes ⅛ inch above the stock to be cut.

3. Place the saw guard over the blade.

4. Be certain the rip fence is moved over, out of the way. Remove it from the saw if necessary.

5. Place the stock to be cut on the table and firmly against the mitre gauge.

6. Start the saw. Do not begin to cut until the spinning blade reaches its full speed.

7. Holding the board firmly against the mitre gauge, slide it into the saw. Sight through the guard to see that the mark on the board lines up with the saw blade and that the blade will cut on the waste side of the line.

8. Push the board and mitre gauge on past the saw. Then remove the board from the mitre gauge.

9. If the scrap end cut off is small, use a stick to push it off the table or wait until the blade stops turning to remove it.

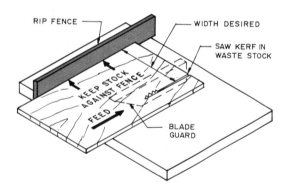

3-6 *When ripping, keep the stock firmly against the rip fence.*

Ripping

Following are steps for ripping stock.

1. Measure the required distance between the saw blade and the rip fence. Measure from the edge of the teeth bent towards the fence.

2. Raise the blade so that it is ⅛ inch above the thickness of the stock to be cut.

3. Place the guard over the blade.

4. Start the saw. Do not begin to cut until the spinning blade has reached full speed.

5. Place the straight, smooth edge of the board against the fence. Do not try to rip stock with curved or warped edges.

6. Hold the stock against the fence and feed it into the saw. Keep an even pressure (see 3-6).

7. Have someone on the other side of the saw to receive long boards. They must only support the stock and should not pull on it.

8. When the end of the stock nears the saw, use a push stick to move the stock past the saw. If the board is 12 inches or wider, you can safely move the stock with your hand if you keep your hand against the rip fence.

Radial-Arm Saw

A radial-arm saw is a type of circular saw that has the blade above the table, and it moves on an arm that extends over the table. A typical radial-arm saw is shown in 3-7. This will rip and crosscut as well as cut mitres.

3-7 *A typical lightweight radial-arm saw.* (Courtesy Delta International Machinery Corporation)

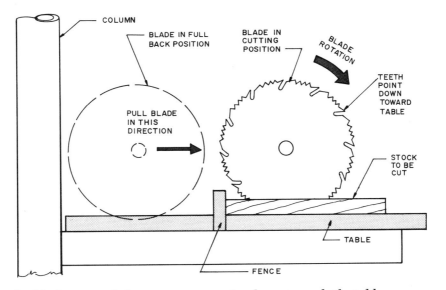

3-8   *The teeth on the blade on a radial-arm saw must point down towards the table.*

The blade is mounted directly onto the motor. The motor and blade are raised and lowered by a crank on the top of the column. They also move horizontally by gliding along the arm. The blade can be tilted to cut on an angle. The blade must be installed with the teeth pointing down towards the table and rotated towards the fence. This action helps hold the stock being cut against the fence (see 3-8).

Radial-Arm Saw Safety

Following are safety recommendations for using a radial-arm saw.

1. Never operate unless all guards are in place.

2. Be certain the blade is installed so that it rotates in the proper direction. If it is not, the saw will tend to run out towards the operator.

3. When ripping, be certain to feed the stock into the blade from the proper direction (see 3-9).

4. When crosscutting, hold the stock firmly until the blade is clear of the stock.

5. Keep both hands clear of the blade at all times. Never reach across the front of the saw.

6. Always return the blade/motor assembly to the full rear position after crosscutting a board.

7. Set the anti-kickback device so that it is slightly below the surface of the stock.

8. When ripping, be certain the blade is parallel with the fence. If not, binding will occur which will produce a damaging kickback.

9. Be certain to use the spreader device when ripping to keep the stock from binding behind the blade after it has been cut.

10. When ripping stock, use a push stick to feed stock past the saw.

11. Never cut anything freehand. Always keep the stock tight to the fence.

12. Do not cut wet, cupped, or warped wood.

13. When ripping, make certain the blade is rotating towards you.

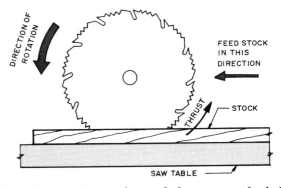

3-9   *When ripping with a radial-arm saw, feed the stock into the blade from the side where the teeth are rotating upwards.*

Crosscutting

1. Adjust the arm to the desired angle of the cut. Lock it tightly in place.

2. Lower the blade so that it cuts a slight kerf in the wood table.

3. Adjust the anti-kickback device so that the fingers are just above the surface of the stock.

4. Place the blade/motor yoke back against the column so that the blade is clear of the front of the fence.

5. Place the stock firmly against the fence. Do not cut warped stock.

6. Turn on the saw.

7. Hold the stock to the fence with one hand. Be certain your hand is clear of the path of the saw. With the other hand move the saw forward into the stock. Hold it firmly so that you control the rate of cut.

8. When the cut is complete, return the yoke to the rear position with the blade behind the fence. Then you can move the cut pieces of stock from the table.

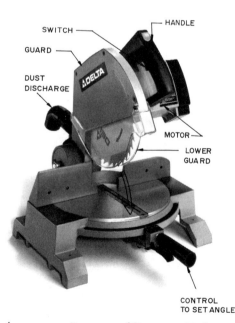

SWITCH
HANDLE
GUARD
DUST DISCHARGE
MOTOR
LOWER GUARD
CONTROL TO SET ANGLE

3-10 A power mitre saw. (Courtesy Delta International Machinery Corporation)

Ripping

1. Move the yoke out on the arm. Release the clamp and rotate it 90 degrees. Lock it to the arm so that the distance between the blade and the fence is the size desired. Set it so that the blade is rotating towards the board as the board is fed into the saw (see 3-9).

2. Be certain all adjustments are locked tight.

3. Lower the blade so that it just touches the wood table. It should cut a shallow kerf in the table when turned on.

4. Adjust the anti-kickback device so that it is slightly below the surface of the stock.

5. Adjust the blade guards so that the blade is covered.

6. Turn on the power. Recheck to be certain the blade is rotating upwards towards you.

7. Place the smooth edge of the stock against the fence and feed into the blade. Do not rip curved, warped, or wet stock.

8. When the end of the stock approaches the blade use a push stick to feed it past the blade.

Mitre Saw

The mitre saw is used to cut mitres and crosscut narrow stock. It resembles the radial-arm saw except that the blade/motor unit swings up and down on a pivot and can be adjusted to swing right and left on various angles (see 3-10).

Mitre saws are specified by the diameter of the blade. A 12-inch saw will crosscut 2×8 stock at 90 degrees and 2×6 and 4×4 stock at a 45-degree mitre. It will also mitre 5¼-inch crown moulding and 5½-inch base moulding. A 10-inch saw will crosscut 2×6 stock at 90 degrees and 2×4 stock at 45 degrees.

Mitre Saw Safety

1. Always leave all guards in place.

2. Be certain the blade revolves down towards the table.

3. Since the saw swings down, it is necessary to be especially alert and keep your hands well clear of the cutting area.

4. Hold the stock firmly against the fence.

5. As soon as a cut is complete, release the switch.

6. Always hold stock against the fence. Never try to cut freehand.

7. Be certain the spring that lifts the saw to an upright position is properly adjusted. Do not use the saw if it will not automatically raise to the up position when released.

Cutting Mitres

1. Set the saw on the desired angle. Lock it tightly in place.

2. Place the stock firmly against the fence.

3. Turn on the saw.

4. Once you are certain your hands are clear, and the stock is firm against the fence, lower the blade and complete the cut (see 3-11).

5. Release the switch and raise the saw. Be careful of the blade, because on most saws it will still be rotating. Some models have a brake to cut short the slowdown.

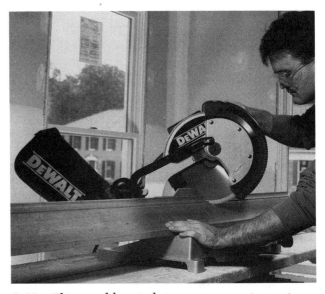

3-11   *This moulding is being cut on a mitre using a power mitre saw.* (Courtesy DeWalt Industrial Tool Company)

Frame-and-Trim Saw

A versatile saw that can crosscut and mitre wide stock is the frame-and-trim saw (see 3-12).

3-12   *A framing and trim saw.* (Courtesy Delta International Machinery Corporation)

3-13 The framing and trim saw will mitre stock up to 12 inches wide. (Courtesy Delta International Machinery Corporation)

3-14 The framing and trim saw can crosscut and cut dadoes. (Courtesy Delta International Machinery Corporation)

The frame-and-trim saw will crosscut stock up to 2¾ inches thick and 16 inches wide, and mitre 1¾-inch stock 12 inches wide at 45 degrees (see 3-13). It can also be used to cut dadoes that are commonly used for stair and cabinet construction (see 3-14). The saw head also can be tilted to cut compound mitres.

When using the frame-and-trim saw, observe safety rules for the use of mitre and radial-arm saws.

Sabre Saw

The sabre saw is primarily used to cut curves and internal cuts. However, the sabre saw can be used for crosscutting, ripping, and mitring, but it is not as accurate as other types of saws (see 3-15). Light-duty sabre saws are used to cut thin materials such as plywood sheets. Heavy-duty sabre saws can be used to cut 2-inch stock. Several brands will cut stock up to 5 inches thick (see 3-16).

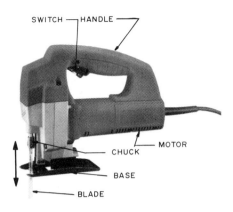

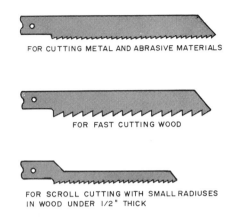

For cutting metal and abrasive materials

For fast cutting wood

For scroll cutting with small radiuses in wood under 1/2" thick

3-15 *A sabre saw.* (Courtesy Milwaukee Electric Tool Corporation)

3-17 *A few of the many blades used with sabre saws.*

Manufacturers provide a variety of blades for various purposes (see 3-17). Thin wood is best cut with a fine-tooth blade, such as one with 12 teeth per inch. A blade with 10 teeth per inch is used on thicker panels. If cutting 2-inch stock, a blade with 6 teeth per inch will produce the fastest cut. Some blades will cut metal and plastics and can be used to cut through nails. Thin, hard metals and very thin woods are cut with a blade having 24 teeth per inch. Thicker, softer metals require a blade with 14 teeth per inch. A blade should always have 2 teeth in contact with the material.

Internal cuts can be made by drilling holes at the corners of the area to be removed. The blade is lowered into the hole and the cut proceeds in a normal manner (see 3-18).

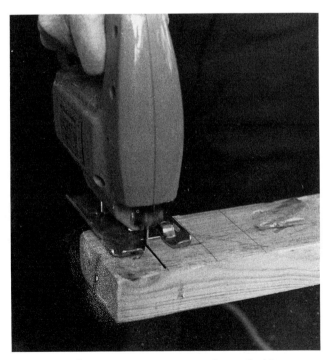

3-16 *A sabre saw can cut two-inch stock.* (Courtesy Black & Decker, Inc.)

3-18 *Internal cuts are made by drilling holes at each corner and cutting from hole to hole.* (Courtesy Black & Decker, Inc.)

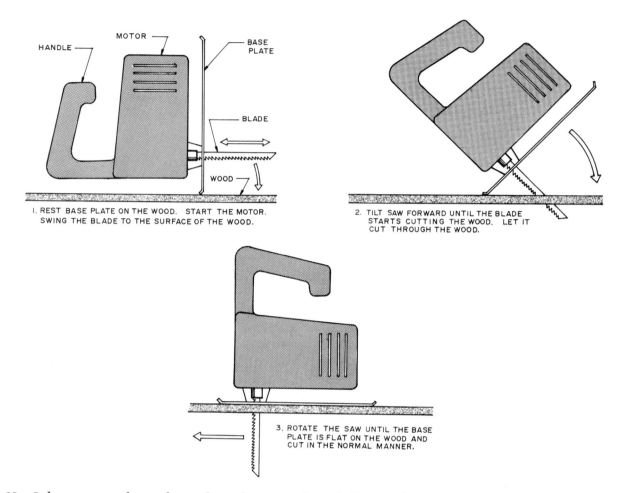

1. REST BASE PLATE ON THE WOOD. START THE MOTOR.
   SWING THE BLADE TO THE SURFACE OF THE WOOD.

2. TILT SAW FORWARD UNTIL THE BLADE
   STARTS CUTTING THE WOOD. LET IT
   CUT THROUGH THE WOOD.

3. ROTATE THE SAW UNTIL THE BASE
   PLATE IS FLAT ON THE WOOD AND
   CUT IN THE NORMAL MANNER.

3-19   Sabre saws can be used to make a plunge cut through thin panels.

Internal cuts in thin stock can also be made by plunge-cutting. The back edge of the base is placed on the panel surface. The saw is started and the blade slowly lowered to the wood surface. It cuts its way through the panel until the saw base is flat on the surface. The cut proceeds in the normal manner (see 3-19).

Sabre Saw Safety

1. Unplug the saw before changing blades.

2. Check to be certain the blade is securely held in the chuck.

3. As you cut, keep the cord out of the way.

4. When beginning a cut, place the base firmly on the wood surface before touching the blade to the wood.

5. If the blade gets stuck, turn off the power and slide the blade clear.

6. When plunge-cutting, use blades designed for that purpose.

7. After cutting, the blade is very hot, so do not touch it.

8. Do not force the saw to cut faster than normal.

9. Do not use dull blades.

10. Be sure the wood to be cut is held so that it will not slip.

11. Let the saw get to full speed before starting to cut.

12. Keep all fingers on the top of the board.

Reciprocating Saw

A reciprocating saw operates much like the sabre saw. A blade is held in a chuck and moves back and forth to produce a cutting action (see 3-20). It will saw

3-20 *A reciprocating saw.* (Courtesy Milwaukee Electric Tool Corporation)

wood, metal, and plastic. A variety of blades is available for cutting various materials. The saw does not produce accurate cuts, but rather it is used for rough cutting operations, such as cutting notches for pipes, holes for electrical outlet boxes, cutting metal duct work, sawing wood, and cutting pipe. It is a versatile saw and useful for many operations (see 3-21).

Reciprocating Saw Safety

1. Observe the safety rules listed for the sabre saw.

2. Use the shortest blade that will do the job.

3. When plunge-cutting, use the foot piece and blade specified by the manufacturer.

4. Before making a blind cut, such as into a wall, be certain no electrical wires or plumbing are behind the surface.

5. Hold the tool by the insulated gripping surfaces.

3-21 *This reciprocating saw is being used to cut a hole in the subfloor.* (Courtesy DeWalt Industrial Tool Company)

Portable Circular Saw

The portable circular saw is probably the most frequently used power tool on a framing job. It is also the *most dangerous*. Carelessness and improper use cause serious accidents.

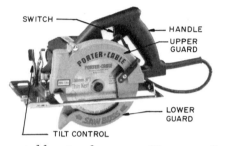

3-22 *A portable circular saw.* (Courtesy Porter-Cable)

A typical saw is shown in 3-22. Popular saw sizes are 7¼-inch and 8¼-inch diameters. However, they are available from 5 to 10 inches in diameter. They are used for crosscutting and ripping solid lumber, plywood, and other panel products. There are many types available, and the purchaser needs to consider possible uses in selection. Factors to consider are the

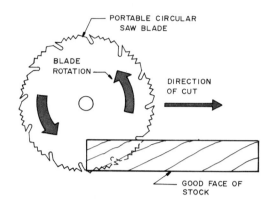

3-23 *The blade of a portable circular saw cuts up from the bottom of the stock.*

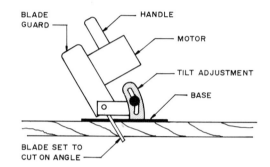

3-24 *The portable circular saw can be tilted on its base to cut bevels.*

NOTE: BOTTOM GUARD IS NOT SHOWN BUT MUST ALWAYS BE IN PLACE.

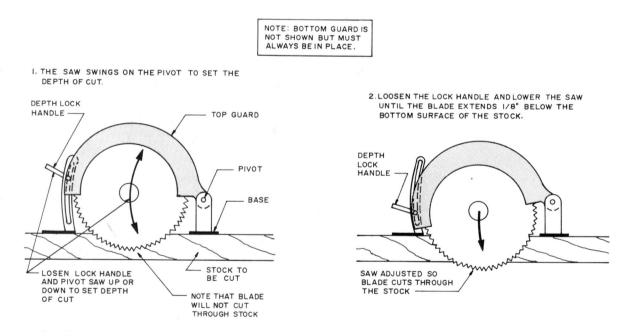

3-25 *The depth of cut on a portable circular saw is set by raising or lowering the saw in relation to the base plate.*

blade size, power available to the blade, guards, provision for grounding, whether it has a brake on the blade, weight, and type of drive.

The saw cuts from the bottom of the material, so that it produces a smoother cut at the bottom. This means the best surface of the stock should be placed down, and the cut made from the other side (see 3-23).

The angle the blade makes with the surface can be adjusted from 90 degrees to 45 degrees. This permits producing bevel cuts on ends and edges. To do this the base is unlocked and pivoted to the angle desired (see 3-24). The depth of cut can be adjusted by loosening a lock on the base, and pivoting it up or down to expose more or less of the blade below the base (see 3-25).

When installing a blade, be certain it is on the arbor, so that the teeth cut up from the bottom, as shown in 3-23. Usually the blade is marked with an arrow on the outside face indicating the direction of rotation.

Crosscutting can be done freehand, if accuracy is not important (see 3-26). A straightedge clamped to the stock will provide a fence against which the saw can slide. This provides a more accurate cut (see 3-27). Ripping can also be done freehand, keeping the blade cutting along a line drawn on the surface. Long straightedges or straight stock can be clamped to the surface to produce a more accurate cut.

The same types of blades described for stationary circular saws are available for use on portable saws.

3-26 *The portable circular saw can be used to crosscut stock.* (Courtesy DeWalt Industrial Tool Company)

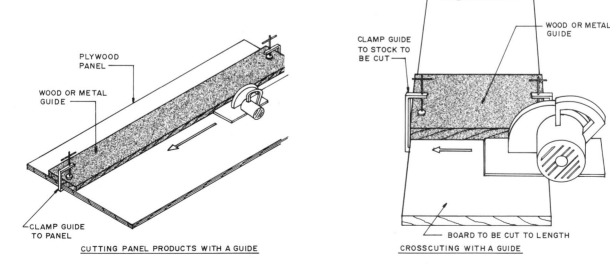

3-27 *Use guides with portable circular saws when an accurate cut is required.*

Portable Circular Saw Safety

1. Do not use blades that are dull, cracked, or that wobble.

2. Keep the extension cord clear of the work. Be certain the cord is long enough to let you finish the cut. A short cord may jerk the saw back, causing a kickback.

3. The piece being cut must be clamped or otherwise held firmly in place.

4. Never hold a piece of wood in your hand while trying to cut it. It must be firmly held on some stationary object.

5. Do not try to cut small pieces of wood.

6. Set the depth of cut so that the blade protrudes no more than ⅛ inch below the wood being cut.

7. Never *ever* place your hands below the wood being cut.

8. Allow the blade to reach full speed before starting to cut.

9. A bind between the saw and wood could cause a kickback. If the saw binds, release the switch immediately. Put a wood wedge in the kerf to hold it open before trying to continue the cut.

10. Do not use the saw if the guards are not working.

11. After finishing a cut, let the guard close and the blade stop, before moving it to another position.

12. A dull blade will cause kickbacks and burning of the blade. Never use a dull blade.

13. Do not force the saw to cut faster than its normal pace.

14. Remove pitch and resin buildup from the blade.

15. Do not cut wet wood. This increases friction and loads the blade with wet sawdust.

16. When cutting large pieces, have provision to keep the pieces from falling when the cut is completed. Having a helper is often a good solution.

Portable Electric Plane

Portable electric planes are used to smooth edges of stock and faces of narrow boards. They can be used to cut chamfers, rabbets, butt joints, and tenons. The width of the cutter is generally about 3 inches and a typical depth of cut in a single pass is ¹¹⁄₆₄ inch. The depth of cut is regulated by raising or lowering the front shoe (see 3-28).

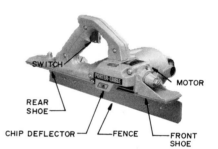

3-28 *A portable electric plane.* (Courtesy Porter-Cable)

To use the electric plane, set the desired depth of cut as specified by the manufacturer. Do not set it too deep. It is better to take two light cuts than one overly deep cut. The fence slides along the face of the board and keeps the plane moving in a straight line. Start the motor, and let it reach full speed. Place the front shoe on the board, and slide the plane along the surface. Hold the plane as specified by the manufacturer. Large planes are usually held with two hands. Smaller planes can be held in one hand. At the start of the cut keep most of the downward pressure on the front shoe. As the end of the surface is reached, keep most of the pressure on the rear shoe (see 3-29).

Portable Electric Plane Safety

1. Be certain the cutters are sharp and installed as recommended by the manufacturer.

2. Allow the cutter head to reach full speed before starting a cut.

3. Use thinner cuts on harder woods.

4. Hold the tool as recommended by the manufacturer. Large planes require two hands. Small block planes can be held with one hand.

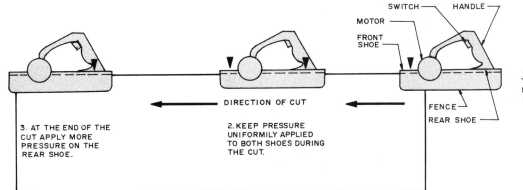

3-29 *How to use the portable electric plane.*

5. Be certain the stock is held securely. Otherwise the plane will throw it back.

6. Keep both hands above the plane.

7. Do not feed faster than it seems to cut easily.

8. When possible avoid cutting knots, especially with deep cuts.

Portable Electric Drill

Portable electric drills are available in a wide range of sizes and features. Some have electric motors that are connected to 120V outlets by a cord, and others are battery operated and are called cordless drills. Most small drills have a pistol-grip handle and can be operated with one hand (see 3-30). Larger, more powerful drills have a pistol grip and a second handle to

3-30 *A portable electric drill.* (Courtesy Porter-Cable)

control the torque produced by large-diameter drills. A heavy-duty drill that is used to bore large-diameter holes and other heavy-duty work is shown in 3-31. Notice the use of two handles to hold the tool firmly and that the chuck is at right angles to the motor.

3-31 *A heavy-duty right-angle drill.* (Courtesy DeWalt Industrial Tool Company)

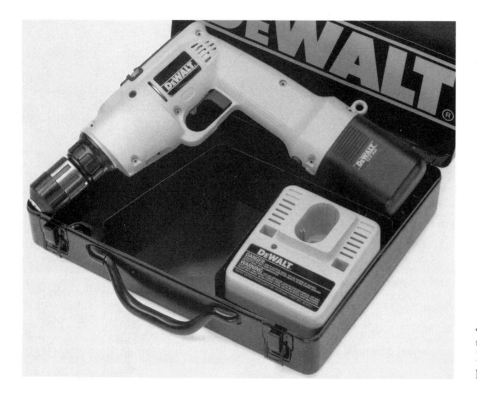

3-32 *A cordless electric drill with a keyless chuck.* (Courtesy DeWalt Industrial Tool Company)

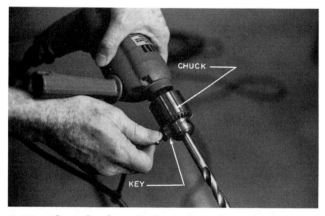

3-33 *This chuck is tightened with a chuck key.* (Courtesy Black & Decker, Inc.)

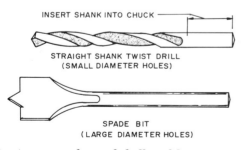

3-34 *A commonly used drill and bit.*

Electric drills operating on 120V current are specified by the chuck size and the amperage of the electric motor. The chuck size indicates the maximum diameter drill shank it will hold. Most frequently used sizes are ⅜ and ½ inch. Typical amperage ratings run from 3 to 10 amps. Battery-operated cordless drills are specified by chuck size and the available voltage. Common chuck sizes are ⅜ inch and ½ inch and voltages of 7 to 13 are typical. The one shown in 3-32 has a keyless chuck.

Bits are installed in key-type chucks which are then tightened with a key (see 3-33). When using straight-shank twist drills, insert the round shank into the chuck but do not let any of the twisted flutes enter. Drills with no flutes, such as a spade bit, are inserted into the chuck as far as they will go (see 3-34). It is recommended that the chuck be tightened by inserting the key and tightening at all three holes in the chuck. The bit can be released by inserting the key in any one of the holes.

When drilling holes, be certain to keep the drill perpendicular to the work. If it drifts off to an angle, the bit may break or may bind in the work. When bits in large, powerful drills bind, the tool could twist out of your hands, causing injury.

Some drills can have the speed of rotation varied and the direction of rotation can be reversed. These can be equipped with a screwdriver bit and used to drive screws. A very low speed of rotation is used.

Portable Electric Drill Safety

1. Do not use a drill if the switch does not operate properly.

2. Remove the chuck key before starting the drill.

3. Always hold the tool securely.

4. Do not force the drill bit into the work.

5. Use sharp drill bits.

6. If the drill bit binds in the work, immediately release the switch. Free the bit from the work before proceeding.

7. When the drill is about to break through the back of the stock, reduce the pressure.

8. Drill bits get very hot, so do not touch them immediately after finishing a hole.

9. Keep drill bits clean and free of wood chips or resin deposits.

10. Be certain the work being drilled is firmly supported.

Electric Drywall Screwdriver

Gypsum wallboard is commonly secured to wood and metal studs with special screws. These are driven with an electric screwdriver. When the screw is tight the clutch releases the drive (see 3-35).

Power Nailers and Staplers

Power nailers are widely used by carpenters when framing a building (see 3-36). While the features vary depending upon the manufacturer, some drive nails up to 16d.

3-35 *An electric drywall screwdriver.* (Courtesy De-Walt Industrial Tool Company)

3-36 *This power nailer operates on compressed air and drives nails up to 3½ inches (16d) long.* (Courtesy ITW Paslode Company)

3-37 *Power nailers are widely used by framing crews. Notice the framer is wearing safety glasses.* (Courtesy ITW Paslode Company)

Most operate on compressed air and are connected to a compressor by an air hose. Power nailers are used to nail wood framing, wood members to concrete, and to install subfloor, sheathing, and roof decking (see 3-37). They are also used in factories assembling door and window units, cabinets, and other related products.

Another type of power nailer is a cordless model which gives great freedom of movement around the construction site and all over the building. It uses an internal combustion engine fueled with disposable fuel cells and has a rechargeable battery providing needed electric power (see 3-38).

Heavy-duty power staplers used for heavy fastening jobs are also driven by compressed air. They can drive staples with legs up to 1½ inches long (see 3-39). The staples used must meet local building codes. Manufacturers produce a wide variety of staples and specify their approved uses. Power staplers are used to join wood framing and to install subflooring and wall and roof sheathing. Shingles are often stapled to the sheathing. Before using staples be certain the building code permits their use. In some places screw-type nails are required for roof sheathing or shingles. Staples are widely used in the assembly of cabinets and door and window units.

It is important to have an air compressor that will supply a constant air stream at the required **pressure**. Air pressures from 80 to 100 psi are common. The air supply must also provide the required **lubrication** to the power tool as specified by the manufacturer. Water condenses in the air tank and must be regularly drained. Filters are used to keep the air clean and remove abrasive sludge created by rust and dust in the air supply system. The air intake filter must be frequently cleaned.

Power Nailer and Stapler Safety

1. Before operating, study the owner's manual and observe all operating recommendations.

2. Treat the tool as you would a gun. Never point it at anyone even as a joke. The projected fastener can cause serious physical damage.

3. Keep both hands behind the nail-ejecting tube.

4. Keep your feet and legs behind and clear of the tool.

5. Wear safety glasses.

6. Use only the fasteners designed for the tool and recommended by the manufacturers (refer to 2-29).

7. Keep the tool tight against the surface being fastened. Do not let it bounce.

8. Maintain the recommended air pressure.

9. When making repairs or adjustments, disconnect the tool from the air line.

10. Do not use a nailer that will allow the discharge of a nail when the end of the tool is not against a surface.

3-38 *This is a cordless framing nailer which uses an internal combustion motor and disposable fuel cells. It has a rechargable battery providing electrical power. It can drive 4000 nails before recharging.* (Courtesy ITW Paslode Company)

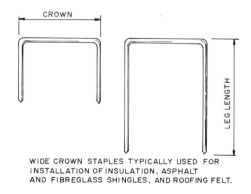

WIDE CROWN STAPLES TYPICALLY USED FOR INSTALLATION OF INSULATION, ASPHALT AND FIBREGLASS SHINGLES, AND ROOFING FELT.

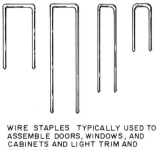

WIRE STAPLES TYPICALLY USED TO ASSEMBLE DOORS, WINDOWS, AND CABINETS AND LIGHT TRIM AND MOULDING.

3-39 *A few of the many types of staples available.*

4

Safety

Working in the construction industry exposes individuals to a vast array of dangerous situations. The contractor is responsible for overseeing that the construction site meets recommended safety regulations. On large jobs a full-time safety supervisor is present. Regardless of the actions of others, the prevention of accidents falls largely upon the knowledge and skills of each individual worker. Regulations alone will not protect the individual unless everyone on the job observes them. Many accidents occur due to the improper use of tools, ladders, and scaffolding.

In 1970 the United States government acted to assure safe and healthful working conditions by passing the Occupational Safety and Health Administration Act, which established the Occupational Safety and Health Administration (OSHA).

U.S. Occupational Safety and Health Administration

OSHA regulations applicable to the construction industry are available in a single volume. It is titled *Construction Industry, OSHA Safety and Health Standards (29 CFR 1926/1910)* and can be purchased from the Superintendent of Documents, Congressional Sales Office, U.S. Government Printing Office, Washington, D.C. 20402. Other specialized publications are available such as *Personal Protective Equipment, OSHA 3077,* and *Hand and Power Tool Safety, OSHA 3080.*

On-Site Housekeeping

Many accidents can be averted by proper on-site housekeeping. Following are some recommendations.

1. Keep the area around the building clear of debris.

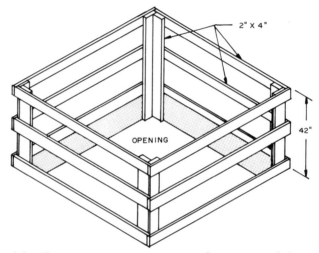

4-1 *Temporary openings must be protected by a guardrail.*

2. Keep the interior of the building, including stairs, halls, aisles, walkways, and open floor areas, free of debris.

3. Remove all nails from scrap lumber.

4. Avoid fires by removing flammable materials or storing them in fire-safe containers.

5. Keep all electrical cords free of entanglement with loose materials and in good repair.

6. Wipe up spilled liquids on areas that may cause workers to slip.

7. Build protective barriers around openings on the site or in the building that may cause falls (see 4-1).

8. When dropping materials to the ground, barricade the drop area. Drops over 20 feet high should be made using a chute.

Worker Safety

The employer is responsible for requiring the wearing of appropriate personal protective equipment in all operations where there is an exposure to hazardous conditions. Each individual should have the proper safety equipment. In some cases the contractor provides some equipment, but basic safety items are usually provided by each worker. Following are some things to observe:

1. Always wear a hard hat in areas designated as "Hard Hat Areas." The hard hat lining must be adjusted so it sits firmly on the band inside (see 4-2). Protective hats are available in two types. Type 1 has a full brim not less than 1¼ inches wide and Type 2 is brimless with a peak extending forward.

2. Purchase hard hats certified to meet the specifications in *American National Standards Institute, Z89.1-1969, Safety Requirements for Industrial Head Protection.*

3. Never wear a hard hat over another hat.

4. Wherever it is not feasible to reduce the noise levels or duration of exposures to those specified by OSHA regulations, ear protective devices shall be provided and used. Plain cotton is not an acceptable protective device (see 4-3).

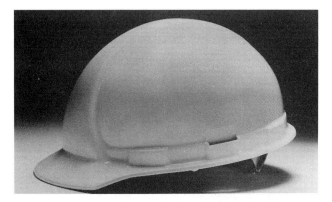

4-2 *This is a Type 2 hard hat. Notice the head rest mounted inside the shell of the hat.* (Courtesy Cabot Safety Corporation)

4-3 *Examples of ear protection devices required for noise levels above those considered safe by OSHA regulations.* (Courtesy Cabot Safety Corporation)

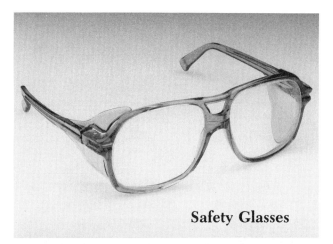

Safety Glasses

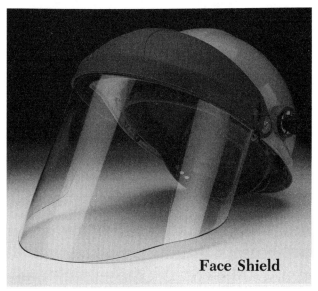

Face Shield

Spectacle Protection Glasses

4-4   *Eye protection can be accomplished with several types of approved eye-shielding equipment.* (Courtesy Cabot Safety Corporation)

5. Eye and face protection equipment shall be required when machines or operations present potential eye or face damage. Eye and face protective equipment must meet the requirements specified in *American National Standards Institute, Z87.1-1989, Practice for Occupational and Educational Eye and Face Protection* (see 4-4).

6. Face and eye protection equipment must be kept clean and in good repair.

7. When employees are exposed to harmful respiratory substances, respiratory protective devices must be used. Selection of a respirator should be made according to the guidelines in *American National Standard Practices for Respiratory Protection Z88.2-1980* (see 4-5).

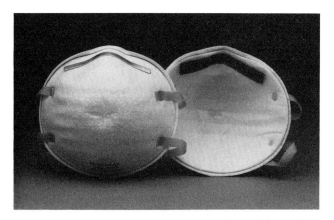

4-5   *Two types of respiratory protection devices.* (Courtesy Cabot Safety Corporation)

8. When working aboveground where falls are likely, lifelines, safety belts, or lanyards should be used for employee safeguarding. These should be sized and secured as specified in OSHA requirements.

9. Many situations require that the worker wear safety shoes having a steel toe covering.

10. Clothes should be loose enough to permit easy bending but not loose enough to get caught in moving tools.

11. Long hair should be enclosed in a hair net.

12. Never wear any jewelry, scarves, or ties.

13. Stay alert when heavy equipment is being operated on the site. The beeping sound it emits means it is backing. Since the operator has limited vision, be especially alert when you hear this warning.

Power Tool Safety

The use of power woodworking tools is covered in Chapter 3. It includes general safety recommendations as well as specific requirements for each tool.

Ladders

The most commonly used ladders on light-frame construction jobs include step ladders, straight ladders, and extension ladders (see 4-6). It is important to purchase high-quality ladders that meet OSHA requirements. Detailed OSHA information on ladders and stairways is available in the publication *Stairways and Ladders, OSHA 3124*. Order from OSHA Publi-

Straight Ladder

Extension Ladder

Step Ladder

4-6 Commonly used types of ladders. (Courtesy Aluminum Ladder Company)

cation Office, 200 Constitution Ave., NW, Room N-3647, Washington, D.C. 20210.

National safety codes for portable ladders available from the American National Standards Institute include *ANSI-14.1-14.2-56, Safety Code for Portable Metal Ladders.*

General Requirements for Manufactured and Site-built Ladders

1. A double-cleated ladder or two or more ladders must be provided for access when ladders are the only way to enter or exit a work area for 25 or more employees or where a ladder serves simultaneous two-way traffic.

2. Ladder rungs, cleats, and steps must be parallel, level, and uniformly spaced when the ladder is in position of use.

3. Rungs, cleats, and steps of portable and fixed ladders (except step stools) should not be spaced less than 10 inches apart or more than 14 inches apart.

4. Ladders must not be tied together to create longer sections unless they have been designed to be extended.

5. Wood ladders must not be coated with an opaque coating because this hides defects that may occur.

6. The minimum clear distance between the side rails of portable ladders must be 11½ inches.

7. The rungs, cleats, and steps of manufactured ladders must be corrugated, knurled, dimpled, coated with skid-resistant material or treated to minimize slipping.

8. Portable ladders must support at least four times the maximum intended load.

Using Straight and Extension Ladders Safely

Following are recommendations to be observed when using ladders.

1. Never use a ladder that is defective. Examine regularly for cracked, broken, or missing parts.

2. Place ladders where they are out of the normal traffic pattern followed by workers on the job. This prevents them from accidentally being bumped or knocked down.

3. The feet of the ladder must be placed on a firm, nonslippery surface.

4. The ladder must have an approved type of nonskid feet.

5. When necessary, nail blocking to keep the feet from sliding.

6. Clear the area of debris where the ladder is to be used.

7. When raising a straight or extension ladder place the feet against something to keep them from sliding (see 4-7).

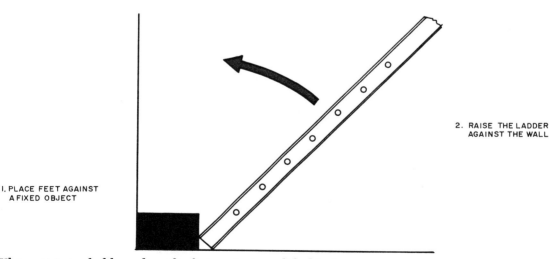

1. PLACE FEET AGAINST A FIXED OBJECT

2. RAISE THE LADDER AGAINST THE WALL

4-7 *When raising a ladder, place the feet against a solid object.*

8. The top of the ladder should extend three feet above the top of a wall. This provides support for activities such as going up on a roof (see 4-8).

9. Use a ladder that is the correct length for the job. Extension ladders are adjustable and make it easy to vary the length (see 4-9).

10. The feet of the ladder should be away from a wall a distance equal to one-fourth of the working distance (as shown in 4-8).

11. When ascending or descending a ladder, keep your hands on both rails and face the ladder.

12. Move heavy materials to a roof or other high place with a forklift, crane, or hoist rather than trying to carry them up a ladder.

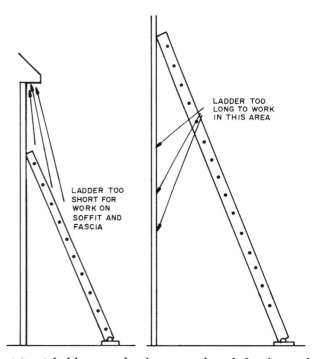

4-9   *A ladder must be the proper length for the work to be accomplished safely.*

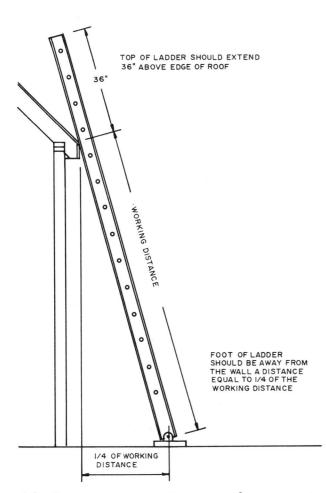

4-8   *Proper way to position a straight or extension ladder.*

13. Observe the load limitations specified for the ladder. They must support at least four times the maximum intended load.

14. Ladders are not designed to carry loads when they are in a horizontal position, so do not use them as scaffolding.

15. Do not lean out away from the ladder. If you cannot reach something, move the ladder closer to it.

16. Keep your shoes clean and dry.

17. Do not stand on the top three rungs of a straight or extension ladder.

18. Allow a 3-foot overlap between sections of a 36-foot extension ladder. A 4-foot overlap is required when using 48-foot extension ladders.

19. The minimum clear distance between side rails of portable ladders is 11½ inches.

20. Metal ladders that could conduct electricity should not be used near energized lines or equipment. Conductive ladders must be prominently marked as conductive.

Using Step Ladders Safely

1. Observe the maximum load-carrying capacity specified.

2. Be certain the ladder is fully open and the braces are fully extended, locking the legs in place.

3. All four legs must be firmly set on a level surface.

4. Do not stand on the top two steps. These are usually marked "no step."

5. Observe the recommendations listed for extension ladders, such as keeping the ladder in good repair, that apply to step ladders.

Site-Built Ladders

If site-built ladders are used, they must be made from quality materials. Stock with splits, warp, and large knots should be avoided. A typical site-built ladder design is shown in 4-10. They must not exceed 30 feet in length. This requires the rails to be at least 3 × 6 stock. Ladders with 2 × 4 rails cannot exceed 16 feet in length. OSHA specifies that site-built ladders must have the same strength requirements as those that are specified for manufactured ladders.

Scaffolding

The most commonly used scaffolding is commercially made from metal pipe welded into units that are assembled on the job. These are freestanding and do not rely on attachment to the building for vertical support. It is important that the feet be placed on a solid material such as 4-inch concrete blocks or heavy wood members set level on the ground. The scaffolding is usually tied to the building to stabilize it and help resist tilting (see 4-11).

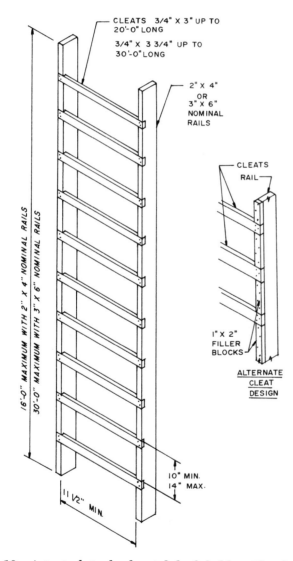

4-10 *A typical single-cleat job-built ladder. This design is not approved by OSHA unless it meets strength requirements.*

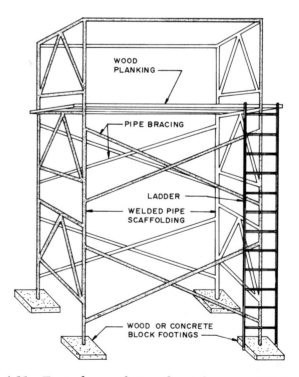

4-11 *Typical manufactured metal pipe scaffolding.*

Sometimes site-built scaffolding is used. It may be freestanding (independent) or built to fasten to the wall of the building (single pole) and rely on the wall for part of the structural frame.

Detailed OSHA regulations for scaffolding are given in the publication *Construction Industry, OSHA Safety and Health Standards (29 CFR 1926/ 1910)*. It is available from the Superintendent of Documents, U.S. Government Printing Office, Washington, D.C. 20402. Design data presented are abstracted from this publication.

Design data for a light-duty, single-pole site-built wood scaffolding with a maximum height of 20 feet are given in table 4-1.

Table 4–1 Minimum nominal size and maximum spacing of members of single-pole scaffolds, light duty.*

Member	20′–0″ Maximum height of scaffold**
Uniformly distributed load	not to exceed 25 psf
Poles or uprights	2″ × 4″
Pole spacing (longitudinal)	6′0″
Maximum width of scaffold	5′0″
Bearers or putlogs to 3′0″ width	2″ × 4″
Bearers or putlogs to 5′0″ width	2″ × 6″ or 3″ × 4″
Ledgers	1″ × 4″
Planking	1¼″ × 9″ (rough)
Vertical spacing of horizontal members	7′0″
Bracing, horizontal and diagonal	1″ × 4″
Tie-ins	1″ × 4″
Toeboards	4″ high minimum
Guardrail	2″ × 4″

* All sizes dressed except as noted. (From *Construction Industry*, OSHA, U.S. Department of Labor)

** *All members except planking are used on-edge.*

Table 4–2 Minimum nominal size and maximum spacing of members of independent-pole scaffolds, light duty.*

Member	20′–0″ Maximum height of scaffold**
Uniformly distributed load	not to exceed 25 psf
Poles or uprights	2″ × 4′
Pole spacing (longitudinal)	6′0″
Pole spacing (transverse)	6′0″
Ledgers	1¼″ × 4″
Bearers to 3′0″ span	2″ × 4″
Bearers to 10′0″ span	2″ × 6″ or 3″ × 4″
Planking (rough)	1¼″ × 9″ (rough)
Vertical spacing of horizontal members	7′0″
Bracing, horizontal and diagonal	1″ × 4″
Tie-ins	1″ × 4″
Toeboards	4″ high (minimum)
Guardrail	2″ × 4″

* All sizes dressed except as noted. (From *Construction Industry*, OSHA, U.S. Department of Labor)

** *All members except planking are used on-edge.*

An example of site-built, light single-pole scaffolding is shown in 4-12. Design data for a light-duty, independent wood scaffolding with a maximum height of 20 feet are given in table 4-2 (previous page). A typical scaffolding is shown in 4-13.

Design data for medium-duty and heavy-duty scaffolding are in the previously mentioned publication. These are for scaffolding carrying heavier loads and to a maximum of 60 feet high.

There are a variety of manufactured scaffolding brackets designed to be clamped to wood posts. These are for light duty. The height of the scaffold is changed by loosening the locks and sliding the bracket up or down the post (see 4-14 on page 74).

Rules for the Construction and Use of Scaffolding

1. Scaffolding must have a firm footing so that it will have no motion when in use. The footing should be wide enough to spread the load over an area large enough to prevent settlement.

2. Scaffolding must be plumb and level.

3. Wood scaffolding must be built to OSHA requirements.

4. Wood scaffolding must support four times the intended load.

5. All load-carrying timber members shall be construction lumber with a rating of 1500 psi extreme fibre stress in bending.

6. All planking shall be Scaffold Grade.

7. Maximum permissible spans for 2×10 or wider planks are in table 4-3.

8. The ends of planking shall be overlapped a minimum of 12 inches.

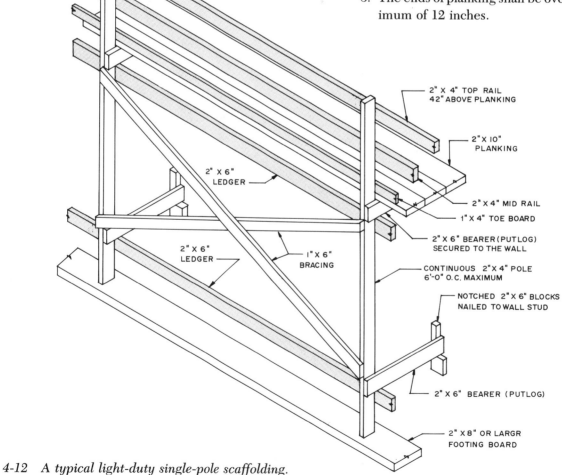

2" X 4" TOP RAIL
42" ABOVE PLANKING

2" X 10" PLANKING

2" X 6" LEDGER

2" X 4" MID RAIL

1" X 4" TOE BOARD

2" X 6" BEARER (PUTLOG) SECURED TO THE WALL

2" X 6" LEDGER

1" X 6" BRACING

CONTINUOUS 2" X 4" POLE 6'-0" O.C. MAXIMUM

NOTCHED 2" X 6" BLOCKS NAILED TO WALL STUD

2" X 6" BEARER (PUTLOG)

2" X 8" OR LARGR FOOTING BOARD

4-12 A typical light-duty single-pole scaffolding.

Table 4–3 Maximum spans for planking.*

Working load (psf)	Planking (2″ × 10″ and wider) (span in feet)	
	Full thickness (undressed)	Dressed thickness
25	10	8
50	8	6
75	6	———

* (From *Construction Industry*, OSHA, U.S. Department of Labor)

9. Scaffolding must have some form of access ladder to reach the planking. Do not climb up on the cross-bracing.

10. Planking shall extend beyond the end supports at least 6 inches, but not more than 12 inches.

11. Planking must be kept clean and free from debris and slippery material.

12. Scaffolding should be secured to the wall of the building to prevent tilting.

13. Horizontal bearers or putlogs must be placed with their greater dimension vertical and must project over the ledger on the inner and outer rows of vertical poles at least 3 inches.

A **bearer** is a horizontal wood member which supports a load. A **putlog** is a horizontal piece of timber used in bricklaying to support scaffold planking.

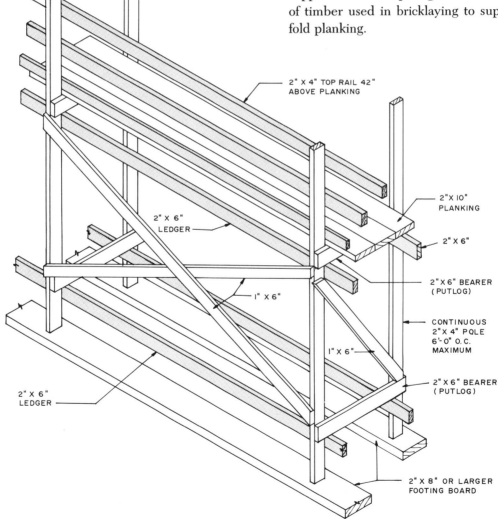

2" X 4" TOP RAIL 42" ABOVE PLANKING

2" X 6" LEDGER

2"X I0" PLANKING

2" X 6"

1" X 6"

2" X 6" BEARER (PUTLOG)

CONTINUOUS 2" X 4" POLE 6'-0" O.C. MAXIMUM

1" X 6"

2" X 6" BEARER (PUTLOG)

2" X 6" LEDGER

2" X 8" OR LARGER FOOTING BOARD

4-13   Construction for a typical light-duty, independent wood scaffolding.

One end of a putlog rests on a ledger secured to wood poles and the other end of the putlog is in a putlog hole. A **putlog hole** is a hole left in a masonry or concrete wall to support a horizontal scaffold framing member (a putlog). The putlog hole is filled to match the wall after the scaffolding has been dismantled and removed.

14. Ledgers must be long enough to extend over at least two poles. They must not be spliced between poles.

15. Poles are stabilized with diagonal bracing.

16. Platform planks must be laid with their edges tight together so that nothing can drop down between them.

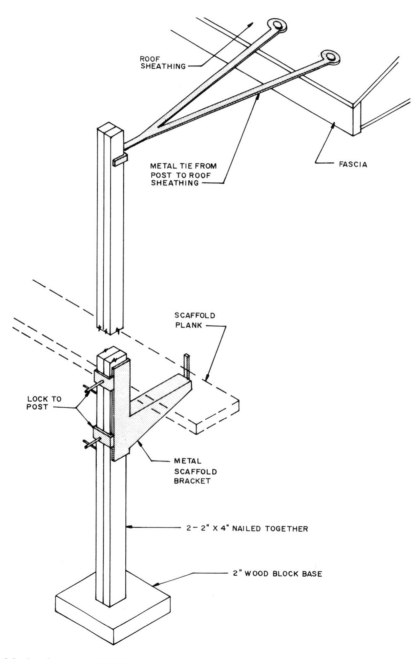

4-14 *A typical metal light-duty scaffold bracket.*

17. Guardrails are 42 inches high and made of 2×4 lumber. A midrail can be a 1×6 stock, and the toeboard must be at least 1×4 (see 4-15). Toeboards are required on all scaffolding more than 10 feet above the ground.

Wall Brackets

Wall brackets are metal units that are nailed to the wall studs. They are used for light-duty work and must be carefully installed. The nails used to secure them to the stud must be at least 16d common. Any nails that bend during installation should be removed and replaced. They use planking as discussed for scaffolding (see 4-16). A guardrail is built by joining 2×4 wood rails to metal posts that are part of the metal scaffold wall bracket.

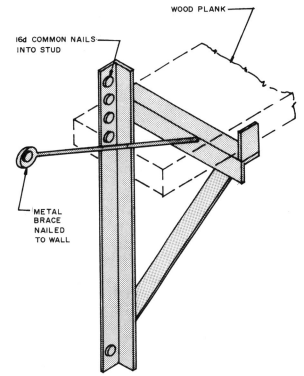

WOOD PLANK

16d COMMON NAILS INTO STUD

METAL BRACE NAILED TO WALL

4-16   A typical scaffold wall bracket.

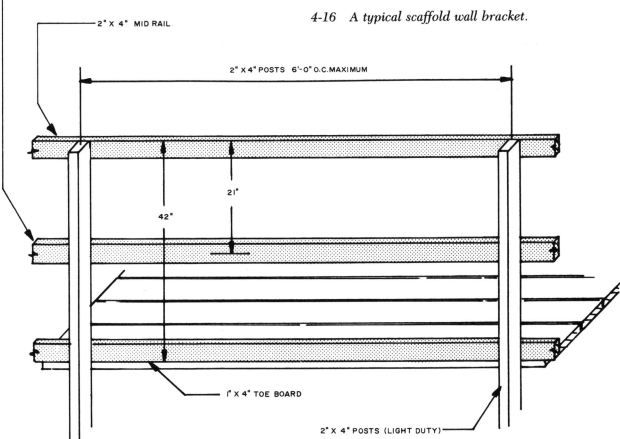

2"x 4" TOP RAIL

2" X 4" MID RAIL

2" X 4" POSTS 6'-0" O.C. MAXIMUM

42"

21"

1" X 4" TOE BOARD

2" X 4" POSTS (LIGHT DUTY)

4-15   A typical guardrail.

Roof Brackets

Roof brackets are used to provide a foot support when working on steeply sloped roofs. Some types go over the ridge, and others are nailed into the rafters. Usually working under these conditions requires the worker to wear a safety belt that is tied to the building above where the worker is located (4-17).

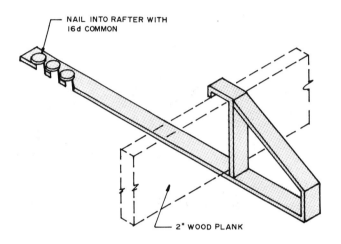

NAIL INTO RAFTER WITH
16d COMMON

2" WOOD PLANK

4-17 A typical roof bracket.

PART II
Floor, Wall, and Ceiling Framing

5

Framing Systems

Following are descriptions of light-frame construction systems in general use. Individual contractors may have other features that they have adopted based on experience and regional differences. However, overall these systems are descriptive and representative of the basic systems in use.

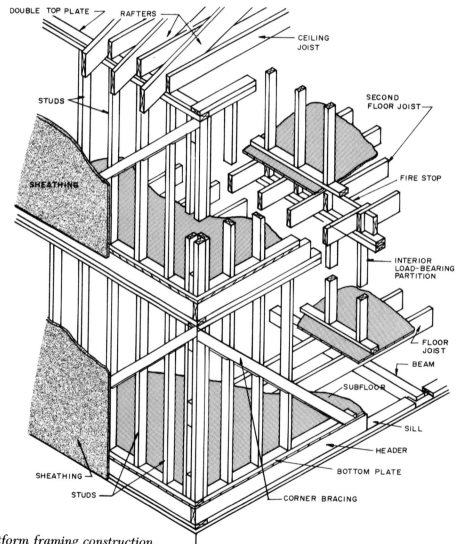

5-1   *Typical platform framing construction.*

Platform Framing

Platform framing is most commonly used in residential construction. Each wall is one-storey high. A two-storey house resembles building a one-storey house on top of another one-storey house (see 5-1). Platform framing has the advantage of using shorter pieces of lumber, and at each floor level it provides a solid platform upon which the carpenter can work.

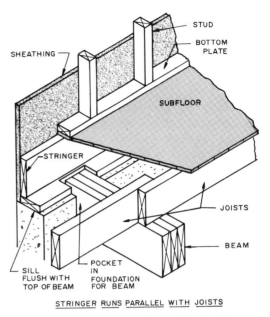

STRINGER RUNS PARALLEL WITH JOISTS

5-3 *The stringer runs parallel with the joists and is toenailed to the sill.*

After the floor joists are in place, the subfloor is glued and nailed to the joists. The first-floor walls rest on top of the subfloor. If the house has a second floor, another box sill platform is built on top of the first-floor wall (see 5-4).

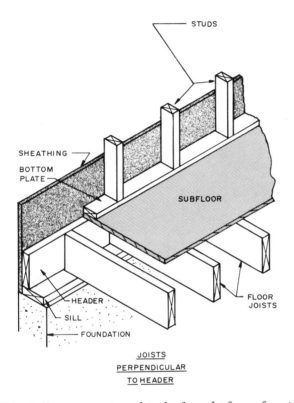

JOISTS
PERPENDICULAR
TO HEADER

5-2 *Sill construction details for platform framing with joists perpendicular to the header.*

The first floor is built as a complete platform using **box sill** construction (see 5-2). The **header** is end-nailed to the joints with three 16d nails. A header is a member that runs perpendicular to the joists. Each joist is toenailed to the sill with three 8d nails. The header is toenailed to the sill with 8d nails placed every 16 inches. The placement of the **stringer** is shown in 5-3. A stringer is the outer member of the platform frame which runs parallel with the floor joists. The stringer is set flush with the outer edge of the sill. It is toenailed to the sill with 8d nails spaced every 16 inches.

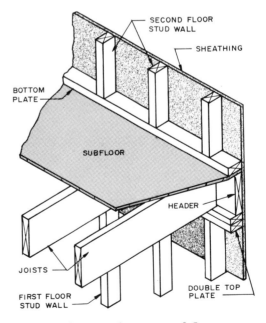

5-4 *Platform framing for a second floor.*

79

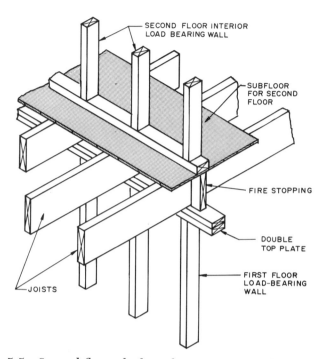

5-5 *Second-floor platform framing supported by an interior load-bearing partition.*

The exterior wall has a double 2 × 4 top plate. The second-floor joists are placed directly above the studs in the wall. The second-floor joists are usually supported inside the structure by interior load-bearing partitions (see 5-5).

Balloon Framing

Balloon framing uses a continuous stud running from the sill to the top plate (see 5-6). The weight of the roof and the second-floor ceiling joists is transmitted directly to the foundation through the studs. The studs rest on the sill, which should be 2-inch-thick material and anchored to the foundation.

Two types of sill construction are used. The **standard sill** has the floor joists face-nailed to the studs with two 10d nails. The studs are toenailed to the sill with two 10d nails (see 5-7).

The **T-sill** construction joins the joists to a header, which also serves as a draft and fire stop (see 5-7). The header is end-nailed to each joist with three 16d nails. The header is toenailed to the sill with 8d nails spaced 16 inches O.C. In both standard and T-sill construction the subfloor is extended over the area between the studs.

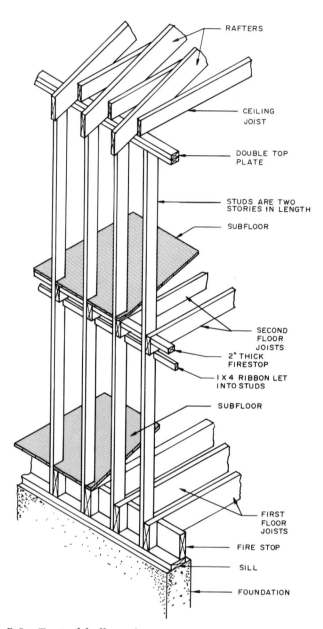

5-6 *Typical balloon framing construction.*

Since the exterior wall in balloon framing is open from the sill to the roof, **fire stops** must be nailed in place. Fire stops are wood members nailed between joists or studs which will break the natural draft or chimney-like effect. This retards the spread of a fire inside the wall to the roof. Fire stops are shown in 5-6, 5-7, and 5-8.

Construction details at the second-floor exterior wall are shown in 5-8. A **ribbon** is let in (notched into) the studs in the exterior wall, and the floor joists rest

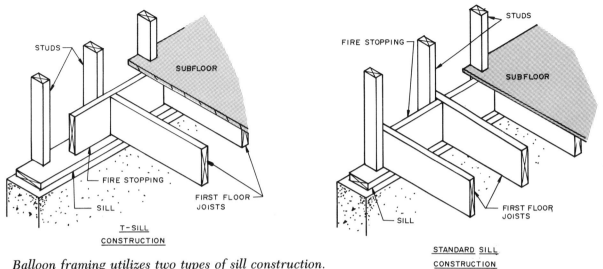

5-7 *Balloon framing utilizes two types of sill construction.*

on it. The joists are face-nailed to the studs with three 10d nails. The ribbon is face-nailed to the studs with two 8d nails. A 2 × 4 fire stop is nailed between the studs. Another fire stop is nailed between joists in the same manner as was done at the sill.

Generally the second-floor joists will rest on an **interior bearing partition** (see 5-8). Each joist will be placed directly above a stud in the partition. A **single 2 × 4 plate** can be used, although some prefer a **double plate**. The joists overlap the thickness of the stud. They are nailed to each other with three 16d nails. Each joist is toenailed to the plate with two 10d nails. Notice the fire-stopping used at this interior supporting wall in 5-8.

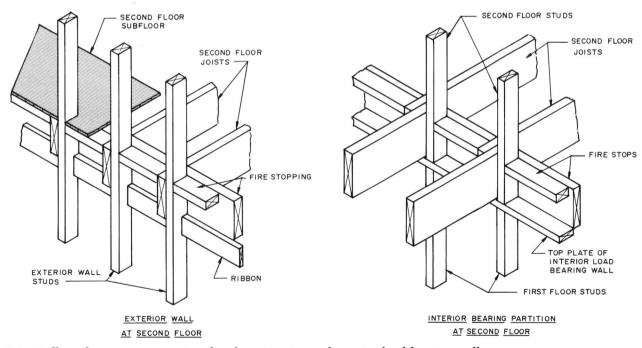

5-8 *Balloon framing construction details on interior and exterior load-bearing walls at the second floor.*

Post, Plank, and Beam Framing

Post, plank, and-beam framing uses wood beams to support the floor and floor load, and wood posts to support the ceiling and roof. The floor is decked with 2-inch-thick wood planks. One commonly used system has the floor and roof beams running the width of the building. The structural floor planks and the strutrual roof planks run the length of the building (see 5-9).

The exterior walls are built between the posts supporting the roof. These are nonload-bearing walls. They can be of any suitable material. See Chapter 9 for additional information.

Truss-Framed System

The **truss-framed system** can be used for light wood-framed buildings. The conventional unit consists of a floor truss and roof truss joined by studs (see 5-10). These factory-assembled units span the width of the foundation, and give an interior free of posts or load-bearing walls. The units are erected on the foundation and spaced 2 feet O.C. They are connected with plywood sheathing, which provides the needed structural support (see 5-11). Windows can be selected to fit between the studs, or a stud can be cut and standard headers used above each of the openings (see 5-12).

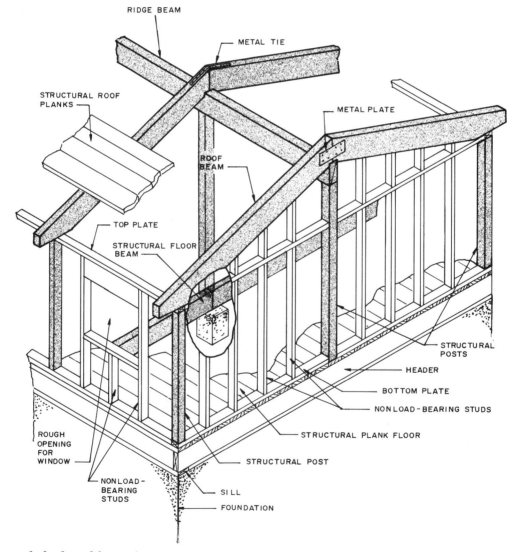

5-9   *One type of plank-and-beam framing system.*

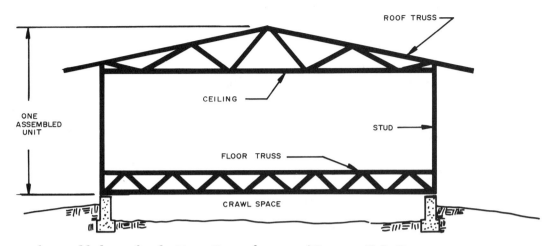

5-10   *A typical assembled unit for the Truss-Framed system.* (Courtesy U.S. Forest Products Laboratory, Forest Service, USDA)

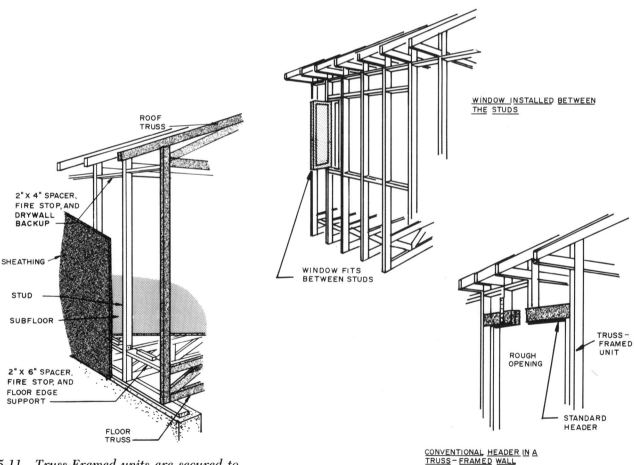

5-11   *Truss-Framed units are secured to the sill and joined with plywood or oriented strand board sheathing.* (Courtesy U.S. Forest Products Laboratory, Forest Service, USDA)

5-12   *Windows can fit between the Truss-Framed units or the units can be cut and headers installed.* (Courtesy U.S. Forest Products Laboratory, Forest Service, USDA)

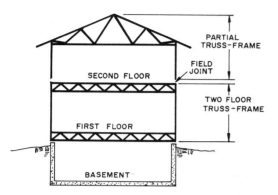

5-13 *This is how Truss-Framed units are used to build a two-storey building. (Courtesy U.S. Forest Products Laboratory, Forest Service, USDA)*

Two-storey buildings can be built using a two-floor and wall unit and a partial truss-frame and wall unit. After the two-floor unit is in place and the second-floor subfloor is installed, a second unit consisting of a roof truss and wall studs is set on top (see 5-13).

This type of construction can be used with either crawl space or basement foundations. For design information consult the Forest Products Laboratory, U.S. Forest Service, U.S. Department of Agriculture or the National Association of Home Builders Research Foundation, Inc.

Panellized Construction

Panellized construction utilizes standard, factory-manufactured components. Exterior wall components are built on a 16-inch module (see 5-14). These components include solid wall units and those containing doors and windows. The common widths are 16, 30, 64, 80, 96, and 144 inches. A typical assembly example is shown in 5-15. Some units are installed with the windows and doors already secured to the component. Others install these after the wall component is erected. Gable-end panels are also factory-built, and set in place on the job (see 5-16). Consult component manufacturers for sizes available.

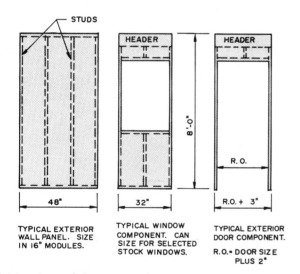

5-14 *Typical factory-made panel units.*

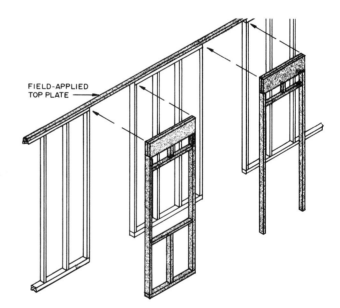

5-15 *Panel units are assembled into walls on the job site.*

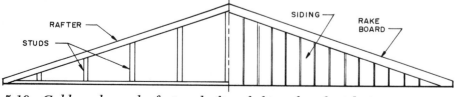

5-16 *Gable ends can be factory-built and shipped to the job site.*

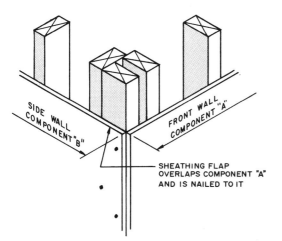

5-17 *Panels are designed to have an overlapping flap at the corner.*

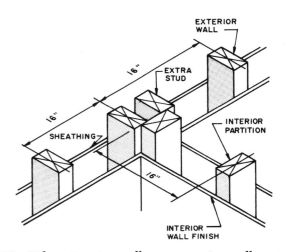

5-18 *Where interior walls meet exterior walls, extra studs are required.*

Panels that form an exterior outside corner require that an extra stud in one panel be set in the thickness of the wall it will meet, plus an allowance for nailing interior wall finish material, such as gypsum board. The other panel has the end stud set over, allowing the sheathing to form a flap that overlaps to form the corner (see 5-17). The framing used when an exterior wall and a partition meet is shown in 5-18.

A typical plan for designing a building using panel construction is shown in 5-19. The building is planned on a 48-inch module. The standard wall panels are used in various combinations to provide door and window locations. The roof is built with trusses spaced 2 feet O.C., and it is sheathed after the trusses are set in place.

Component manufacturers will have variations of this type of construction. For example, the floor can be constructed of factory-assembled panels consisting of joists and plywood subfloor that are set in place on the foundation with a small crane.

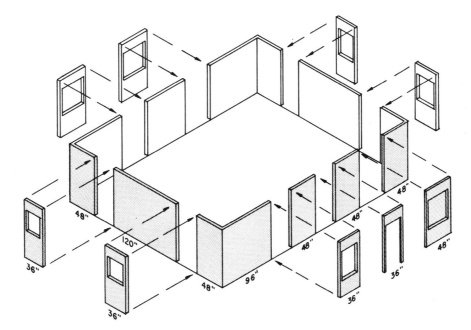

5-19 *An example of a house planned to use panel construction.*

Steel Framing

Lightweight cold-formed steel structural members are used to provide structurally sound framing for load-bearing walls, curtain walls, partitions, floors, and roofs. There are a number of systems available, and design data is available from the various manufacturers. Lightweight **steel framing** provides for passage of electrical wiring and other utilities through openings in the studs, is incombustible, is easily insulated, will accommodate most types of exterior siding, and can be preassembled into panels permitting speedy erection. It can be used for multistorey buildings.

Various systems include studs, tracks, joists, and accessories, such as bracing, angles, and joist hangers, needed to complete the installation (see 5-20).

5-20   *Typical components of a lightweight steel framing system.*

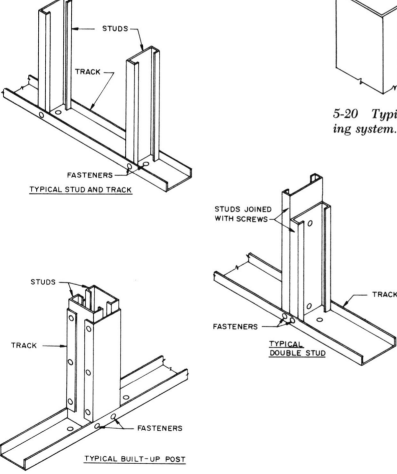

5-21   *Selected wall construction details for lightweight steel framing.*

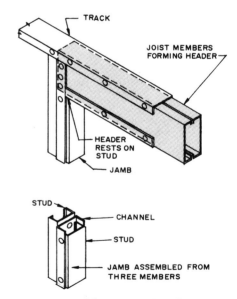

5-22   *Load-bearing headers are made from assemblies of lightweight steel joists.*

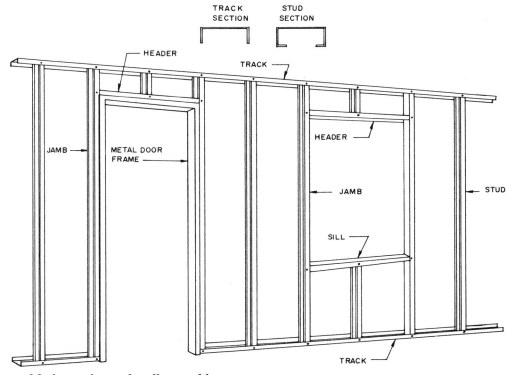

5-23 *A typical lightweight steel wall assembly.*

Bearing walls can use single or double studs depending upon the design load. An assembly of studs and track is used to build a post (see 5-21). Load-bearing headers are assembled from joist sections and track (see 5-22). A sill, as occurs below a window opening, can be secured with clip angles or a short section of stud.

A typical wall assembly is shown in 5-23. Bridging used in wall construction can be strap or channel material (see 5-24). Other types of bridging are used.

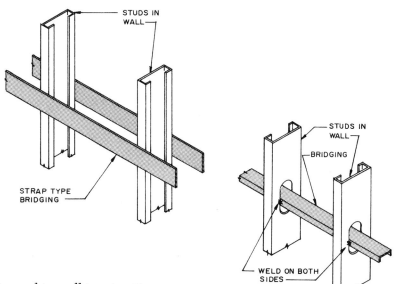

5-24 *Bridging is used in wall construction.*

Floors can use solid channel bridging or strap bridging (see 5-25). A typical installation for a building with more than one floor is shown in 5-26. Lightweight steel framing members are also used to assemble roof trusses as shown in 5-27.

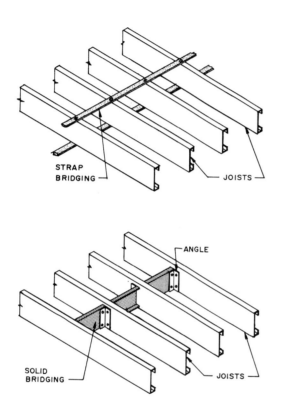

5-25 *Floor bridging can be steel straps or steel channels.*

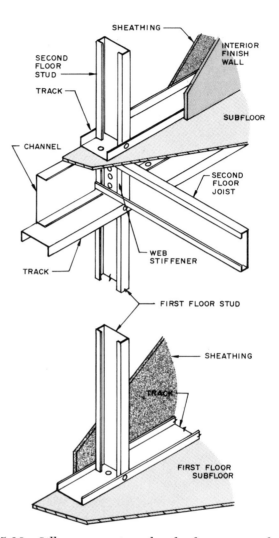

5-26 *Sill construction details for a second floor using lightweight steel framing.*

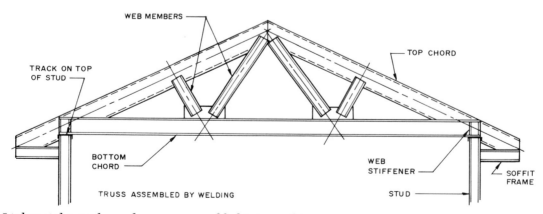

5-27 *Lightweight steel members are assembled into roof trusses.*

6

Floor Framing

Floor framing includes setting columns, beams, sills, headers, joists and applying the subfloor. These form a strong, solid base on which the interior and exterior walls rest, and they carry other loads such as cabinets, stairs, appliances, bath fixtures, water heater, furnace, and eventually furniture. The floor also forms a diaphragm to resist the lateral pressure from the earth and subsurface water that is pressing on the foundation wall, tending to push it inward.

In basement construction, steel columns are most commonly used, though wood posts can provide adequate support. Beams may be steel, solid wood, carpenter-built from 2-inch lumber, or some form of glued, laminated member. Second-floor loads are carried to the foundation through the exterior walls and through load-bearing walls on the interior of the building. These rest on the floor structure and require support below the floor.

The Sill Plate

The sill plate is a pressure-treated wood member, usually 2 × 6 inches, that is bolted or strapped to the foundation. If bolts are used they should be ½ inch in diameter, embedded 7 inches into the concrete or 15 inches into unreinforced grouted masonry and spaced not more than 6 feet apart. Bolts shall be located within 12 inches of the end of each piece of sill lumber, and each piece should have at least 2 bolts (see 6-1).

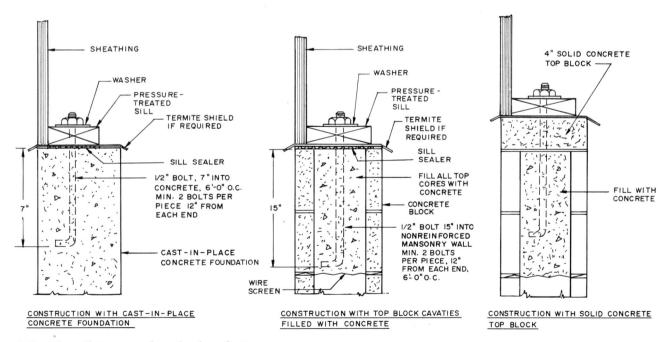

6-1 *The sill is secured to the foundation.*

89

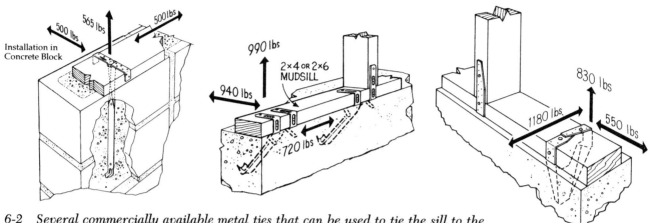

6-2   *Several commercially available metal ties that can be used to tie the sill to the foundation.* (Courtesy Simpson Strong-Tie Company, Inc.)

The sill plate can be anchored with metal straps that are set into the concrete (see 6-2). They are spaced 6 feet apart. They are bent around the wood plate and nailed to it. If used with concrete blocks, they must extend two blocks into the foundation. In some areas codes approve the use of power-driven fasteners which penetrate the concrete foundation.

Some codes permit the sill plate to be omitted. The floor joists then rest directly on top of the cast-in-place concrete foundation, a concrete floor, or on the webs of the top course of concrete blocks that have

the cores filled with concrete. Metal anchors tie the stud wall to the foundation (see 6-3).

Installing the Sill Plate

1. Lay the sill plate on top of the foundation. It is best to use pieces up against the bolts 14 to 16 feet or longer. Position plates so that no joints occur over an opening, such as a vent, in the foundation. They should meet with a square butt joint.

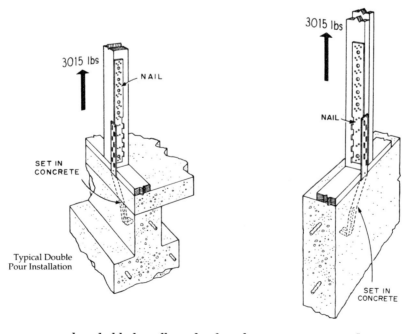

6-3   *Strap anchors are used to hold the sill to the foundation or concrete floor.* (Courtesy Simpson Strong-Tie Company, Inc.)

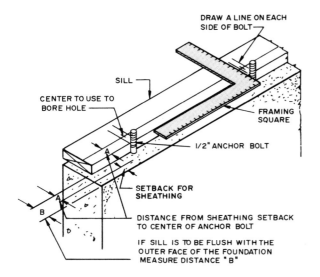

6-4 *Lay the sill next to the anchor bolts and mark the location of each.*

2. Draw square lines on the plate from each bolt (see 6-4). Measure in from the outside edge of the foundation to the center of the bolt, and mark this. This locates the spot to bore the bolt hole. Examine the construction drawing to see if an additional setback allowance must be made for sheathing. Some have the sheathing set flush with the foundation (see 6-5). Others prefer to let it overlap.

3. Bore the bolt holes a little larger than ½ inch so that the sill can be moved a little, permitting it to be set square with abutting pieces.

4. If a termite shield and sill sealer are to be used, place these over the bolts. A termite shield is a metal piece that extends beyond the faces of the foundation. A sill sealer is a thin layer of insu-

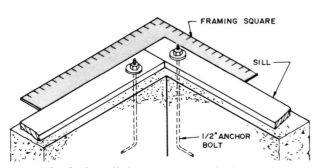

6-6 *Check the sill for squareness before tightening the bolts.*

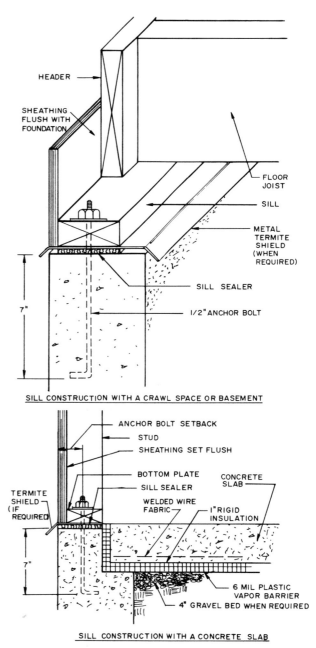

SILL CONSTRUCTION WITH A CRAWL SPACE OR BASEMENT

SILL CONSTRUCTION WITH A CONCRETE SLAB

6-5 *When the sheathing is to be flush with the face of the foundation, the sill is set in a distance equal to the sheathing thickness.*

lation that seals the air spaces that occur between the sill plate and the foundation. Some prefer to caulk this joint.

5. Place the sill plate over the bolts, put a washer on and finger-tighten the bolt. Check to be certain the corners are square and adjust as necessary (see 6-6).

6. Place a level on the sill plate. If it is not level, place metal shims between it and the foundation, and adjust until it is level. If the top of the foundation is very irregular, trowel a thin coat of mortar over it, and level the sill in the fresh mortar. Finger-tighten the bolts to hold the sill in place as the mortar sets.

7. Tighten the bolts with a wrench just enough to firm up the connection. Too much tightening might pull the bolt out of the concrete.

Table 6–1 Wide flange steel beam allowable loads in kips.*

Unsupported span (in inches)	W835**	W820**
8	62.2	34.0
10	49.8	27.2
12	41.5	22.7
14	35.5	19.4
16	31.1	17.0
18	27.6	——
20	24.9	——

* A kip is 1000 pounds

** W means wide flange beam, 8 means it is 8 inches high, and 35 means it weighs 35 pounds per lineal foot.

Floor Beams

Usually the span from one foundation wall to the other is so long that floor joists cannot reach and carry the expected loads. Beams are installed in the foundation to shorten the distance joists must span.

Beams in light construction could be a standard or wide-flange steel beam, solid wood, built-up, or some form of laminated wood (see 6-7).

Steel Beams

Steel beams are frequently used because they can span long distances using members that are smaller in size than wood beams. This often helps give additional head room in basements.

The two types used are standard (S) and wide flange (W). The wide flange has a wider surface on which to rest the floor joists. Typical load-carrying capacities for two sizes of wide-flange beams are given in table 6-1. The size of the beam will be determined by the architect and will be found on the drawing. If the framing carpenter installs the beam, it will be necessary to check and make certain it is as specified.

Solid and Built-Up Wood Beams

Wood beams can be solid wood members or made from assembled 2-inch lumber, producing what is called a built-up beam. These are usually assembled by the carpenter. The stock should be of high quality. The joints should be staggered and if possible occur

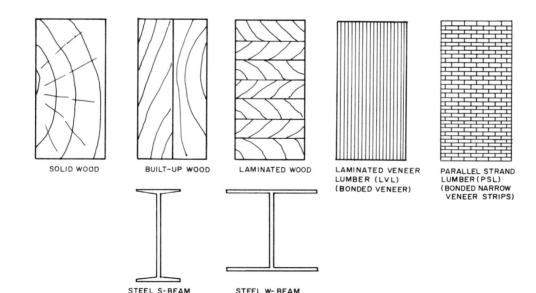

SOLID WOOD   BUILT-UP WOOD   LAMINATED WOOD   LAMINATED VENEER LUMBER (LVL) (BONDED VENEER)   PARALLEL STRAND LUMBER (PSL) (BONDED NARROW VENEER STRIPS)

STEEL S-BEAM   STEEL W-BEAM

6-7 *Beams used in floor construction.*

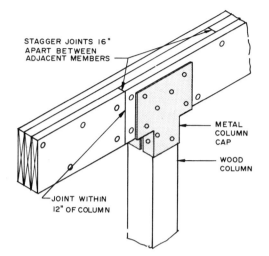

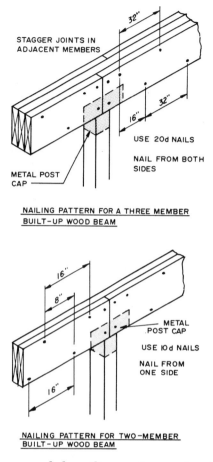

NAILING PATTERN FOR A THREE MEMBER
BUILT-UP WOOD BEAM

6-8 *Joints in built-up beams should be over a column or post or within 12 inches of it and be staggered.*

over piers or columns or at least not more than 12 inches from a pier or column (see 6-8). Solid wood beams are seldom used because they are difficult to secure in the large sizes required and are not seasoned in the interior cross section. They tend to check and crack as they dry after installation.

Allowable spans for built-up beams are found in Appendices H and L. The lumber must always be dry, and the lumber used must be the grade indicated on the table.

Built-up beams are often glued. The nails should follow the nailing patterns shown in 6-9. Two-piece beams are joined with 10d nails, all driven from one

NAILING PATTERN FOR TWO-MEMBER
BUILT-UP WOOD BEAM

6-9 *Recommended nailing patterns for built-up beams.*

side. Two nails are driven at each end. Three-piece beams are nailed from both sides using 20d nails. Two nails are driven at each end.

Span data for solid wood beams is found in Appendices G and E.

Glued Laminated Beams

Glued laminated beams are referred to as **glulams**. They are made by gluing, under carefully controlled conditions, high-quality wood strips that have defects cut away. The strips range from about ¾ to 1½ inches in thickness and are kiln-dried. This produces a high-quality beam that will carry heavy loads over long distances (see 6-10). They are more dimensionally stable than solid wood beams and carry more weight than the other types of wood beams over the same span. Typical span data for selected sizes are found in Appendices I and P. Consult manufacturers for specific data.

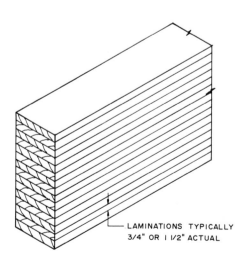

6-10 *Glulam beams span longer distances than solid or built-up beams.*

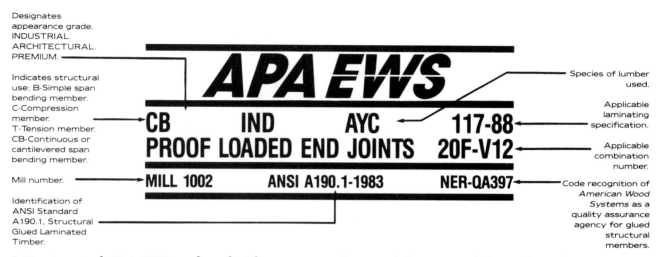

Designates appearance grade. INDUSTRIAL. ARCHITECTURAL. PREMIUM.

Indicates structural use: B-Simple span bending member. C-Compression member. T-Tension member. CB-Continuous or cantilevered span bending member.

Mill number.

Identification of ANSI Standard A190.1, Structural Glued Laminated Timber.

Species of lumber used.

Applicable laminating specification.

Applicable combination number.

Code recognition of *American Wood Systems* as a quality assurance agency for glued structural members.

APA EWS

CB   IND   AYC   117-88
PROOF LOADED END JOINTS   20F-V12

MILL 1002   ANSI A190.1-1983   NER-QA397

6-11 *A typical APA-EWS trademark. The meanings of some of the parts of the trademark: 117-88—The manufacturing standards and specifications published by the American Institute of Timber Construction; 20F—The allowable bending stress in fibre (00,000 psi); V12—The lamination layup; AYC—The wood species (Alaskan yellow cedar).*

The American Plywood Association has expanded to incorporate this family of wood products including glulams. The American Wood Systems was created by the APA to serve the needs of the engineered wood systems industry. A new trademark has been created, APA-EWS (Engineered Wood Systems). The APA-EWS trademark appears on glued laminated beams and may be used on prefabricated wood I-beams, structural composite lumber, and other engineered wood products (see 6-11). Products bearing the APA-EWS trademark are supported with the same technical and promotional services APA provides to manufacturers of structural wood products.

Parallel Strand Lumber

Parallel strand lumber is used for beams, headers, columns, and posts. They are made from Douglas fir and southern pine (see 6-12). The logs are peeled into veneer sheets $\frac{1}{10}$ and $\frac{1}{8}$ of an inch in thickness. These sheets are clipped into strands up to 8 feet in length. Defects are removed, and the strands are coated with a waterproof adhesive. The oriented strands are fed into a rotary belt press and cured using microwave energy. This produces a billet that is cut into standard sizes up to 66 feet in length (see 6-13). One such product is marketed under the name Parallam®. It has been extensively tested for fire resistance,

6-12 *Beams are made from parallel strand lumber (PSL).* (Courtesy Trus Joist MacMillan, Limited)

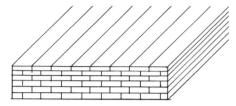

WOOD STRANDS 1/8" OR 1/10" THICK
ARE BONDED WITH AN ADHESIVE FORMING
PARALLEL STRAND LUMBER.

6-13   Parallel strand lumber is made by bonding narrow wood veneer strips with a waterproof adhesive.

Table 6–2 Parallam® beams are made in these sizes.

Thickness (inches)	Depth (inches)
1¾	7¼
3½	9¼
5¼	9½
7	11¼
	11½
	11⅞
	12
	12½
	14
	16
	18

fastener-holding, moisture response, long-term loading, flexural response, stiffness, and internal bond. It has exceeded the performance of competing wood products. It can be sawed, drilled, and nailed like solid wood. It has been accepted by major building codes in the United States and Canada (see table 6-2).

Laminated Veneer Lumber

Laminated veneer lumber (LVL) is another form of manufactured structural member. It is made from wood veneers, usually southern pine, bonded with an exterior adhesive to form a structural member that has virtually no shrinkage, checking, twisting or split-

ting. It has more load-bearing capacity per pound than solid sawn lumber. It has a high allowable bending stress (3100 psi) and a modulus of elasticity (E) of 2.0. It is made in many depths and long lengths (see 6-14). Typical depths range from 9¼ to 18 inches and thicknesses are 1½ and 1¾ inches. Design data on spans are available from manufacturers.

16-14   Laminated veneer lumber is made by bonding sheets of veneer with a waterproof adhesive. (Courtesy Louisiana-Pacific)

6-15 These I-joists have laminated veneer lumber flanges and oriented strand board webs. (Courtesy Louisiana-Pacific)

I-Joists

Another manufactured wood structural member is the I-joist. It is made using an oriented strand board web with flanges of solid kiln-dried lumber or laminated veneer lumber (see 6-15). I-joists are lightweight, need no midspan bridging, and allow greater on-center spacing than solid sawn joists (see 6-16).

They are useful as floor and ceiling joists, cantilever beams in balconies, cathedral ceiling joists, or other high-pitched roof construction. They are available in depths from 11⅞ to 24 inches and 2¼ inches wide. Detailed design specifications are available from manufacturers.

6-16 I-joists provide long spans for roof and floor construction. (Courtesy Louisiana-Pacific)

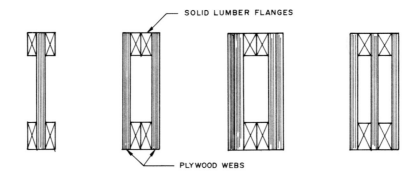

6-17 *Typical sections for glued panel-lumber beams.* (Courtesy American Plywood Association)

Structural Use Panel-Lumber Beams (Box Beams)

Panel-lumber beams (also called box beams) are made by combining lumber and structural panels in various combinations. They are made following specific design requirements as prescribed by the American Plywood Association. They may be assembled by nailing, gluing, or gluing and nailing.

Glued beams require the lumber flanges be glued together with rigid structural adhesive and the plywood webs be glued to the lumber flanges under pos-

itive mechanical pressure, which is not practical outside of a factory (see 6-17).

Nailed panel-lumber beams can be constructed on the job site and glue may be added to provide additional stiffness. A typical use is a header over a garage door opening. Nailed panel-lumber beams use 2×4 lumber flanges and APA-Rated Sheathing, Exposure 1, nonveneer Com-Ply®, .4- or 5-ply plywood. These panels are all made with exterior adhesive (see 6-18).

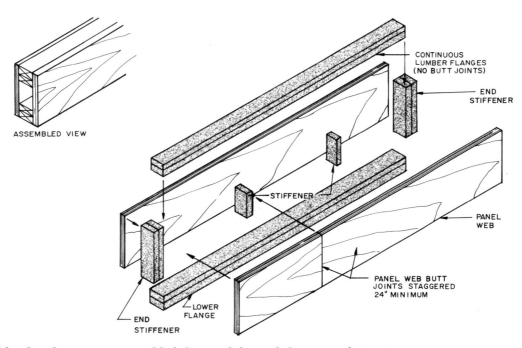

6-18 *Panel-lumber beams are assembled from solid wood flanges and American Plywood Association-rated panel products.* (Courtesy American Plywood Association)

Typical allowable loads for selected sizes of nailed box beams are given in 6-19. These designs are based on the use of No. 1 Douglas Fir or southern pine kiln-dried lumber. Reduced loads by 19 percent for No. 2 Douglas fir, or No. 2 KD15 southern pine.

To select a nailed box beam:

1. Figure the load on the beam. For this example assume a load of 260 pounds per lineal foot on an 18-foot beam.

2. Select the beam design. Examine the load design data in 6-19. The 18-foot-length column

shows that a 16-inch beam with double top and bottom flanges and 23/32-inch and 48/24-inch panel webs with Cross Section B will carry 274 pounds per lineal foot. This is the design closest to the required design load. In some cases several designs would be appropriate.

To build this panel-lumber beam:

1. Select the correct layout of stiffeners as shown in 6-20. The panel joint locations require a minimum of a 2-foot stagger between the panel butt joints on opposite sides of the beam. All vertical joints are located in the center half of the beam.

ALLOWABLE LOAD(a) FOR 12″-DEEP ROOF BEAM OR HEADER (lb/lin ft)

| Structural Wood Panel | Cross-Section | Approx. Wt. per Ft (lb) | Span (ft) | | | | | | | |
			10	12	14	16	18	20	22	24
15/32″ 32/16	A	6	301*	251	199	153	121	98	81	68
15/32″ 32/16	B	8	310*	259*	222*	194	172	148	122	103
23/32″ 48/24	B	10	354*	295*	253	221	183	148	122	103
23/32″ 48/24	C	12	—	—	232*	203*	180	162	138	116

ALLOWABLE LOAD(a) FOR 16″-DEEP ROOF BEAM OR HEADER (lb/lin ft)

| Structural Wood Panel | Cross-Section | Approx. Wt. per Ft (lb) | Span (ft) | | | | | | | |
			10	12	14	16	18	20	22	24
15/32″ 32/16	A	7	430*	358	284	218	172	139	115	97
15/32″ 32/16	B	9	435*	362*	311*	272*	242	217	188	158
23/32″ 48/24	B	11	494*	412*	353*	309	274	227	188	158
23/32″ 48/24	C	14	—	—	—	288*	256*	230	209	191

ALLOWABLE LOAD(a) FOR 20″-DEEP ROOF BEAM OR HEADER (lb/lin ft)

| Structural Wood Panel | Cross-Section | Approx. Wt. per Ft (lb) | Span (ft) | | | | | | | |
			10	12	14	16	18	20	22	24
15/32″ 32/16	A	8	569*	474	370	283	224	181	150	126
15/32″ 32/16	B	10	—	466*	399*	349*	310	279	254	214
23/32″ 48/24	B	13	633*	527*	452*	395	352	309	255	214
23/32″ 48/24	C	15	—	—	—	376*	334*	300*	273	250

ALLOWABLE LOAD(a) FOR 24″-DEEP ROOF BEAM OR HEADER (lb/lin ft)

| Structural Wood Panel | Cross-Section | Approx. Wt. per Ft (lb) | Span (ft) | | | | | | | |
			10	12	14	16	18	20	22	24
15/32″ 32/16	A	9	693*	577	456	349	276	223	184	155
15/32″ 32/16	B	11	—	568*	487*	426*	378*	341	310	271
23/32″ 48/24	B	14	769*	641*	550*	481*	427	385	323	271
23/32″ 48/24	C	17	—	—	—	—	412*	370*	337*	309

Cross Sections

A

B

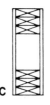
C

(a) Includes 15% snow loading increase.
 * Lumber may be No. 2 Douglas-fir or No. 2 KD15 southern pine.

6-19 *Span and load data for selected APA-approved panel-lumber beams. (Courtesy American Plywood Association)*

Web Joint Layouts

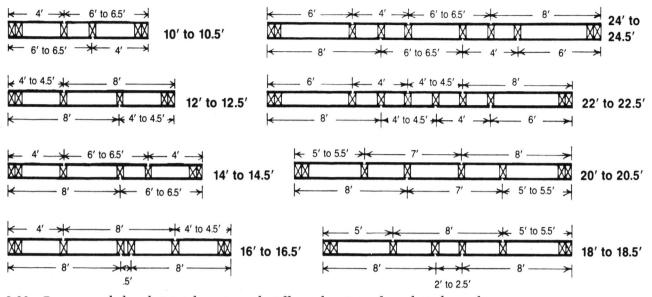

6-20 *Recommended web joint layouts and stiffener locations for selected panel-lumber beams.* (Courtesy American Plywood Association)

Vertical stiffeners should be added in the layouts so that they are no more than 4 feet apart. Place vertical stiffeners behind the butt joints between panel webs. Six inches is added to the clear span to allow the double-bearing-end vertical stiffeners to rest on the double-load-carrying studs on each end of the beam.

2. Build the framework of lumber flanges and stiffeners. Use dry lumber having a moisture content of 19 percent or less for Douglas fir and 15 percent or less for southern pine. Lumber should be free of warp or characteristics that produce gaps greater than ⅛ of an inch between the lumber and the panel. Nail the flanges to the stiffeners with 8d common nails.

3. Fasten the panel webs to the framework with the face grain or strength axis (8-foot dimension) in the long direction (same direction as the flanges) using 8d common nails. The required nailing pattern is shown in 6-21.

Nailing Layout

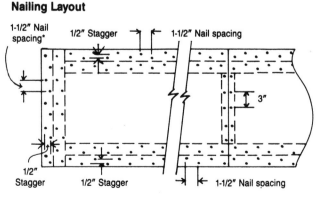

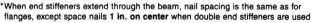

*When end stiffeners extend through the beam, nail spacing is the same as for flanges, except space nails **1 in. on center** when double end stiffeners are used

in beams with three members per flange (cross-section C). When end stiffeners are inserted between flanges, nails may be spaced 3 in. on center.

6-21 *The required nailing pattern for carpenter-built panel-lumber beams.* (Courtesy American Plywood Association)

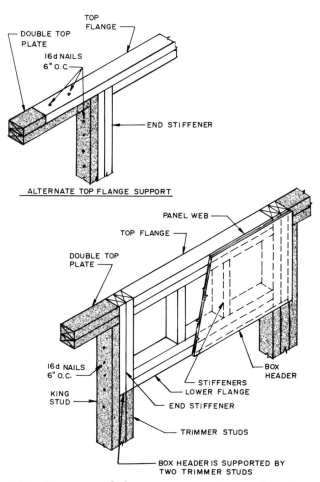

6-22 *Recommended ways to attach panel-lumber headers to frame walls.* (Courtesy American Plywood Association)

Panel-lumber beam headers are installed as shown in 6-22. The beam rests on two 2 × 4 trimmer studs on each end and is face-nailed to a full-length stud with 16d common nails 6 inches O.C. An alternate design has the top flange extend above the double vertical stiffeners on each end and lap over the top plate.

For additional information contact the American Plywood Association.

Posts, Columns, and Piers

Buildings with crawl spaces usually use piers to support beams. These are usually concrete block with the cores filled with concrete. However, cast concrete piers also find some use (see 6-23). Concrete block piers are usually 8 × 16 inches or 16 × 16 inches depending on the load to be carried.

Steel columns are most commonly used to carry beams over basement space. They will have a steel plate on top to carry the wood beam. If steel beams are used, they are often welded to the column (see 6-24). Steel columns have a square steel plate on the bottom which may be bolted to the footing.

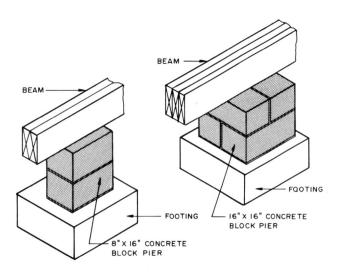

6-23 *Floor beams can be given intermediate support with concrete block piers.*

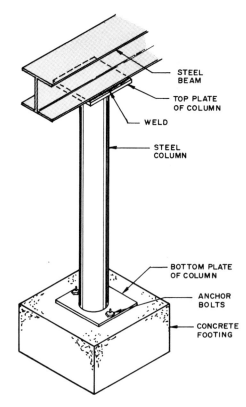

6-24 *Beams in construction with basements often use steel columns.*

Wood posts and columns are joined to wood beams and concrete footings with metal connectors (see 6-25). The posts and columns can be solid wood, glued laminated members, or parallel strand lumber (PSL) as discussed in the section on beams. PSL columns are available in square and rectangular shapes ranging from 3½ inches square to 7 inches square. They are worked in the same manner as solid wood columns and use the standard metal connections.

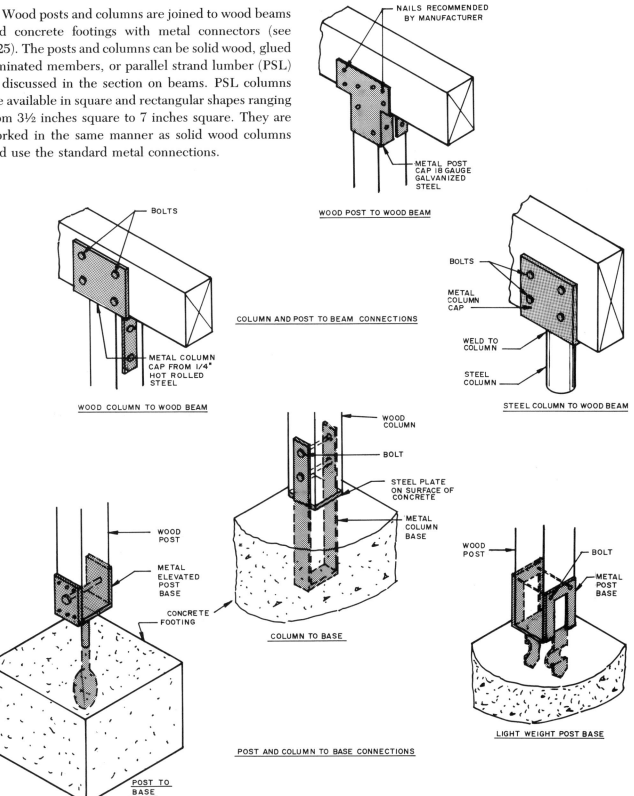

6-25 *Wood posts and columns are most effectively installed using standard metal connections.*

Installing Beams

Beams are set in pockets built in the foundation wall. The end of the beam should rest at least 4 inches on the foundation. Wood beam pockets should be large enough to allow a ½-inch air space around it on all sides. This helps provide circulation to keep the wood dry (see 6-26). A ¼-inch steel plate is usually placed in the pocket under the wood beam. Steel beams are set in the same way, except that the depth of the pocket must allow for the 2×4 or 2×6 wood member fastened to the top of the beam. The top of either beam must be level with the top of the sill plate (see 6-27).

If it is not possible to get adequate support for a beam on the foundation wall, a pilaster can be built as part of the foundation. While it can be any size required, a 4-inch $\times$ 12-inch pilaster is commonly used with concrete block construction (see 6-28).

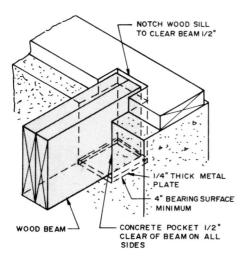

NOTCH WOOD SILL TO CLEAR BEAM 1/2"

1/4" THICK METAL PLATE

4" BEARING SURFACE MINIMUM

WOOD BEAM

CONCRETE POCKET 1/2" CLEAR OF BEAM ON ALL SIDES

6-26 *Wood beams are set in pockets in the concrete foundation with the top above the foundation so that it is flush with the sill.*

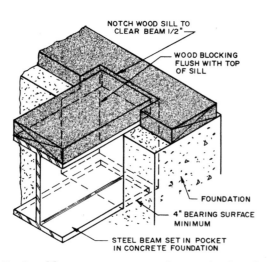

NOTCH WOOD SILL TO CLEAR BEAM 1/2"

WOOD BLOCKING FLUSH WITH TOP OF SILL

FOUNDATION

4" BEARING SURFACE MINIMUM

STEEL BEAM SET IN POCKET IN CONCRETE FOUNDATION

6-27 *Steel beams are set in pockets in the foundation with their top flush with the top of the foundation.*

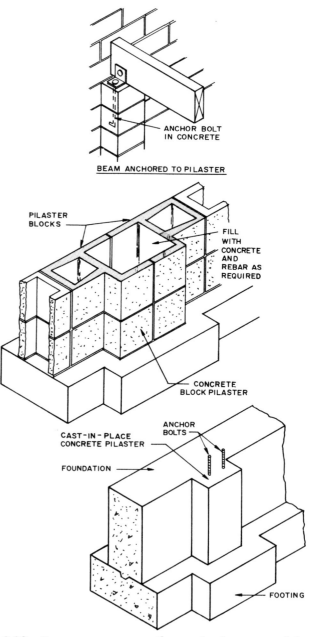

ANCHOR BOLT IN CONCRETE

BEAM ANCHORED TO PILASTER

PILASTER BLOCKS

FILL WITH CONCRETE AND REBAR AS REQUIRED

CONCRETE BLOCK PILASTER

CAST-IN-PLACE CONCRETE PILASTER

ANCHOR BOLTS

FOUNDATION

FOOTING

6-28 *Beams can rest on pilasters built as part of the foundation.*

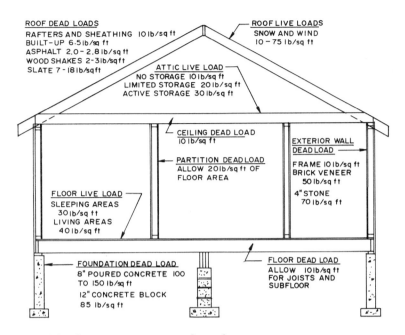

6-29 *Typical live and dead loads occurring in residential construction.*

Floor Joists

Floor joists must span the required distances and carry the design loads. For typical residential work joists must carry a total weight of around 100 pounds per square foot. This includes the weight of the floor materials, live load (furniture, people), partitions, ceiling materials, and attic storage (see 6-29). These will vary some with the actual design, but are typical. Generally, bedroom areas are figured to have a live load of 30 pounds per square foot, and living areas 40 pounds per square foot.

Joists must have sufficient strength to carry the design loads. In addition, stiffness must be considered. Sometimes designers choose a joist a size larger than required for strength, to get a firmer floor. Joists are generally 2-inch-thick solid lumber. Other products are now on the market, such as I-joists and laminated veneer lumber, for this use. The actual size of solid wood joist chosen depends therefore upon the loading, span, spacing between joists, and the grade and species of lumber used. The most common spacings used are 16 and 24 inches center to center. Span data were developed by the *In-Grade Testing Program* discussed in Chapter 2.

Tables giving allowable spans for lumber manufactured in the United States are found in Appendices J through O. To use these tables you must know the size of the member, the joist spacing, the live and dead loads, and the grade of the lumber. For example, a 2×8 southern pine floor joist with a grade of No. 1 spaced 16 inches O.C. with a 40-pound live load and a 10-pound dead load will span 13'-1".

Span data for other species of wood, such as those harvested in the western part of the United States, are available from various wood product associations, such as the Western Wood Products Association.

The Canadian Wood Council has developed extensive design tables for wood structural members in metric and English units. The selected span data found in Appendices F through I have been calculated in metric units for Spruce-Pine-Fir to meet the requirements of buildings covered in *Part 9* of the *National Building Code of Canada (NBCC) 1990*. Floor joists are in many cases limited by both **deflection** and **vibration** performance, producing spans slightly less than those in span tables for products used in the United States, which only considers deflection.

Canadian metric lumber span ratings for floor joists vary with the specie, whether the subfloor is nailed or nailed and glued, and the type of bridging and strapping used. Data found in Appendices F through I give only a limited example.

Metric loads are given in kilopascals (kPa). Metric sizes are given in millimetres. Metric conversion factors are found in Appendix Q. Detailed data is available from the Canadian Wood Council, 1730 St. Laurent Blvd., Ottawa, Ontario, Canada, K1G 5L1.

Canadian lumber manufacturers also produce lumber to match the sizes and grades used in the United States. Span data for their Spruce-Pine-Fir classification are found in Appendices C through E. Refer to Chapter 2 for information on the *In-Grade Testing Program*.

Nail Sizes to Use

The size of nail to be used for structural framing depends on the lateral strength required. This is es-

Table 6–3 Typical nail penetration requirements.

Nail size	Box nail penetration (inches)	Common nail penetration (inches)
6d	1⅛	1¼
8d	1¼	1½
10d	1½	1⅝
12d	1½	1⅝
16d	1½	1¾
20d	1⅝	2⅛
30d	1⅝	2¼
40d	1¾	2½

tablished by the building codes, which also specify the required penetration. Examples of typical penetration requirements are given in table 6-3. The actual size and number of nails required for various assemblies will vary somewhat in different localities, but those shown in Appendices A and B are typical of those found in various codes.

Installing Floor Joists

Before installing joists on the foundation, each joist should be inspected for straightness. Those with any twist, cup, or large bow should not be used (see 6-30). If a joist has a slight crook, it can be used, but the crown should be placed up so that load will tend to straighten it out (see 6-31). If a joist has a large knot near an edge, place this edge on top, because the top of the joist is in compression and the knot will have less effect on the strength.

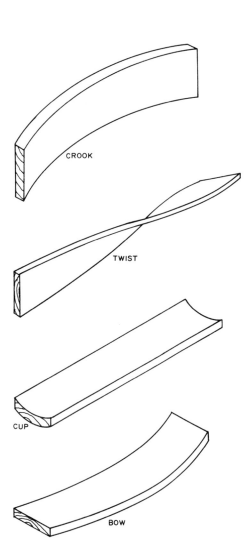

6-30 *Lumber warps in several ways.*

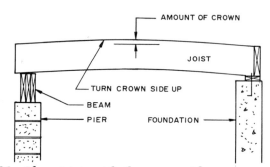

6-31 *Place joists with the crown side up.*

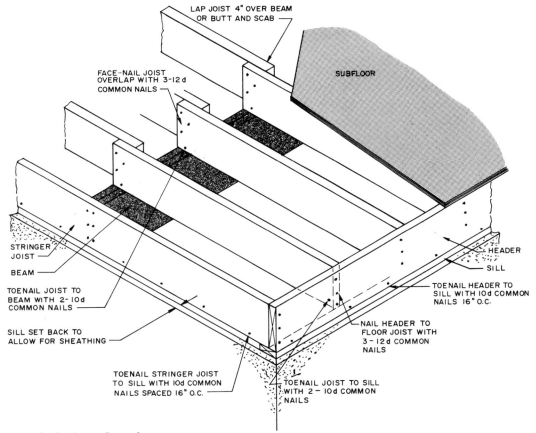

6-32 *A typical platform floor framing system.*

The most common way floors are framed is shown in 6-32. The joists are lapped on the beam a minimum of 4 inches. The header joist is nailed to the ends of the joists with three 16d common nails. The header joist and the stringer joist are toenailed to the sill plate with 10d common nails, 16 inches O.C. Joists are toenailed to the beam and sill plate with two 16d common nails. The joist overlap is nailed with two 16d common nails on each side, at the end of the joist.

Joist locations are laid out on the header. While joist spacing is given by the on-center distance, this is difficult to use. Therefore, the edge of the joist is located (see 6-33). The stringer joist is set flush with the end of the header. The next joist is set 15¼ inches from the end of the header. This allows the subfloor to cover the stringer joist. Mark a line here, representing the right side of the joist, and place an X to its left. The X shows on which side of the mark to place the joist. Locate all other joists at 16-inch spaces, as specified. If joists are to be 24 inches O.C., set in the first joist 23¼ inches, and locate the rest 24 inches apart.

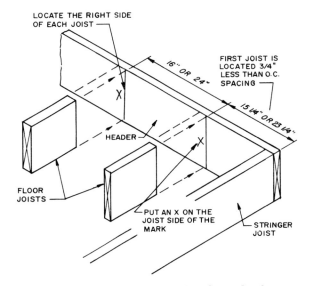

6-33 *Locate each joist on the header. The first joist is ¾ inch less than the specified on-center (O.C.) spacing.*

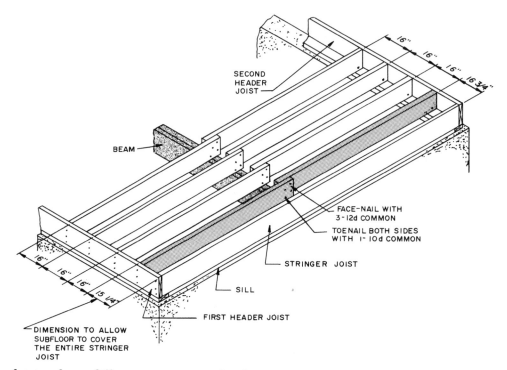

6-34 *Lapped joists have different spacing on the first joist on each side of the building.*

A typical layout for joists that are lapped on the beam is shown in 6-34. Notice that the layout on the header on the other end of the floor is different from the first because the joists are lapped. The first joist is set in 16¾ inches, which allows for the 1½-inch lapped floor joist.

Typical joist layouts for a floor with lapped joists are shown in 6-35. It shows the evenly spaced, regular floor joists. Additional joists will be needed for other structural features, such as load-bearing walls and openings in the floor. These are shown as trimmer joists, extra regular joists, and tail joists.

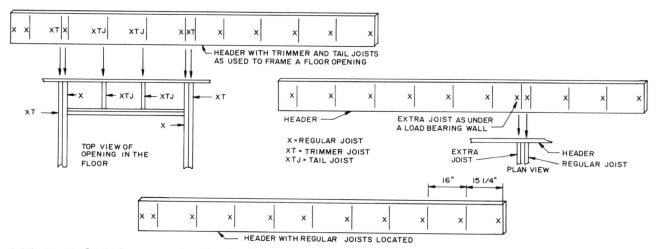

6-35 *Typical joist layouts on headers for floors with lapped joists when double joists are required for a floor opening.*

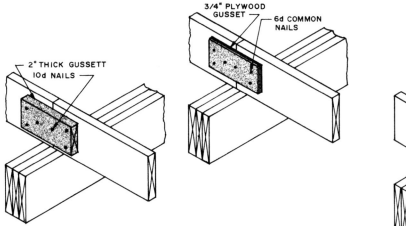
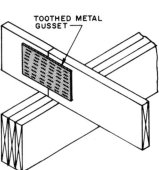

6-36 *When floor joists are butted they are joined with a splice plate.*

In some cases the designer prefers to butt the joists on the beam. This keeps them in line and makes it easier to apply the subfloor. When this is done the butting joists are joined with a 2-inch-thick wood splice plate, ¾-inch plywood, or a manufactured metal splice plate (see 6-36). In this case the layout of joists is the same on both headers.

Balloon Framing Layout

The joist layout for balloon framing is done on the sill, because the studs rest on it. The floor joists are placed next to the studs and nailed to them. The first or end joist is nailed to the wall studs in the end wall.

A corner framing detail for balloon framing is shown in 6-37.

To lay out the joist and stud locations, study 6-38. Locate the wall studs first. The width of the end exterior wall (typically 3½ inches) is located first. Then the next stud is located 15¼ inches from the end of the plate. All other studs are located 16 inches from this. Put an S to the left of the marks to indicate the location of the stud. Now mark the location of the joists to the left of the stud. Indicate this with an X to the left of the stud location.

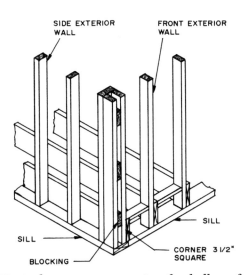

6-37 *Typical corner construction for balloon framing.*

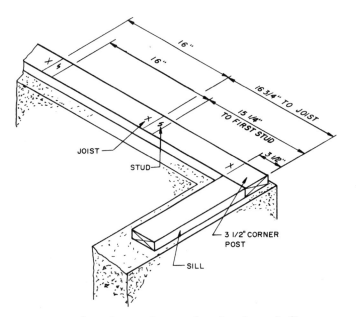

6-38 *Stud and joist layout for the front balloon-framed exterior wall shown in 6-37.*

107

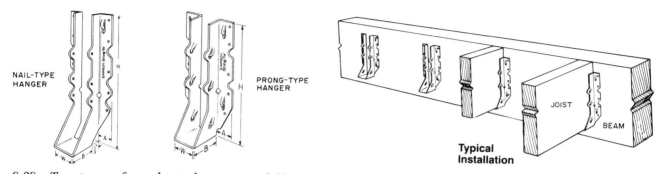

6-39 *Two types of metal joist hangers available.* (Courtesy Simpson Strong-Tie Company, Inc.)

Framing Joists to the Beam

There are a number of ways a joist can be framed to a beam. The most common, as just discussed, is to rest them on top of the beam and overlap or butt them. Sometimes it is desired to have the bottom of the joists flush with the bottom of the beam, as when preparing a basement ceiling. One way to do this with wood beams is to use metal joist hangers (see 6-39). Ledger strips can be used to reduce the amount the beam shows or to adjust the ceiling height (see 6-40). Joists can be framed around a steel beam as shown in 6-41. If an S-beam is used, a steel plate must be welded to the bottom to give an adequate bearing surface.

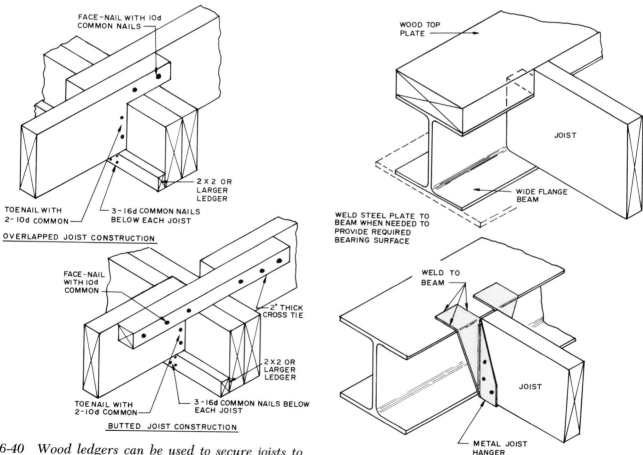

6-40 *Wood ledgers can be used to secure joists to wood beams.*

6-41 *Two ways to frame wood joists to steel beams.*

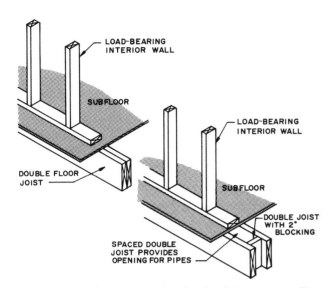

6-42   *Double floor joists under load-bearing walls.*

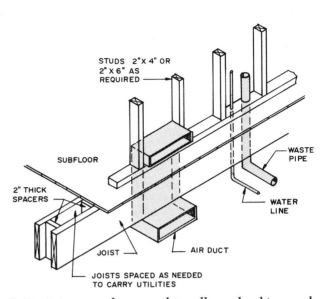

6-43   *Joists can be spaced to allow plumbing and ducts to pass up into the wall above.*

Supporting Interior Partitions

Nonload-bearing interior partitions do not need blocking or an extra joist below them if ⅝-inch or thicker plywood subfloor is used. Joists should be doubled under load-bearing interior partitions running parallel with the joists (see 6-42). Solid blocking between two joists is used when it is necessary to have access to the partition, such as a need to install heating ducts (see 6-43).

Framing Floor Openings

It is often necessary to frame an opening in a floor for a stair or fireplace. The joists are doubled on each side of the opening and are called **trimmer joists**. The shortened joists abutting the opening are called **tail joists**. The tail joists are nailed to **headers**. If the opening is less than 4 feet wide, a single header is used. Double headers are required for openings 4′0″ or larger (see 6-44).

Tail joists shorter than 6 feet are nailed to the header with three 16d common end nails and two 10d nails toenailed. Tail joists longer than 6 feet are hung with metal joist hangers or ledger strips. Headers are joined to trimmers with three 16d common nails and two 10d toenails.

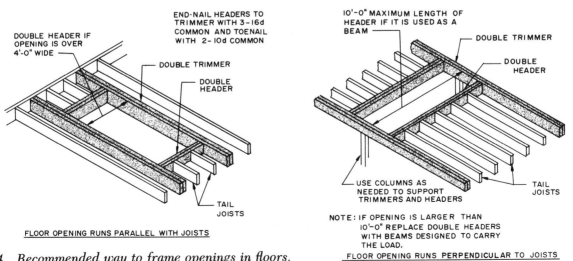

6-44   *Recommended way to frame openings in floors.*

Order of Assembly

A. End-nail trimmers 3 and 4 to header 1 with three 16d comon nails.

B. End-nail header 1 to tail joists with three 16d common nails and two 10d inside toenails.

C. Face-nail header 2 to header 1 with 12d common nails staggered 12 inches O.C.

D. End-nail trimmers 3 and 4 to header 1 with three 16d common nails.

E. Face-nail trimmers 5 and 6 to trimmers 3 and 4 with 12d common nails 12 inches O.C. staggered.

6-45 *Typical nailing sequence for installing headers and trimmers.*

When nailing framed openings, first frame the opening with single headers and trimmers. Then face-nail the second header and trimmers to those in place (see 6-45).

Framing Floor Projections

Floors often cantilever over the foundation where bay windows or balconies are required. Some house styles have the second floor cantilever over the first floor. When joists run in the direction of the projection, they are extended beyond the foundation (see 6-46). Under normal conditions a 2-foot projection is maximum. Projections of a second floor seldom extend beyond 12 inches. Anything longer than this will need special design consideration. Notice that the joists on the outside edges are doubled and a single header is used. The subfloor extends out over the projection and is cut flush with the outside of the framing. The same nailing pattern that is used on the rest of the floor is used.

When the projection runs parallel with the joists, it must be framed by extending the joists in the projection back into the floor to the second joist (see 6-47), which is doubled. The joists on the ends of the projection are also doubled. All joists are hung using metal joist hangers.

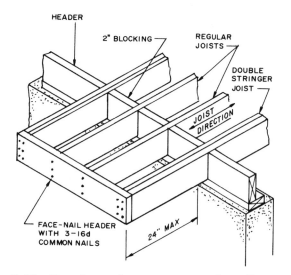

6-46 *Framing a floor projection that allows floor joists to extend beyond the foundation.*

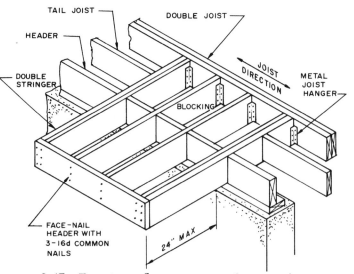

6-47 *Framing a floor projection having joists that run perpendicular to the floor joists.*

Framing for a Bath

The floor below a bathroom requires extra strength because of loads heavier than normal. When the floor is to have a wood subfloor and tile, carpet, or composition finish, the only extra framing is to double the joists under the edges of the bathtub (see 6-48). If the wall is to hold plumbing, the joists are spaced apart with blocking.

Notching Joists and Beams

Occasionally it is necessary to cut a notch or hole in a joist or beam to run through plumbing or other utilities. Notching of joists should be avoided whenever possible. Notches on the ends of joists should not exceed *one fourth* of the joist depth. Notches in the top or bottom of joists should not exceed *one sixth* of the depth and should not be located in the middle third of the joist (see 6-49).

Holes bored in joists should not be within 2 inches of the top or bottom of the joist. The diameter of the hole should not exceed *one third* of the depth of the joist (see 6-49).

If larger cuts are needed, the joist will need reinforcing. Sometimes sections of 2-inch-thick lumber are nailed on both sides of the notched section, or the joist can be doubled. It is also possible to cut out the joist and frame the area in the same way as for an opening in the floor.

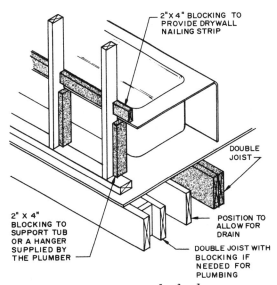

6-48 *Framing to support a bathtub.*

Notching of beams should also be avoided. When necessary the notches in sawn lumber shall not exceed *one sixth* the depth of the member and not be located in the middle third of the span. Notches in the ends of beams should not exceed *one fourth* the beam depth. Notching of I-joists, laminated veneer, parallel strand, and other manufactured beams and joists should be according to the instructions of the manufacturer.

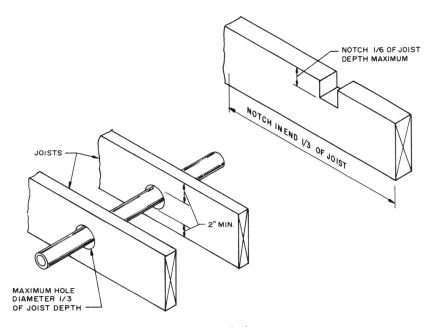

6-49 *Recommended allowances for notching or boring holes in joists.*

Table 6–4 Typical spans for I-joists.*

Spacing, O.C. (inches)	Joist depth			
	9½	11⅞	14	16
12	18′2″	21′9″	24′8″	27′3″
16	16′6″	19′9″	22′5″	24′10″
19.2	15′6″	18′6″	21′1″	23′4″
24	14′4″	17′1″	19′8″	21′7″
32	11′4″	14′4″	———	———

* Based on a floor load of 40 psf and 10 pounds dead load. Consult manufacturer for specific data.

I-Joist Floor System

An I-joist is a structural wood member used for floor, ceiling, and roof framing. It is manufactured using plywood or oriented strand board webs and laminated veneer lumber flanges. These joists have long span capabilities, and on many residential installations they eliminate the need for a center beam. Typical construction details are shown in 6-50. When a heavy load is to be applied to a section of the floor, the joists can be doubled or spaced close together. Spans for representative sizes are given in table 6-4.

Other manufactured joist, beam, and column systems such as laminated veneer lumber, parallel strand lumber, glued laminated members, and various other laminated wood structural products are worked in the same manner as solid lumber. (These products are described earlier in this chapter.)

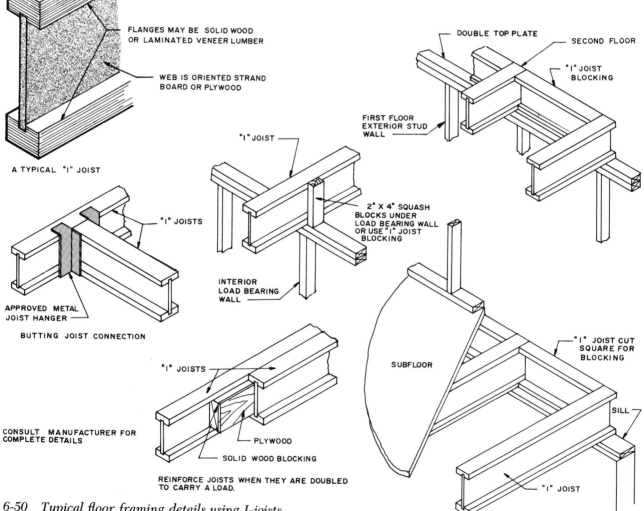

6-50 *Typical floor framing details using I-joists.*

Wood Floor Trusses

Wood floor trusses are used for floor joists. They can carry reasonably high floor loads for long spans (see 6-51). These joists will span the width of a typical residence, eliminating the need for a center beam. Since they have open space between the members, heating, plumbing, and electrical wires can be easily run. Typical span data are given in table 6-5. Secure this information from the company manufacturing the trusses.

Table 6–5 Span and load data for truss-type floor joists spaced 24″ O.C.*

Clear Span (in feet)	Joist depth					
	12	14	16	18	20	22
14	120	118				
16	83	100				
18	66	79	92	105	117	120
20	53	63	74	85	95	103
22	—	52	61	70	79	88
24	—	—	51	59	67	74
26	—	—	—	50	57	63
28	—	—	—	—	49	—
30	—	—	—	—	—	47

* Pounds per square foot (psf). (*Alpine Engineered Products, Inc.*)

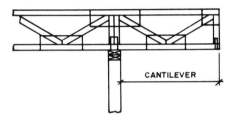

CANTILEVER FRAME

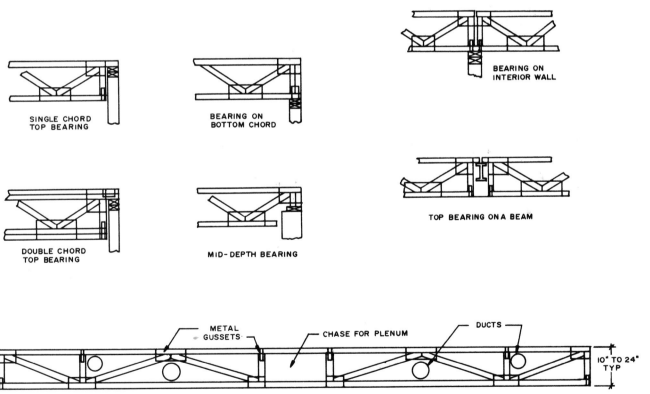

SINGLE CHORD TOP BEARING

BEARING ON BOTTOM CHORD

BEARING ON INTERIOR WALL

DOUBLE CHORD TOP BEARING

MID-DEPTH BEARING

TOP BEARING ON A BEAM

METAL GUSSETS CHASE FOR PLENUM DUCTS

10" TO 24" TYP

TYPICAL FLOOR OR ROOF TRUSS
SPANS TO 40'-0" COMMON

6-51 *Construction details for truss-type wood floor joists.* (Courtesy Alpine Engineered Products, Inc.)

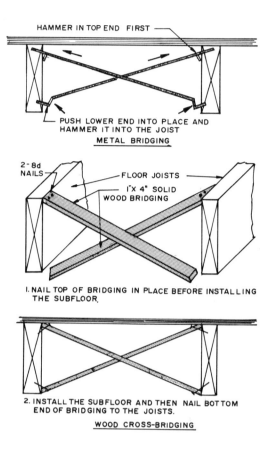

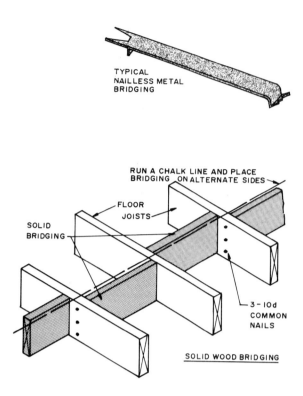

6-52   *Commonly used types of floor bridging.*

Bridging

Bridging is usually required when the ratio of joist depth to thickness is six to one or greater. Solid blocking or cross-bracing is required. It is installed in rows not more than 8 feet apart. Typical types of bridging are shown in 6-52. Local codes specify bridging requirements.

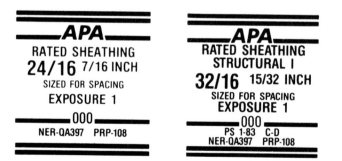

6-53   *Grade marks for APA-Rated Sheathing and APA Structural Panels used for subflooring.* (Courtesy American Plywood Association)

Installing the Subfloor

The subfloor is secured to the joists forming a strong, stiff platform. While solid wood boards nailed on a diagonal can be used, subfloors are now almost entirely plywood or some type of reconstituted wood panel.

Plywood Subfloor

A plywood subfloor may be APA-Rated Sheathing or APA-Rated Sturd-I-Floor.

APA-Rated Sheathing and APA Structural I panels are used as a subfloor, if a separate underlayment panel or strip flooring is to be nailed over them. The stamp on the panel indicates the maximum span. For example, a span rating of $32/16$ means the panel can be used as roof sheathing for rafters up to 32 inches O.C. and floor sheathing for joists up to 16 inches O.C. Generally, ½-inch-thick plywood is used for joists spaced 16 inches O.C. and ¾ inch for joists 24 inches O.C. Underlayment plywood should be APA Underlayment Int or one of several other grades available (see 6-53).

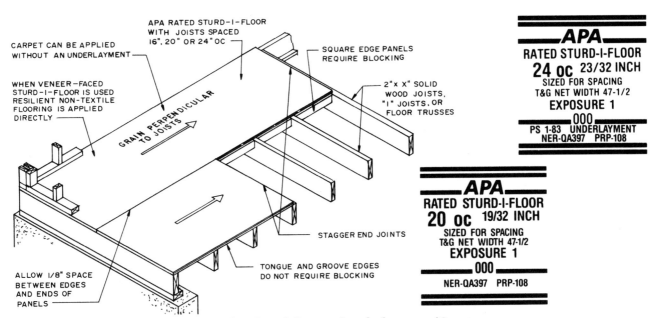

CARPET CAN BE APPLIED
WITHOUT AN UNDERLAYMENT

WHEN VENEER-FACED
STURD-I-FLOOR IS USED
RESILIENT NON-TEXTILE
FLOORING IS APPLIED
DIRECTLY

APA RATED STURD-I-FLOOR
WITH JOISTS SPACED
16", 20" OR 24" OC

SQUARE EDGE PANELS
REQUIRE BLOCKING

2"x X" SOLID
WOOD JOISTS,
"I" JOISTS, OR
FLOOR TRUSSES

GRAIN PERPENDICULAR
TO JOISTS

STAGGER END JOINTS

ALLOW 1/8" SPACE
BETWEEN EDGES
AND ENDS OF
PANELS

TONGUE AND GROOVE EDGES
DO NOT REQUIRE BLOCKING

APA
RATED STURD-I-FLOOR
24 OC 23/32 INCH
SIZED FOR SPACING
T&G NET WIDTH 47-1/2
EXPOSURE 1
_000_
PS 1-83 UNDERLAYMENT
NER-QA397 PRP-108

APA
RATED STURD-I-FLOOR
20 OC 19/32 INCH
SIZED FOR SPACING
T&G NET WIDTH 47-1/2
EXPOSURE 1
_000_
NER-QA397 PRP-108

6-54   *APA-Rated Sturd-I-Floor provides the subfloor and underlayment.* (Courtesy American Plywood Association)

APA-Rated Sturd-I-Floor is a combination subfloor-underlayment providing the strength required and a smooth surface for the application of carpet or composition floor-covering materials. It also has a stamp indicating a span rating. It is available with span ratings of 16, 20, 24, 32, and 48 inches O.C. The spans from 16 through 32 inches are framed with 2-inch joists or manufactured joists of plywood webbing and solid wood stringers. These panels range in thickness from $^{19}/_{32}$ to $^{7}/_{8}$ inch (see 6-54). Panels spanning 48 inches O.C. are placed on girders spaced 48 inches O.C. These girders may be 4-inch solid wood, 2-inch thick stock nailed together, wood floor trusses, or lightweight steel beams (see 6-55).

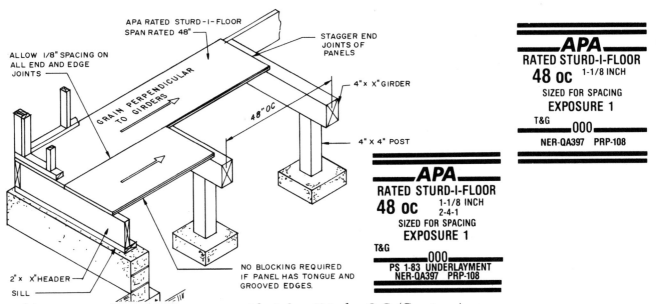

ALLOW 1/8" SPACING ON
ALL END AND EDGE
JOINTS

APA RATED STURD-I-FLOOR
SPAN RATED 48"

STAGGER END
JOINTS OF
PANELS

GRAIN PERPENDICULAR
TO GIRDERS

4" x X" GIRDER

48" OC

4" X 4" POST

2" x X" HEADER

SILL

NO BLOCKING REQUIRED
IF PANEL HAS TONGUE AND
GROOVED EDGES.

APA
RATED STURD-I-FLOOR
48 OC 1-1/8 INCH
SIZED FOR SPACING
EXPOSURE 1
T&G _000_
NER-QA397 PRP-108

APA
RATED STURD-I-FLOOR
48 OC 1-1/8 INCH
2-4-1
SIZED FOR SPACING
EXPOSURE 1
T&G _000_
PS 1-83 UNDERLAYMENT
NER-QA397 PRP-108

6-55   *APA-Rated Sturd-I-Floor system with girders 48 inches O.C.* (Courtesy American Plywood Association)

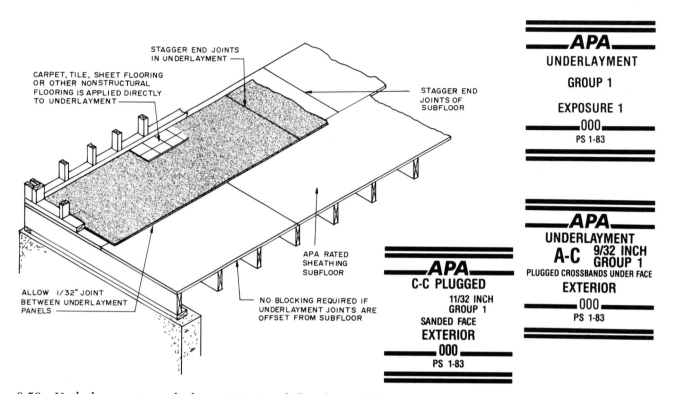

6-56 *Underlayment is applied over APA-Rated Sheathing subfloor to give a smooth finished surface.* (Courtesy American Plywood Association)

Plywood is installed with the face grain at right angles to the joists. Tongue-and-groove sheets are joined, leaving ⅛-inch spacing on all joints. If square-edge sheets are used, blocking must be installed below each joint (see 6-55).

Plywood sheathing is nailed to floor joists using 6d ring- or screw-shank nails for panels up to ¾ inch thick and 8d ring- or screw-shank nails for thicker panels. Nails are spaced 6 inches apart on all edges and 12 inches apart on intermediate members for panels that are nailed only.

Underlayment is installed with the face grain of the panels perpendicular to the joists. End joints should be staggered and a 1/32-of-an-inch space left between the edges of panels. The underlayment is nailed 6 inches O.C. along the edges and 8 inches O.C. on the interior, with 3d shank nails for panels ½ inch or thinner. Panels up to ¾ inch thick are nailed with 4d shank nails 6 inches O.C. on the edges and 12 inches O.C. on the interior. Fill and sand the joints, producing a smooth surface (see 6-56).

The American Plywood Association has a thoroughly tested glued floor system using field-applied construction adhesives to permanently secure wood-based subfloor panels to wood joists. The glue bond joins the joists and subfloor so that they behave like integral T-beam units. This increases the stiffness of the floor and is especially effective when tongue-and-groove panels are used (see 6-57). The tongue-and-groove joint should also be glued. If square-edge panels are used, 2 × 4 blocking must be placed below unsupported joints. Gluing not only produces a stiffer floor but helps eliminate squeaks, bounce, and nail-popping.

A ¼-inch-diameter bead of adhesive is applied to the sill and joists. When panel ends butt, apply two beads of adhesive. As soon as a panel is set in place, it should be nailed using 6d ring- or screw-shank nails for panels up to ¾ inch thick and 8d ring- or screw-shank nails for thicker panels. The nails on glued panels are spaced 12 inches O.C. on the edges and intermediate joists for panels up to 23/32 inch thick. Thicker glued panels require edge nails every 6 inches on the edge and 12 inches on any intermediate supports. Subfloors are generally nailed with pneumatic nailers (see 6-58).

6-58 *Pneumatic nailers drive a wide range of fasteners including plain shank, ring shank, screw shank, coated, and galvanized nails.* (Courtesy Stanley-Bostitch)

6-57 *Installing plywood subflooring with an adhesive.* (Courtesy American Plywood Association)

Reconstituted Wood Panels

Reconstituted wood panels are made using compressed, bonded-wood chips and strands. Those used for floor sheathing include composite panels, oriented strand board, and waferboard. They are graded and installed in the same manner as discussed for plywood panels (see Chapter 2 for details).

Plank Subfloors

Planks are 2- to 4-inch-thick wood members used for floor and roof decking. They are usually tongue-and-grooved on the edges.

The floor framing system is made of girders with spans of 6 feet and more (see 6-59). The span used

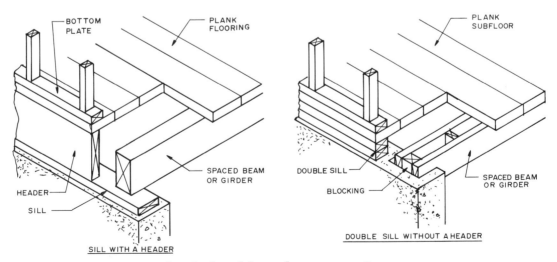

6-59 *Sill details for construction for plank-and-beam floor construction.*

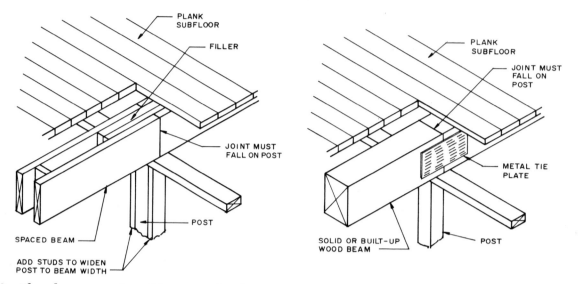

6-60   *Floor beams may be solid or spaced and can rest on posts in the interior of the building.*

depends on the load-carrying capability of the planks (see 6-60). The plank flooring is usually covered with an underlayment such as plywood. The lower face often is used as the ceiling of rooms below (see 6-61).

Planks 4 to 6 inches wide are face-nailed with one 16d common nail at each support. Eight-inch planks are face-nailed with two 16d nails, and 10- and 12-inch planks require three 16d nails.

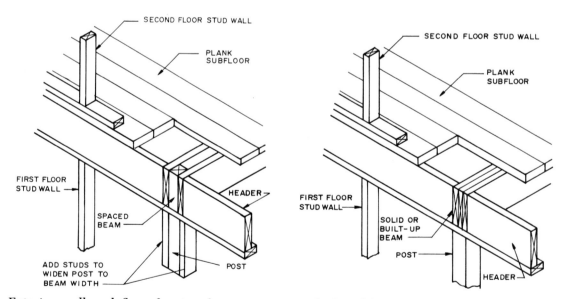

6-61   *Exterior wall and floor framing for a two-storey plank-and-beam framed building.*

7

Wall and Partition Framing

Since most light-frame buildings are constructed using platform framing, this system of framing will be emphasized in this chapter. After the floor joists are in place and the subfloor is glued and nailed to them, the framers begin constructing the exterior walls and interior partitions. The exterior wall frame serves as the base on which sheathing and siding is applied and carries most of the roof load. It also carries the weight of the second floor, if there is one. Some of the interior partitions may support the ceiling framing while most serve as room dividers and as a base to carry the interior wall finish material. Any partitions that carry loads are called load-bearing partitions.

Framing the Exterior Wall

A typical exterior wall for platform framing is made up of a bottom or sole plate, studs, double top plates, and headers. They are generally covered with some type of sheathing. Generally the framing material is 2×4 stock; however, 2×6 stock is often used. The studs are spaced 16 or 24 inches O.C. The 2×6 material enables extra insulation to be placed in the wall. A typical wall framing plan is shown in 7-1. When a wall is framed, there should be a stud every 16 inches (or 24 inches), even though other studs, such as for a window, may break the pattern (see 7-2).

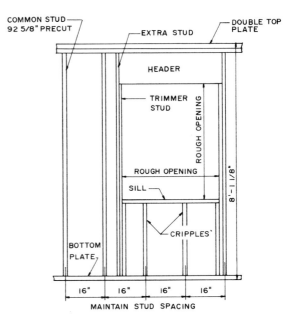

7-2 *The specified stud spacing is maintained even when extra studs break the sequence.*

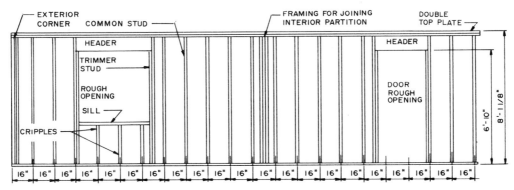

7-1 *A typical wall framing plan.*

119

The spacing of studs on 16- or 24-inch centers must be done accurately, because sheathing materials, such as plywood, are made in 4 foot × 8 foot sheets and should span from the center of one stud to the center of another without having to be cut (see 7-3).

Framing lumber is available in 2-foot lengths, such as 10 feet and 12 feet. However, precut studs, 92⅝ inches long, are available for framing walls when an 8-foot ceiling is desired. Using precut studs saves the framer a lot of time, because no studs have to be cut to length (see 7-4).

Framing Door and Window Openings

Openings in walls, such as those needed for doors and windows, must be spanned by **headers** strong enough to carry any imposed loads. Headers are required only in load-bearing walls and partitions. Framing for a typical window opening is shown in 7-5. The studs on each side are doubled, and the header rests on the **trimmer** stud. The header may be one that, while it is large enough to carry the imposed load, does not fill the space up to the top plate. If this design is used, **cripples** are placed as shown in 7-6. The cripples are spaced to maintain the 16- or 24-inch O.C. spacing. A sill is placed on the bottom side of

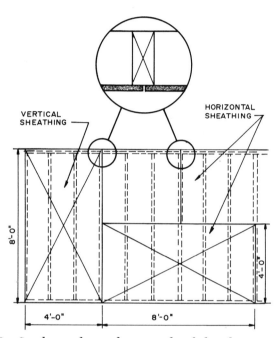

7-3 *Studs are located so panels of sheathing material need not be cut.*

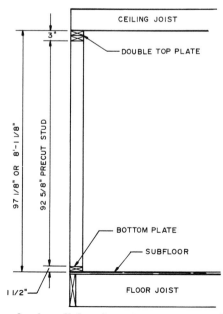

7-4 *The standard wall height using precut studs.*

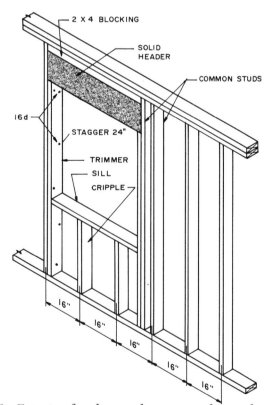

7-5 *Framing for the rough opening of a window using a solid header. Notice the trimmer stud nailing requirements.*

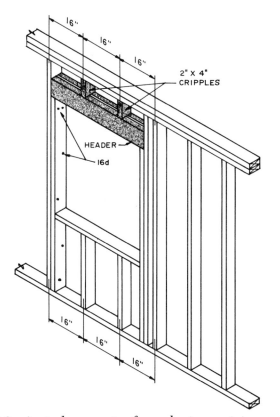

the window opening. Some framers prefer to double the sill. Below the sill cripple studs are located, maintaining the 16- or 24-inch O.C. spacing.

Several variations of headers using 2-inch-thick material are shown in 7-7 (this page and next). One commonly used type is built using an assembly of 2-inch-thick stock with ½-inch plywood spacer strips between them. This assembly is nailed together giving a 3½-inch-thick header, which is the same thickness as a 2×4 stud. Other lumber header designs are also shown in 7-7 (this page and next).

7-6   A window opening framed using a minimum-size header and cripples.

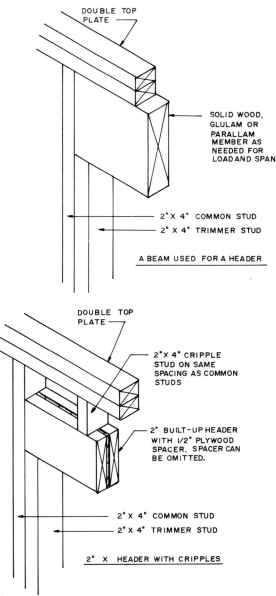

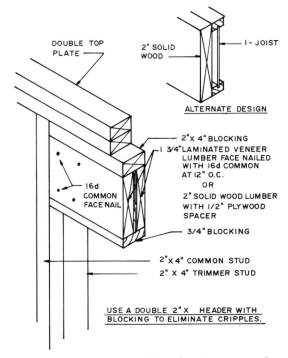

7-7   Commonly used types of header. (Continued next page.)

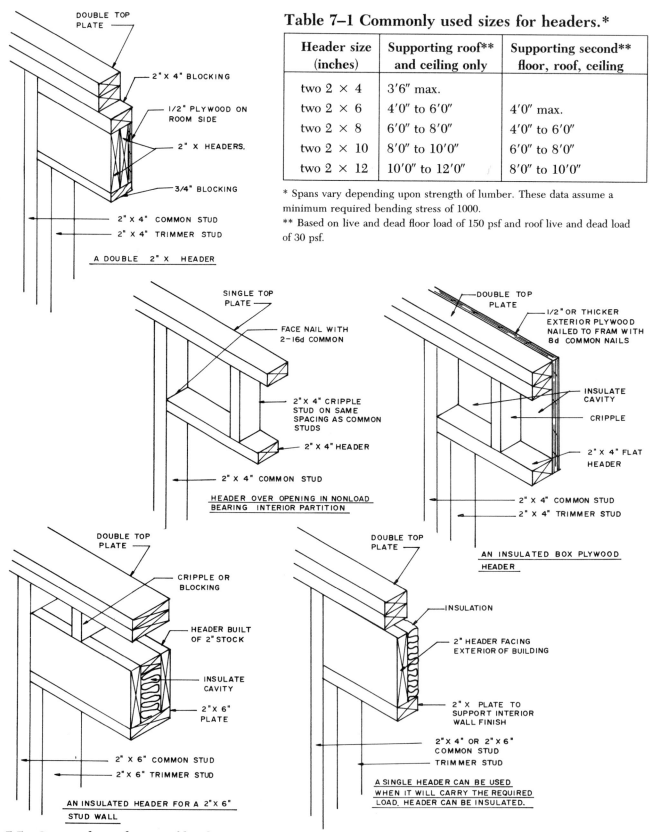

Table 7–1 Commonly used sizes for headers.*

Header size (inches)	Supporting roof** and ceiling only	Supporting second** floor, roof, ceiling
two 2 × 4	3'6" max.	
two 2 × 6	4'0" to 6'0"	4'0" max.
two 2 × 8	6'0" to 8'0"	4'0" to 6'0"
two 2 × 10	8'0" to 10'0"	6'0" to 8'0"
two 2 × 12	10'0" to 12'0"	8'0" to 10'0"

* Spans vary depending upon strength of lumber. These data assume a minimum required bending stress of 1000.

** Based on live and dead floor load of 150 psf and roof live and dead load of 30 psf.

7-7 *Commonly used types of header (continued).*

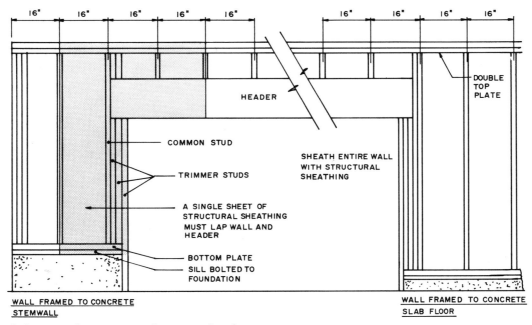

7-8 *Rough framing for a garage door or other large opening.*

When load conditions permit, such as for an exterior wall that has no load imposed, the header can be a single 2-inch-thick member with a 2 × 4 nailing strip on the bottom. The size of the header will depend on the span of the opening and the load to be imposed on it. Typical header sizes in common use are given in table 7-1 (opposite page).

Plywood box beams can also be used as headers. They are light in weight, and the cavity can always be filled with insulation. (Box beams are discussed in Chapter 6.)

Headers for long spans, such as a garage door, require special design considerations. A manufactured beam such as a glulam or Parallam® will span the distance as will a plywood box beam. (These are illustrated in Chapters 2 and 6.) A suggested framing plan for a garage door or other large opening is shown in 7-8.

Headers for spans 9 feet to 12 feet are supported by double trimmer studs on each side. Triple trimmers are used on openings over 12 feet. In addition to the use of manufactured beams, other types of engineered headers are used where loads exceed the normal roof and floor loads. Some examples of these designs are shown in 7-9.

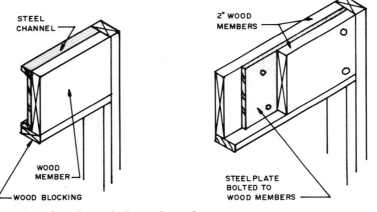

7-9 *These headers are reinforced with steel channel or plate.*

When framing a rough opening, the height of the header above the floor is usually 6'10" to 6'11". Normally the height of the rough opening for windows is the same as for doors. If it is different, this should be noted on the plans. The header is placed on trimmer studs to provide the opening (see 7-10). There are many ways to frame this and several are illustrated. Frequently the framer will use oversize headers to avoid the trouble of installing cripples, or will frame around the headers with 2 × 4 and 1 × 4 stock instead of using cripples.

Framing for a typical exterior door opening is shown in 7-11. It is framed just like the window opening. Notice that the sole plate continues across the opening. This is needed to stiffen the wall frame until it is raised, braced, and sheathed. Then it is cut away. The size of the rough opening is determined by the size of the door to be used. While framers vary in the allowances they use, it is typical to make the rough opening 2 inches wider and 2⅝ inches higher than the

actual size of the door. For interior doors the height of the opening will vary some depending on the thickness of the flooring to be used. For a door opening in a nonload-bearing partition a large header is not required, as shown in 7-12. Commonly used door framing dimensions are given in table 7-2.

Framed openings for **balloon framing** are shown in 7-13. The header must carry the weight of the second floor, the ceiling, and the roof. The actual framing can

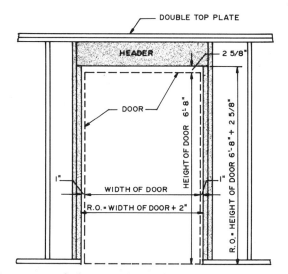

7-11   Rough framing for a door in an exterior load-bearing wall.

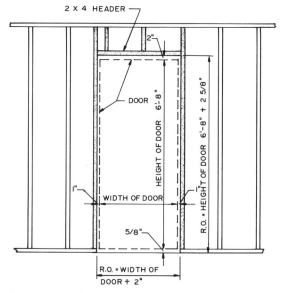

7-12   Rough framing for a door in an interior nonload-bearing partition.

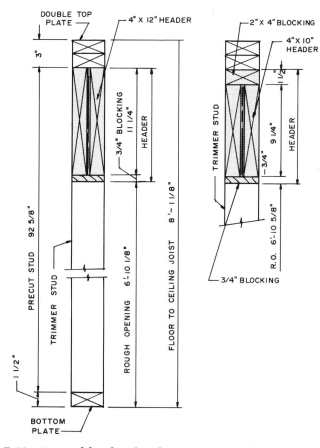

7-10   Typical lumber header installation details.

Table 7–2 Standard framing dimensions for rooms with an 8'0" finished ceiling.

Wall height with per-cut stud (92⅝") (subfloor to top of double plate)	97⅛"
Type of door	Rough opening size
Rough opening of exterior doors	Door width plus 2" Door height plus 2⅝"
Rough opening of sliding doors	Door width equals size of unit Height for 6'8" door 80⅝"
Rough opening for interior doors	Door width plus 2" Door height plus 2⅝"
Rough opening for pocket doors	Door width actual size of door Door height plus 2⅝"
Rough opening for bypass doors	Door width actual size of door Door height plus 2⅝"

be done several ways. The studs, which extend from the sole plate to the roof, could be erected first. Then the openings could be cut and the headers, rough sills, and cripple studs installed. Another way is to erect only the full-length studs and then install the headers, rough sills, and cripple studs in the open areas. Notice in 7-13 that the studs are all spaced evenly. The headers continue past the side of the rough opening to the next full stud. The side of the rough opening is framed with shorter double studs.

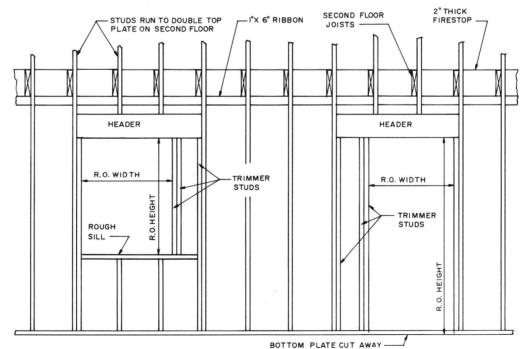

7-13 *Framing wall openings when using balloon construction.*

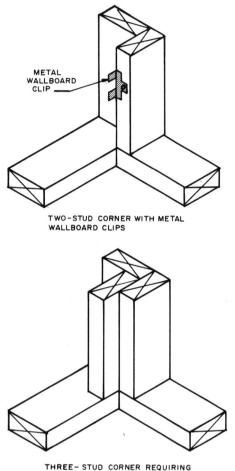

TWO-STUD CORNER WITH METAL
WALLBOARD CLIPS

Framing Exterior Corners

There are several ways to frame the corners where exterior walls meet. It is important to provide some means for securing the interior wall finish material. Several ways to frame the corner when using platform construction are shown in 7-14. When using balloon framing, the corner can be framed with an extra stud and blocking (see 7-15).

THREE-STUD CORNER REQUIRING
NO BLOCKING

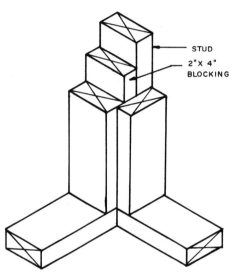

THREE-STUD CORNER WITH BLOCKING

7-14   *Common ways to frame the corners of exterior walls.*

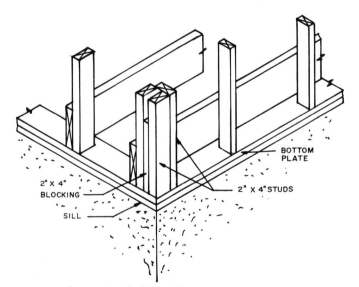

7-15   *Framing an exterior corner when using balloon framing.*

Framing Interior Partitions

Some interior partitions are load-bearing and carry the weight of the ceiling structure and a second floor, if one is required. Most partitions are nonload-bearing and only support the finish wall material such as gypsum board.

Interior load-bearing partitions are framed in the same manner as exterior walls, including the use of headers. Nonload-bearing partitions use the same framing, except that large headers over door openings are not required. Generally 2×4 studs are used for partition construction. When extra soundproofing is needed, 2×6 or 2×8 studs can be used. Staggered studs are also used to improve soundproofing. In most cases, a 2×6 top and bottom plate and 2×4 studs are used. Sound-deadening insulation can be placed between the studs (see 7-16). As a space-saving technique 2×3 studs or 2×4 studs placed flatwise can be used. A typical example is in the wall separating clos-

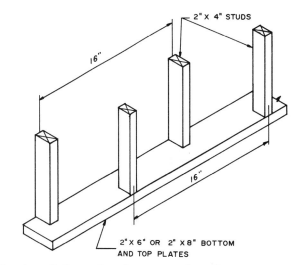

7-16   *A wall framed with staggered studs.*

ets. Typical load-bearing and nonload-bearing partitions are shown in 7-17.

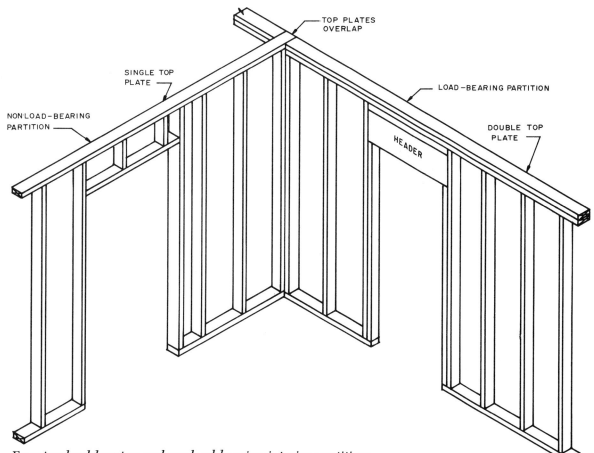

7-17   *Framing load-bearing and nonload-bearing interior partitions.*

Wider partitions are often necessary when the partition will contain plumbing. Generally a 2×6 stud partition will be adequate. If cast-iron soil pipes are used, a 2×8 stud partition is needed. If pipes are to be run parallel to the partition, the studs can be turned flatwise (see 7-18).

Partitions that run perpendicular to the ceiling joists can be nailed to the joist (see 7-19). Notice the use of 2-inch blocking on the top plate to provide a nailing surface for ceiling finish material.

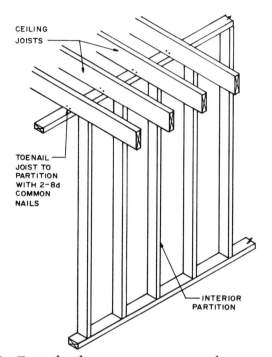

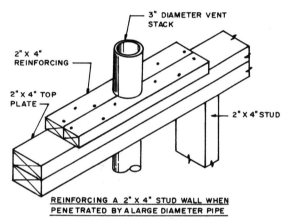

REINFORCING A 2" X 4" STUD WALL WHEN PENETRATED BY A LARGE DIAMETER PIPE

7-19 Toenail ceiling joists to partitions that run perpendicular to them.

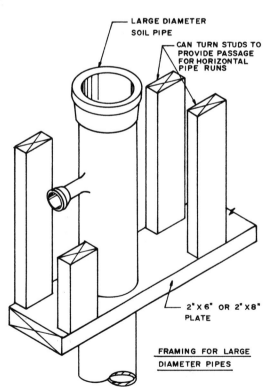

FRAMING FOR LARGE DIAMETER PIPES

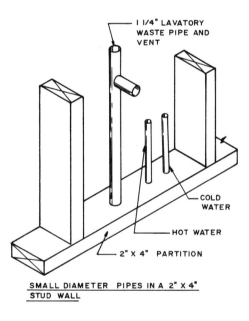

SMALL DIAMETER PIPES IN A 2" X 4" STUD WALL

7-18 Typical framing for plumbing.

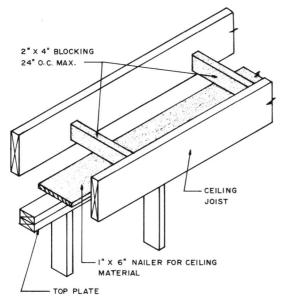

7-20 *How to secure interior partitions when they run parallel with the ceiling joists.*

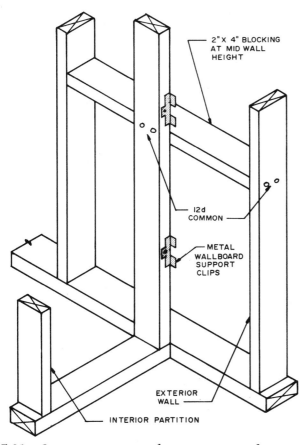

7-21 *One way to secure the intersection of interior partitions with the exterior wall.*

Partitions running parallel to the ceiling joists must be anchored to 2×4 nailers (see 7-20). Notice the one-inch-thick boards on top of the partitions that provide a nailing surface for the finished ceiling.

Nonload-bearing partitions are adequately supported by the subfloor even if they run between, and parallel to, the floor joists, if the subfloor is ⅝ inch or thicker. They are nailed through the bottom plate into the subfloor. Floor joists should be doubled under load-bearing partitions that run parallel with the joists. Loads greater than normal may require that a beam be placed below the partition.

Intersecting Partitions

Partitions intersect each other and the exterior wall. The union must provide a surface to which the interior wall finish material can be installed. There are several ways this is done. One way uses 2×4 blocking between studs. Usually one piece at the midpoint of the wall is adequate. Metal gypsum-board backup clips are nailed to the stud. The clips provide a nonrigid joint which tends to minimize cracking (see 7-21). A variation of this is shown in 7-22. An extra stud is inserted and a 2×4 block used to support a 1×6 nailer. The nailer provides the needed supporting surface for the interior wallboard.

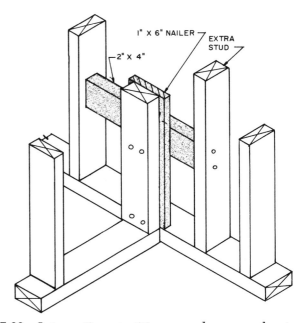

7-22 *Intersecting partitions can be secured using horizontal blocking and a 1×6 nailer.*

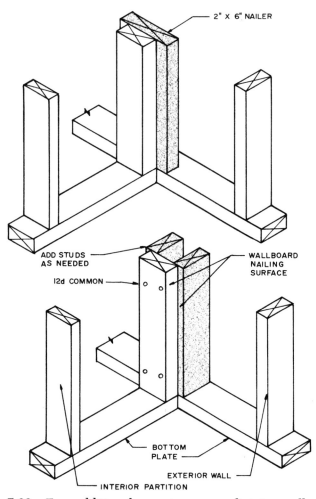

7-23 *Two additional ways to secure adjoining walls and partitions.*

Possibly the most commonly used framing techniques are shown in 7-23. Extra studs are used to provide the needed supporting surface. They are not needed for structural purposes. A variation of these uses a 2×6 nailer placed in the wall. This is a quick way to provide needed supporting surfaces. Backup and nailing surfaces for wall finish materials such as plywood panelling should be built as recommended by the manufacturer.

The top plate of the interior partition overlaps the lower top plate of the exterior partition. This provides a strong tie and structural support (see 7-24).

Laying Out the Plate

Wall and partition construction is begun by locating the studs, rough openings, trimmers, and cripples on the top and bottom plates. Select straight stock, since it often takes several pieces to run the length of a wall. Place the joint so that it will be below a stud. When possible locate the studs so that they are directly above the floor joists and so that the rafters are directly above them.

First lay out the location of the walls and partitions on the subfloor with a chalk line. This must be carefully and accurately done. Consult the plans often and measure several times before actually marking the locations. Rub blue or red chalk on the line and snap it to produce a line on the subfloor (see 7-25).

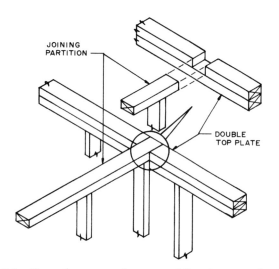

7-24 *Top plates overlap, providing increased rigidity in the structural frame.*

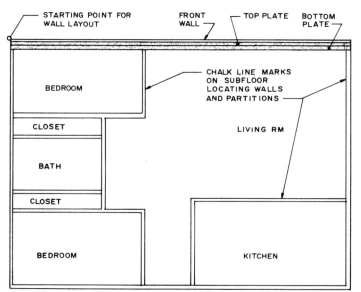

7-25 *Walls and partitions are laid out on the subfloor.*

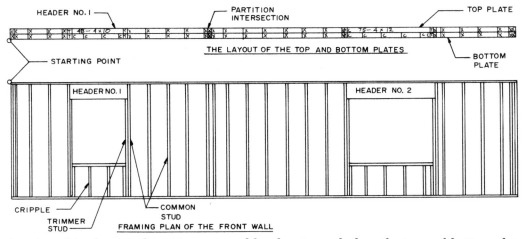

7-26 *The location of studs, cripples, trimmers, and headers is marked on the top and bottom plates.*

To lay out the plates, place them along the chalk line and locate the partition backers, stud trimmers, and cripples for any openings. Then locate the studs (see 7-26). Symbols frequently used to mark the plates are shown in 7-27. Other symbols may be used in various localities.

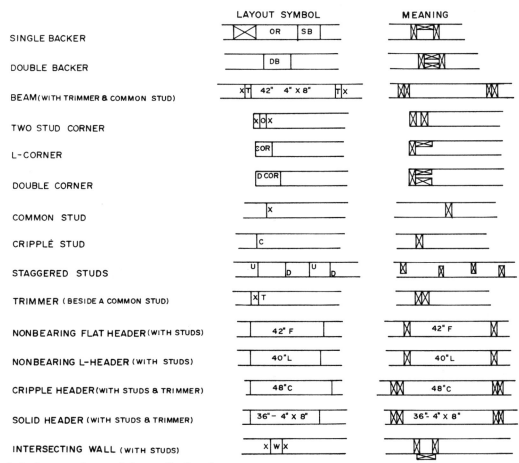

7-27 *Symbols frequently used for wall plate layout.*

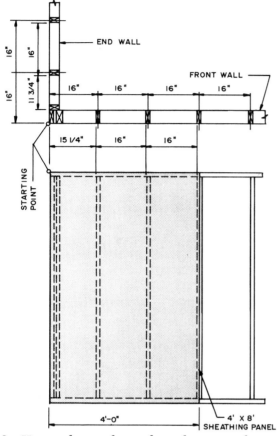

7-28   *How to locate the studs at the corner framing so that the sheathing panels need not be cut.*

The wall layout starts at a corner of the front wall. The location of the studs should be such that when the stock 4'0" sheathing panels are set flush with the outside face of the end stud, they hit the center of a stud down the wall. This means the first stud beyond the corner framing is set 15¼ inches from the outside face of the end stud (see 7-28). In order to maintain the 16-inch O.C. spacing on the *end wall*, the first stud beyond the corner stud is located 11¾ inches from the outside face of the end stud.

Building the Walls

There are many ways to assemble the parts that make up the wall framing. Most framers develop a system that suits their needs. The following is a general plan.

Usually the long exterior walls are framed first. In most cases these are the front and rear walls. The exact procedure depends on the way the framer prefers to do the job. After these long walls are assembled and raised into place, the end walls are assembled and set in between the long walls. Interior partitions are generally erected after the exterior walls are in place.

Begin the exterior-wall assembly by laying the top and bottom plates on the subfloor about 8 feet apart.

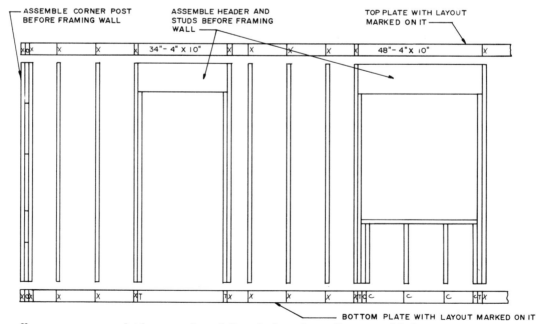

7-29   *The wall components are laid out on the subfloor before the wall is assembled.*

Lay the precut studs, trimmers, cripples, and headers in their approximate location (see 7-29). Beginning at one end of the wall, nail the top and bottom plates to each full-length stud with two 12d or 16d common nails. Some prefer to use box nails because they are less likely to split the wood. Next, nail the trimmers to the common studs with 12d or 16d common nails (see 7-30). Nail these assemblies to the plates and set the headers on the trimmer studs. Nail through the common stud into the header with 12d or 16d common nails (see 7-31). Some prefer to assemble the header, trimmers, and adjacent full-length studs before placing them in the wall assembly (see 7-32). Install any sills, and then nail the cripples in place.

Another variation of this assembly procedure is to nail the bottom plate in place on the edge of the subfloor. Assemble the studs, trimmers, headers, sills, and cripples by nailing to the top plate. Then this assembly is raised into place on top of the bottom plate and the studs are toenailed to the bottom plate. Since the studs are swinging loose, this assembly must be handled carefully.

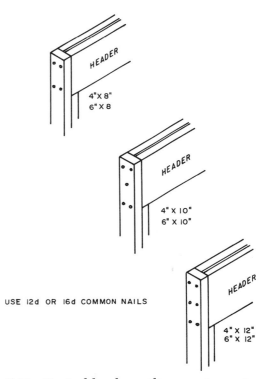

7-31   Typical header nailing requirements.

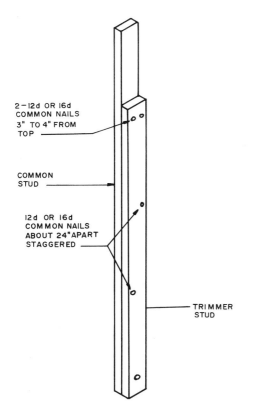

7-30   Face-nail the trimmer stud to the common stud.

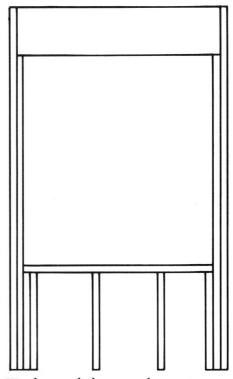

7-32   Window and door rough opening assemblies are often assembled before they are placed in the wall framing.

It is common practice to add bracing and sheathing to the frame while it is still on the subfloor. Before doing this make certain the frame is square by measuring the diagonals (see 7-33). If the diagonals are the same length, the frame is square. Bracing and sheathing can then be added.

Some framers prefer to erect the frame, and apply the bracing and sheathing after it is raised into place. Others prefer to not only sheath the frame, but install the windows before raising it.

Partitions are framed and erected in the same way as exterior walls.

Bracing the Exterior Wall

Possibly the most common way to brace the frame is to apply 4 foot × 8 foot sheets of plywood, oriented strand board, or Com-Ply® sheathing on each end and in the center if it is a long wall. The strongest possible construction would be to sheath the entire wall with these materials.

A second way to brace the wall is to notch the studs to receive 1×4 wood strips that are set at approximately 45 degrees (see 7-34). If a window interferes, two shorter braces can be used (see 7-35). Metal straps nailed to the outer face of the studs are also used as bracing. They are on a 45-degree angle and run from the top plate to the bottom plate.

Building codes will specify the requirements for exterior wall bracing. While these may vary in different localities, those shown in 7-36 are typical. In addition there are specific requirements as to the size of

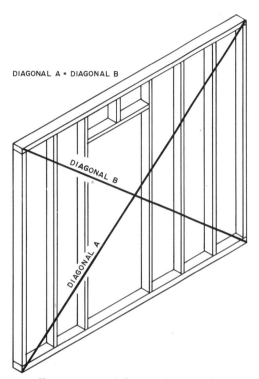

7-33 *A wall is square if diagonals A and B are the same length.*

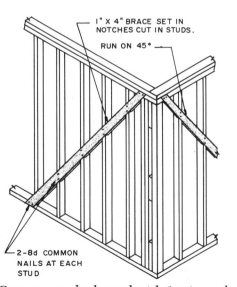

7-34 *Corners can be braced with 1×4 wood members set into notches cut in the stud.*

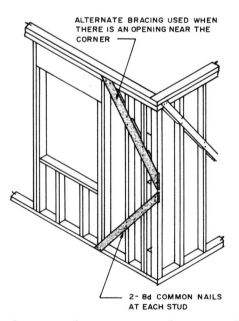

7-35 *This is an alternate way to brace a wall with 1×4 bracing when an opening is near the corner.*

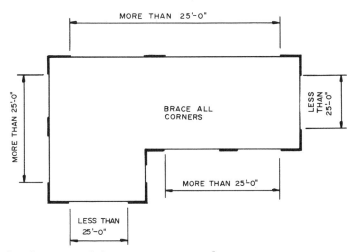

7-36   *Typical examples of code-required frame construction bracing.*

nails used for panels, let-in wood braces, and metal strapping. If a frame building is more than two stories, wall bracing must be with structural sheathing panels. Special considerations are necessary if building on a seismic zone or area subject to high winds. For example, one code specifies that braced sheathing in Seismic Zones 3 and 4 should cover 40 percent of the length of the wall. The designer and framer must consult local codes before proceeding with construction.

Erecting the Assembled Walls

The assembled walls are raised to a vertical position. This requires the efforts of several persons (see 7-37). A wall is carefully set on the edge of the sub-

7-37   *The assembled wall frame is lifted into position. (Courtesy Western Wood Products Association)*

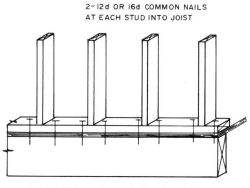

2-12d OR 16d COMMON NAILS
AT EACH STUD INTO JOIST

WHEN PARTITION IS PARALLEL WITH JOIST

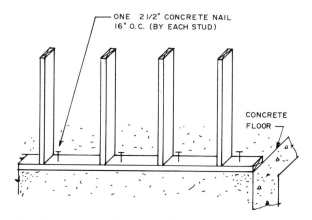

ONE 2 1/2" CONCRETE NAIL
16" O.C. (BY EACH STUD)

CONCRETE
FLOOR

7-39 *Securing a frame wall or partition to a concrete floor.*

WALL
STUDS

2 - 12d OR
16d NAILS
INTO JOIST

BOTTOM
PLATE

WHEN STUDS FALL BETWEEN JOISTS

WALL STUDS

BOTTOM
PLATE

TOENAIL ONE
12d OR 16d
NAIL ON
EACH SIDE

FLOOR
JOISTS

WHEN STUDS LINE UP WITH JOISTS

7-38 *Securing a frame wall or partition to a wood framed floor.*

floor, and nailed through the bottom plate and sub-floor into a floor joist with 16d common nails or into concrete floors with 2½-inch concrete nails (see 7-38 and 7-39). While the wall is held in a vertical position, temporary braces are nailed to hold it erect. The wall is checked for plumb with a carpenter's level, and the braces are adjusted until the wall is plumb (see 7-40). Continue erecting exterior-wall sections until the building is enclosed.

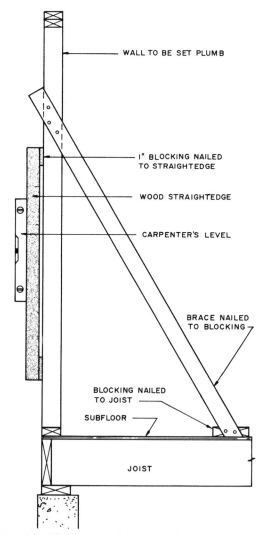

WALL TO BE SET PLUMB

1" BLOCKING NAILED
TO STRAIGHTEDGE

WOOD STRAIGHTEDGE

CARPENTER'S LEVEL

BRACE NAILED
TO BLOCKING

BLOCKING NAILED
TO JOIST

SUBFLOOR

JOIST

7-40 *A wall is checked for plumb with a carpenter's level and a long straightedge.*

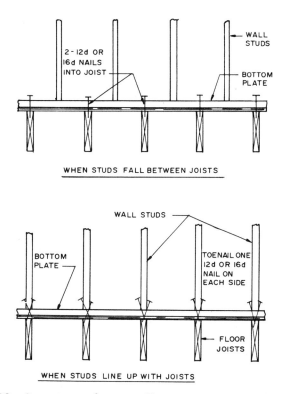

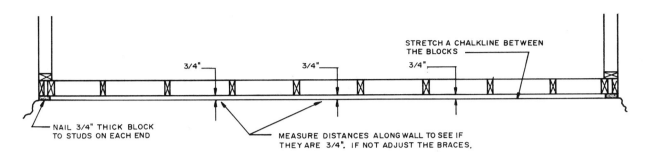

7-41 A chalk line is used to check walls for straightness.

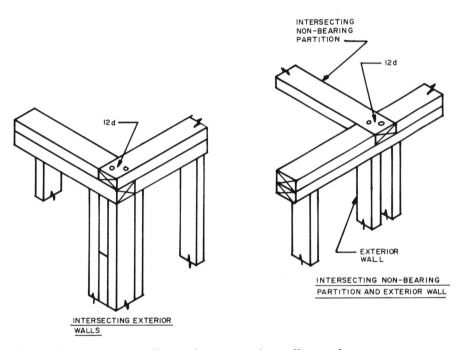

7-42 The top plates of intersecting walls overlap, tying the walls together.

If roof trusses are to be used and the walls are sufficiently braced, the trusses can be set in place before the interior partitions are built. If the roof is constructed with individual rafters, several of the interior partitions will be load-bearing and should be erected before the roof is in place. The interior partitions also help brace the exterior walls and resist the outward thrust produced by the rafters.

Straightening a Wall

A wall may be checked for straightness by running a chalk line parallel to it (see 7-41). Nail a ¾-inch wood block at each end of the wall, and pull the chalk line tightly over them. Adjust the wall by loosening the temporary braces and moving the wall until it is ¾ inch from the chalk line over its entire length. Then renail the braces or add additional braces.

The Top Plate

After the exterior walls and interior partitions are erected, plumbed, and braced, the top plate is nailed in place, tying them together. This plate provides resistance to forces that tend to push the walls outward. Wherever walls meet, the top member of the double top plate overlaps the intersecting wall and is nailed to it (see 7-42). The top plate can be nailed onto the wall unit before it is erected, but provisions for the overlaps must be made.

137

Special Framing Considerations

As partitions are framed, there are many special framing applications. If plumbing fixtures are to be hung from the partition, blocking is installed (see 7-43). It is important to get the correct height and make the blocking large enough to support the fixture. Generally, by the time the plumber hangs the fixture, the blocking is hidden by the finish wall material. Openings for medicine cabinets are also framed so that the cabinet can be recessed into the wall. This may require cutting a stud. The framer must know the size of the rough opening (see 7-44). If safety bars, such as those used by the handicapped, are to be installed, blocking is required at each location. Bathtubs and whirlpools require supporting material (see 7-45). Consult the recommendations of the manufacturer for specific instructions.

Sheathing the Exterior Wall

As mentioned earlier, the sheathing can be applied before or after the wall is erected. The commonly used structural sheathing—plywood, oriented strand board, and Com-Ply®—are discussed in Chapter 2.

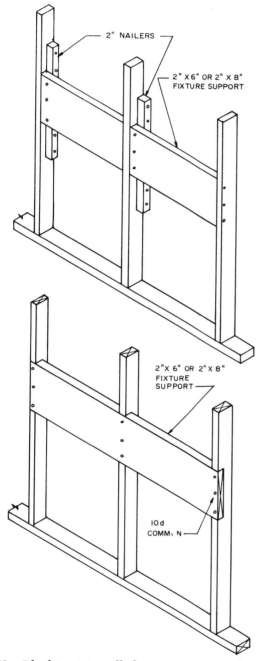

7-43 Blocking is installed to give a means of support to wall-hung plumbing fixtures or other items needing support.

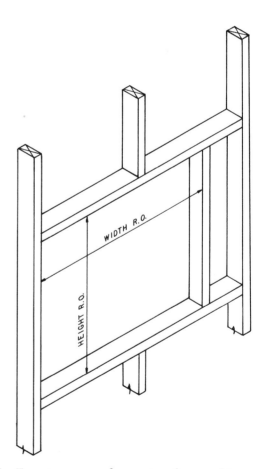

7-44 Framing a rough opening for a cabinet to be set into the wall.

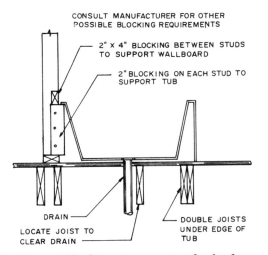

CONSULT MANUFACTURER FOR OTHER
POSSIBLE BLOCKING REQUIREMENTS

2" X 4" BLOCKING BETWEEN STUDS
TO SUPPORT WALLBOARD

2" BLOCKING ON EACH STUD TO
SUPPORT TUB

DRAIN

LOCATE JOIST TO
CLEAR DRAIN

DOUBLE JOISTS
UNDER EDGE OF
TUB

7-45 *Typical blocking to support a bathtub.*

APA-Rated Siding can be nailed directly to the studs and serves as bracing, sheathing, and the finished siding (see 7-46). Other sheathing materials used include fibreboard, gypsum, and rigid foam plastic sheets (see 7-47). These serve to enclose the structure and, generally, are not used as bracing. They also do not hold nails, so that wood, plastic, or aluminum siding must be nailed into the studs. Information on the various types of sheathing is summarized in table 7-3 on the following page.

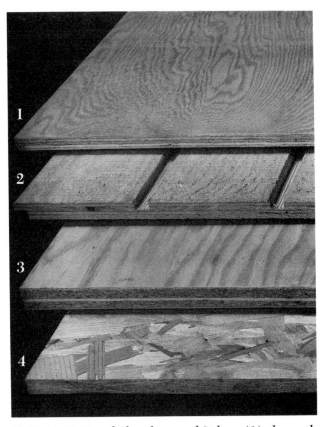

7-46 *APA-Rated Sheathing and Siding: (1) plywood, (2) siding, (3) Com-Ply®, (4) oriented strand board.* (Courtesy American Plywood Association)

7-47 *This rigid foam plastic sheathing has a layer of reflective foil bonded to the exterior surface.* (Courtesy The Celotex Corporation)

Table 7–3 Characteristics of wall sheathing material.

	Gypsum	Rigid foam plastic	Fibreboard	APA Structural Panels (plywood, oriented strand board, Com-Ply®)
Panel sizes (ft)	2 × 8, 4 × 8, 4 × 9, 4 × 12	2 × 4, 2 × 8, 4 × 8 , 4 × 9	2 × 8, 4 × 8, 4 × 9, 4 × 10 4 × 12	4 × 8, 4 × 9, 4 × 10
Thickness (in.)	½, ⅝	¾ to 4	½, 25/32	5/16, 3/8, 7/16, 15/32, ½, 19/32, ⅝, 23/32, ¾
Hold nails	no	no	no	yes
Serve as a vapor barrier	no*	yes	only if asphalt-impregnated	no
Serve as structural wall bracing	only under special conditions	no	only high-density type	yes
R-Value per ½ in. thickness	0.5	4.00 and higher**	1.3	0.5 to 1.2

* Covered with water-repellant paper.
** Some types have aluminum foil reflective insulation bonded to the foam plastic panel.

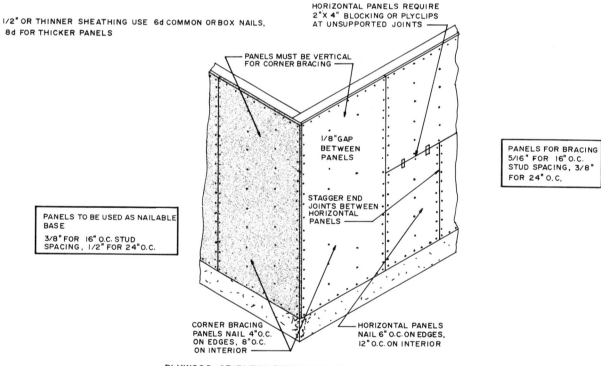

7-48 Installation of plywood oriented strand board, and Com-Ply® sheathing.

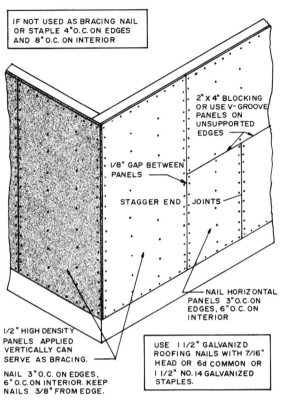

IF NOT USED AS BRACING NAIL OR STAPLE 4"O.C. ON EDGES AND 8"O.C. ON INTERIOR

2" X 4" BLOCKING OR USE V-GROOVE PANELS ON UNSUPPORTED EDGES

1/8" GAP BETWEEN PANELS

STAGGER END JOINTS

NAIL HORIZONTAL PANELS 3"O.C. ON EDGES, 6"O.C. ON INTERIOR

1/2" HIGH DENSITY PANELS APPLIED VERTICALLY CAN SERVE AS BRACING.

NAIL 3"O.C. ON EDGES, 6"O.C. ON INTERIOR. KEEP NAILS 3/8"FROM EDGE.

USE 1 1/2" GALVANIZD ROOFING NAILS WITH 7/16" HEAD OR 6d COMMON OR 1 1/2" NO.14 GALVANIZED STAPLES.

FIBREBOARD SHEATHING

7-49   *Installation of fibreboard sheathing.*

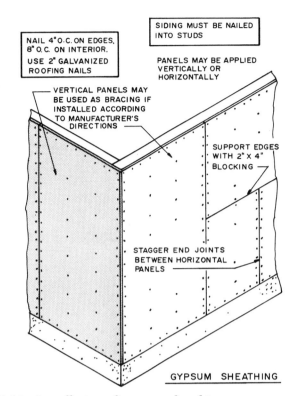

SIDING MUST BE NAILED INTO STUDS

NAIL 4"O.C. ON EDGES, 8"O.C. ON INTERIOR. USE 2" GALVANIZED ROOFING NAILS

VERTICAL PANELS MAY BE USED AS BRACING IF INSTALLED ACCORDING TO MANUFACTURER'S DIRECTIONS

PANELS MAY BE APPLIED VERTICALLY OR HORIZONTALLY

SUPPORT EDGES WITH 2" X 4" BLOCKING

STAGGER END JOINTS BETWEEN HORIZONTAL PANELS

GYPSUM SHEATHING

7-50   *Installation of gypsum sheathing.*

APA-Rated Structural Sheathing panels when used as wall bracing must be applied vertically. If applied horizontally, joints between panels must be blocked or held with plyclips (see 7-48). Gypsum or fibreboard panels can be applied vertically or horizontally. Any unsupported edges must have wood blocking (see 7-49 and 7-50). Rigid foam sheathing panels that are 2 feet wide are applied horizontally. Panels, 4 feet × 8 feet, are applied vertically (see 7-51).

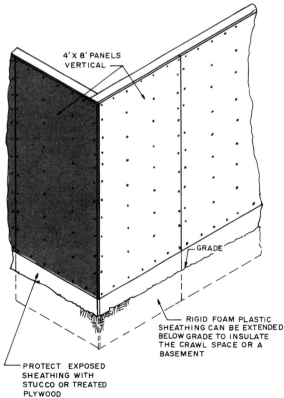

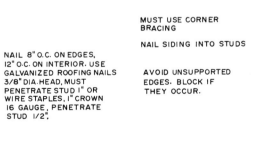

MUST USE CORNER BRACING

NAIL SIDING INTO STUDS

NAIL 8"O.C. ON EDGES, 12"O.C. ON INTERIOR. USE GALVANIZED ROOFING NAILS 3/8"DIA.HEAD, MUST PENETRATE STUD 1" OR WIRE STAPLES, 1"CROWN 16 GAUGE, PENETRATE STUD 1/2".

AVOID UNSUPPORTED EDGES. BLOCK IF THEY OCCUR.

4' X 8' PANELS VERTICAL

GRADE

RIGID FOAM PLASTIC SHEATHING CAN BE EXTENDED BELOW GRADE TO INSULATE THE CRAWL SPACE OR A BASEMENT

PROTECT EXPOSED SHEATHING WITH STUCCO OR TREATED PLYWOOD

RIGID FOAM PLASTIC SHEATHING

7-51   *Installation of rigid foam plastic sheathing.*

Metal Wall Connectors

There are a wide variety of metal connectors used to strengthen the wall structure and tie it to the floor and roof (see 7-52). These greatly strengthen the con-nections and are required by code in localities having unusual conditions such as high winds. Local codes should be consulted to determine the wind speeds that your design must take into account for your locality.

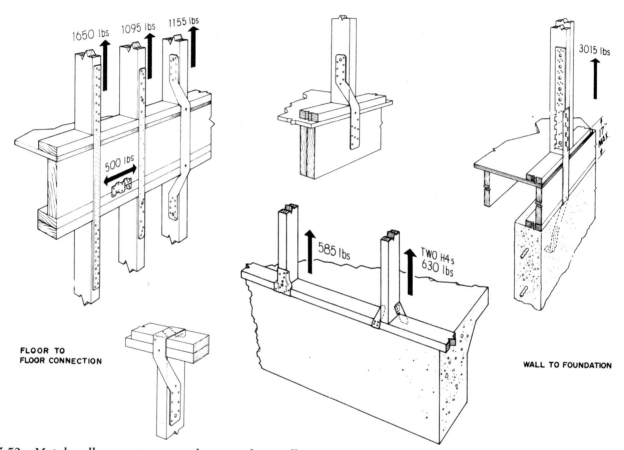

FLOOR TO FLOOR CONNECTION

WALL TO FOUNDATION

7-52   *Metal wall connectors greatly strengthen wall construction.* (Courtesy Simpson Strong-Tie Company, Inc.)

8

Framing the Ceiling

Ceiling framing usually consists of joists that are supported by the exterior wall and interior load-bearing partitions (see 8-1). These joists are usually smaller than floor joists because they carry little load other than possible attic storage. The load to be placed on them and their span is considered when selecting their size. In a two-storey building the joists support the ceiling of the first floor as well as carry the loads imposed by the second floor. Again, these loads and the span influence the size of joists used.

If a building uses *roof trusses*, the bottom chord of the truss serves as the ceiling joist.

Selecting Ceiling Joist Sizes

Ceiling joists are usually spaced 16 inches O.C., but in some cases they may be 24 inches O.C. The attic load to be carried, the type of finished ceiling, and the unsupported span must be known. Typically a 10-pound-per-square-foot live load is used for attics

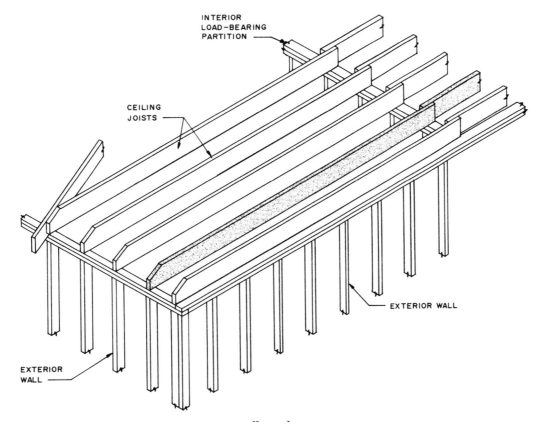

8-1   *Ceiling joists are run between supporting walls or beams.*

143

with no anticipated storage. If the attic will be used for storage but not be a living area, 20-pound-per-square-foot live load is used. If it is to serve as living areas, 30-pound-per-square-foot live load is used for bedrooms and 40-pound-per-square-foot for uses such as a living room, dining room, or kitchen. For the 30- and 40-pound-per-square-foot live loads, floor joist tables would be used to select the joist size (see Chapter 6).

The designer must consider the location and support of unusual items on ceiling joists such as placing a water heater or furnace in the attic. That section of the ceiling may require double joists or joists spaced closer together.

Span tables for ceiling joists for one specie of lumber are found in Appendices E, F, K, and N. The left column gives the spacing of the joists. These tables assume a drywall ceiling. Additional tables are available for plaster ceilings. The grade of lumber is located across the top of the table, and the unsupported span is in the table body.

Running the Ceiling Joists

Ceiling joists are generally run across the width of the building, but there will be times when they may have to run parallel with the length (see 8-1 on the previous page). The end that rests on the top plate of the exterior wall usually must have the top edge sloped so that it is below the height of the rafter (see 8-2). This cut is laid out using the distance from the bird's-mouth to the top of the rafter and the slope of the roof. The slope is set by locating the rise and run of the rafters on a framing square, as shown in 8-3. Cut the joist so that the sloped surface is a little below the top of the rafter.

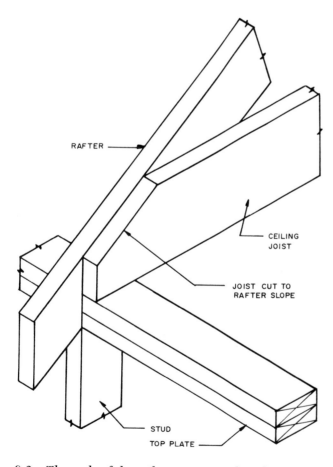

8-2 *The ends of the ceiling joists are sloped to match the slope of the rafter.*

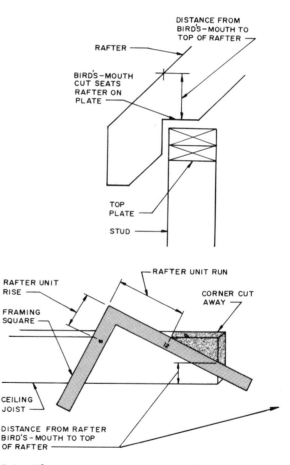

8-3 *These measurements are used to lay out the slope on the end of ceiling joists.*

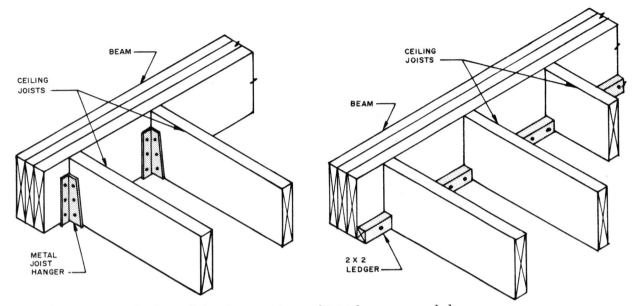

8-4   *Ceiling joists can be framed to a beam with metal joist hangers or a ledger.*

A large room may have a span that is beyond the span distance of normal ceiling joists. The ceiling is framed by running a beam across the room and butting the joists to it (see 8-4). They can be secured using metal joist hangers or a ledger.

Where ceiling joists run parallel to the edge of a roof and the roof has a steep slope, such as occurs with a hip roof, the last joist can be omitted and 2 × 4 blocking is nailed on the top plate to provide a nailer for the interior ceiling material (see 8-5). When the roof has a low pitch, short joists can be run perpendicular to the ceiling joists, as shown in 8-6. Blocking is nailed between them to support the finished ceiling material.

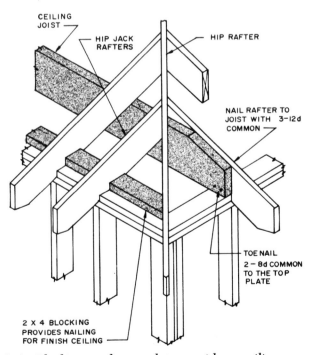

8-5   *Blocking on the top plate provides a nailing surface for the finish ceiling material.*

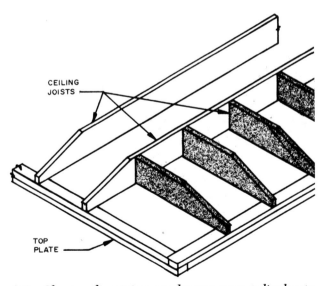

8-6   *Short ceiling joists can be run perpendicular to regular joists when low-pitched roofs require it.*

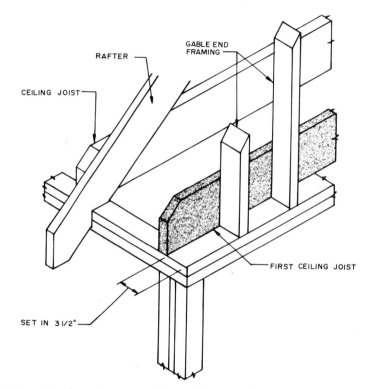

8-7 *The first ceiling joist is set in from the outer face of the top plate.*

Installing Ceiling Joists

As just mentioned, the end joist is set in to provide a nailing surface, and the other joists are located next to the rafter marks on the top plate (see 8-7).

Ceiling joists rest on interior load-bearing walls, and they may be butted and secured with a splice plate or lapped and nailed as shown in 8-8 and 8-9.

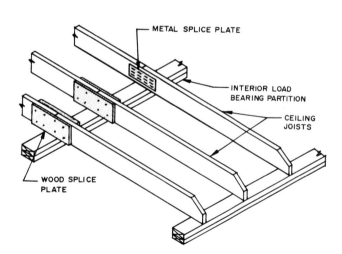

8-8 *Butted ceiling joists can be joined using metal or wood splice plates.*

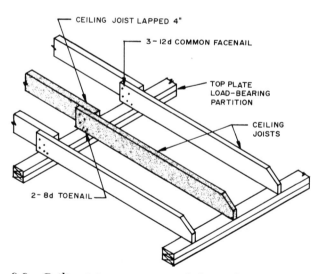

8-9 *Ceiling joists are commonly lapped over interior load-bearing partitions.*

When butted, they are joined with ⅜- or ½-inch-plywood splice plates 24 inches long or metal splice plates. When lapped, they are end-nailed on each side with three 12d nails and toenailed to the top plate with two 8d nails. Remember to set joists with the crown side up (see 8-10).

Nonload-bearing partitions that run perpendicular to the ceiling joists are nailed to the joists through the top plate (see 8-11). When they run parallel and between ceiling joists, 2 × 4 blocking is nailed between the joists, and a 1 × 6 nailing strip is nailed to the top of the partition. This gives a nailing surface for ceiling material (see 8-12).

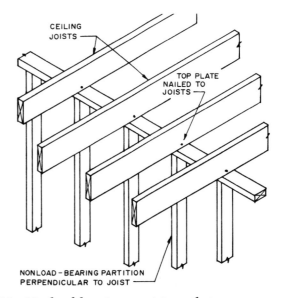

8-11 Nonload-bearing partitions that run perpendicular to ceiling joists are nailed to the joists.

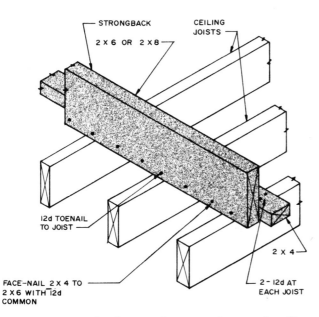

8-10 A strong back is used to straighten and stiffen ceiling joists.

Trusses

As mentioned earlier, a building framed with trusses uses the bottom chord of the truss as a ceiling joist. (Trusses are discussed in Chapter 15.)

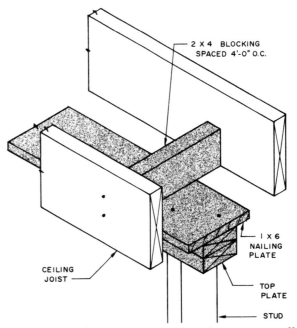

8-12 Nonload-bearing partitions that run parallel with, and between, ceiling joists are secured by blocking.

9

Post, Plank, and Beam Construction

Post, plank, and beam construction uses beams widely spaced to form the floor and roof structural system. The roof beams are supported by posts located directly below them. The posts can transmit the load to piers or to a conventional foundation. The space between the posts is framed with stud walls which contain the doors and windows (see 9-1).

The *advantages* of the post, plank, and beam system is that it has fewer members, which can reduce the labor costs. Many people like the exposed-wood structural system and the wood ceiling formed by the roof decking. The thick floor and roof decking provide good fire resistance.

The *limitations* to this system include difficulty in finding concealed places to run wiring, piping, and ducts. Sometimes a beam is made up of two wood members with spacers forming a cavity for wires and pipes.

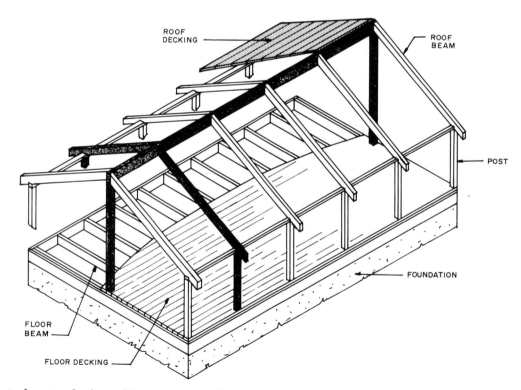

9-1   *A typical post, plank, and beam structural frame.*

148

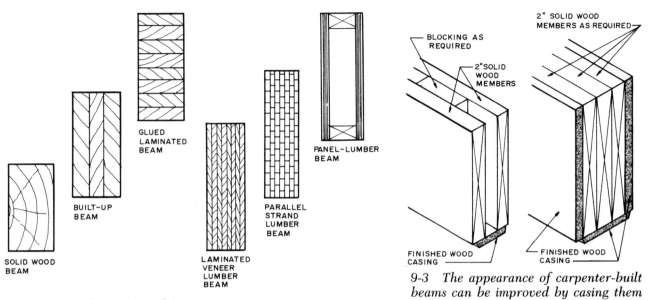

9-2 *Commonly used wood beams.*

9-3 *The appearance of carpenter-built beams can be improved by casing them with a quality wood.*

Floor and Roof Beams

Beams may be solid wood, built-up, glued laminated (glulam), laminated veneer lumber (LVL), parallel strand lumber (PSL), and panel-lumber beams (see 9-2). (These are discussed in detail in Chapter 6.) Since roof beams are often left exposed to the inside of the building, the choice of which material to use includes not only strength but the quality of the exposed surface. Exposed beams are stained or sealed with a clear, natural finish. Some beams are made using 2-inch stock and spacers to permit the passage of wires and plumbing. Built-up beams are often cased with high-quality finished lumber (see 9-3). The size of the beam depends on the type used, the loads, the specie of wood, and the span. These decisions must be made by an engineer.

Posts

Posts may be solid wood, built-up, glued laminated, or parallel strand lumber. They may be exposed to the interior, in which case the quality of the exposed surface is important. The size depends on the type of post, the loads it will carry, the specie of wood, the length of the post, and the spacing between posts. The longer the post, the greater it must be in cross-sectional area.

As the engineer does the calculations to select the post size, one factor of great importance is the **slenderness ratio** (see table 9-1). The slenderness ratio is the number found by dividing the post length in inches by the actual size of the smallest dimension of the cross section of the post. It is represented by the formula l/d.

Table 9–1 Examples of column slenderness ratios.

Nominal size (inches)	Actual size (inches)	Slenderness ratio for 8'0" post	Slenderness ratio for 10'-0" post	Slenderness ratio for 12'0" post
4 × 4	3½ × 3½	27.4	34.3	41.1
4 × 6	3½ × 5½	27.4	34.3	41.1
6 × 6	5½ × 5½	17.4	21.8	26.2
8 × 8	7¼ × 7¼	13.2	16.5	19.8

Table 9–2 Total allowable uniformly distributed roof loads for
3-inch nominal (2½-inch actual) laminated wood decking.*

Span (deflection 1/240)	Inland red cedar E 1.2	Southern pine E 1.8	Douglas fir/larch E 1.8
	(pounds per square foot, psf, of roof area)		
8′0″	54	80	80
10′0″	27	44	41
12′0″	16	25	24

* Simple span with end joint falling on supports.

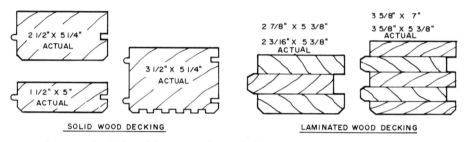

9-4   *Typical types and sizes of solid and laminated wood decking.*

As an example, a 6 × 6 wood post 10 feet long would be 120 inches divided by 5½ inches, giving a slenderness ratio of 21.8. The *smaller* the slenderness ratio, the *greater* the load that can be carried. Examples of typical slenderness ratios are given in table 9-1 on the preceding page.

Planks and Decking

The words *plank* and *decking* are used interchangeably to describe wood members over one inch thick. They are used to cover the roof beams and support the finished roofing, and they are also used to cover the floor beams and carry the live loads imposed on the floor. Commonly used wood decking is 2, 3, or 4 inches

thick. Two-inch-thick decking usually has a single tongue-and-groove. Thicker types will have two tongue-and-grooves (see 9-4).

The distance decking can span depends on the specie and grade of wood and the loads to be carried. A general example is given in table 9-2. Consult manufacturer's data for specific capacities. Decking is installed as single span or continuous span of random lengths (see 9-5). Single-span installation requires that the decking span at least two beams, because this increases the stiffness. The end joints in each row should be staggered.

Random lengths are most commonly used because they reduce waste. To use random lengths, the deck must span three or more supports. The distance be-

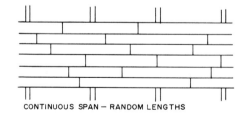

CONTINUOUS SPAN – RANDOM LENGTHS

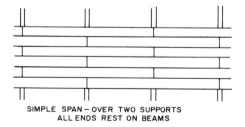

SIMPLE SPAN – OVER TWO SUPPORTS
ALL ENDS REST ON BEAMS

9-5   *Common ways to install wood decking.*

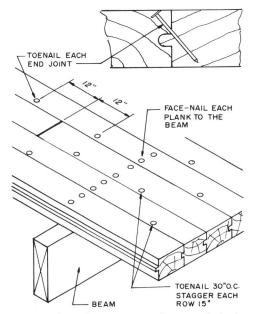

9-6 *A typical nailing pattern for wood decking.*

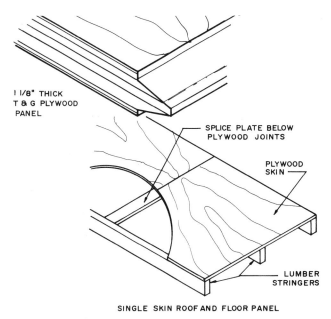

9-7 *Plywood panels used to deck floors and roofs.*

tween end joints in adjacent rows of decking should be at least 2 feet and between decking separated by one row at least one foot. The decking should have tongue-and-groove end joints. When decking sloped roofs, the edge with the tongue should face up the slope. Spans will vary for floor and roof construction and manufacturer's instructions should be observed.

Observe the manufacturer's directions for nailing solid-wood and laminated-wood decking. The following is a typical example. Face-nail the decking to the beam with two nails. A 20d nail is used for 3-inch decking. Then toenail each row together through the tongue. Space these 30 inches apart and toenail within 12 inches of any end joints (see 9-6).

In addition to wood decking, other products used include wood fibre roof planks, plywood, and wood panel and composite stressed-skin panels. **Wood fibre planks** are made by bonding long wood fibre strands. They are available in 2-, 2½-, and 3-inch thicknesses, 48 to 96 inches long, and as square-edge or tongue-and-groove-edge panels. **Plywood** sheets 1⅛ inch thick with tongue-and-groove edges can span up to 4 feet (as shown in Chapter 6). Lumber-panel stressed-skin panels use solid-lumber stringers and plywood skins to produce panels that can span long distances (see 9-7). They can be fabricated on the ground, and their use speeds up the erection of the building. They must be designed following preengineered specifica-

tions. The panels may have a panel skin on one or two sides. Lumber blocking is required wherever there is a joint in the skin. Stressed-skin panels should be built following American Plywood Association design specifications. Composite stressed-skin panels are made in a variety of ways. One type has an isocyanurate foam insulation core with a nail base board bonded on top and a structural board bonded on the bottom (see 9-8). Install following manufacturer's nailing instructions.

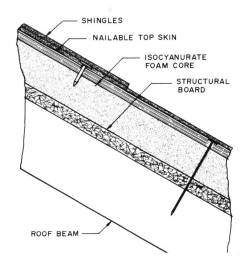

9-8 *A typical composite stressed-skin panel having an insulating core used for roofing.*

151

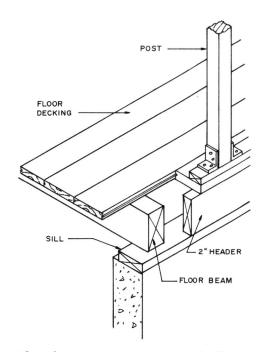

9-9 *Floor beams can rest on a wood sill.*

9-10 *Floor beams can be set in pockets in the foundation.*

Floor Construction

The floor framing system is built several ways. One way is to rest the floor beam on a wood sill (see 9-9). A header is nailed across the ends of the beam, as is done in conventional framing with floor joists. If it is desired to lower the building, the beams can be set in pockets. The pockets should allow a ½-inch air space on all sides. Some prefer to place a ¼-inch thick steel plate between the bottom of the beam and the concrete pocket. The beam should bear at least 4 inches on the foundation (see 9-10). Beams can be supported in the interior of the building by columns (see 9-11) or piers (see 9-12). If the building is to have concrete slab floor construction, it appears as shown in 9-13. Several types of post anchors are available.

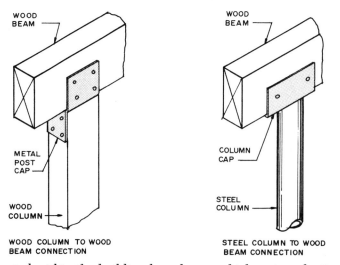

9-11 *Beams can be supported within the building by columns which rest on footings.*

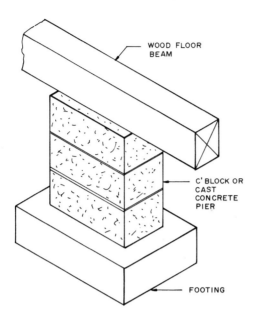

9-12 *Floor beams can be supported with cast concrete or concrete block piers.*

If the floor is subject to concentrated loads, such as a heavy whirlpool, or if a nonload-bearing interior partition runs on the decking between and parallel with the floor beams, supporting framing is required above or below the decking (see 9-14). No extra support is required for nonload-bearing interior partitions running perpendicular to the floor beams.

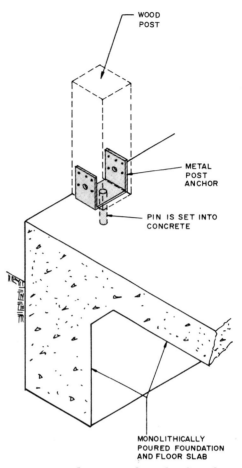

9-13 *Posts can be secured to the foundation when concrete slab floor construction is used.*

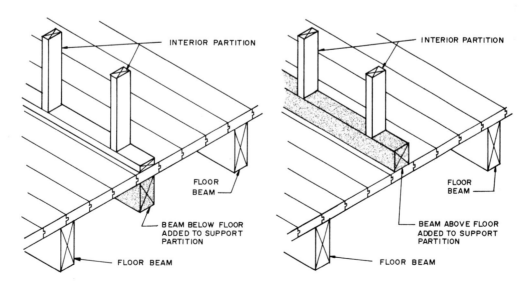

9-14 *Interior partitions running parallel with, and between, floor beams require additional support.*

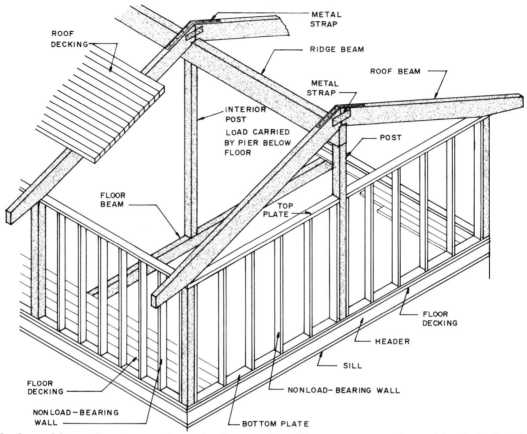

9-15 *Post, plank, and beam framing can have the floor and roof beams running the width of the building.*

Roof Construction

The roof in post, plank, and beam construction may be built in two ways. The roof beams may run from a ridge to the exterior wall similar to rafter framed roofs or they may run parallel (longitudinally) with the exterior side walls and the ridge beam (see 9-15 and 9-16). The longitudinal beams are usually larger than the beams running from the ridge to the exterior wall, because they generally have to span longer distances. They can be reduced in size if supported by posts within the building.

An alternative structure for a parallel or longitudinal structure is shown in 9-17. Rafters span the longitudinal beams and are sheathed with plywood. This provides a space for insulation in the roof and does not require expensive, heavy decking. The interior ceiling will have to be covered with gypsum or some other material.

The typical post, plank, and beam framing system does not provide for running electrical or plumbing service. If this is necessary in the roof, spaced beams

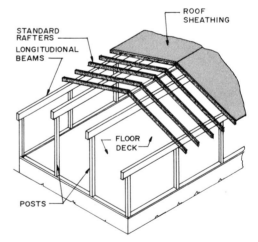

9-17 *Standard rafters and roof sheathing can be used with longitudinal-beam roof framing.*

can be used instead of solid beams (see 9-18). This influences the spacing of beams and posts, because the load-carrying capacities will be different from solid beams.

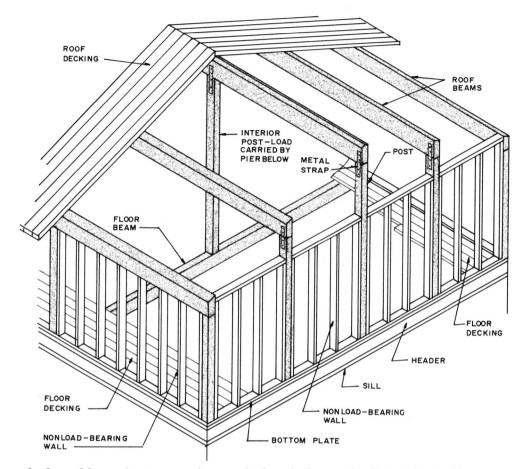

ROOF DECKING

ROOF BEAMS

INTERIOR POST—LOAD CARRIED BY PIER BELOW

METAL STRAP

POST

FLOOR BEAM

FLOOR DECKING

FLOOR DECKING

HEADER

SILL

NONLOAD—BEARING WALL

NON LOAD—BEARING WALL

BOTTOM PLATE

NONLOAD—BEARING WALL

9-16 *Post, plank, and beam framing can be run the length (longitudinally) of the building.*

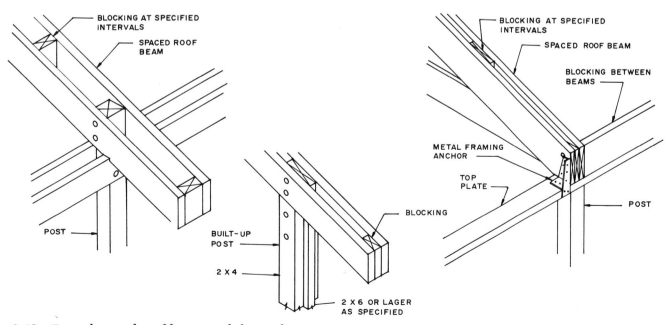

BLOCKING AT SPECIFIED INTERVALS

SPACED ROOF BEAM

POST

BUILT-UP POST

2 X 4

2 X 6 OR LAGER AS SPECIFIED

BLOCKING

BLOCKING AT SPECIFIED INTERVALS

SPACED ROOF BEAM

BLOCKING BETWEEN BEAMS

METAL FRAMING ANCHOR

TOP PLATE

POST

9-18 *Typical spaced roof beams and their column connections.*

155

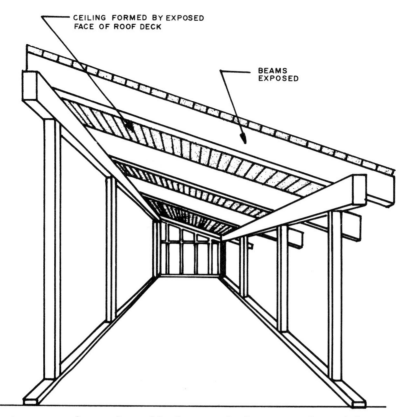

CEILING FORMED BY EXPOSED
FACE OF ROOF DECK

BEAMS
EXPOSED

9-19   *Generally the interior ceiling is formed by leaving the bottom surface of the roof decking exposed.*

Generally, the bottom side of the roof decking is left exposed, forming the finished ceiling. The roof beams and bottom of the decking are stained or finished in an attractive manner (see 9-19).

Various methods for joining roof beams to the ridge beam and supporting posts are used. Beams joining the ridge may butt it (see 9-20) and be secured with metal hangers, or they may rest on top of it and be

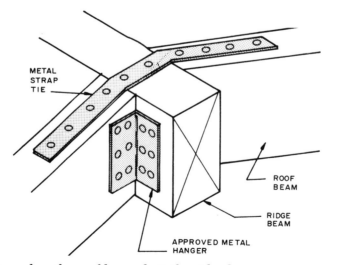

METAL
STRAP
TIE

ROOF
BEAM

RIDGE
BEAM

APPROVED METAL
HANGER

9-20   *Typical construction when the roof beams butt the ridge beam.*

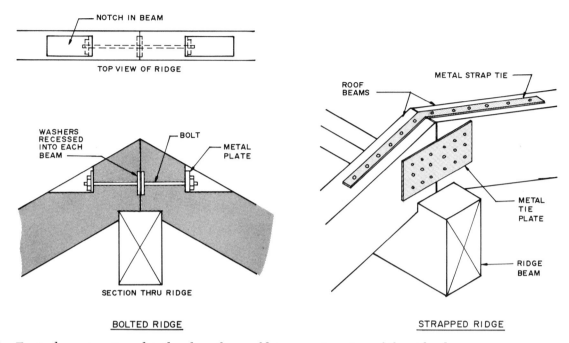

9-21 *Typical construction details when the roof beams rest on top of the ridge beam.*

secured with metal gussett plates with a tie strap over the top (see 9-21). Beam-to-post connections are shown in 9-22. The choice of connectors is important, because they are an important part of the structural system.

Decking is secured to roof beams in the same manner as described for floors. While wood is a good insulating material, the roof will require additional insulation. Since it is desired for the roof beams and wood decking to be visible from inside the building, the insulation is placed on the top side of the decking (see 9-23). The rigid sheets of insulation are secured to the decking. A vapor barrier is placed between the decking and the insulation. Frequently a built-up roof is laid over the insulation.

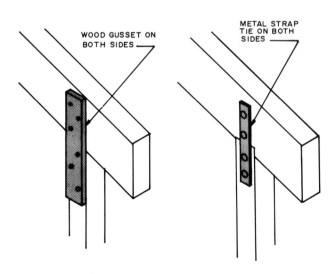

9-22 *Typical roof beam-to-post connections.*

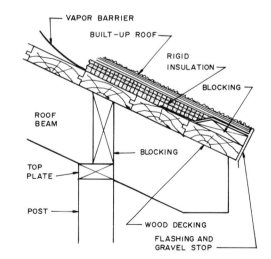

9-23 *The roof can be insulated by nailing rigid insulation on the top of the deck and installing a built-up roof membrane over it.*

157

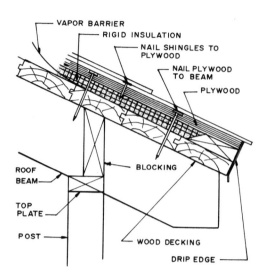

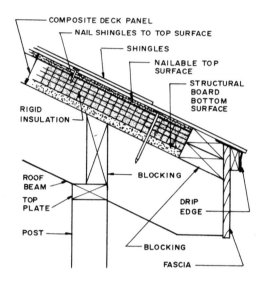

9-24 *Nailable panels can be nailed over the rigid insulation to provide a surface for the installation of shingles.*

9-25 *An example of a composite roof panel as used on post, plank, and beam construction.*

Exterior Wall Construction

If shingles are to be used, nailable panels are laid over the insulation and nailed through the insulation into the decking. The shingles are nailed to these panels in the usual way (see 9-24). If composite panels are used, they are nailed through the panel into the roof beam (see 9-25).

The exterior structural wall posts are placed directly below a roof beam. The posts usually rest on a bottom plate directly above a floor beam (see 9-26). If the posts are between floor beams, blocking is placed below them (see 9-27). A wood top plate ties the top of the posts together.

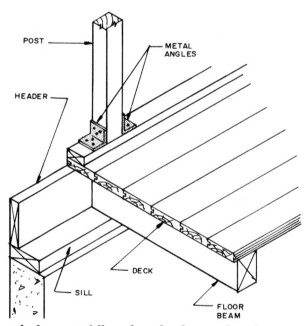

9-26 *Typical wall framing with the posts falling directly above a floor beam.*

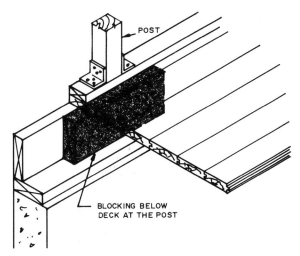

9-27 *If a post does not rest directly above a floor beam, blocking below it is required.*

When possible, posts and beams are spaced on standard distances (48, 72, or 96 inches) used in conventional construction, because construction materials are manufactured to fit these distances. The size of the posts and beams used depends on the engineering design of the building, which includes the distance between these members.

The spaces between the posts are filled with stud-framed walls, which may have door and window openings. Since these are nonload-bearing walls, large headers are not needed. The exterior walls not only enclose the structure, but also provide lateral stability for the entire wall. The posts alone will not resist lateral forces causing racking. APA-Rated Sheathing provides the strength needed. It is advisable to have some sections between posts with no openings. These are needed to provide the required wall bracing (see 9-28).

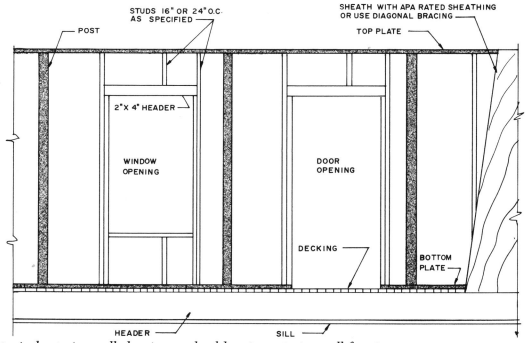

9-28 *A typical exterior wall showing nonload-bearing exterior wall framing.*

Typical framing details for a two-storey post, plank, and beam structure are shown in 9-29. The posts are placed directly above each other and must rest on a solid, secure base such as a beam. This is built much the same as conventional platform construction. The second floor is built on a platform formed on top of the first-floor framing. Insulation is placed between the exterior wall studs, as in conventional construction.

Interior partitions are framed in the same manner as explained for conventional construction. They generally are nonload-bearing. They do provide rigidity and lateral stability to the structure. When they run parallel with the floor beams the floor must have additional framing (see 9-14).

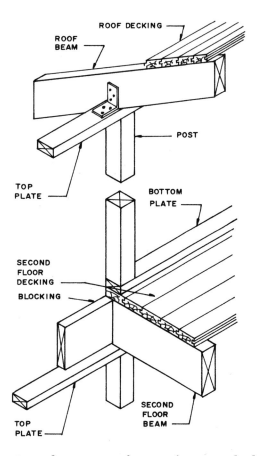

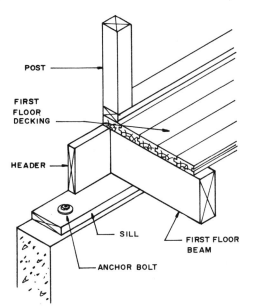

9-29 *Typical two-storey framing for post, plank, and beam construction.*

PART III
Roof Framing

10

Roof Types

Framing a roof is one of the more difficult parts of constructing a building. It involves careful calculations of linear distances and angles as well as precise layout on the rafter stock. Much preplanning is required before layout and cutting is begun.

This chapter gives an introduction to the types of roofs and the technical aspects of their design. Additional chapters in Part III explain how to lay out and cut rafters for commonly used roof designs.

Types of Roofs

The most commonly used types of roofs are shown in 10-1.

The **flat roof** is built either absolutely flat or with a slight slope. It is the type most likely to eventually leak. The rafters serve as both ceiling joists and roof joists, and therefore they are often larger than those used in other types of roofs. The insulation is placed between the ceiling and roof deck, and an air space must remain between it and the roof deck (see 10-2 on page 164).

A **gable roof** is possibly the most commonly used type. It is not difficult to build, sheds rain and snow, and permits insulation to be placed between ceiling joists, allowing a large area to be ventilated (see 10-3 on page 164).

A **hip roof** has four sloping sides. The main roof is much like the gable roof, but the ends are sloped and shingled, eliminating the gable end.

A **shed roof** is a single sloping surface. It is built like the flat roof but has slope.

A **Dutch** or **modified hip roof** has the ridge extended to produce a small vertical surface, which usually contains a louvre.

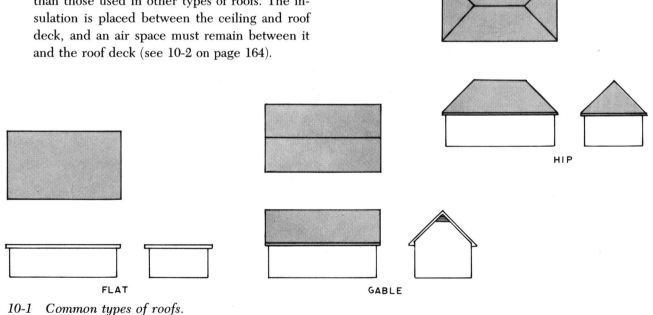

FLAT   **GABLE**   **HIP**

10-1 Common types of roofs.

162

The **gambrel roof** is a variation of the gable. It has two sloped surfaces, each with different pitches. This provides more space on the second floor for living area. Dormers are frequently added to provide light and ventilation.

The **mansard roof** resembles both the hip roof and the gambrel roof. It has two sloped surfaces on each side of the building. Therefore it does not have a gable end. Dormers are frequently added.

The **pyramid roof** slopes from each side of the building to a center point. It eliminates the need for a gable end.

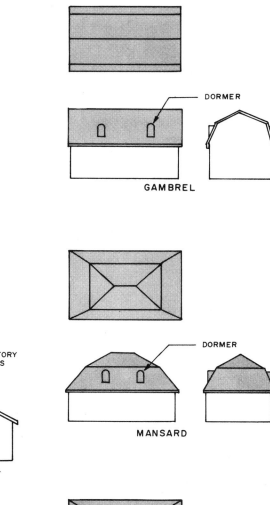

GAMBREL

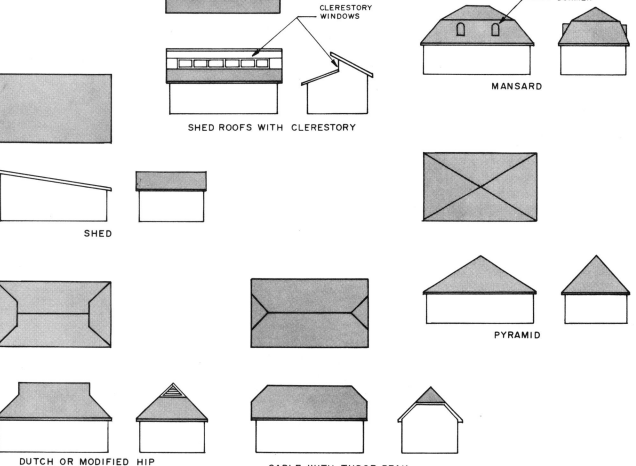

10-1 Common types of roofs (continued).

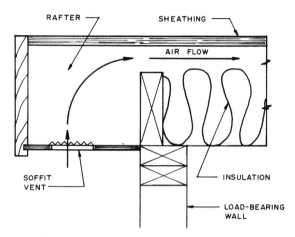

10-2 *Flat roofs require air space for ventilation.*

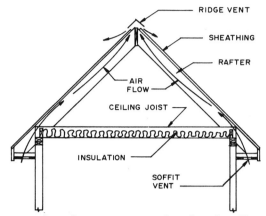

10-3 *Roofs with attics are ventilated with soffit vents and some form of roof vent.*

Types of Rafters

A **rafter** is the structural member used to frame a roof and carry the sheathing and shingles. It must carry their load plus loads from snow and wind. The common types of rafters are shown in 10-4.

Common rafters run from the top plate to the ridge at right angles to both (see 10-5).

Hip rafters run on a 45-degree angle from the top plate to the ridge, forming the line of intersection for the two surfaces of a hip roof.

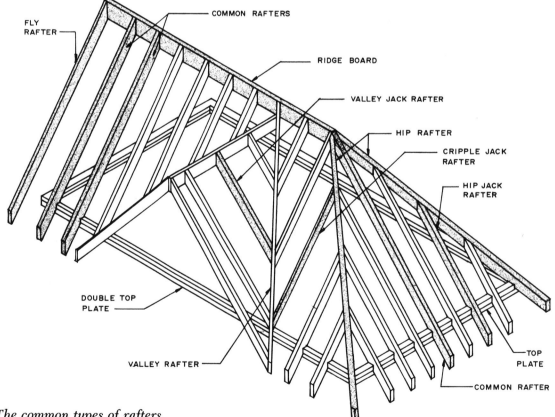

10-4 *The common types of rafters.*

Valley rafters run from the top plate on an angle to the ridge or an intersection with an adjoining gable roof. Rafters from two intersecting gable roofs run to the valley rafter.

Hip jack rafters run from the top plate to a hip rafter.

Valley jack rafters run from the top plate to a valley rafter.

Cripple jack rafters run between valley jack and hip jack rafters.

Parts of a Rafter

The rafter has a notch called a bird's-mouth which sits on top of the top plate. The rafter meets the ridgeboard with an angle called the ridge line. The **tail** is the overhang beyond the supporting wall. If there is no overhang, the end of the rafter has a **seat cut** (see 10-6). The outer end of the rafter is the **fascia surface**, and the cut on the bottom of the tail that establishes the length of the fascia surface is the **plancher**.

Framing Plans

Some architectural designers will prepare a roof framing plan. A roof framing plan shows the location of each rafter (see 10-7). If the working drawings do not have a plan, the framer will have to prepare one.

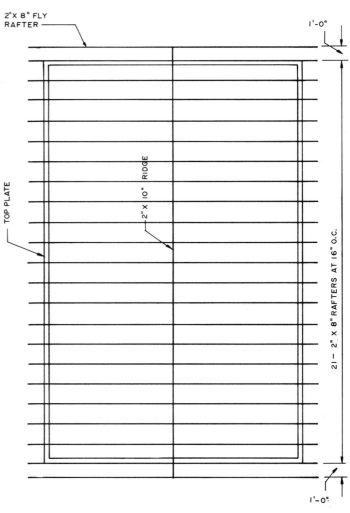

10-7 A typical roof framing plan for a simple gable roof.

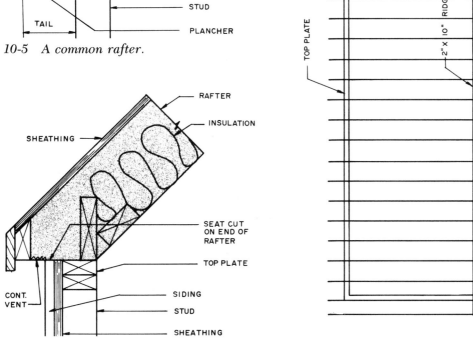

10-5 A common rafter.

10-6 The rafter ends with a seat cut, if there is to be no overhang.

It is well worth the short time it takes to prepare a plan before starting construction of the roof. The plan will show how many rafters are needed and uncover possible framing problems that can be resolved before the actual framing starts. The easiest way to develop a framing plan is to lay a sheet of tracing paper over the floor plan, and locate each member. Thumbnail plans can be drawn as shown in 10-8.

Determining Rafter Sizes

The size of a rafter depends on the distance that it must span, the roof slope, the spacing between rafters, the weight of the roofing material, wind load, snow load, and specie and grade of the lumber used. Wind and snow loads vary a great deal across the country. Rafter span tables refer to **dead loads** and

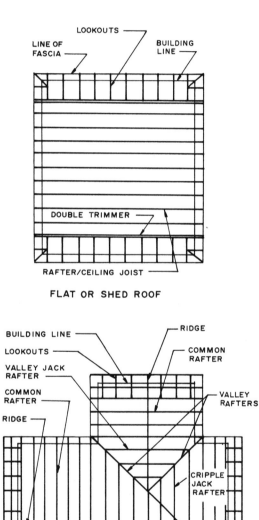

FLAT OR SHED ROOF

INTERSECTING GABLE ROOFS

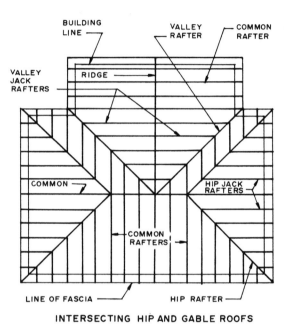

INTERSECTING HIP AND GABLE ROOFS

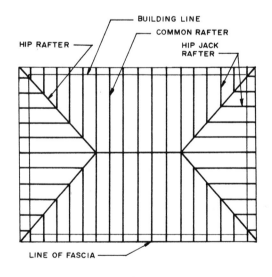

HIP ROOF

10-8 Thumbnail roof framing plans.

live loads. Dead loads are the weight of materials, such as sheathing and shingles. Live loads are those which are movable, such as snow, but do not include

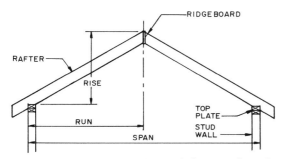

10-9 *Terms used to specify roof slope and pitch.*

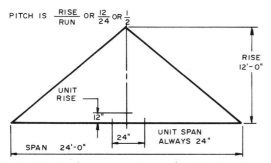

10-10 *Pitch is the proportion of unit rise to unit span.*

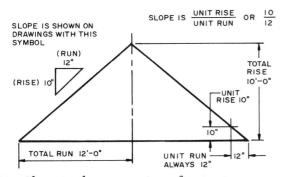

10-11 *Slope is the proportion of unit rise to unit run.*

wind loads. Tables giving selected examples of data available are shown in Appendices G, L, M, N, and O. Detailed information is available from various organizations, such as the Southern Forest Products Association, the National Association of Homebuilders Research Foundation, the National Forest Products Association, and the Western Wood Products Association.

Technical Terms

Following are the technical terms used in the layout and cutting of rafters (see 10-9).

Pitch is the angle the surface of the roof makes with the horizontal. It is a ratio of the **unit of rise** to the **unit of span**. A roof with a unit rise of 12 inches and a unit span of 24 inches has a pitch of $^{12}/_{24}$ or ½. It is referred to as having a ½ pitch (see 10-10).

Rise is the vertical distance from the top of the plate to the top of the ridgeboard (see 10-9).

Run is the horizontal distance from the outside face of the top plate to the centerline of the ridgeboard (see 10-9).

Span is the distance from the outside faces of the double top plates across the width of the building (see 10-9).

Slope is the incline of the roof given in **units of rise** to **units of run**. A roof with a unit rise of 10 inches and a run of 12 inches has a slope of 10 in 12 (see 10-11). The unit of run is always 12 inches.

The **unit of rise** is the number of inches a roof rises per foot of run (see 10-11).

The **unit of run** is a 12-inch horizontal distance used to describe the slope (see 10-11).

The **unit of span** is a 24-inch horizontal distance used to describe pitch (see 10-11).

11

Roof Construction with Common Rafters

Roofs constructed using individual rafters are often referred to as *stick built*. They are rapidly being replaced with factory-assembled roof trusses (see Chapter 15). The following discussion tells how to lay out common rafters and shows how they are assembled to form the roof structure for a gable roof. Common rafters are also used on other types of roofs, such as a hip roof.

Getting Approximate Rafter Length

The approximate length of a rafter can be found by locating the total rise in feet and total run in feet on the body and tongue of the framing square (see 11-1).

Each inch represents one foot. In 11-1, the total rise is 8 feet and the total run is 12 feet. To find the approximate rafter length, measure the hypotenuse, and add the length of the overhang. In this case the length of the hypotenuse is 14.5 feet, and a 6-inch overhang was added, so that the rough length is 15'0". The framer will know to order 16'0" long rafter material.

Laying Out a Rafter

The two commonly used methods for finding rafter length are by using rafter tables and the step-off method.

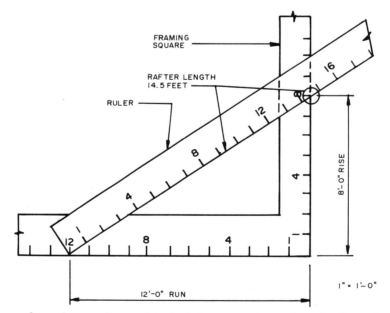

11-1 A framing square and a ruler can be used to find the approximate length of a rafter.

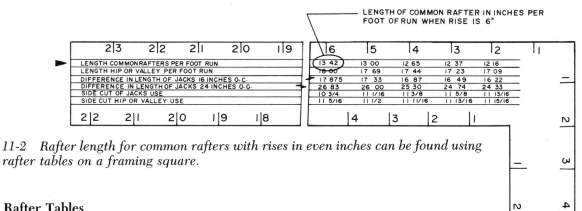

2|3	2|2	2|1	2|0	1|9	1|6	1|5	1|4	1|3	1|2	1|1
LENGTH COMMON RAFTERS PER FOOT RUN					13 42	13 00	12 65	12 37	12 16	
LENGTH HIP OR VALLEY PER FOOT RUN					18 00	17 69	17 44	17 23	17 09	
DIFFERENCE IN LENGTH OF JACKS 16 INCHES O.C.					17 875	17 33	16 87	16 49	16 22	
DIFFERENCE IN LENGTH OF JACKS 24 INCHES O.C.					26 83	26 00	25 30	24 74	24 33	
SIDE CUT OF JACKS USE					10 3/4	11 1/16	11 3/8	11 5/8	11 13/16	
SIDE CUT HIP OR VALLEY USE					11 5/16	11 1/2	11 11/16	11 13/16	11 15/16	

LENGTH OF COMMON RAFTER IN INCHES PER FOOT OF RUN WHEN RISE IS 6"

11-2 Rafter length for common rafters with rises in even inches can be found using rafter tables on a framing square.

Rafter Tables

Steel framing squares have rafter tables stamped on the body. These show rafter lengths for several types of rafters. Examine the square in 11-2. The first row of numbers gives the lengths of common rafters that have rises in even inches. For example, if a rafter has a 6-inch unit rise, find the 6 on the square. Below it on the "common rafter" line is the figure 13.42. This means that the length of the rafter is 13.42 inches for each foot of run. If the run were 10 feet the rafter would be 13.42 × 10, or 134.2 inches, or 11.183 feet—or 11 feet 2³⁄₁₆ inches long. The final length of the rafter will have the length of the tail added and one-half the thickness of the ridgeboard subtracted (see 11-3).

Rafter Step-Off When Span Is an Even Number

The following instructions are for laying out a common rafter for a building having a *run in an even number of feet.* For this example, the span is 20 feet. The roof has a slope of 8 inches of rise per 12 inches of run and a 10-inch overhang is required.

1. Set the framing square so that the 8-inch and 12-inch marks are on the top edge of the rafter. Fasten stair gauges to the square so that it retains this position (see 11-4). A stair gauge is a metal clip that is fastened to the square with a set screw. Check the rafter for straightness. If it has a slight crown, place the crown side up. If it has much warp or twist do not use it.

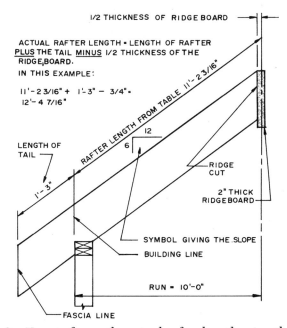

11-3 How to figure the actual rafter length using the rafter table on the framing square.

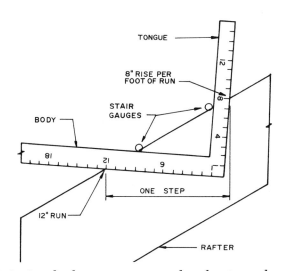

11-4 Set the framing square so that the rise and run in inches are on the top edge of the rafter.

2. Draw the line representing the center of the ridgeboard near the end of the rafter. If the material has splits in the end, cut it back to remove them (see 11-5).

3. Step off one 12-inch step for each unit of run. In this example it will be 10 steps. Mark this last step. This is the outside face of the top plate (the building line) (see 11-5).

4. Measure an additional 10-inches, and mark the fascia line. This provides the overhang (see 11-5).

5. Return to the ridgeboard centerline. Mark off half the thickness of the ridgeboard. This is the actual ridge cutting line (see 11-6). Now mark the bird's-mouth as shown in 11-7.

Rafter Step-Off When Span Is an Odd Number

Many times the run is not an even number of feet, but will be somewhere between, such as 10 feet 6 inches. The procedure for this layout is the same as

described for the even foot span except for one additional partial step, since 6 inches, in this case, is needed (see 11-8).

Marking the Bird's-Mouth

Return to the mark locating the building line. Measure a distance equal to the width of the top plate. Place a framing square on the building line, and mark a line perpendicular to it that runs through the point where the plate width line meets the bottom edge of the rafter. This is the seat cut for the bird's-mouth (see 11-7).

Laying Out a Common Rafter Using Rafter Tables

Rafter tables give the length of rafters per foot of run for various slopes. They are stamped on the body of some framing squares or published in table form as shown in table 11-1.

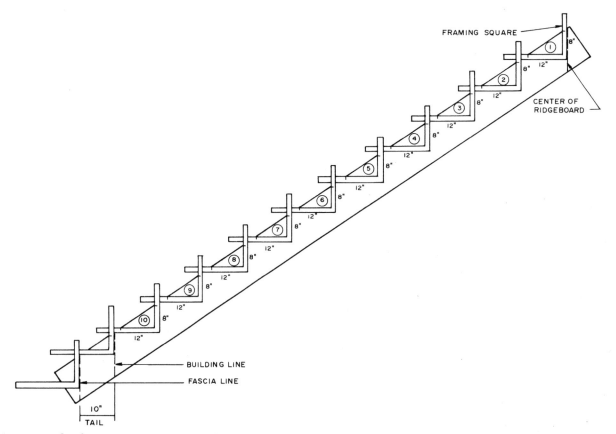

11-5 Using the framing square, step off one step for each foot of run and add the length of the tail.

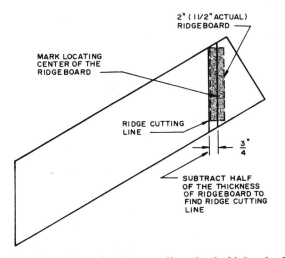

11-6 *Adjust the ridge line to allow for half the thickness of the ridgeboard.*

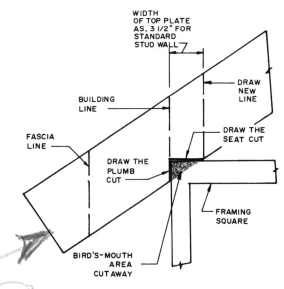

11-8 *How to lay out a rafter when the run is not an even number of feet such as 10'6".*

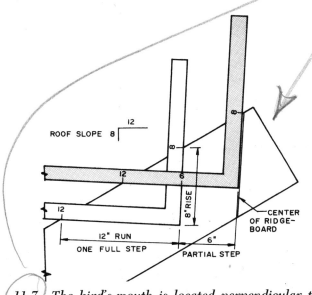

11-7 *The bird's-mouth is located perpendicular to the building line.*

Table 11–1 Length of rafter per foot run (in inches).

Rise (inches)	Common rafters	Hip valley rafters
1	12.04	17.03
2	12.16	17.09
3	12.37	17.23
4	12.65	17.44
5	13.00	17.69
6	13.42	18.00
7	13.89	18.36
8	14.42	18.76
9	15.00	19.21
10	15.62	19.70
11	16.28	20.22
12	16.97	20.78
13	17.69	21.38
14	18.44	22.00
15	19.21	22.65
16	20.00	23.32
17	20.81	24.02
18	21.63	24.74
19	22.47	25.47
20	23.32	26.23
21	24.19	27.00
22	25.06	27.78
23	25.94	28.58
24	26.83	29.39

The lengths given in table 11-1 are the length of the rafter per foot of run for a given rise. For example, assume a roof with a run of 15 feet and a rise of 10 inches per foot of run for a common rafter. The length opposite the rise of 10 is 15.62 inches. Multiplying this by 15 feet (15.62 × 15) gives a rafter length of 234.30 inches, or 19.525 feet, or 19'6.3"—or 19'6⁵⁄₁₆". To convert 0.525 feet to inches, multiply it by 12, which gives 6.3 inches. To get this to a 16th of an inch multiply 0.3 inches by 16, giving 4.8/16th—then rounding to ⁵⁄₁₆ inch.

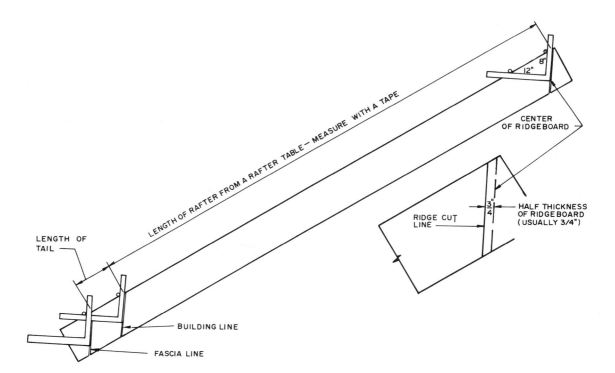

11-9   *Laying out a common rafter using lengths from a rafter length table.*

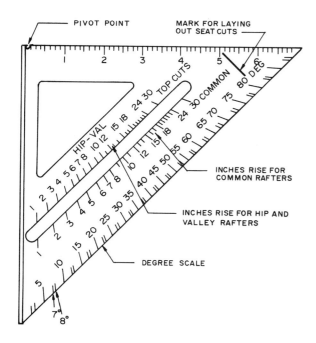

11-10   *The Swanson Speed® Square has scales for laying out hip, valley, and common rafters. It also has a scale for laying out rafter cuts given in degrees. (Courtesy Swanson Tool Co., Inc.)*

When using rafter tables, the length calculated is to the center of the ridgeboard. Therefore half the thickness of the ridgeboard must be removed from the length of the rafter, as shown in 11-9.

Common Rafter Layout Using a Swanson Speed® Square

The Swanson Speed® Square is shown in 11-10. It is designed with scales for laying out common, hip, jack, and valley rafters using the unit of slope, such as a $\frac{5}{12}$ slope, or in degrees.

To lay out a common rafter the procedure is the same as shown in 11-9. The difference is that the ridge, building line, and fascia lines are located with the Swanson Speed® Square.

The way to place the Swanson Speed® Square is shown in 11-11. The notch in the 90-degree corner is placed tightly against the edge of the stock. The square is pivoted until the number representing the rise touches the top edge of the stock. The line (ridge, building, or fascia) is drawn along the hypotenuse of the square.

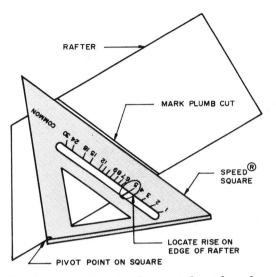

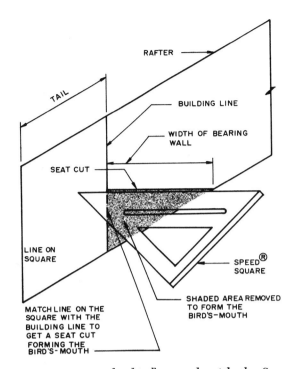

11-11 *Locating the plumb cut at the ridge of a common rafter using the Swanson Speed® Square. (Courtesy Swanson Tool Co., Inc.)*

The bird's-mouth is located with the Swanson Speed® Square on the building line as shown in 11-12.

Locating the Plancher Line

The end of the rafter tail usually requires a plancher cut to reduce it to the size required for the

11-12 *Laying out the bird's-mouth with the Swanson Speed® Square. (Courtesy Swanson Tool Co., Inc.)*

fascia. If the fascia board is as wide or wider than the fascia plumb cut, no plancher is needed (see 11-13).

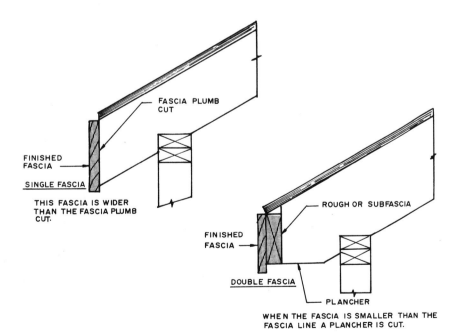

11-13 *The size of the fascia determines if a plancher is needed.*

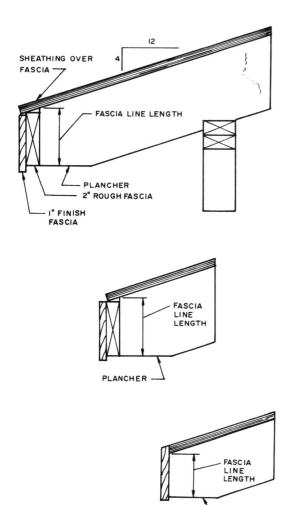

11-14   *Typical ways to frame the fascia.*

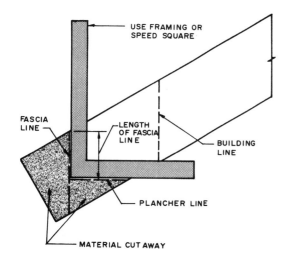

11-15   *Laying out the plancher line.*

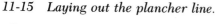

The size of the fascia determines the location of the plancher cut. This will depend upon how the fascia is to be framed. Three commonly used ways are shown in 11-14. The length of the fascia line will be determined by the framing method. Once the length is determined, draw the plancher line perpendicular to the fascia line (see 11-15).

Duplicating and Cutting Rafters

After the first rafter is laid out, cut it to size, and check to make certain it is correct. When certain it meets the ridgeboard and sits on the top plate properly, use it as a pattern to mark the remainder of the rafters of that size. The rafters can be cut with a radial-arm saw or a portable circular saw. The radial-arm saw will produce more uniform, accurate cuts.

Erecting Common Rafters

1. First mark the rafter locations on the plate. Usually the ceiling joists are in place, and the rafter is located next to them and directly above a stud.

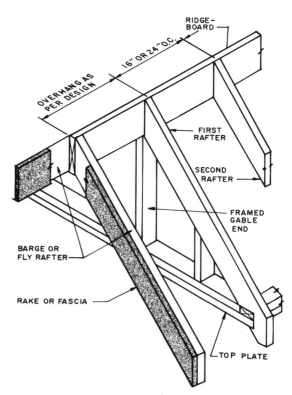

11-16   *The ridgeboard extends beyond the gable end to support the fly rafter and rake board.*

174

The first rafter is set flush with the outside face of the top plate. It is often notched to receive lookouts which support the rake fascia. (This is discussed later in this chapter.)

2. Next, erect the ridgeboard. First mark the location of each rafter using the marks on the top plate. The ridgeboard is usually 2-inch-thick stock and wider than the ridge plumb cut. The ridge must extend beyond the exterior wall an amount equal to the overhang on the gable end with an allowance for the barge or rake board (see 11-16). If there is no overhang on the gable end, the ridgeboard is cut flush with the outside surface of the plate (see 11-17). Sheathing is applied and one-inch-thick blocking is added to allow for the siding.

The ridge is supported with braced, temporary 2 × 4 posts. Be certain it is level and in the center of the area to be roofed (unless an irregular roof is being framed) (see 11-18). Generally the ridge is made from two or more long pieces of 2-inch stock. The joints should fall where a pair of rafters will meet, or they can be joined between rafters with splice plates (see 11-19). Plywood or solid wood decking can be temporarily laid on the ceiling joists to provide a safe work platform.

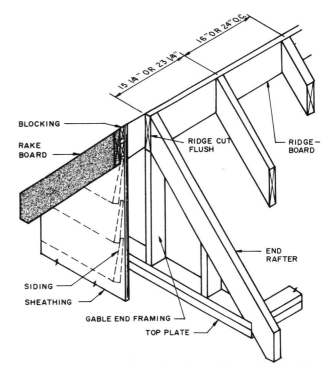

11-17　Framing the roof at the gable end when there is no overhang.

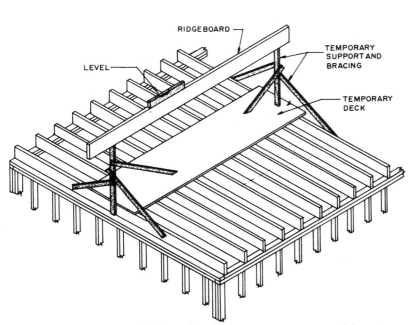

11-18　Support the ridgeboard with temporary posts and bracing.

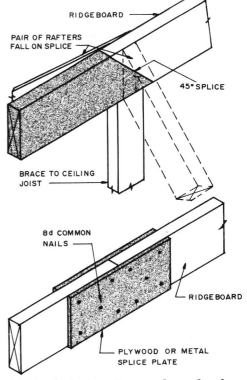

11-19　Ridgeboards can be spliced using splice plates or a splice cut.

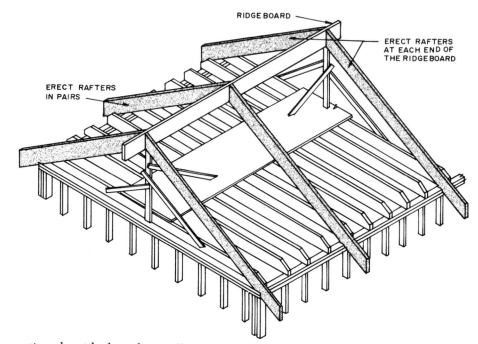

11-20 After erecting the ridgeboard, install the rafters in pairs, beginning with a pair at each end and in the center.

3. Nail the rafter to the ridgeboard by end-nailing the first rafter with three 12d common nails and toenailing the matching rafter on the other side with three 12d common nails. Some framers angle a 10d nail through the top of the rafter into the ridgeboard. Always erect rafters in pairs. Place a pair of rafters on each end of the section of ridgeboard and one pair in the center (see 11-20). Then fill in the remainder in pairs.

Rafters are toenailed to the top plate with two 8d common nails and face-nailed to the ceiling joist with three 12d common nails. There are a variety of metal anchors used for making these connections (see 11-21).

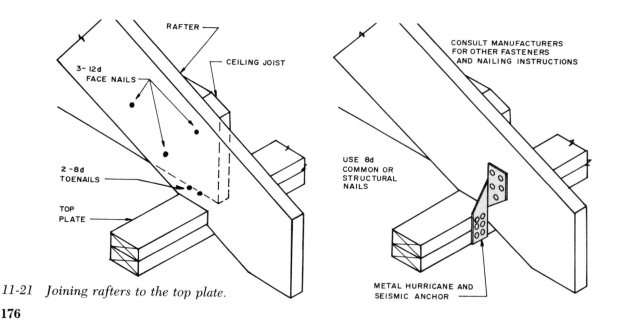

11-21 Joining rafters to the top plate.

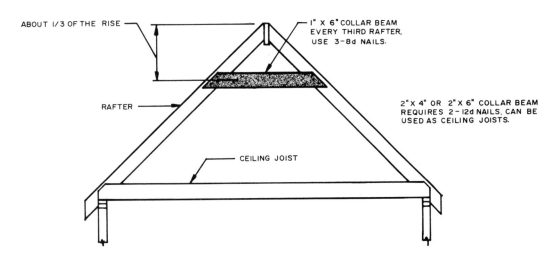

ABOUT 1/3 OF THE RISE

1" X 6" COLLAR BEAM EVERY THIRD RAFTER. USE 3-8d NAILS.

RAFTER

2" X 4" OR 2" X 6" COLLAR BEAM REQUIRES 2-12d NAILS. CAN BE USED AS CEILING JOISTS.

CEILING JOIST

11-22   Collar beams are placed on every third pair of rafters in normal roof construction.

4. After the rafters are in place, collar beams and sway bars are installed. Collar beams (also called collar ties) are used to help resist the tendency of the roof to push the exterior walls outward. The ceiling joists also contribute a great deal to resisting this force. Normally collar beams are 1 × 6 or 2 × 4 material nailed to every third rafter, about one third of the distance down the rafter from the ridge (see 11-22). Roofs under greater than normal loads may require collar beams on every pair of rafters. Collar beams also can serve as ceiling joists for rooms on the second floor. In this case, they are usually 2 × 6 stock.

Sway braces are used to stabilize the ridgeboard. They can be 2 × 4 or 2 × 6 material and are on about a 45-degree angle. They are nailed to the ridge and the top plate of an interior wall or 2 × 6 blocking nailed between ceiling joists (see 11-23). They are spaced about every 6 feet.

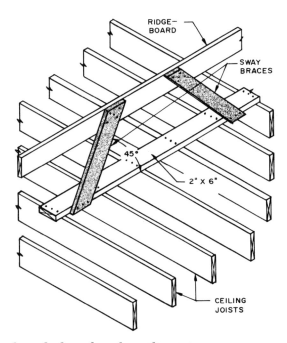

RIDGE-BOARD

SWAY BRACES

45°

2" X 6"

CEILING JOISTS

11-23   Sway braces are run from the ridgeboard to the ceiling joists.

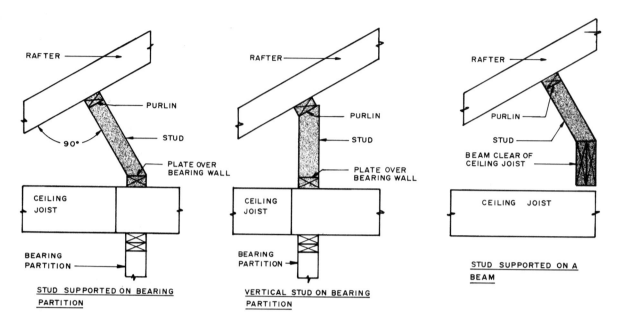

11-24   *Various types of bracing are used to enable the rafters to carry an increased load.*

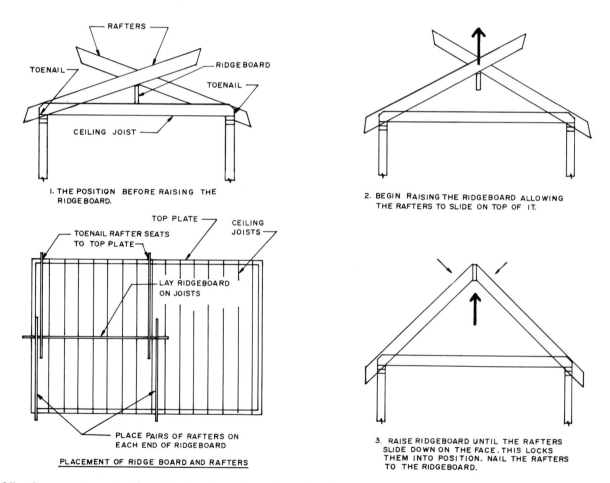

11-25   *One way to raise the ridgeboard and set the end rafters.*

Truss-Type Bracing

The structural designer may specify additional bracing for rafters. In areas of high winds, a truss-type bracing may be specified. This has the effect of reducing the span of the rafters, thus increasing their ability to carry a wind load (see 11-24). This bracing can also provide needed support when the span equals the maximum allowed for a rafter or exceeds it somewhat. In all cases the load must be transferred to a beam that clears the ceiling joists or to an interior bearing wall. It must never be transferred to the ceiling joists unless they have been sized to carry this extra load. Normal size ceiling joists are inadequate for this purpose.

Another Framing Technique

Some framers erect the ridgeboard and the end rafters by laying the ridgeboard across the ceiling joists. Toenail the end rafters at each end to the top plate at the seat cut. The ridge cut end overlaps the ridgeboard. Raise the ridgeboard, allowing the rafters to slide back until they slide down on the face of the ridge. Release the ridgeboard, allowing its weight to bind the rafters against it. Carefully nail the rafters to the ridgeboard, being watchful to stay clear of it in case it might fall. It helps to have some temporary plywood decking on top of the ceiling joists to provide a safe footing. This system makes it difficult to adjust the ridge if it is not level; however, it does speed construction (see 11-25). It is also difficult to use on high-pitched roofs.

Building the Gable End Projection

There are several ways the roof projection over the gable end (also referred to as the overhanging rake) is framed. When the overhang is in the range of 12 inches or less, the overhang is framed on the ground as a ladder-type unit, and nailed to the end rafter (see 11-26). The blocking is spaced 24 inches O.C. to support the soffit on the bottom. The finished fascia is nailed over the fly rafter after the ladder is in place.

Larger overhangs built when a rafter is located on the end of the building are framed as shown in 11-27.

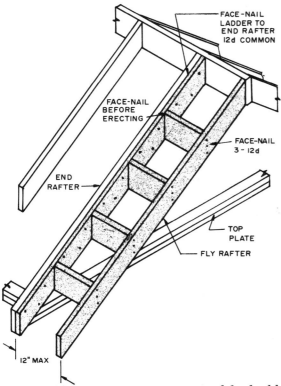

11-26   Ladder-type construction is used for building small roof overhangs.

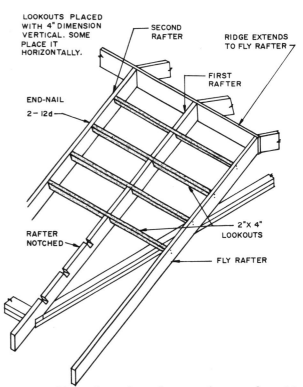

11-27   Gable end roof overhangs of more than 12 inches are constructed using lookouts.

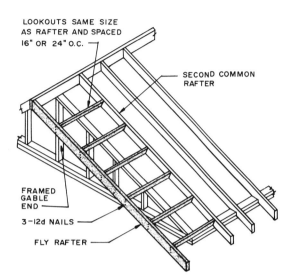

11-28   *Large overhangs can be framed with the lookouts resting on top of the gable-end top-plate framing.*

The end rafter is notched to receive 2 × 4 lookouts which run to the second rafter and can be end-nailed to it. Usually the lookouts are extended into the roof a distance equal to the amount of the overhang. The lookouts are spaced 24 inches O.C. The finished fascia is nailed over the fly rafter (rough fascia).

Another framing technique is to omit the end rafter, and build in its place the gable end with the top plate in line with the bottom of the rafter. The lookouts rest on this plate and are nailed to it as shown in 11-28.

Sometimes there is no overhang at the rake and the rake is constructed as shown in 11-29.

Framing the Gable End

There are several ways commonly used to frame the gable end. The first consideration is whether it will have a louvre. The opening for the louvre is framed so that the louvre can be installed later (see 11-30). When the roof is framed with an end rafter, the gable-end studs can be notched and placed 16 inches O.C. as shown in 11-31. If a rafter is not used, the gable-end framing forms the support for the lookouts on the roof overhang as shown in 11-28.

Framing Openings in the Roof

Openings in the roof are framed the same as described for floor openings. The most common opening is for a fireplace chimney. The rafters on each side and the headers between the rafters are doubled. The wood framing must clear the chimney a distance specified by local codes. A clearance of 1 to 2 inches is generally required by local code (see 11-32).

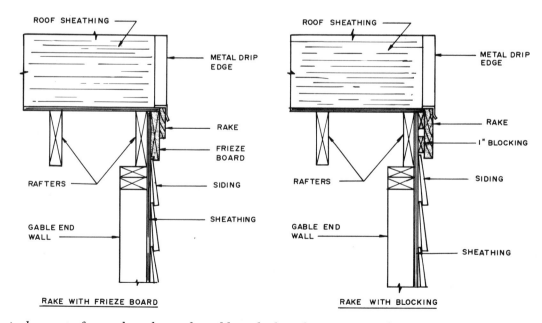

11-29   *Typical ways to frame the rake on the gable end when there is no overhang.*

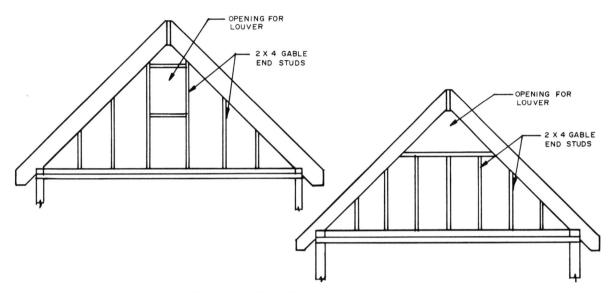

11-30   *Louver openings are framed in the gable end.*

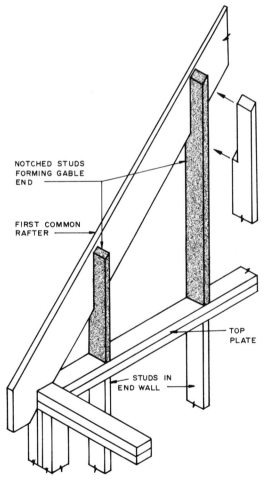

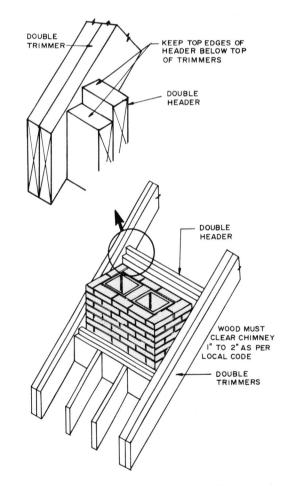

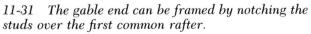
11-31   *The gable end can be framed by notching the studs over the first common rafter.*

11-32   *Openings in a roof are framed the same as openings in floors.*

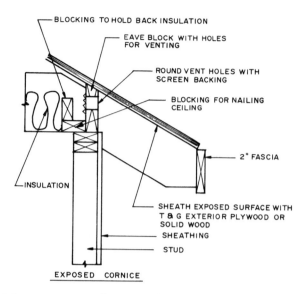

11-33 *An exposed cornice has no soffit and exposes the roof sheathing on the overhang.*

11-34 *A soffited cornice has a horizontal soffit usually with vents.*

Framing the Cornice

The cornice is the overhang of a pitched roof at the eave line. It usually consists of a fascia board, soffit, and sometimes moulding. There are several ways a cornice can be framed. It may be an **exposed cornice** (see 11-33), allowing the roof sheathing to be seen; **soffited** (see 11-34); **boxed** (see 11-35), using the rafter to hold the soffit material; or a **narrow box cornice** (see 11-36) giving little or no overhang. The details desired will be shown on the architect's working drawings. Details for framing with a cathedral ceiling are shown in 11-37. Other methods of construction than those shown are used.

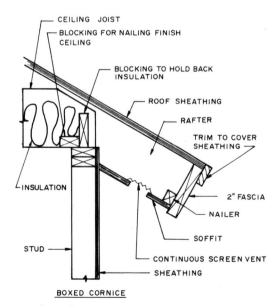

11-35 *A boxed cornice has the soffit material nailed to the rafter.*

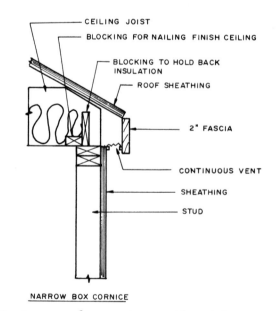

11-36 *A narrow box cornice provides minimum ventilation and no protective overhang.*

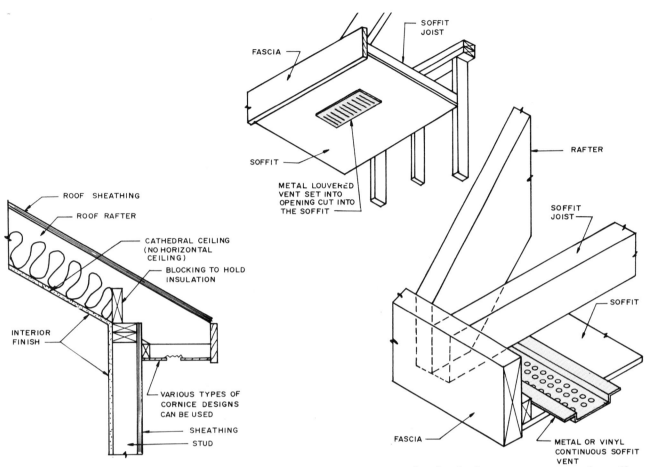

11-37 Typical cornice framing for a cathedral ceiling construction.

11-38 Continuous and individual vents are set into the soffit to provide attic ventilation.

Some framers prefer to install a rough fascia, usually 2-inch-thick stock, and then install a 1-inch-thick finish fascia board over it. This usually gives a better-looking fascia, and the 2-inch rough fascia is needed to hold gutters. A 1-inch single fascia applied with no backup will often warp.

Soffit material can be hardboard, plywood, gypsum, vinyl, or aluminum. Vents installed in the soffit may be individual units or continuous strip vents (see 11-38).

Framing a Cornice Return

The cornice return is the underside of the cornice at the corner of the building where the gable end roofline meets the wall. It serves no structural purpose but provides a neat, decorative transition from the horizontal eave line to the sloped roofline of the gable. Framing details are shown in 11-39.

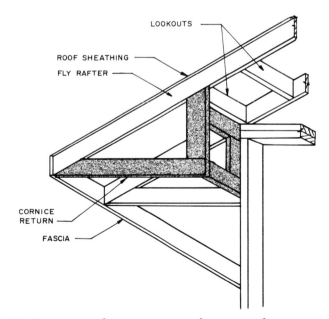

11-39 A typical cornice-return framing technique.

The fly rafter is connected to cornice return nailers extending out from the wall. The rake fascia and cornice fascia meet. Shingle moulding, if used, is carried around the corner and up the slope of the rake board to the ridge (see 11-40).

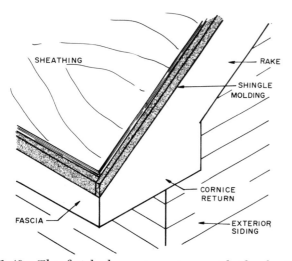

11-40 *The finished cornice return with the fascia boards in place.*

Framing a Cricket

A **cricket** (also called a saddle) is a double-sloped structure built on the high side of a chimney to divert water away from the chimney (see 11-41). It is usually framed with 2 × 4 members and covered with copper or aluminum.

Roof Framing with I-Joists

Manufactured I-joists are strong and lightweight and also suited for use as rafters. (They are described and their use in floor construction is illustrated in Chapter 6.) They can be joined to each other with metal straps and hangers. They are cut in the same manner as wood rafters. Since they are thin in cross section, they do not have as much strength in compression as solid wood rafters. Therefore, wood stiffeners are added between the flanges. The same principles used for framing with solid wood rafters apply to I-joist rafters. However, manufacturer's specifications and assembly instructions must be carefully followed. Typical construction details for a few applications are shown in 11-42.

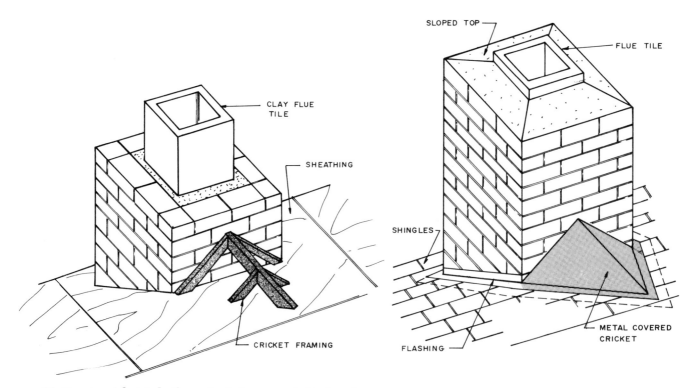

11-41 *A cricket is built to shed the water behind a chimney.*

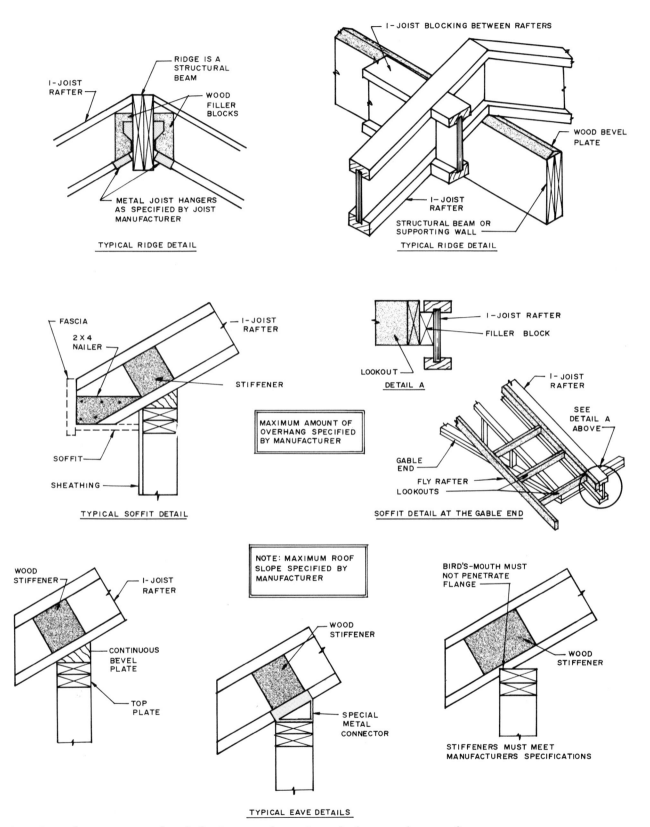

11-42   Typical construction details for I-joist rafters. Consult the manufacturer for specific requirements.

Sheathing the Roof

After the framing is complete the sheathing is applied. It is normally 4 × 8 foot sheets of plywood or oriented strand board. The sheathing greatly stiffens and increases the strength of the roof. While manufacturer's recommendations should be observed when selecting sheathing, specifications typical for rated sheathing panels are given in table 11-2.

Table 11–2 Typical specifications for rated sheathing panels (measurements in inches).

Rafter O.C.	Thickness	Maximum unsupported edge length
12	5/16	12
16	5/6, 3/8	16
24	3/8, 1/2	20 for 3/8 24 for 1/2

If the unsupported-edge span exceeds the specified distance, aluminum H-clips are inserted in the center of the span (see 11-43). Panel ends are spaced 1/16 of an inch apart and edges 1/8 inch apart. Panels 1/2 inch or less in thickness require 6d common smooth, ring-shank or spiral-thread nails. Panels 5/8 to 1 inch use 8d common nails. The nails are spaced 6 inches apart on the edges of the panel and 12 inches apart on intermediate supports.

The sheathing is applied with the long dimension (8 feet) perpendicular to the rafters. The joints between panels should be staggered (see 11-44). On roofs with overhangs at the gable end, the sheathing should extend at least two rafter or truss spaces into the roof to provide adequate support for the overhang. Sheathing not made with waterproof adhesive must have any exposed edges protected from the weather by trim or a metal drip edge. Sometimes, spaced boards are used for roofs to be covered with wood shakes, concrete, or clay tile. Normally the roof boards are 1 × 4 square-edged and spaced the same distance on center as the shingles are laid to the weather (see 11-45). Consult the manufacturer of the wood shakes, clay, and concrete roof tile for sheathing recommendations.

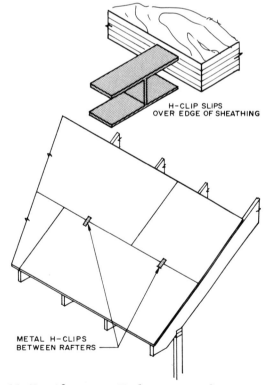

11-43 Aluminum H-clips are used on unsupported edges of roof sheathing panels, eliminating the need for wood blocking.

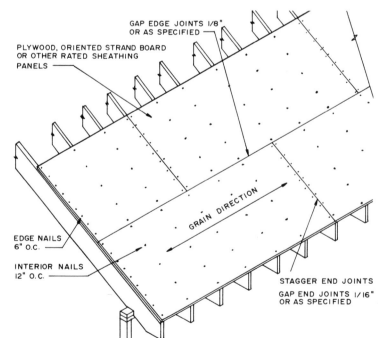

11-44 Sheathing panels are applied perpendicular to the rafters.

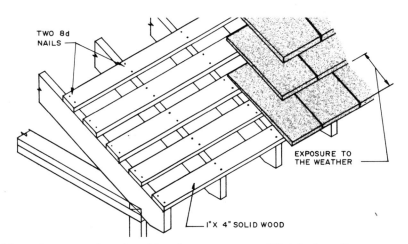

11-45   Spaced wood boards are used as sheathing for some types of finished roofing.

Valleys

When two gable roofs intersect, a **valley** is formed. The line of intersection between the two roofs is located with a valley rafter. Valley jack rafters run between the ridge and the valley rafter (see 11-46). Details for laying out valley and valley jack rafters are in Chapter 12, which follows.

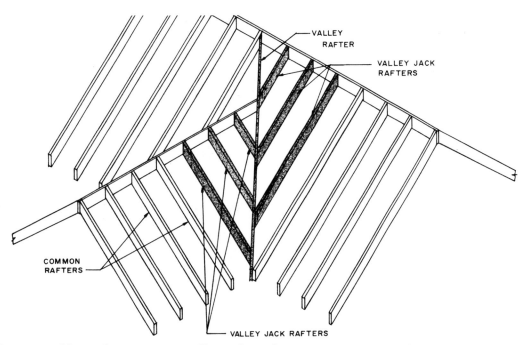

11-46   When two gable roofs intersect, a valley is formed.

12

Hip and Valley Rafters

A hip roof is actually formed by intersecting gable roofs. It eliminates the gable end. It is made up of common, hip, and hip jack rafters (see 12-1). If it has an intersection with another roof, it will have valley and valley jack rafters.

Hip Rafters

Generally all the roof surfaces on a hip roof have the same slope. The construction of a hip roof begins by erecting the ridgeboard and the common rafters as discussed in Chapter 11. Hip rafters are usually 2 inches wider than common and jack rafters because they carry a heavier load (see 12-2).

The centerlines of the first common rafters are located in from the end of the building a distance equal to the run of the common rafter. The length of the ridge is equal to the length of the building minus twice the run of the rafters, plus the thickness of the rafters (see 12-3).

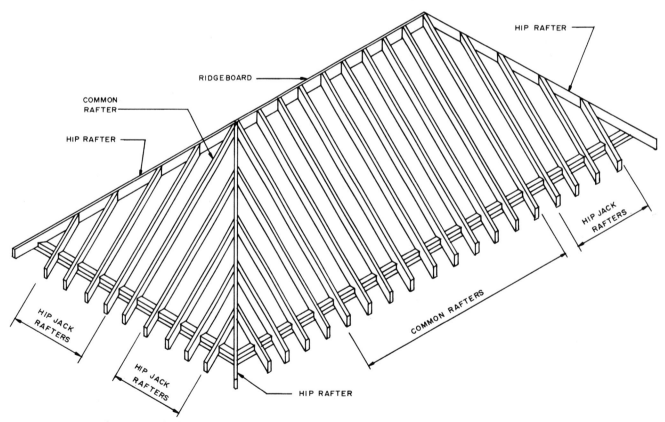

12-1   *Framing for a simple hip roof.*

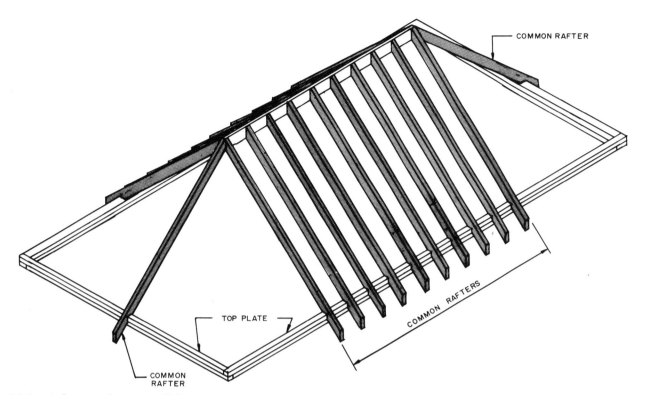

12-2   A hip roof is erected by raising the ridgeboard and common rafters before installing the hip rafters.

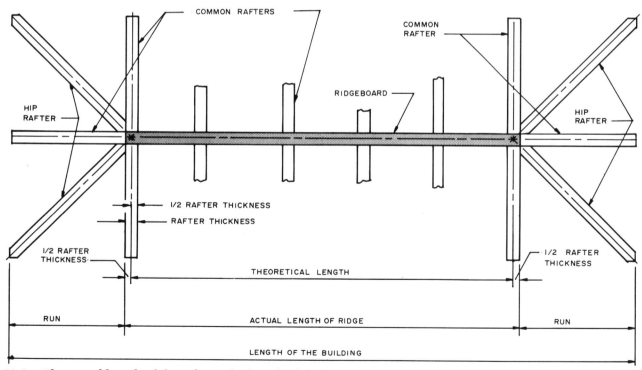

12-3   The actual length of the ridge is the length of the building minus two times the run of the rafters—plus the thickness of the rafters.

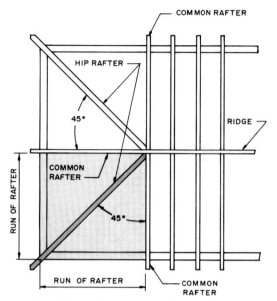

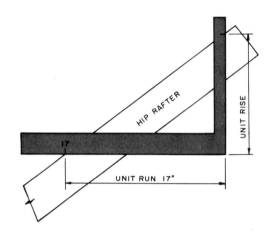

12-6   The hip rafter can be laid out using the step method, as explained for the common rafter.

12-4   The hip rafter is the diagonal of a square formed by common rafters and the double top plate.

Hip rafters run from the end of the ridge to the corner of the double top plate, forming an angle of 45 degrees with the adjoining common rafter. Actually it is the diagonal of a square (see 12-4). The unit of run for common rafters is 12 inches. The unit of run for the hip rafter is 16.97 inches (use 17 inches) for 12 inches of rise, because it is the diagonal of the square.

Valley rafters are in the same position and also have a run of 17 inches (see 12-5).

The hip rafter is laid out in the same way as a common rafter (see Chapter 11) except that the unit run is 17 inches. The procedure using the *step-off method* is shown in 12-6. Remember the unit of run is 17 inches. Generally, there are a few inches left over after laying out the 17-inch units of run. These are called *odd units*. To lay out odd units, locate the distance left over on the body and tongue of the square (see 12-7). Measure the diagonal. This becomes the

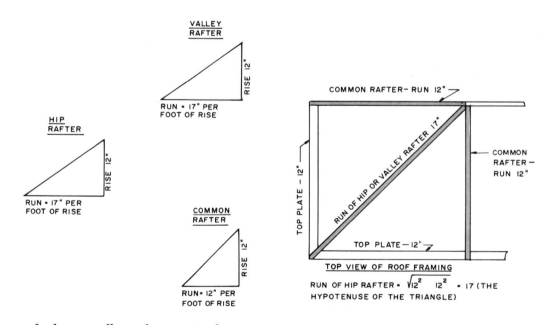

12-5   The run of a hip or valley rafter is 17 inches.

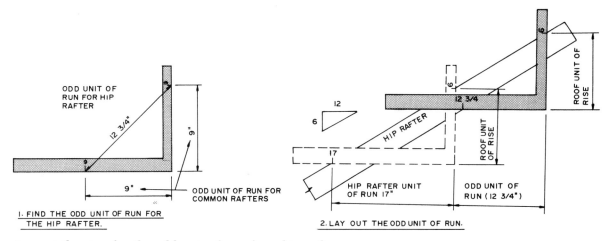

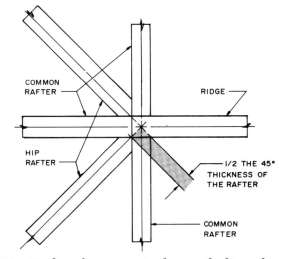

12-7 *Laying out the step for the odd unit of run for a hip rafter.*

unit of run for the odd units. For example, if a span was 12′9″, then the 9-inch run would be left over. Lay this out on the square, and measure the diagonal. This dimension, 12¾ inches, is the odd unit of run for the hip rafter. Locate it on the rafter as shown in 12-7.

The hip rafter must now be shortened a distance equal to one half the 45-degree thickness of the ridge. This measurement is shown in 12-8.

The length of the hip or valley rafter can also be found on the table on the framing square. The second line on the table is marked "length hip or valley per foot run." Find the rise on the inch scale on the outside edge of the square. Follow this down into the table. Where it meets the hip or valley row is the length of the rafter per one foot of run. For example, if the roof rise is 6 inches, the length of the hip or valley rafter is 18 inches per foot of run (see 12-9).

12-8 *Finding the amount to shorten the hip rafter at the ridges.*

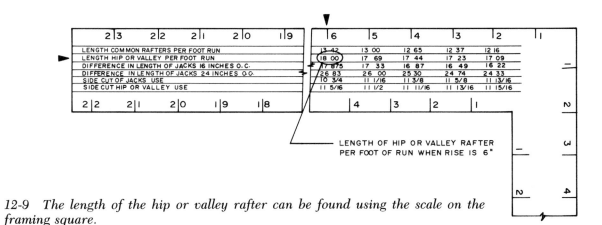

12-9 *The length of the hip or valley rafter can be found using the scale on the framing square.*

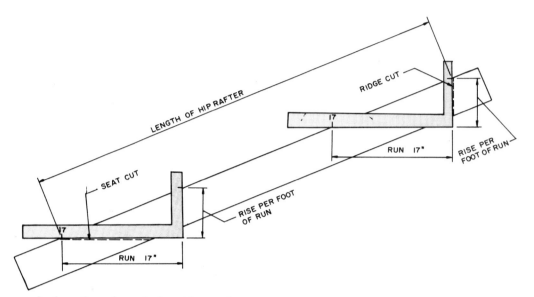

12-10   *Measure the length and mark the ridge and seat cuts.*

Now mark the ridge plumb and seat cuts as shown in 12-10. The unit rise is that specified for the roof, and the unit run is 17 inches. The plumb cut must be an angle cut because it butts the ridgeboard and two common rafters. These angled surfaces are called *cheek cuts.* To get the required angle use the table on the framing square marked "side cut hip or valley use." Use the figure under the column identified by a number representing the unit rise. In 12-9, a rise of 6 inches was used. The run shown on the square is 11 5/16 inches. Place the framing square on the top of the rafter, and mark the cheek cuts as shown in 12-11. The measurements are located from the centerline of the rafter.

After the angles are located, draw the plumb cuts. Place the square with the unit rise 6 inches, and the run 17 inches, on the rafter as shown in 12-12. The tail cuts on the ends of the rafters are drawn at the same angle.

Ordinarily, the hip rafter will have a tail extending beyond the seat cut. The length of the tail is found by drawing a square with sides equal to the desired over-

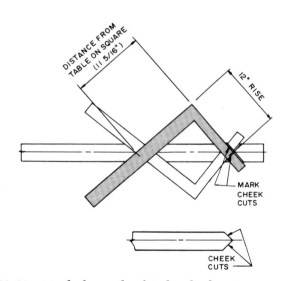

12-11   *Mark the angles for the cheek cuts.*

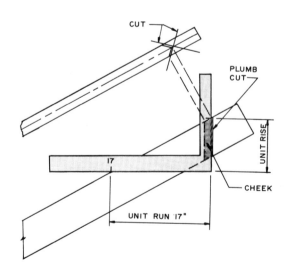

12-12   *Mark the plumb cut on each side of the rafter.*

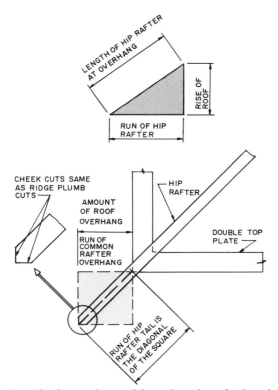

12-13 *The hip rafter tail length is found after finding the run of the tail.*

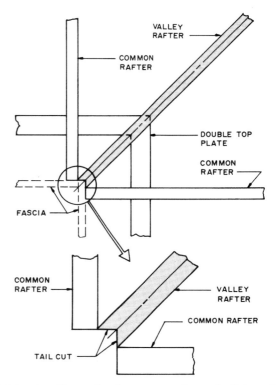

12-14 *A valley rafter has cuts at the end of the tail to receive the fascia board.*

hang. The length of the diagonal is the run of the tail of the hip rafter (see 12-13). The length of the tail of the rafter is the hypotenuse of a right triangle having sides equal to the run of the common rafter (12 inches). The length of the overhang can be found by stepping off the length with the framing square as shown in 12-6 and 12-7. It can also be found by using the unit length of a hip rafter shown on the second scale on the framing square. Multiply the unit length by the number of feet of run. For example, for a roof with a 6-inch rise, the unit length would be 18.00. If the overhang was to be 18 inches (1½ feet), the length of the rafter tail would be 18 × 1.5 or 27 inches.

The end of the hip rafter tail has cheek cuts on the same angle as the ridge plumb cut. The same procedures are used for laying out a valley rafter, except the tail cut is made as shown in 12-14. The plancher is laid out and cut as described for common rafters.

Next, locate and draw the bird's-mouth in the manner described for common rafters. Generally, it is preferred to vee the end of the bird's-mouth to fit the corner of the top plate (see 12-15). Mark and cut the plancher, if one is required.

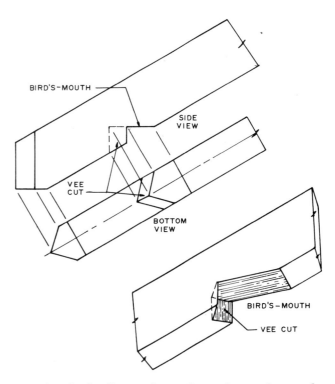

12-15 *The bird's-mouth on a hip rafter is often made with a vee cut.*

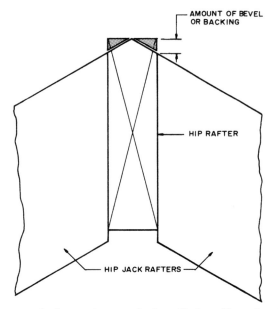

12-16 *The hip rafter can be bevelled to allow sheathing to fit smoothly to it.*

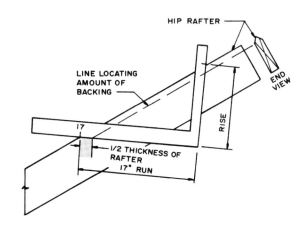

12-17 *Finding the amount of backing to bevel a hip rafter.*

parallel with the edge of the rafter gives the amount of bevel or backing.

Another technique is to cut the bird's-mouth deeper, dropping the height of the rafter (see 12-18). To find the amount of drop, position a square on the rafter, placing the rise and run as shown in 12-19. Measure horizontally one half the thickness of the rafter. The vertical distance between the square and this mark on the top of the rafter is the amount of drop.

Since the hip rafter will sit above the height of the jack rafters, an adjustment must be made. The edges of the hip rafter could be bevelled (see 12-16). To find the amount of bevel (also called backing), place the square on the rafter as shown in 12-17. From the unit run, 17 inches, measure horizontally one half the thickness of the rafter. A line drawn through this point

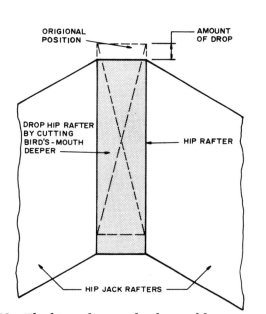

12-18 *The hip rafter can be dropped by cutting the bird's-mouth deeper.*

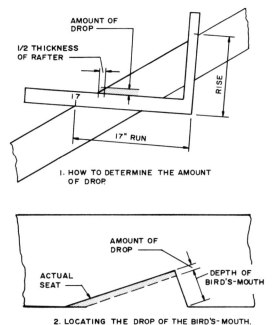

1. HOW TO DETERMINE THE AMOUNT OF DROP.

2. LOCATING THE DROP OF THE BIRD'S-MOUTH.

12-19 *Finding the amount of drop for a hip rafter.*

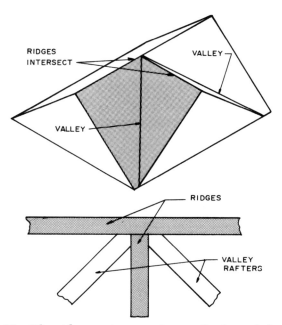

12-20   *The ridges on intersecting roofs of equal slope and span intersect.*

Valley Rafters

Valley rafters serve the same basic function as hip rafters, which is to be the line of intersection of roofs. A valley occurs when the intersecting roofs make an inside angle. If the intersecting roofs have the same slope and span, the valley rafters butt against both ridgeboards (see 12-20). If the slope and span are unequal, one valley rafter reaches the ridge of the larger roof (see 12-21).

The layout of the valley rafter is much the same as the hip rafter. The valley rafter is shortened at the ridge a distance equal to one half the 45-degree thickness of the ridge (see 12-22). The side cuts are on a

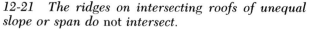

12-21   *The ridges on intersecting roofs of unequal slope or span do* not *intersect.*

45-degree angle and equal to one half the rafter thickness. When the valley rafter meets both ridges, equal side cuts are made on the rafter.

The main valley rafter for roofs of unequal slope or span has a single side cut. Its length is reduced as shown in 12-23. The butting valley rafter has a square-end plumb cut where it meets the main valley rafter. It is shortened one half the valley rafter thickness.

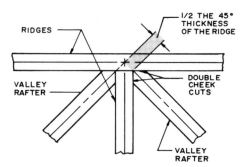

12-22   *Determining the amount to shorten the valley rafter for roofs of equal slope and span.*

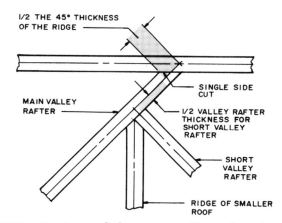

12-23   *Cutting and shortening valley rafters for intersecting roofs of unequal slope or span.*

195

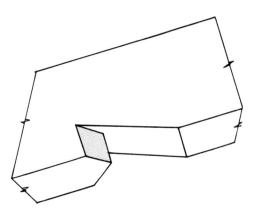

12-24 *The bird's-mouth detail for a valley rafter with an overhanging tail.*

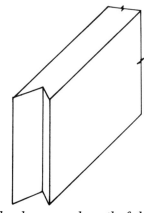

12-25 *The plumb cut on the tail of the valley rafter to receive the fascia board.*

The bird's-mouth is laid out as described for hip rafters except that the side cuts are angled as shown in 12-24. The overhang is figured the same as the hip rafter (detailed in 12-13 and 12-14). The end cuts on the tail are made to support a fascia board (see 12-25).

Jack Rafters

The three types of jack rafters are hip jack, cripple jack, and valley jack. **Hip jack** rafters run from the hip

rafter to the top double plate. **Valley jack** rafters run from the ridgeboard to the valley rafter. There are two types of **cripple jack** rafters, hip valley cripple jacks and valley cripple jacks. **Hip valley cripple jacks** run between hip and valley rafters. **Valley cripple jacks** run between two valley rafters (see 12-26). Hip jacks have a cheek cut on one end and a bird's-mouth and a plumb fascia cut on the other. Valley jack rafters have a cheek cut on one end and a plumb ridge cut on the other. Cripple jacks have cheek cuts on both of the ends.

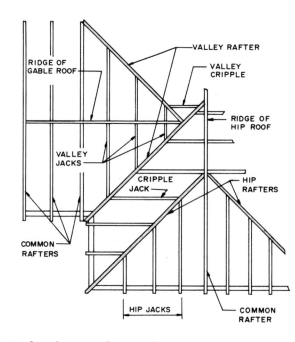

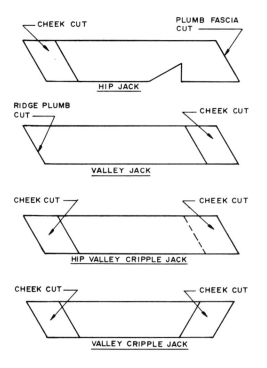

12-26 *Jack rafters used in roof construction.*

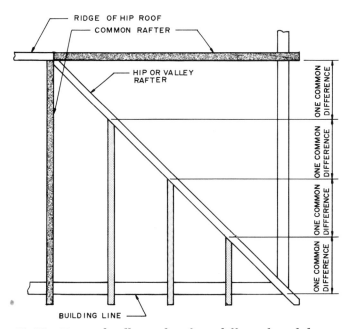

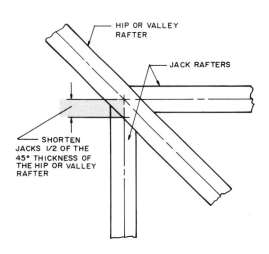

12-27   Hip and valley jack rafters differ in length by one "common difference."

12-29   Jack rafters are shortened by half the 45-degree thickness of the hip or valley rafter.

Common Difference of Hip and Valley Jack Rafters

Jack rafters are usually spaced the same, 16 or 24 inches O.C., as are common rafters. When they are equally spaced each will have a **common difference** in length (see 12-27). The longest jack rafter will be one common difference shorter than the common rafter. The second-longest jack rafter will be two common differences shorter than the common rafter. This continues until the shortest jack rafter, which is equal to one common difference, is laid out.

The common difference can be found on the third and fourth lines of the framing square table. Line three is for rafters 16 inches O.C., and line four is for those 24 inches O.C. (see 12-28). To find the common difference, locate the rise of the roof on the inch line of the square. For example, assume a rise of 6 inches. On the third line of the table below the 6-inch mark, a common difference of 17.875 inches for rafters 16 inches O.C. is found. The shortest jack rafter is 17.875 inches. The longest is the length of the common rafter minus 17.875 inches. In addition it is necessary to subtract one half of the 45-degree thickness of the hip or valley rafter (see 12-29).

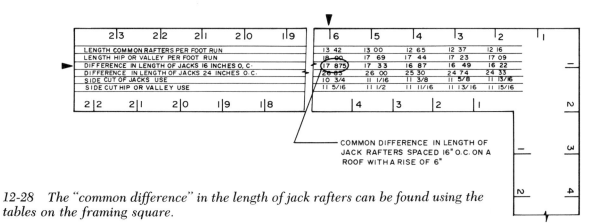

12-28   The "common difference" in the length of jack rafters can be found using the tables on the framing square.

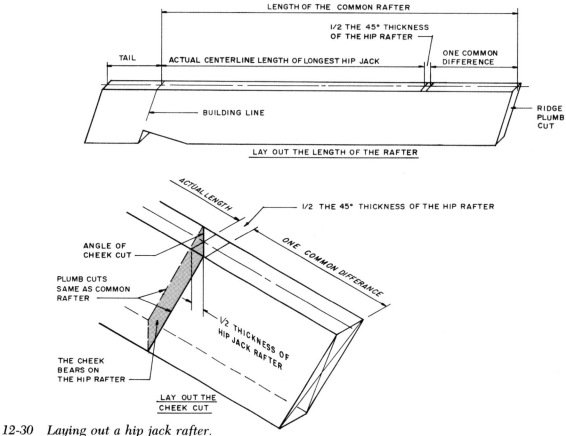

LENGTH OF THE COMMON RAFTER

1/2 THE 45° THICKNESS OF THE HIP RAFTER

TAIL

ACTUAL CENTERLINE LENGTH OF LONGEST HIP JACK

ONE COMMON DIFFERENCE

BUILDING LINE

RIDGE PLUMB CUT

LAY OUT THE LENGTH OF THE RAFTER

ACTUAL LENGTH

1/2 THE 45° THICKNESS OF THE HIP RAFTER

ANGLE OF CHEEK CUT

ONE COMMON DIFFERENCE

PLUMB CUTS SAME AS COMMON RAFTER

1/2 THICKNESS OF HIP JACK RAFTER

THE CHEEK BEARS ON THE HIP RAFTER

LAY OUT THE CHEEK CUT

12-30   *Laying out a hip jack rafter.*

Hip Jack Rafters

Some prefer to lay out the longest hip jack first, and then the others, by shortening the length one common difference. Following is a suggested procedure.

Use a common rafter as a pattern. Lay out the bird's-mouth and fascia plumb cut. They will be the same as the common rafter. To find the first (longest) jack rafter measure from the ridge plumb cut a distance equal to one common difference (see 12-30). Mark this on the centerline of the top of the rafter. Then shorten the rafter again to allow for the thickness of the hip rafter. This distance is equal to one half

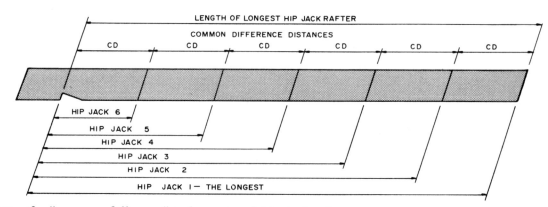

LENGTH OF LONGEST HIP JACK RAFTER

COMMON DIFFERENCE DISTANCES

CD   CD   CD   CD   CD   CD

HIP JACK 6

HIP JACK 5

HIP JACK 4

HIP JACK 3

HIP JACK 2

HIP JACK 1 — THE LONGEST

12-31   *Use the "common difference" to lay out each hip jack rafter.*

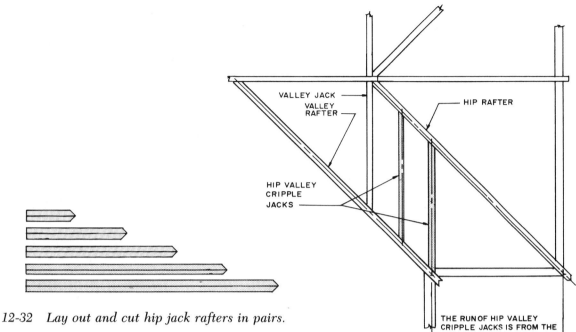

12-34   Finding the run of a hip valley cripple jack.

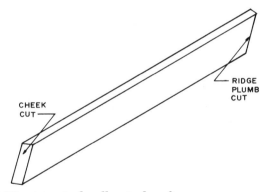

12-32   Lay out and cut hip jack rafters in pairs.

12-33   A typical valley jack rafter.

the 45-degree thickness of the hip rafter. Draw this line square across the rafter, and mark the center point. Then measure from it a distance equal to one half the thickness of the jack rafter. Draw a diagonal from this through the point, locating the actual length of the jack rafter on the centerline. This gives the angle of the cheek cut. Draw plumb cuts parallel with those at the ridge of the common rafter.

To lay out the second jack, shorten the length of the first by one common difference. Repeat until all rafters are laid out (see 12-31). Since the hip jack rafters are the same length on both sides of the hip rafter except for the angle of the cheek cut, lay out and cut in pairs (see 12-32).

Valley Jack Rafters

The valley jack rafter is laid out in the same manner as the hip jack rafter. The same tables are used to find the common difference. The ridge plumb cut is the same as that used on the common rafter. The other end has a cheek cut where it meets the valley rafter (see 12-33). The length of the valley jack rafter is measured from the cheek cut. The longest rafter is the same as a common rafter, except that it has a cheek cut instead of a bird's-mouth.

The allowances for shortening and cheek cuts are the same as those used on hip jack rafters. Cut valley jack rafters in pairs.

Hip Valley Cripple Jacks

Hip valley cripple jacks run between hip and valley rafters. Since these are parallel, all cripple jacks are the same length. The **run** of the cripple jacks is found by measuring from the center of the hip rafter to the center of the valley rafter along the top plate. The length is then found as explained for common rafters (see 12-34). The shortening allowance is one half the 45-degree thickness of the hip rafter on one end and the 45-degree thickness of the valley rafter on the other end.

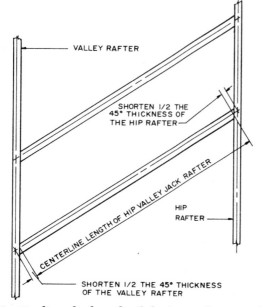

12-35 *Finding the length of the hip valley cripple jack.*

The length of the cripple jack is marked on the centerline of the rafter, and then each end is shortened by one half the 45-degree thickness of the hip and valley rafters. The cheek cuts are located in the same manner as for hip jacks (see 12-35).

Installing Jack Rafters

First mark the location of the rafters on the plate and hip and valley rafters. Install the rafters in pairs to help keep the hip or valley rafter straight. The first pair is usually installed near the center of the hip or valley rafter. Toenail each jack rafter with three 10d common nails. It is important that the hip and valley rafters remain straight. This may require temporary bracing. When installing valley jacks, some framers raise them slightly above the valley rafter to help the sheathing meet in a smooth, tight corner (see 12-36).

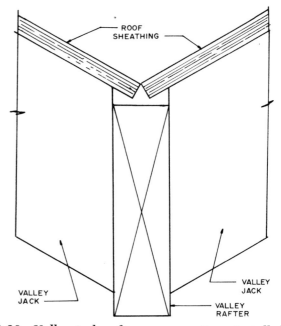

12-36 *Valley jack rafters are sometimes installed a little above the valley rafter.*

13

Framing Dormers

A **dormer** is a framed structure projecting from a sloping roof to house a window or ventilating louvre. This admits light and ventilation into the area under the roof (the attic). Dormers make it possible to have satisfactory living space in the attic area.

The style of dormer depends on the style of the house. The common types of dormer are shed, gable, and hip (see 13-1). Shed dormers can be made very long and run almost the entire length of the house with roof overhang or no overhang.

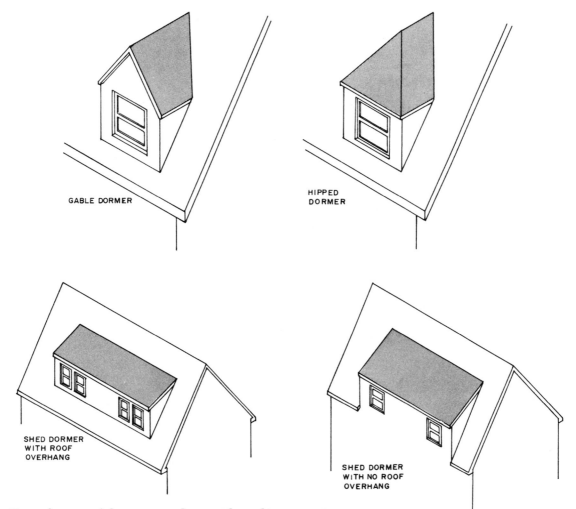

GABLE DORMER

HIPPED DORMER

SHED DORMER WITH ROOF OVERHANG

SHED DORMER WITH NO ROOF OVERHANG

13-1 Typical types of dormers used in residential construction.

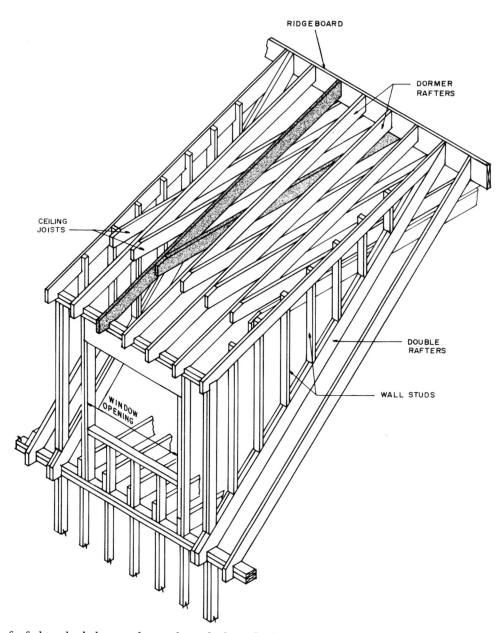

13-2   The roof of this shed dormer butts the ridgeboard of the main house roof.

Shed Dormers

The roof of **shed dormers** may run to the ridge (see 13-2) or fall short of the ridge (see 13-3). Notice in 13-3 that a roof overhang was added as a design feature. The rafters are laid out and cut as described for common rafters in Chapter 11. The side walls are framed the same as for the gable ends of gable roofs. The common rafter on which the side wall rests must be doubled. Ceiling joists are face-nailed to the dormer roof rafters and extend across the attic to the common rafters on the other side (see 13-4).

The end wall usually rests on the double top plate of the exterior wall below. If this is not the case, the attic floor joists must be sized large enough to carry this extra load or doubled in the area to carry the roof load. The window openings are framed in the normal manner.

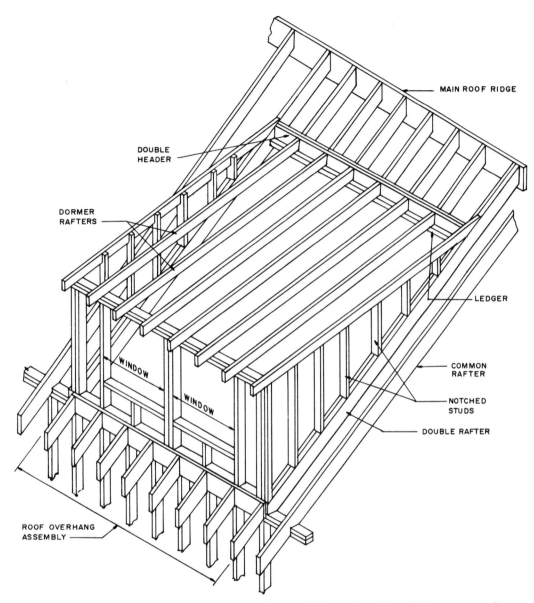

MAIN ROOF RIDGE

DOUBLE
HEADER

DORMER
RAFTERS

LEDGER

WINDOW

WINDOW

COMMON
RAFTER

NOTCHED
STUDS

DOUBLE RAFTER

ROOF OVERHANG
ASSEMBLY

13-3   *The roof of this shed dormer butts a header located below the ridge of the main roof.*

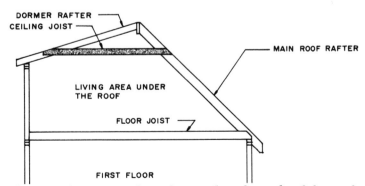

DORMER RAFTER
CEILING JOIST

MAIN ROOF RAFTER

LIVING AREA UNDER
THE ROOF

FLOOR JOIST

FIRST FLOOR

13-4   *The ceiling joist can extend across the area to the rafter on the other side of the roof.*

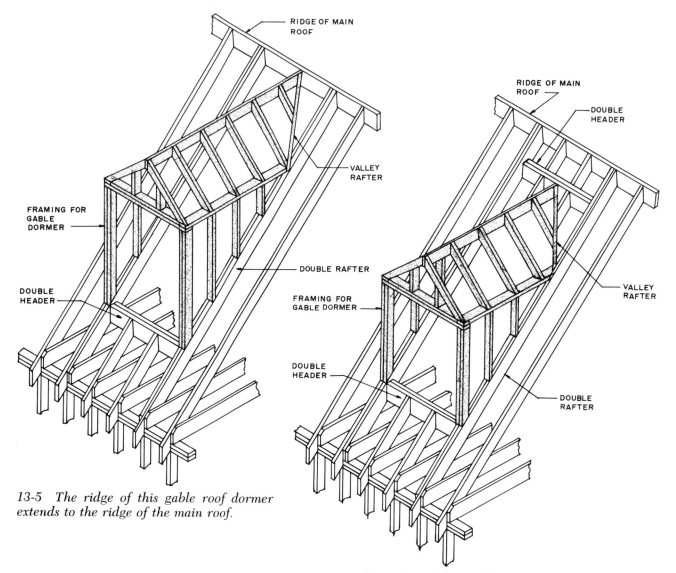

13-5 *The ridge of this gable roof dormer extends to the ridge of the main roof.*

13-6 *The ridge of this gable roof dormer extends to a double header located below the ridge of the main roof.*

Gable Dormers

Gable dormers are smaller than shed dormers and usually are designed to contain one window, although more could be used, if the main house roof has sufficient rise to accept the higher dormer roof needed by the wider dormer. The dormer roof is built as described in Chapter 11 for gable roofs. It has a ridge which may run to the ridge of the main roof (see 13-5) or fall below the ridge (see 13-6). Notice that the gable dormer roof has a ridgeboard and common valley jack, and valley rafters. Often the bird's-mouth is not cut. If the dormer ridge does not extend to the ridge of the main roof, a double header must be installed.

A typical framing plan for the header, valley rafter, and common rafter is shown in 13-7. Notice that an allowance must be made for the double side rafters when shortening the valley rafter. Usually a double top plate is used on the front wall, because it must be framed for a window. The side walls generally have a single top plate.

204

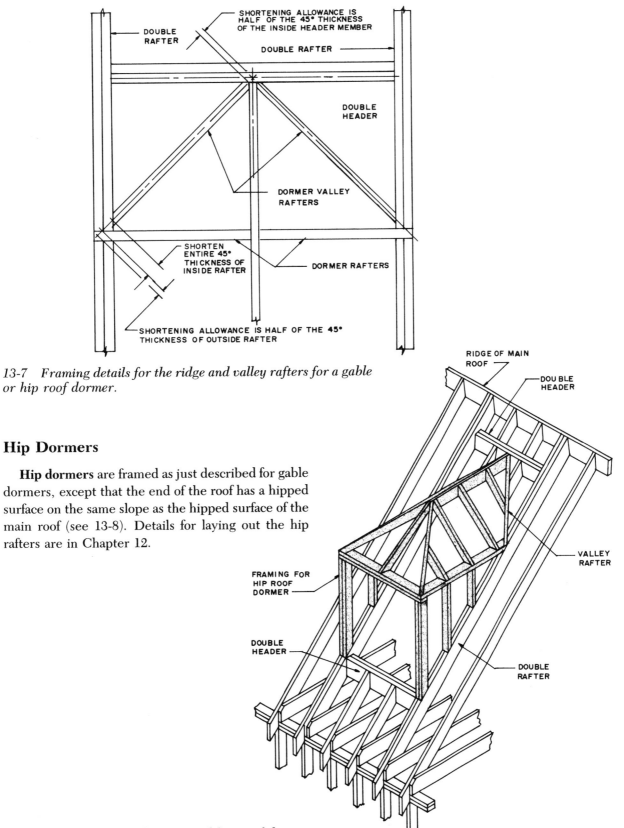

13-7   Framing details for the ridge and valley rafters for a gable or hip roof dormer.

Hip Dormers

Hip dormers are framed as just described for gable dormers, except that the end of the roof has a hipped surface on the same slope as the hipped surface of the main roof (see 13-8). Details for laying out the hip rafters are in Chapter 12.

13-8   Framing details for a typical hip roof dormer.

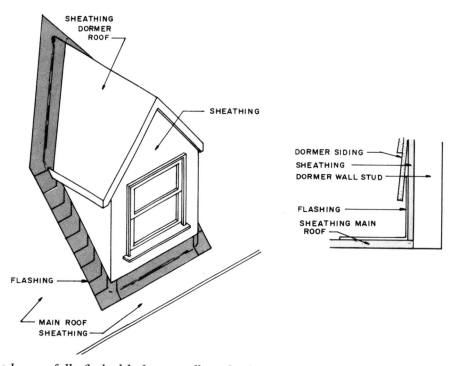

13-9   Dormers must be carefully flashed before installing the finished siding and the roof shingles.

Finishing the Dormer

The dormer is sheathed in the same manner as the exterior of other frame walls. A major factor is the installation of flashing, which is usually done by the roof-ers. Flashing details are shown in 13-9. After the flashing is in place the framers nail the siding so that it overlaps the flashing.

14

Framing Other Types of Roofs

Other types of roofs in common use include shed, flat, gambrel, and mansard. However, these are not as commonly used as the gable and hip roof.

Framing a Shed Roof

A **shed roof** is actually half of a gable roof. While most designs using shed roofs have low slope, some house styles require steeply sloped shed roofs (see 14-1). Shed roofs are also used on porches, shed dormers, and roof additions.

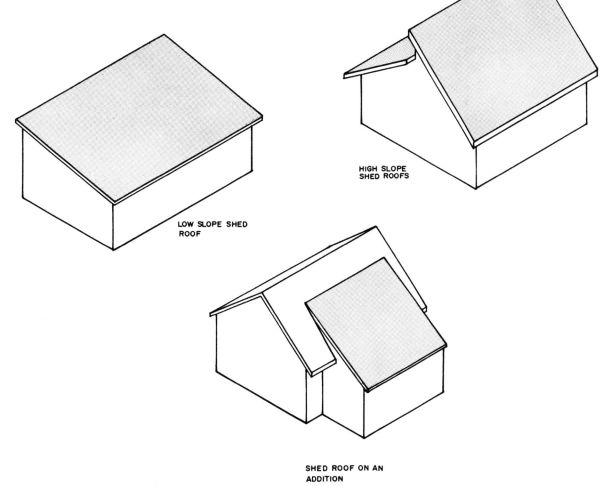

LOW SLOPE SHED ROOF

HIGH SLOPE SHED ROOFS

SHED ROOF ON AN ADDITION

14-1 *Typical shed roof applications.*

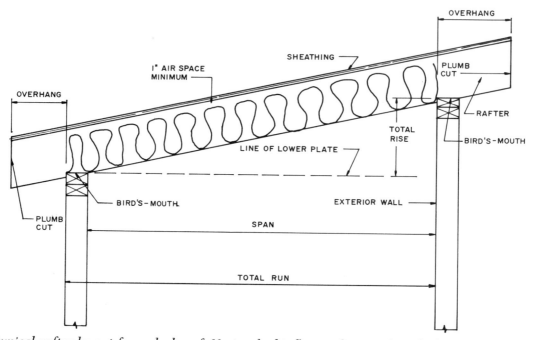

14-2   *A typical rafter layout for a shed roof. Notice the bird's-mouth on each end of the rafter.*

The rafters are much like common rafters, except that they have a bird's-mouth and plumb cut on each end (see 14-2). Each end provides an overhang. The rafter length is laid out the same as for a common rafter. The **run** of the rafter is taken from the inside face of the top plate on the higher wall to the outside face of the plate on the lower wall. When figuring the overhang at the higher wall, include the thickness of the stud wall. The **rise** is the vertical distance from the top of the lower plate to the top of the higher plate. The soffit material is usually nailed to the bottom of the rafter overhang. Overhang on the end walls is constructed in the same manner as described for flat roof construction that follows. The rafters usually support the interior finished ceiling (see 14-3).

Flat Roof Construction

Framing a **flat roof** is much the same as framing a floor. The rafters carry the roof load and the finished interior ceiling. The rafters must be sized to carry this extra load. Usually a flat roof is built with a slight slope to provide some drainage. Normally a slop of ¼ inch per foot is used. Slope can be produced by using oversize joists and cutting them on a taper, adding a bevelled wood strip on top of the high plate, using trusses built with a taper, or building the roof flat and adding tapered rigid foam insulation on the sheathing. Sloped rafters will produce a sloped ceiling. If this is not desired, level ceiling joists can be installed alongside the rafters (see 14-4).

Typical framing details are shown in 14-5, 14-6, and 14-7. When an overhang is required it can be built as shown by these illustrations. The size of the joists and double joists serving as a header must be engineered to carry the loads.

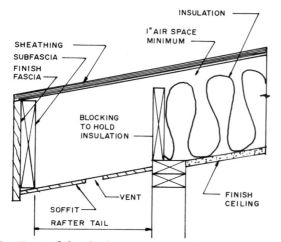

14-3   *Typical finished construction details for a shed roof.*

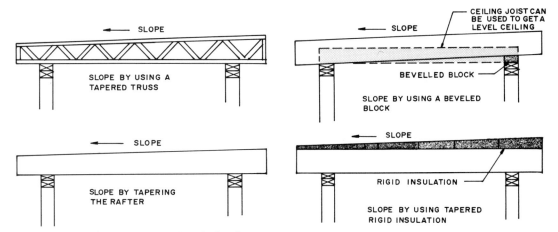

14-4   Typical ways to give a flat roof a slight slope.

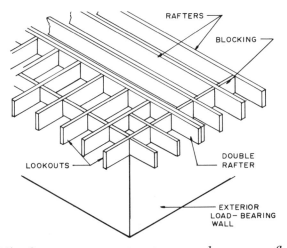

14-5   One way to construct an overhang on a flat roof using lookouts.

14-6   An alternate way to construct an overhang on a flat roof using lookouts.

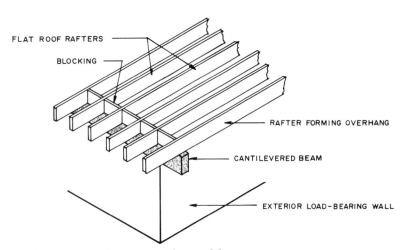

14-7   Flat roof overhang can be supported on a cantilevered beam.

Gambrel Roofs

A **gambrel roof** consists of two gable roofs, each on a different slope. Typically, it is used to provide a large living area on the second level. The roof replaces the wall of a second floor. Normally the upper roof is on a slope of about 20 degrees or approximately 4 or 5 inches of rise to 12 inches of run. The lower roof is very steep and is normally on an angle of about 70 to 75 degrees or a slope of about 35 to 40 inches of rise to 12 inches of run (see 14-8).

The rafters in the upper roof butt the ridgeboard and have a bird's-mouth that sits on a purlin. The top end of the rafter of the lower roof is notched to fit on the purlin and has a bird's-mouth that sits on the top plate of the exterior wall. A typical layout is shown in 14-9. This gives a sloping exterior wall. The rafters are laid out as explained for common rafters.

An alternate method of framing is shown in 14-10. It uses a double plate instead of a purlin and a vertical stud interior wall. A framing drawing of the complete

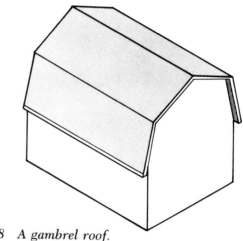

14-8   A gambrel roof.

system is shown in 14-11. Windows can be framed in the vertical end wall.

Windows can be framed into gambrel and mansard roofs (see the following) using dormers, recessed windows, or roof windows (see 14-12).

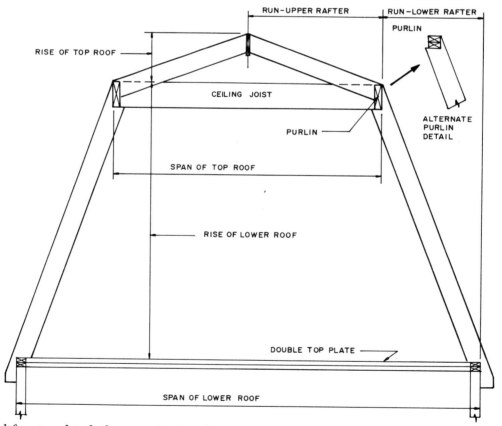

14-9   Typical framing details for a gambrel roof.

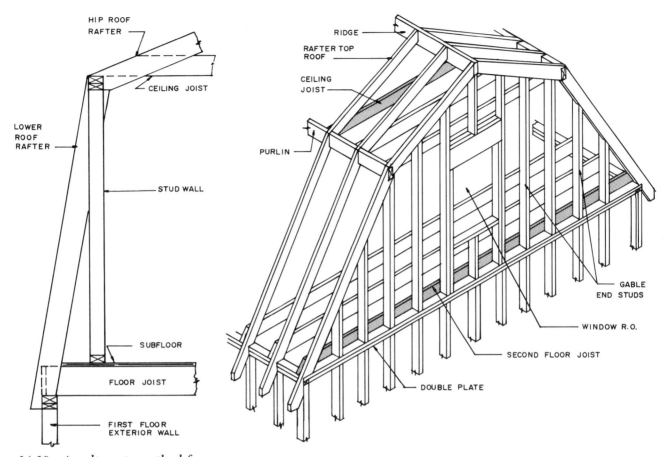

14-10 An alternate method for framing a gambrel roof.

14-11 Typical framing for a gambrel roof.

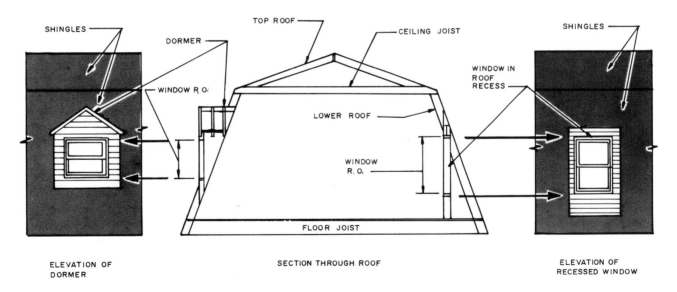

14-12 Windows can be placed in gambrel and mansard roofs by building dormers or recessing them into the roof.

Mansard Roofs

A **mansard roof** provides full ceiling height. It is made of two roof surfaces. The top roof is a hip roof. The lower roof is very steep and serves to protect the interior wall (see 14-13). It is on all sides of the building, eliminating the gable end.

Typical construction details are shown in 14-14. In one design the floor joists are cantilevered beyond the exterior wall. The rafters on the lower roof run from the edge of the floor to rafters on the top roof. The top hip roof is supported by the framing of the second-floor wall. The hip rafters are laid out as described for hip roof construction (see 14-15).

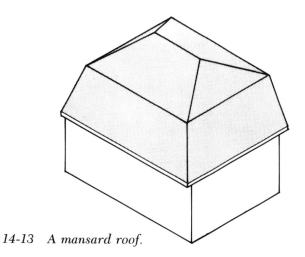

14-13   A mansard roof.

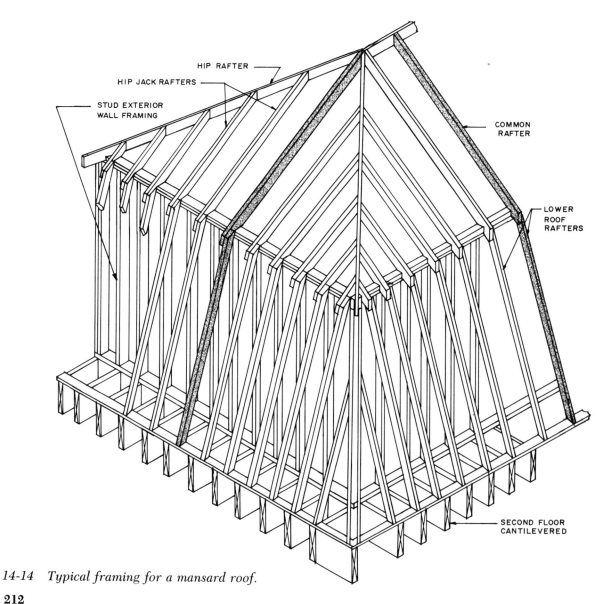

14-14   Typical framing for a mansard roof.

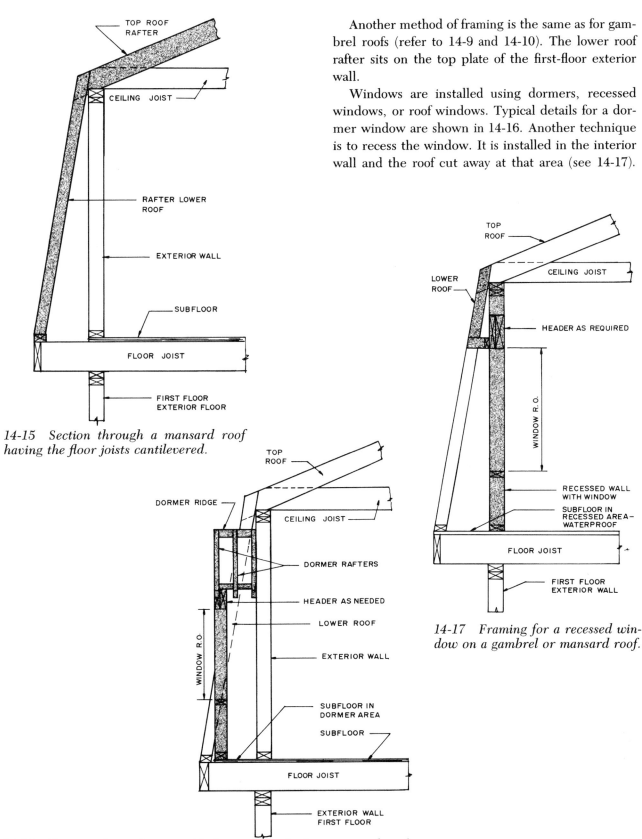

Another method of framing is the same as for gambrel roofs (refer to 14-9 and 14-10). The lower roof rafter sits on the top plate of the first-floor exterior wall.

Windows are installed using dormers, recessed windows, or roof windows. Typical details for a dormer window are shown in 14-16. Another technique is to recess the window. It is installed in the interior wall and the roof cut away at that area (see 14-17).

14-15 Section through a mansard roof having the floor joists cantilevered.

14-17 Framing for a recessed window on a gambrel or mansard roof.

14-16 Framing for a dormer added onto a gambrel or mansard roof.

15

Wood Roof Trusses

A **truss** is a structural unit made up of an assembly of members usually in a triangular arrangement. It forms a rigid framework that will carry a load over a distance between two supports. The triangular shapes enable the various parts of the truss to resist the tension and compression forces produced by the load.

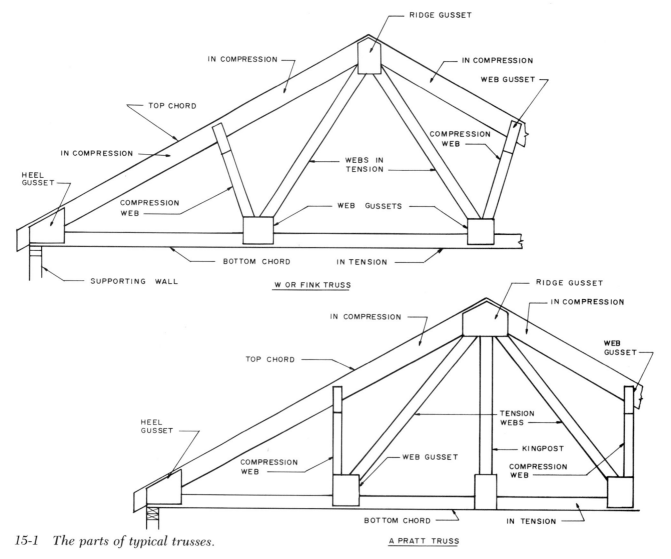

15-1   *The parts of typical trusses.*

A **roof truss** is a structural unit designed to frame a roof (see 15-1) and to support the roof material, interior ceiling, insulation, and forces caused by snow, rain, and wind. Roof trusses are supported by the exterior walls and span the width of the building.

Advantages

Roof trusses save on-site costs because they are rapidly erected, and the building is made weathertight in a minimum of time. Since they span the width of the building, no interior partitions are required for support. This allows complete freedom for room arrangement. Factory-made trusses are carefully engineered for the job and built under controlled conditions in a plant. The quality is more consistent than on-site cut-and-assembled conventionally framed roofs. The members of a truss are usually consider-ably smaller than those used in conventional joist and rafter framing, reducing weight and cost.

Disadvantages

Roof trusses have a series of supporting members that limit the use of attic space. Large trusses require that a crane be used to lift them in place. Since they are generally spaced 24 inches O.C., roof sheathing and interior ceiling finish material must be thicker than for conventional 16 inches O.C. spaced members.

Types of Trusses

There are many types of trusses available. Each type has specific design considerations and advantages and disadvantages. Many special-purpose trusses are designed by engineers working for truss manufacturers. Some of the frequently used trusses are shown in 15-2.

The **king-post truss** is the simplest form used in light-frame construction. It consists of upper and lower chords and a center vertical post called a king post. Its spans are less than the W-truss when the same size members are used.

The **W-** or **Fink truss** is possibly the most commonly used truss for light construction. Since it uses more web members than the king-post truss, it can be made with lower-grade lumber and span greater distances for the same member size.

The **scissors truss** is designed to provide a sloping, sometimes called *cathedral*, ceiling. It provides solid roof construction and space for considerable ceiling insulation and for running heat ducts and electrical wiring.

The **Howe truss** is often called an *M-truss* because of the design of the web members. It is a king-post truss with web members running from the bottom of the center vertical member to the center of the top chord and dropping another vertical member from there to the bottom chord, which gives three vertical supports to the bottom chord. It will carry a heavier ceiling load than the W-truss, if it is designed using the same size material.

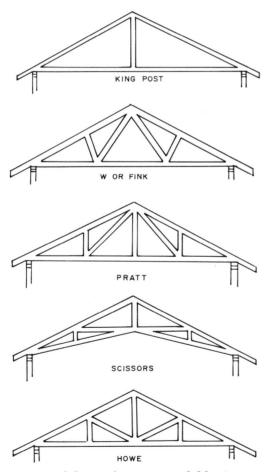

KING POST

W OR FINK

PRATT

SCISSORS

HOWE

15-2 *Some of the roof trusses available. (Continued on next page.)*

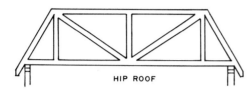

HIP ROOF

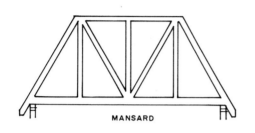

MANSARD

MONO-PITCH 4 PANEL

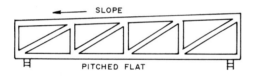

SLOPE

PITCHED FLAT

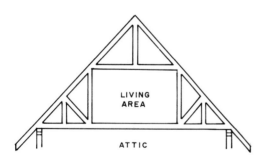

LIVING AREA

ATTIC

DUCT AREA

TRUSS WITH DUCT PASSAGE

A **hip truss** is used to frame a hip roof. Hip trusses are trapezoids with equal slopes on the side members, which connect the horizontal top and bottom chords. Each hip roof uses a series of trusses each smaller than the one before.

A **mono-pitch truss** is used when framing shed roofs.

An **attic truss** is used to provide space for storage or a living area in the attic. To get headroom the roof must have a steep slope. A variation of this for low-sloped roofs is used to provide a space to run air ducts.

A **gable end truss** is built without gusset plates. However, it is not strong enough to support a roof load, if the building length is increased at some future time. If an addition is built, add gusset plates to the truss. It is usually sheathed with structural sheathing.

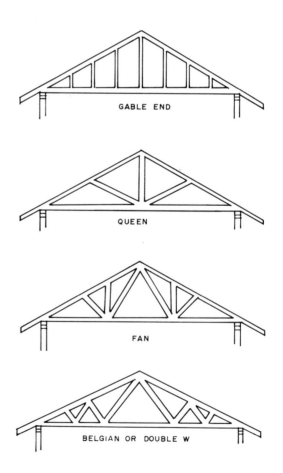

GABLE END

QUEEN

FAN

BELGIAN OR DOUBLE W

15-2   *Some of the roof trusses available (continued).*

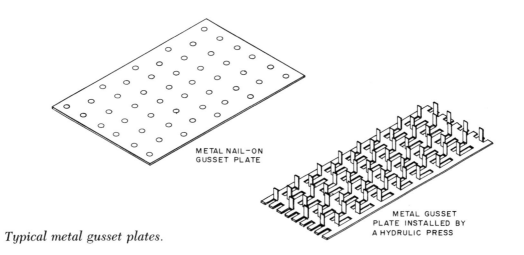

15-3 Typical metal gusset plates.

METAL NAIL-ON
GUSSET PLATE

METAL GUSSET
PLATE INSTALLED BY
A HYDRULIC PRESS

Design and Fabrication

Trusses must be *designed by an engineer*. Factors to be considered include the type of truss to be used, the structural properties of the wood, the imposed loads, both live and dead, the span, the roof slope, and the spacing of the trusses. Imposed loads include dead loads such as the weight of the truss, sheathing, roofing, insulation, and interior ceiling. Live loads include snow and wind. Members for trusses used in light-frame construction are usually 2 × 4 and 2 × 6 stock. Notice that in the truss shown in 15-1 some web members are in compression and others are in tension. The engineer must specify the wood properties and size to carry the calculated loads.

Most trusses are manufactured in factories. The manufacturer can design a wide range of special-purpose trusses. The trusses are assembled from precision-cut parts that are held in jigs. The metal gusset plates are either power-nailed or pressed into place. Machine stress-rated lumber is used.

Two types of metal gussets are used on factory-manufactured trusses. One is a flat metal plate with punched holes for nails, whereas the other is a flat metal plate with prongs (see 15-3). The plate is placed over the union of truss members and pressed in place with a hydraulic press.

While it is best to buy trusses from a reliable truss manufacturer, small trusses can be built on the site. They must follow an approved engineering design. The proper grade of lumber must be used, it must be kiln-dried to 19 percent moisture, and it must be free of any form of warp or twist.

Begin by carefully drawing the truss on a large flat surface, such as the subfloor. Cut each piece to fit, and then place it on the pattern and lightly nail in place. Check to make certain the joints fit and that the left and right sides of the truss are the same. Then nail 2-inch wood blocks to the floor around the truss, forming a jig (see 15-4).

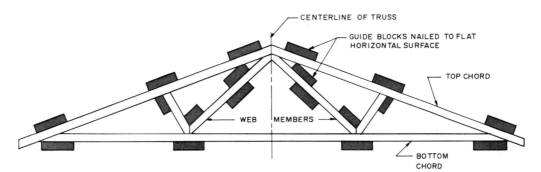

CENTERLINE OF TRUSS

GUIDE BLOCKS NAILED TO FLAT
HORIZONTAL SURFACE

TOP CHORD

WEB MEMBERS

BOTTOM
CHORD

15-4 Truss members assembled in a jig ready for the application of gussets.

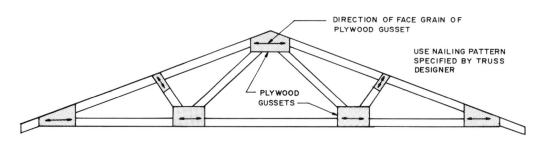

15-5 *The face grain of plywood gussets runs parallel with the webs and chords.*

Now cut the number of pieces required for the series of trusses. Use the parts of the original truss as a pattern. A radial-arm saw will produce more accurate cuts than a portable circular saw. If plywood gussets are to be used, cut them to size. The face grain of the gussets and the heel gussets should be parallel with the chords and webs (see 15-5).

Whenever possible use full-length lumber for the top and bottom chords and the webs. If splices do occur in the chords, they should be located in the middle panels and *never at a panel joint* (see 15-6). A typical splice for a truss using solid wood and plywood gussets is shown in 15-7.

When plywood gussets are used, apply glue to the truss and the gusset. The glue used is a casein type, but if there is danger of exposure to moisture, use a waterproof glue such as a resorcinol type. Almost all roof trusses have possible moisture exposure at the soffit. Spread the glue carefully over the entire surface with a brush. Plywood gussets used on small trusses are usually ⅜ inch or ½ inch thick, as specified on the design drawing. Use 4d galvanized or cement-coated nails for ⅜-inch-thick gussets and 6d for those ½ inch thick. Space the nails 3 inches apart on ⅜-inch gussets and 4 inches on ½-inch gussets. When nailing into 4-inch-wide members, use two rows of nails ¾ inch from each edge of the gusset. Use three rows of nails when the truss member is 6 inches wide.

After the gussets on one side are in place, carefully raise the truss by the peak. Have several workers help turn it over and lay it flat on the floor. Then glue and nail the gussets on the other side. Stock the trusses absolutely flat, and let the glue cure 24 hours.

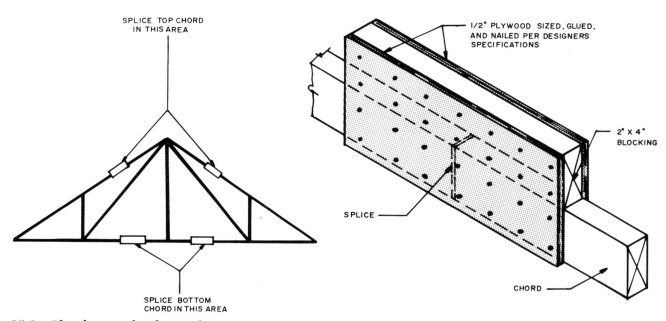

15-6 *Chords are spliced near the center of panels.*

15-7 *A typical chord splice design.*

15-8 *Trusses removed from the truck and positioned to be lifted on the roof.*

Handling Trusses

Trusses are designed to carry a load when they are in a vertical position. They should be stored and lifted in an upright position (see 15-8). If they are stored flat, they must be placed on a firm surface that is flat and dry. They should never be laid flat on the ground. No stress must be placed on trusses during storage and moving. There should be a sufficient number of workers to handle trusses so that they do not twist. Trusses should be covered with plastic when stored on the construction site.

Erecting the Trusses

Small trusses can be lifted into place by several workers. Larger trusses must be lifted with a crane (see 15-9).

15-9 *Large trusses are set in place with a crane.*

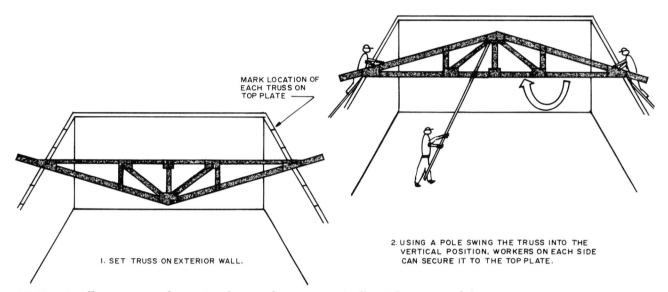

MARK LOCATION OF EACH TRUSS ON TOP PLATE

1. SET TRUSS ON EXTERIOR WALL.

2. USING A POLE SWING THE TRUSS INTO THE VERTICAL POSITION, WORKERS ON EACH SIDE CAN SECURE IT TO THE TOP PLATE.

15-10 *Small trusses can be set in place and swung vertically without a need for a crane.*

If interior partitions are not in place, small trusses can be installed by having workers lift them onto the top plate with the ridge down. One person uses a pole to swing the ridge into a vertical position. A worker is on the wall at each end of the truss. When the truss is erect they position it on the top plate and toenail it in place (see 15-10). Another worker nails a temporary brace near the ridge to tie the truss to the gable end truss and to adjoining trusses. The brace is generally marked with the spaces (usually, 24 inches O.C.) so that no measuring is required.

Each truss is erected in this way in turn (see 15-11). To assist in positioning the trusses, some framers prefer to erect both gable end trusses before continuing. And then run a chalk line at the ridge. Others will install temporary blocking at the top plate and run a chalk line, locating the amount of overhang. Usually, the overhang is ¾ inch more than required. The truss is then set to within ¾ inch of the chalk line. The space is checked with a ¾-inch piece of wood. This keeps the truss from touching the chalk line and possibly pushing it out of position (see 15-12).

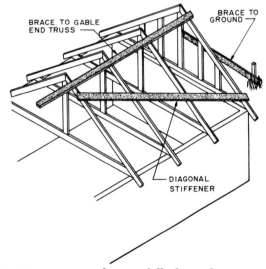

BRACE TO GABLE END TRUSS

BRACE TO GROUND

DIAGONAL STIFFENER

15-11 *Trusses must be carefully braced.*

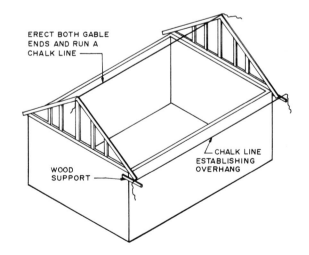

ERECT BOTH GABLE ENDS AND RUN A CHALK LINE

WOOD SUPPORT

CHALK LINE ESTABLISHING OVERHANG

15-12 *Chalk lines can be used to help position the truss.*

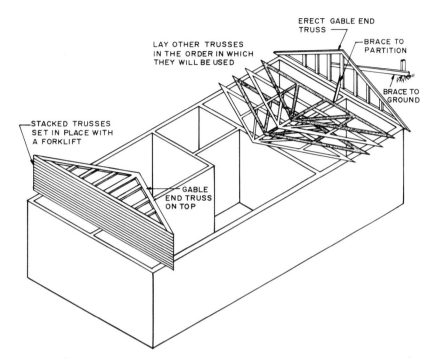

15-13   *Trusses can be laid out on the interior partitions in the order in which they should be erected.*

If the trusses are delivered in stacks and can be set on the top plate with a forklift, they can be laid out as shown in 15-13. This requires that interior partitions be in place to provide support. The gable end truss goes up first; therefore, it must be on top. It can be braced to the interior partitions and to the ground, if needed.

Large trusses are set in place with a crane (see 15-14). Control lines are tied to each end of the truss so that workers on the ground can keep it from swing-

ing and can guide it into the proper position on the top plate. As above, workers are on each wall to nail it to the top plate, and one or more workers nail the needed bracing.

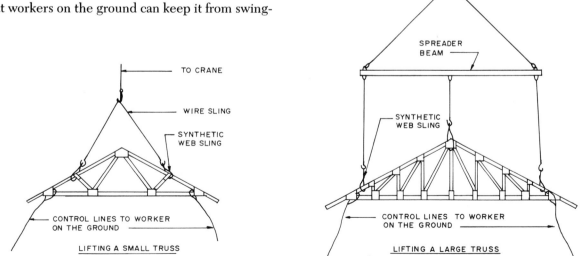

15-14   *When raising trusses with a crane, the slings must be properly installed to prevent damage to the truss.*

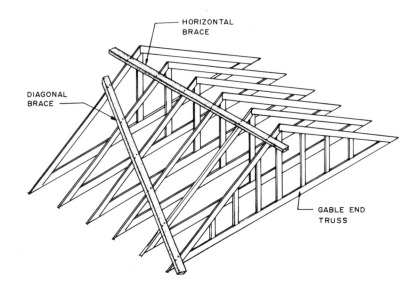

15-15   *Trusses are temporarily braced until permanent bracing and sheathing are installed.*

After several trusses are in place, a diagonal brace is nailed across the top chord running from the bottom of the gable end truss to the ridge of the last truss. Some prefer to do this on both sides of the roof. The brace is nailed to each top chord with duplex nails so that they can be easily removed. They are not removed until permanent bracing is installed and the sheathing is begun (see 15-15). Wind is a big problem when erecting trusses and can cause considerable damage unless the roof is carefully braced.

The truss designer will indicate how the trusses are to be permanently braced. One method uses diagonal braces from the ridge to the lower chord of the next truss (see 15-16). Stiffeners are generally installed on top of the bottom chord at all points where a web meets the bottom chord, and they run the full length

of the building. Cross-bracing is typically installed between the first eight trusses from each end of the building; then eight trusses are skipped and the next eight trusses are braced; or bracing is done as specified by the designer. The truss is toenailed to the double top plate with two 12d or 16d nails. In areas where high winds occur, metal tiedowns are required (see 15-17). It is also difficult to toenail some trusses that have large metal gussets. In these cases metal tiedowns are also used.

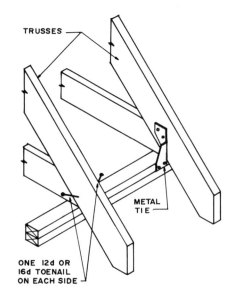

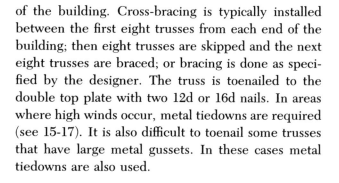

15-16   *Typical wind bracing and stiffener placement for roof trusses.*

15-17   *Methods for anchoring trusses to the top plate.*

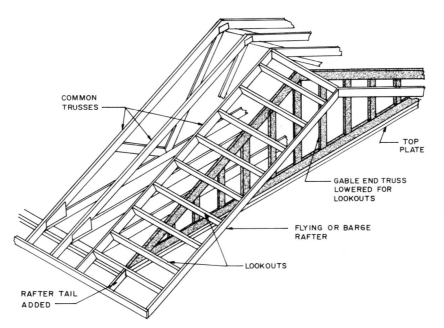

15-18   *The gable end truss can be lowered to allow the use of lookouts to build the overhang.*

Framing a Gable End Overhang

A gable end overhang can be framed by ordering a gable end truss that has been dropped to permit lookouts to rest on top of it and run to the top chord of the next truss (see 15-18).

Framing a Hip Roof

A hip roof is framed using hip and hip jack rafters. Standard rafters can be used instead of the hip jack rafters. A framing plan for a simple hip roof is shown in 15-19. This required three different hip trusses.

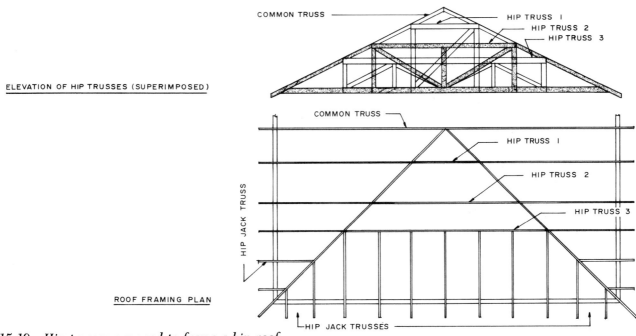

15-19   *Hip trusses are used to frame a hip roof.*

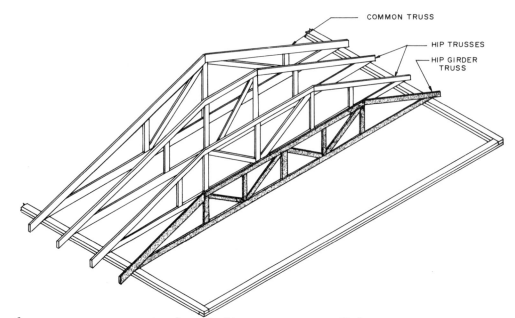

15-20 *After the common trusses are in place the hip trusses are installed.*

After the common trusses are erected in the center of the building, the hip rafters are set in place (see 15-20). Then the hip jack trusses are installed, and blocking is placed between the hip trusses to provide stability and a nailing surface for the sheathing. One of the hip trusses is designed to carry the load imposed by the joining hip jack trusses. The complete assembly is shown in 15-21.

Framing an L-Shaped Roof

An L-shaped roof is produced by the intersection of two gable roofs. This forms valleys at the lines of intersection. It requires the use of a series of special

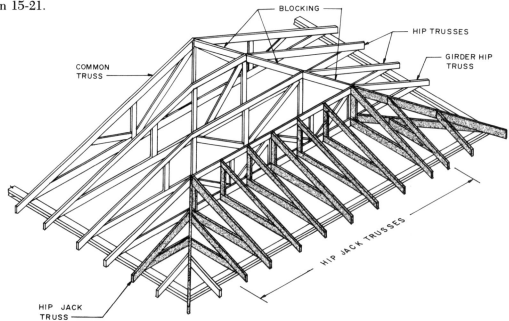

15-21 *The hip jack trusses are secured to the girder hip truss to finish the roof frame.*

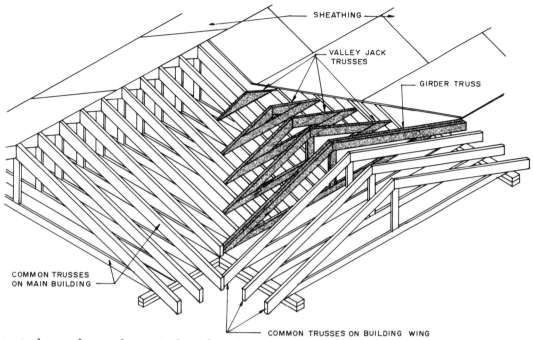

15-22   *A typical truss layout for an L-shaped roof.*

trusses called valley jack trusses. Each gets progressively smaller than the previous one (see 15-22). These special trusses are secured to the top chord of the common trusses in the adjoining roof. The girder truss is placed first and strongly braced. Metal truss hangers are used to secure the bottom chord of the special trusses to the top chord of the common truss. Blocking is placed at the ridge between the trusses and is usually held with metal pocket-type hangers. This gives a nailing surface for the sheathing (see 15-23).

The girder truss is placed across the opening where the two parts of the house intersect. It is installed first and braced. The valley jack trusses are placed on the intersecting roof and the common trusses placed over the adjoining wing of the building (see 15-24).

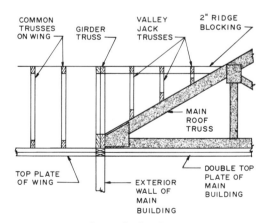

15-23   *A section through the framing of an L-shaped roof.*

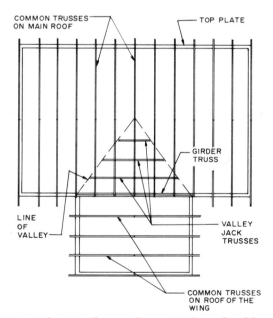

15-24   *A framing layout for an L-shaped gable roof using trusses.*

Other Details

Trusses can be manufactured giving a wide range of soffited eave construction possibilities. Some of these are shown in 15-25.

The installation of a 2-inch-thick nailer to support the finish ceiling material is shown in 15-26.

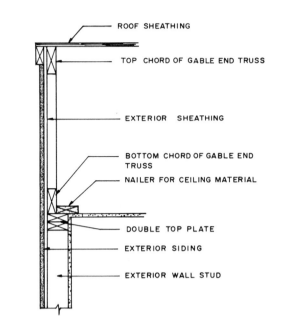

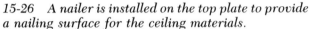

15-26   *A nailer is installed on the top plate to provide a nailing surface for the ceiling materials.*

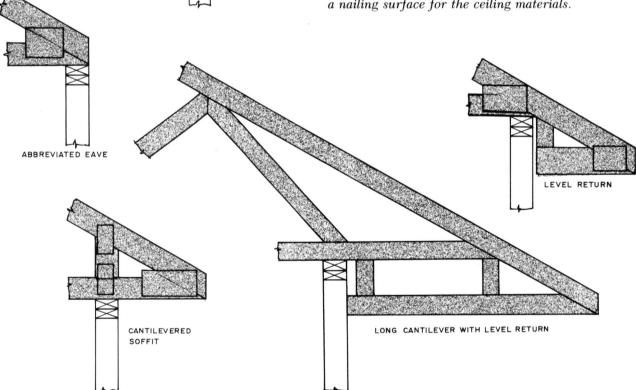

15-25   *Some typical eave framing details for pitched roof trusses.*

PART IV
Finishing the Building

16

Doors and Windows

Exterior doors commonly used in light-frame construction are made with the outer facing of wood, steel, or fibreglass. The steel and fibreglass doors are filled with a rigid foam insulation. Generally, exterior doors are 1¾ inches thick and 6'8" high, though 7-feet-high doors are available. Usually, the main entrance door is 3 feet wide. Other exterior doors, such as from a garage or rear of the house, are often 2'8" wide. All door sizes are shown on the architectural drawings in the door schedule.

Interior doors are made from wood or are moulded hardboard. Generally they are 1⅜ inches thick and 6'8" high. Commonly used widths range from 2 feet to 2 feet 8 inches. An important consideration is the passage of furniture or wheelchairs.

Exterior doors are usually swinging or sliding types. Interior doors may be swinging, bypass, pocket, bifold, multifold, and accordian (see 16-1).

Doors used in light-frame construction are generally wood flush hollow or solid core; panel doors of wood, steel, fibreglass, or hardboard; and louvred (see 16-2). Hollow-core doors are made with a thin wood veneer facing, over a grid of wood or cardboard. They are used for interior purposes only. Flush solid-core doors have wood veneer bonded to a solid wood core. They provide good security and can be used as exterior doors. Solid wood, steel, and fibreglass doors are generally used for exterior applications. Hardboard doors are generally used for interior purposes.

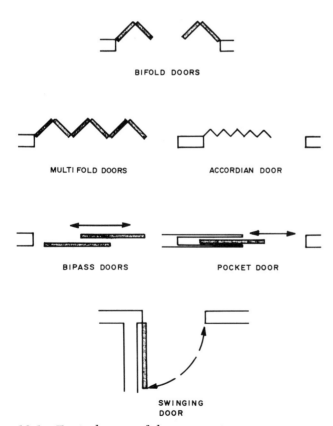

BIFOLD DOORS

MULTI FOLD DOORS   ACCORDIAN DOOR

BIPASS DOORS   POCKET DOOR

SWINGING DOOR

16-1   Typical types of door operation.

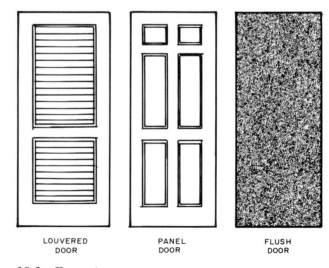

LOUVERED DOOR   PANEL DOOR   FLUSH DOOR

16-2   Doors in common use.

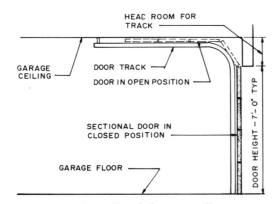

16-3 *A sectional overhead door installation.*

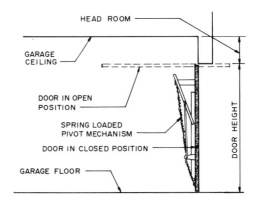

16-4 *A swinging overhead door installation.*

Most garage doors are wood-panel type, steel, aluminum, or fibreglass. The two types in use are the overhead track type and the swinging type. Most garage doors in use are the overhead track type, operated by an electric motor (see 16-3). The swinging type are available but find limited use (see 16-4).

Door swings are indicated in the architectural drawings. They are described as shown in 16-5. The swing is described as *right-hand* or *left-hand* depending on the side containing the hinges. The hand of the door depends on the position of the person facing the door. If the person is outside the building facing the door or inside the building in a hall facing a door and the hinges are on the left side it is a *left-hand* door, and the door should swing away from you into the building or the room. If the door swings towards the person it is called a *left-hand reverse*. The same principles apply to right-hand doors.

Installing Prehung Exterior Doors

The exterior door and frame are usually delivered to the site completely assembled, weatherstripped, and ready for installation. The frame is often braced, and the door held centered in the fame with wedges. Do not remove these until the frame is securely in place on the wall.

There are several types of frames and sills manufactured. Examples of the commonly used sill details are shown in 16-6. One type requires the header and joist to be cut away a little to allow for the sloped sill. Another is designed to sit flat on the subfloor, while another sits on the header and the subfloor butts against it. Some exterior doors are installed with metal sills.

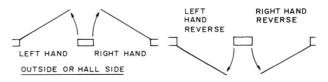

16-5 *Door swings are described by the location of the hinge and the direction of the swing.*

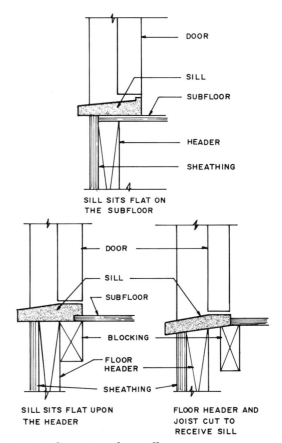

16-6 *Typical exterior door sills.*

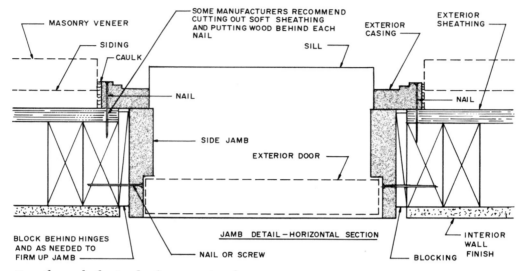

MASONRY VENEER

SIDING

CAULK

SOME MANUFACTURERS RECOMMEND
CUTTING OUT SOFT SHEATHING
AND PUTTING WOOD BEHIND EACH
NAIL

SILL

EXTERIOR
CASING

EXTERIOR
SHEATHING

NAIL

SIDE JAMB

EXTERIOR DOOR

NAIL

JAMB   DETAIL—HORIZONTAL SECTION

BLOCK BEHIND HINGES
AND AS NEEDED TO
FIRM UP JAMB

NAIL OR SCREW

INTERIOR
WALL
FINISH

BLOCKING

16-7   *A section through the jamb of an exterior door.*

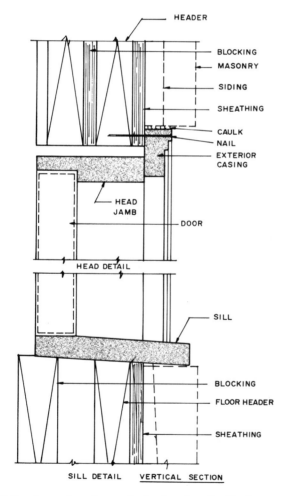

HEADER

BLOCKING

MASONRY

SIDING

SHEATHING

CAULK

NAIL

EXTERIOR
CASING

HEAD
JAMB

DOOR

HEAD DETAIL

SILL

BLOCKING

FLOOR HEADER

SHEATHING

SILL DETAIL   VERTICAL SECTION

16-8   *A section through the head and sill of an exterior door and frame.*

Prehung exterior door units are available as single-door units, double-door units, and units with side-lights. They should be installed following the directions of the manufacturer. Usually a printed instruction sheet accompanies each unit.

Horizontal and vertical sections through typical exterior door frames are shown in 16-7 and 16-8. The exterior casing fits flush against the sheathing. The siding, or masonry veneer, butts against the exterior casing.

Following is a typical procedure for installing prehung exterior doors.

1. Be certain the opening has been covered with building paper and the sill flashed with aluminum.

2. Set the door into the rough opening from the exterior of the building.

3. Check to be certain the sill is level. If it is not, shim it at the floor. Some framers place several rows of caulking below the sill to get a tight seal. Some manufacturers recommend placing a screw through the sill into the subfloor.

4. The door frame must be plumb in two directions. It must be plumb and square so that the door fits properly. It must also be plumb in relationship to the wall so that the door does not swing open by itself or swing closed by itself, when it should stay open (see 16-9).

230

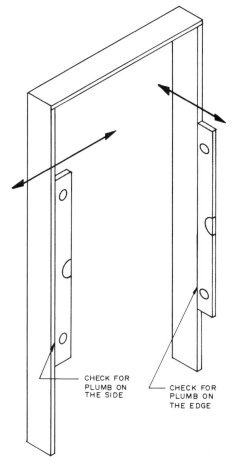

16-9   *The door frame must be plumb in both directions.*

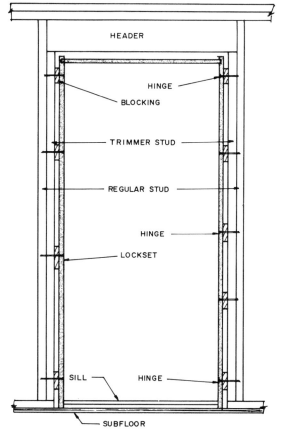

16-10   *Blocking the exterior door frame.*

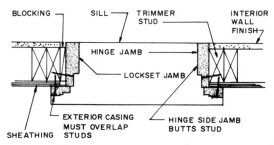

16-11   *An alternate way to install an exterior door frame.*

5. Place wedge-shaped blocking between the door jamb and trimmer stud to hold the frame plumb. Be certain the casing is firm against the sheathing. Drive one casing nail through the casing into the studs on both sides. Do not set the nails at this time, because they may have to be removed for readjustment.

6. Place blocking between the jamb and studs on the hinge side, and, when plumb, nail through the jamb and blocking into the stud. Use 16d galvanized casing nails. Place blocking behind each hinge location, and nail with two 16d casing nails (see 16-10).

7. Now nail the other jamb, placing blocking at the lockset and other locations as shown in 16-10. Place 16d galvanized nails in the lockset area, after making certain that the lockset hole in the door and the hole in the jamb are in line.

The head jamb may require blocking and be nailed to the header to make certain that it is straight and level.

8. Some framers prefer to place the jamb with the hinges tight against the stud, shimming only enough to get it plumb (see 16-11). The rough opening must be narrow enough to allow the exterior casing to lap over the sheathing and trimmer stud on the lockset side.

9. Check to be certain that when the door closes, the opening around the edges is uniform, and that it does not rub on the jamb. Also check to be certain the door hits the door stop uniformly on all sides.

10. If all is plumb and the door fits the opening correctly, set the nails and cut off any shims sticking beyond the frame.

11. Then nail through the casing into the studs on all sides of the frame and set the heads.

Installing Interior Frames with Prehung Doors

Most **interior doors** and frames are assembled in the factory and have the door hung in the frame by hinges. The door usually has holes bored for the lockset. The unit consists of a frame and door and, if ordered, has precut casing (see 16-12). There are two types of frames generally available, a one-piece frame and a split frame (see 16-13).

One-piece jambs are installed by placing the frame in the rough opening, adjusting it so that it is plumb, installing blocking on each side, and nailing through the side jamb and blocking into the stud (see 16-14). Wedge-shaped blocks are often used, because they are easy to adjust when plumbing the frame. The nails are placed in the area to be covered by the door stop. The blocking is placed behind each hinge and the lockset area and in other places as needed to plumb and reinforce the frame (see 16-15). Once the frame is in place, the casing is installed.

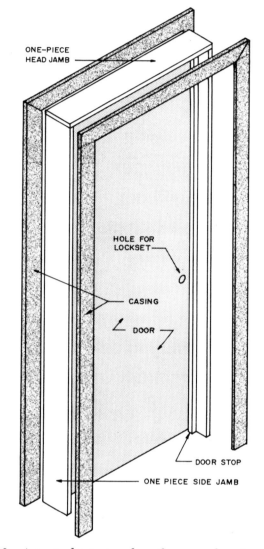

16-12 *A typical interior door frame and casing.*

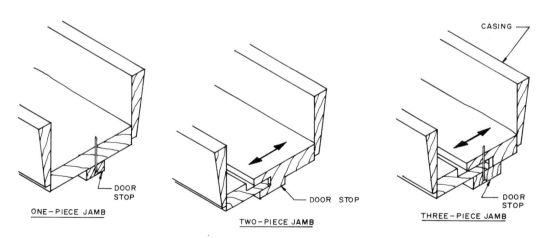

16-13 *Three types of interior door frames.*

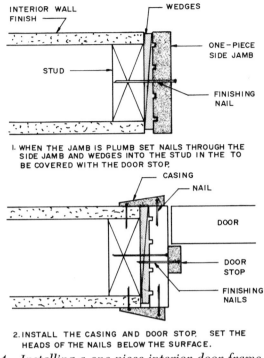

1. WHEN THE JAMB IS PLUMB SET NAILS THROUGH THE SIDE JAMB AND WEDGES INTO THE STUD IN THE TO BE COVERED WITH THE DOOR STOP.

2. INSTALL THE CASING AND DOOR STOP. SET THE HEADS OF THE NAILS BELOW THE SURFACE.

16-14 *Installing a one-piece interior door frame.*

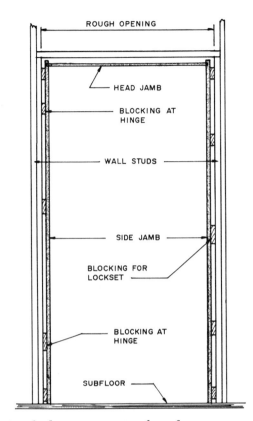

16-15 *Blocking an interior door frame.*

Some types of interior door frames have the casing nailed on one side in the factory. After installation, the precut casing for the other side is nailed in place. The door frame width should be the same as the width of the interior wall. This is specified when ordering. Widths wider than normal may arrive with an extender strip that is glued and nailed to the basic jamb (see 16-16).

Split interior door jambs usually have the casing applied in the factory. One side is installed first, by nailing the casing to the stud. The jamb then has blocking installed as described for one-piece jambs. Then, the other half is inserted from the other side and nailed in place through the casing. The doorstop is nailed as shown in 16-17. The tongue-and-groove slip joint enables the jamb to adjust for variances in wall thickness.

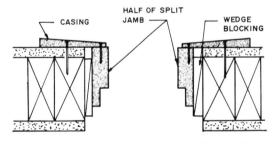

1. INSTALL ONE HALF OF THE SPLIT JAMB BY NAILING THROUGH THE CASING AND BLOCKING.

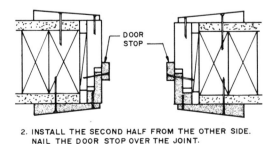

2. INSTALL THE SECOND HALF FROM THE OTHER SIDE. NAIL THE DOOR STOP OVER THE JOINT.

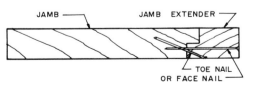

16-16 *Jambs can be made wider by adding a jamb extender.*

16-17 *Installing a split jamb interior door frame.*

233

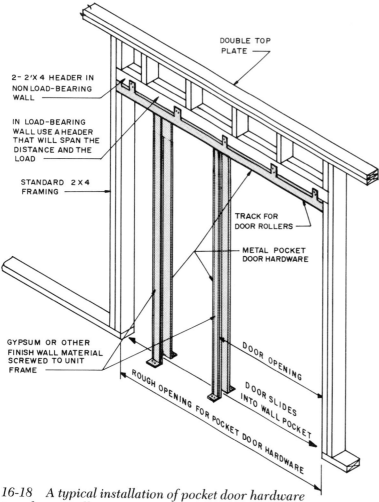

16-18 *A typical installation of pocket door hardware in a frame wall.*

16-19 *A complete set of hardware for a pocket door.* (Courtesy Johnson Hardware)

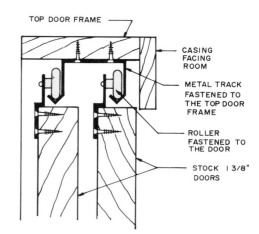

16-20 *Typical hardware for a bypass sliding door installation.*

Installing Pocket Doors

Pocket doors slide into the wall using a special door frame. The pocket frame and track are installed as the wall is rough-framed (see 16-18). Follow the directions that accompany the pocket door frame. The parts of a frame as delivered to the job are shown in 16-19. Hardware for 2 × 4 and 2 × 6 walls is available.

Installing Bypass Sliding Doors

The rough opening for a **bypass sliding door** is framed as described for other doors. The door frame and trim are installed in the normal manner. One-piece frames are used, because door stops are not required.

The door slides on rollers that run in an overhead track (see 16-20). The track is screwed to the top

jamb. The rollers are secured to the doors. Any type door can be used. However, the track selected must accommodate the door. Most commonly 1⅜-inch-thick interior doors are used (see 16-21). After the doors are hung, the floor guides are screwed to the floor. Be certain to have the doors plumb, before securing the floor guide.

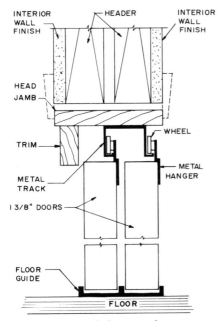

16-21 *A section through bypass doors.*

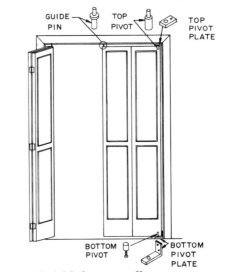

16-22 *A typical bifold door installation.*

Installing Bifold Doors

The opening for **bifold doors** is framed with a solid frame, as discussed for other doors. The doors are hinged, enabling them to fold as they open. The sides of the doors next to the jamb have a metal pivot installed on the top and bottom. A metal pivot plate is installed on the floor and top jamb (see 16-22). A metal track is screwed to the top jamb and runs across the door opening. A pin is placed on the top edge of the interior door. The pin runs in the track, keeping the doors moving in a straight line.

Installing Sliding Exterior Doors

Follow the instructions that come with the **sliding exterior door** unit. Procedures differ with each brand of door. Following is a typical installation procedure.

1. Remove the door from the carton. Leave all shims and braces in place until the door is installed.

2. Check to see that the rough opening is the correct size and that the studs are plumb and the floor level. Be certain that clearances on all sides are those recommended by the manufacturer. A generalized drawing showing a section through a unit is given in 16-23.

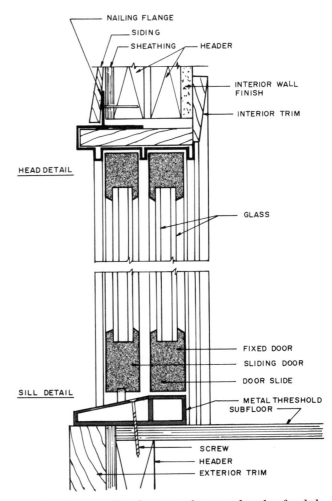

16-23 *A generalized section showing details of a sliding exterior door installation.*

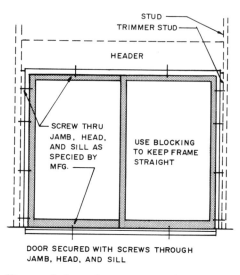

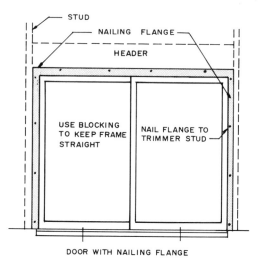

16-24   *Installing a sliding glass exterior door.*

3. If necessary raise the door unit to allow the operating panel to clear the finished floor (carpet, hardwood floors, etc).

4. Clean the area around the door opening so that it is free of dust and debris. Lay three beads of caulking across the opening to seal the sill to the subfloor. Run the caulking several inches up the sides on each side.

5. Slide the door unit into the opening, and center it in the rough opening.

6. Sliding glass doors are secured to the studs and header by either the wood casing, a fin-type flange, or clips. Nail or screw one top corner to the stud. Check the unit to be certain it is plumb and level. Nail or screw each of the other three corners after shimming where needed. Some manufacturers recommend using 8d box nails.

7. Move the door in the unit to be certain it glides smoothly. Adjust the frame with shims, if necessary. Some doors have adjusting screws at the bottom that are used to regulate the gap between the door and the jamb.

8. Nail or screw completely around the frame. Some manufacturers recommend nailing every 10 inches. The metal threshold will have predrilled holes for screws to go into the subfloor (see 16-24).

9. Some units have screws through predrilled holes in the frame that go through the wedges and into the trimmer stud (refer to 16-24). Use as much blocking as necessary to get the frame straight. Drill additional holes as needed to straighten the frame.

10. Caulk around all sides of the frame.

Windows

Wood windows are manufactured to the quality standards established by the National Woodwork Manufacturers Association. These standards cover all aspects of the fabrication and materials used in wood window construction. Aluminum- and plastic-framed windows are also used in light-frame construction.

Types of Windows

The style and type of window is indicated in the architectural drawings on the building elevations and the window schedule. Windows are of three basic types, sliding, swinging, or fixed. Sliding windows move vertically or horizontally. Swinging windows are hinged at the top, bottom, or side (see 16-25).

Double-Hung and Single-Hung Windows

Double-hung windows have two sashes that slide vertically. They are held in position by various devices, such as springs and friction. **Single-hung windows** have the top sash fixed, while the lower sash moves vertically (see 16-26).

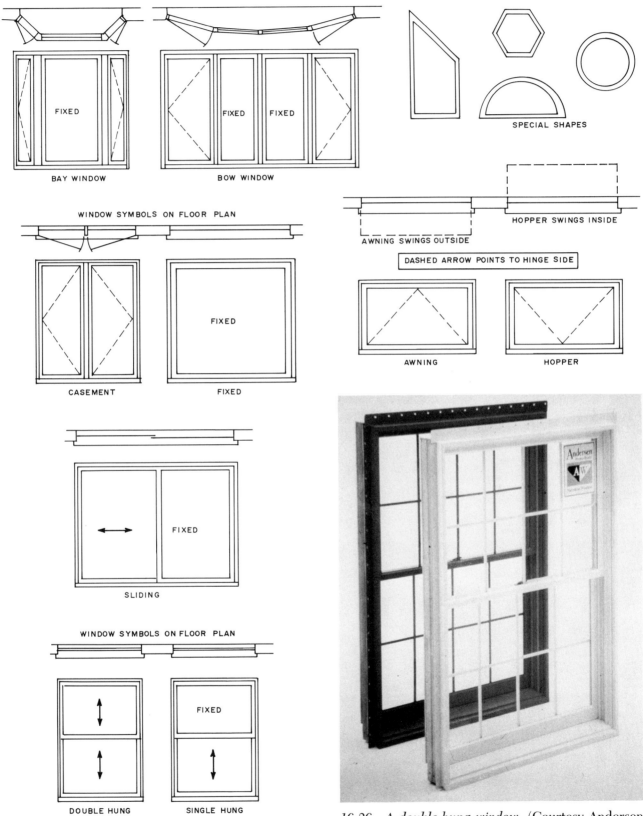

16-25   *Commonly used types of windows.*

16-26   *A double-hung window.* (Courtesy Andersen Corporation)

16-27 *A horizontal sliding window.* (Courtesy Andersen Corporation)

16-28 *A casement window.* (Courtesy Andersen Corporation)

Sliding Windows

Sliding windows move horizontally in a metal track. Generally a two-sash sliding window will have one sash fixed and one that moves (see 16-27).

Casement Windows

Casement windows are a type of swinging window that is hinged on the side. They have some form of crank arrangement to open and close the sash. Casement windows are made in a variety of arrangements, ranging from a single swinging sash to a multiple-sash unit in which some are fixed (see 16-28).

Awning and Hopper Windows

Awning windows are a type of swinging window that hinges from the top. They usually come as single units and can be stacked one above the other or beside the other, to produce multiple openings. They have the advantage of allowing the window to be open during a rain. **Hopper units** have the hinge at the bottom and the top swings out. It permits the window to be open, but blocks the direct flow of air on the people inside the area (see 16-29).

16-29 *A hopper window.* (Courtesy Andersen Corporation)

238

16-30 *A fixed window combined with an awning window.* (Courtesy Andersen Corporation)

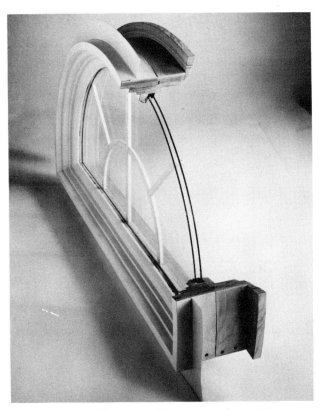

16-31 *A round or circle top window.* (Courtesy Andersen Corporation)

Fixed Windows

Fixed windows are secured to the frame so that they do not move. They allow light to enter the area and permit an unobstructed view from inside. They are often combined with moving types of windows (see 16-30).

Special Windows

Window manufacturers offer an extensive array of special window shapes which are usually fixed in the frame. These include **round tops**, which are generally placed on top of one of the standard types (see 16-31). Other types are illustrated in 16-25.

Roof Windows

Roof windows are installed on the roof and have a framed opening into the building, permitting light and, in some cases, ventilation. Those with moving sash have the hinge on the top of the unit. They are opened with a crank (see 16-32).

16-32 *A roof window.* (Courtesy Andersen Corporation)

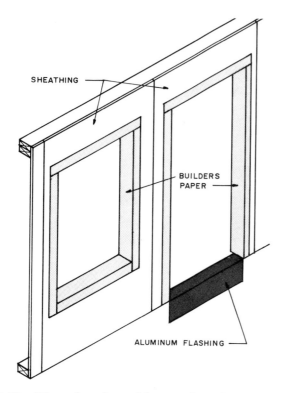

SHEATHING

BUILDERS PAPER

ALUMINUM FLASHING

16-33   Wrap the edges of door and window openings with builder's paper before installing the frames.

Installing Windows

Windows arrive on the job carefully packed to prevent damage. Place the units in the rooms where they will be used. Do not remove from the packing, until they are needed for installation. After removal, examine for damage. Keep all factory-applied bracing and spacer strips on the unit until it has been installed. Windows not shipped in cartons should be wrapped in plastic and stored in a safe, dry place on the job.

Check the rough opening to see if the trimmer studs are plumb and the sill is level. If they are not, shimming may be necessary. Be certain the rough opening is the correct size. Window manufacturers recommend rough opening sizes for their units. These are often recorded on the architectural drawings as part of the window schedule. If this information is not given, framers will typically allow ½-inch clearance on each side and ¾-inch clearance at the top.

Before installing the unit, tack builder's paper around the edges of the rough opening to reduce air infiltration (see 16-33).

Before beginning the installation, study the manufacturer's directions. Many framers keep copies of

CASEMENT & DOUBLE HUNG BOW/BAY INSTALLATION INSTRUCTIONS

1. Remove aligner trim.

2. Insert unit in rough opening. Shim unit square. (**TIP:** Cedar shake or precut wedge shaped shims work best.) Place four shims in each jamb behind the predrilled holes and three shims in the head. Check unit squareness by measuring diagonally from corner to corner. Measure unit width at top, middle, and bottom; all measurements must be equal. Then check to make sure unit is plumb.

3. Secure unit with eight 10 x 4″ screws through predrilled holes in jamb aligner. Also secure through head and seat board with 16 penny finish nails supplied. Recheck unit squareness and plumbness. Adjust shims if necessary.

4. Secure aligner trim to unit with 4 penny finish nails supplied.

IMPORTANT: Support brackets or cables are supplied by others and must be installed for primary support.

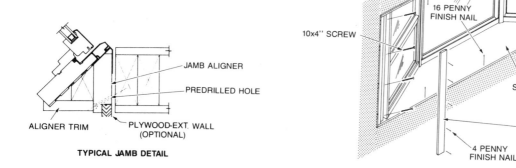

JAMB ALIGNER

PREDRILLED HOLE

ALIGNER TRIM

PLYWOOD-EXT. WALL (OPTIONAL)

TYPICAL JAMB DETAIL

SHIM

HEAD BOARD

16 PENNY FINISH NAIL

10x4″ SCREW

SEAT BOARD

ALIGNER TRIM

4 PENNY FINISH NAIL

16-34   An installation instruction sheet. (Courtesy BiltBest Windows)

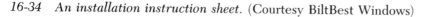

CLAD DOUBLE-HUNGS

INSTALLATION DETAILS—2 x 4 Frame and Wood Siding

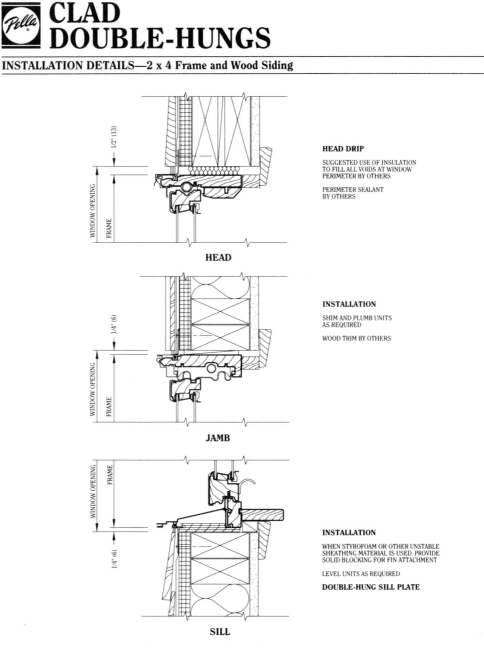

HEAD

HEAD DRIP

SUGGESTED USE OF INSULATION TO FILL ALL VOIDS AT WINDOW PERIMETER BY OTHERS

PERIMETER SEALANT BY OTHERS

JAMB

INSTALLATION

SHIM AND PLUMB UNITS AS REQUIRED

WOOD TRIM BY OTHERS

SILL

INSTALLATION

WHEN STYROFOAM OR OTHER UNSTABLE SHEATHING MATERIAL IS USED. PROVIDE SOLID BLOCKING FOR FIN ATTACHMENT

LEVEL UNITS AS REQUIRED

DOUBLE-HUNG SILL PLATE

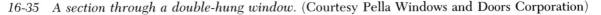

NOTE: THESE DETAILS ARE FOR TYPICAL SINGLE PUNCH OPENINGS. SEE SECTION 25 FOR MULTIPLE UNIT DETAIL CONSIDERATIONS.

16-35 *A section through a double-hung window.* (Courtesy Pella Windows and Doors Corporation)

manufacturer's installation instructions so that they are readily available. Some companies place an instruction sheet with each unit (see 16-34).

Generally, the window heads are aligned with the door heads. The height of the window head can be marked on the trimmer stud. This speeds up the installation of the window.

A section through a double-hung window that is typical of the type of detailed information available from window manufacturers is shown in 16-35. This is useful for architects and builders and available in a variety of bulletins and manuals. It shows how to frame the rough sill, head, and jamb and the blocking required.

CLAD DOUBLE-HUNGS

SIZE TABLE   Window opening dimensions apply to single units only.

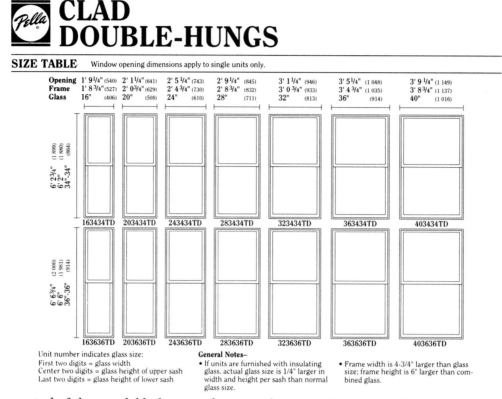

| | 163434TD | 203434TD | 243434TD | 283434TD | 323434TD | 363434TD | 403434TD |

Opening 1' 9¼" (540) 2' 1¼" (641) 2' 5¼" (743) 2' 9¼" (845) 3' 1¼" (946) 3' 5¼" (1 048) 3' 9¼" (1 149)
Frame 1' 8¾" (527) 2' 0¾" (629) 2' 4¾" (730) 2' 8¾" (832) 3' 0¾" (933) 3' 4¾" (1 035) 3' 8¾" (1 137)
Glass 16" (406) 20" (508) 24" (610) 28" (711) 32" (813) 36" (914) 40" (1 016)

| 163636TD | 203636TD | 243636TD | 283636TD | 323636TD | 363636TD | 403636TD |

Unit number indicates glass size:
First two digits = glass width
Center two digits = glass height of upper sash
Last two digits = glass height of lower sash

General Notes–
• If units are furnished with insulating glass, actual glass size is 1/4" larger in width and height per sash than normal glass size.

• Frame width is 4-3/4" larger than glass size; frame height is 6" larger than combined glass.

16-36   Data typical of that available from window manufacturers. (Courtesy Pella Windows and Doors Corporation)

Accompanying the section information are detailed rough-opening sizes for all the double-hung windows available from this manufacturer. An example of these data is in given in 16-36. This information is available for all the types of windows manufactured.

Two types of window sill are in common use. One type sits flat on the rough sill (see 16-37), and the other is at an angle to the sill (see 16-38). Manufacturer's instructions include blocking and nailing instructions.

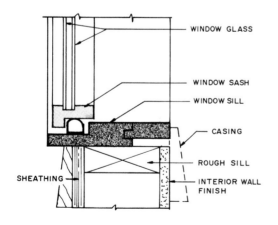

16-37   The sill of this window unit sits flat on the rough sill.

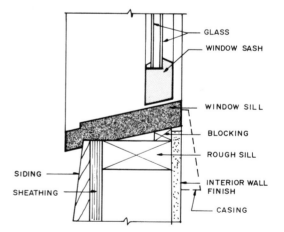

16-38   The sill of this window unit is on an angle to the rough sill.

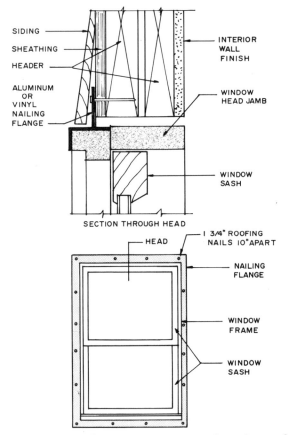

SECTION THROUGH HEAD

SET NAILS BELOW SURFACE OF CASING

16-39 Some window units are secured to the studs and header by nailing through a flange.

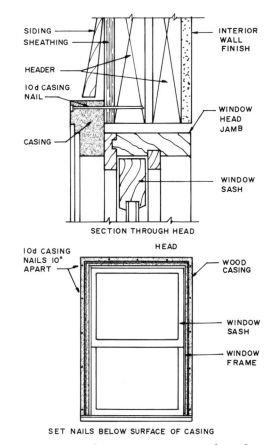

SECTION THROUGH HEAD

16-40 Some window units are secured to the studs and header by nailing through a wood casing.

Most window units are installed from the outside. Since windows are heavy, have several workers involved in moving them outside and lifting them into position in the rough opening. Some install the windows while the wall framing is horizontal on the floor. This eliminates the need of lifting them into position, especially in openings that are quite some distance above the ground.

Once the window unit is in the rough opening, nail it temporarily to the trimmer stud, but do not drive the nail in all the way. Then, using shims at the sill, raise it to the required height. Be certain to place shims at both ends of the unit and in several places in between.

Next, check the side jambs for plumb with a level, and check the corners of the frame with a framing square to be certain that it is still square. It is best to keep the sash closed and locked. This helps keep the unit square. Once the unit is plumb and square, drive several nails through the casing or flange provided for

joining it to the wall. Then see if the sash operates smoothly with no binding. Any sag or bow in the frame should be corrected by placing blocking between the frame and the stud, and nailing through the jamb. Once all is correct, finish nailing the unit to the studs, sill, and header through the casing or flange (see 16-39 and 16-40). Use aluminum or galvanized casing nails when nailing through the casing. When nailing through a flange, use 1¾-inch roofing nails through the predrilled holes in the flange.

When nailing a flange through soft sheathing, such as rigid foam, some manufacturers recommend cutting away the sheathing behind each nail and replacing it with solid wood. This gives the flange a solid connection to the stud. If nails through flanges are set too much with soft sheathing, they may break through the flange. The window will not have a solid base.

Manufacturers' installation manuals also have recommended procedures for caulking the units during installation and specify the type of caulking to use.

243

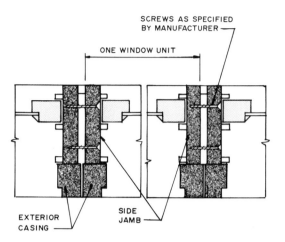

16-41   *Installation details for joining two window units without a wide mullion.*

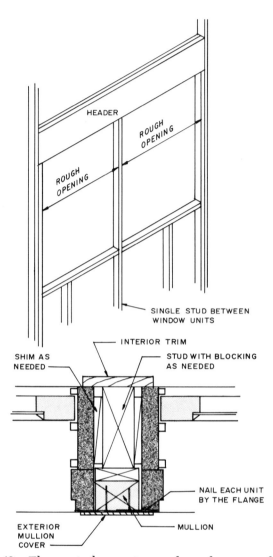

16-42   *These window units are butted to a stud to form a mullion between them.*

Often two or more window units are joined to form a series of windows. Sometimes they are stacked on top of each other. It is important to follow the detailed installation instructions. One type of installation has the jambs butt each other, and these are joined with screws (see 16-41). Another method is to frame the rough opening, placing a stud between each unit. The windows are installed in the normal manner, and some type of mullion trim strip is applied over the area between the windows. Some manufacturers supply a strip for this purpose (see 16-42).

Installing Bow and Bay Windows

Bow and **bay windows** usually arrive on the site fully assembled. If they come knocked down, special instructions from the manufacturer must be followed to assure proper assembly. These units are very heavy. They require several people to move them and to lift them into the rough opening. Be certain that the unit is not allowed to twist or bend.

Installation instructions vary a great deal from one manufacturer to another. It is important to follow the instructions that come with the unit.

Following is a generalized description of an installation process that covers many of the instructions to be followed.

1. The rough opening must be of the size recommended by the manufacturer and be square, level, and plumb. The rough sill should be doubled.

2. Some form of platform is required to provide support. In 16-43 the unit has a ¾-inch plywood platform that is nailed to the sill and a head platform that is nailed to the header. Another system uses a ¾-inch plywood platform that is supported by braces below it (see 16-44). In all cases, the manufacturers recommend a brace be placed below the unit.

3. Slide the unit into the rough opening. Block and shim it, until it is centered in the opening and is level and plumb. Notice that the seat board extends past the stud and covers the interior wall finish material.

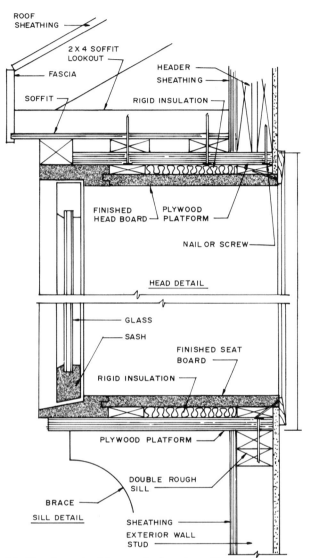

HEAD DETAIL

SILL DETAIL

16-43   *A typical bow window installation.*

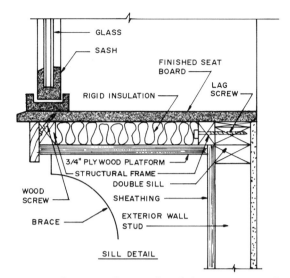

SILL DETAIL

16-44   *Another installation detail for a bow window.*

Installation details for bay windows are very much like those for bow windows.

Installing Roof Windows

The opening in the roof must be framed to support the roof load. Some roof windows fit between rafters spaced 24 inches O.C. Others are wider and require a rafter be cut. A typical framed opening is shown in 16-45.

4. In the unit in 16-43 the platforms are nailed to the sill and header with 10d ring-shank nails spaced 8 inches apart. The top platform is also nailed into the soffit lookouts. The finished head and seat boards are then installed over a layer of rigid insulation.

5. In 16-44 a ¾-inch plywood platform is built, extending from the sheathing. It is supported by braces below. Blocking and insulation are placed on top of this, and the bow window unit is supported by the sill and this platform.

6. Apply exterior trim supplied by the manufacturer.

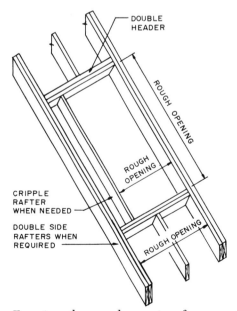

16-45   *Framing the rough opening for a roof window.*

When the opening requires a rafter be cut, double the rafters on each side of the opening. They should be the same size as the regular rafters and run the full span. The headers on each side of the opening must be doubled. The size of the rough opening is specified by the window manufacturer. The opening must be square and very close to the required size.

Some manufacturers size their roof windows 22½ inches to fit between rafters spaced 24 inches O.C. without cutting a rafter. A 30½-inch-wide unit will fit between two 16 inches O.C. rafters, requiring one rafter to be cut and headers installed. A 46½-inch unit will fit between two rafters spaced 24 inches O.C., requiring one rafter to be cut.

The installation can take several forms as shown in 16-46. The one used depends on the design of the architect. The opening is framed with 2 × 4 stock and covered with an interior finish material such as gypsum board.

Following are typical directions for installing a roof window.

1. After the rough opening is built and the roof sheathing is applied, cover the sheathing with roofing felt. Apply roofing cement for about 8 to 10 inches around the perimeter of the rough opening, and press the roofing felt into it. Leave a flap of felt so that it can be turned up on the side of the frame.

2. Center the roof window frame in the rough opening. Temporarily secure it on two sides. Check the diagonals to be certain that it is square. If it is a unit that opens, make certain that it opens and closes properly, before fully securing it in place.

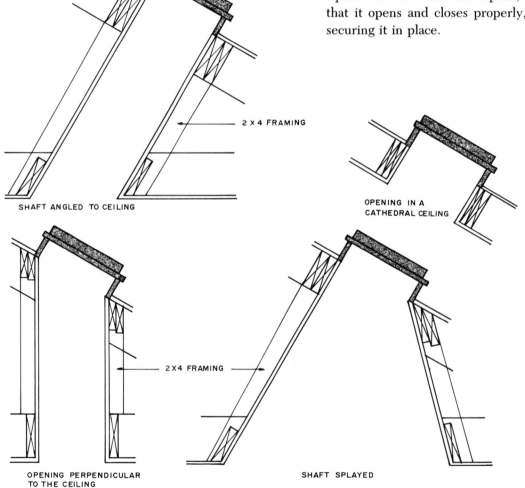

SHAFT ANGLED TO CEILING

2 X 4 FRAMING

OPENING IN A
CATHEDRAL CEILING

OPENING PERPENDICULAR
TO THE CEILING

2 X 4 FRAMING

SHAFT SPLAYED

16-46 *Typical ways to install roof windows.*

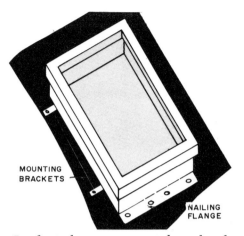

16-47 *Roof windows are secured to the sheathing and rafters with metal mounting brackets or flanges that are on all sides of the unit.*

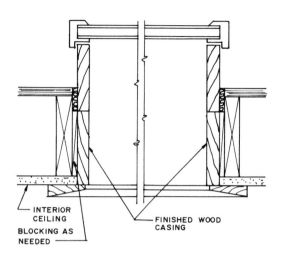

16-48 *A typical roof window installation with wood-cased sides.*

3. When the unit is plumb and square, secure the mounting brackets or flanges to the sheathing and roof framing. Some units use wood screws through mounting brackets. Others use 2-inch roofing nails through a nailing flange (see 16-47).

4. Caulk between the frame and the rough opening.

5. Run the roofing felt up the side of the frame.

6. Install flashing as shown on the instruction sheet.

Typical installation details are shown in 16-48 and 16-49.

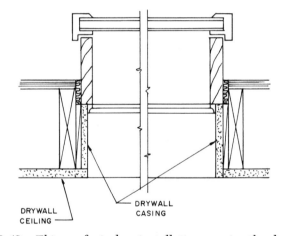

16-49 *This roof window installation carries the drywall into the window opening.*

17

Stairs

The stair design is shown on the architectural working drawings. The designer shows the number of treads and risers and their sizes, the shape of the stair, and the design of the handrail. Simple stairs are built using stock parts bought from a building supply dealer.

Stair Shapes

The basic stair shapes include straight, L-shaped, U-shaped, and spiral or circular. They may be enclosed on all sides by walls or have open side areas that require some type of handrail.

Straight stairs are the most common and easiest to build. They run from one floor to the next with no turns. Straight stairs are often physically tiring for the user, however. A landing can be provided partway up to provide some relief. Building codes limit the rise between landings to 12 feet, but shorter rises are desirable. The size of the landing in the direction of travel should equal the width of the stair but need not be greater than 4 feet (see 17-1).

U-shaped stairs make a 180-degree turn by having a landing midway up the flight and short straight stairs running from the lower floor to the landing and another from the landing to the second floor. They occupy more floor space than a straight stair, and the area occupied may be square or rectangular (see 17-2).

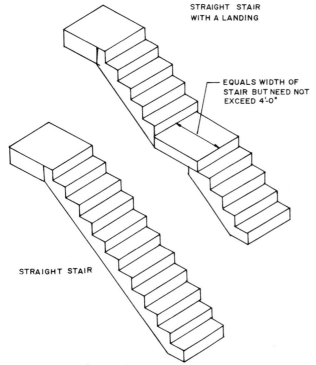

STRAIGHT STAIR
WITH A LANDING

EQUALS WIDTH OF STAIR BUT NEED NOT EXCEED 4'-0"

STRAIGHT STAIR

17-1 *Typical straight stairs.*

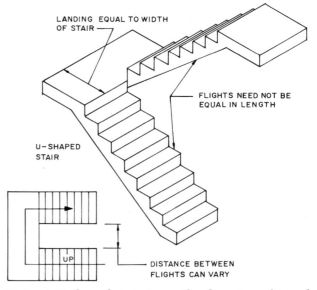

LANDING EQUAL TO WIDTH OF STAIR

FLIGHTS NEED NOT BE EQUAL IN LENGTH

U-SHAPED STAIR

UP

DISTANCE BETWEEN FLIGHTS CAN VARY

17-2 *A U-shaped stair turns the direction of travel 180 degrees.*

L-shaped stairs make a 90-degree turn by placing a landing somewhere in the stair. The landing can be anywhere in the stair needed to make it serve its purpose. An L-shaped stair, as in the U-shaped stair, is made of a landing and two flights of straight stairs (see 17-3). **Winders** may be used on an L-shaped stair instead of a landing (see 17-4). Winders are triangular treads used to turn the direction of the stair. They are *hazardous* because the surface area of the treads is small and their shape is irregular. They are avoided whenever possible. Their advantage is that they reduce the floor area needed by the stair. Building codes specify the requirements for use of winders. A typical specification is given in 17-5.

Spiral or circular stairs are purchased from companies manufacturing units that are assembled on the site. They are available in a variety of diameters and can be adjusted for various heights. Some are made to be freestanding, while others fit inside circular or square-walled enclosures (see 17-6). The treads are all triangular and are *more hazardous* than other types. It is also difficult to move furniture on circular stairs. Building codes limit the use of these in residential buildings by specifying the size of the second-floor room they serve.

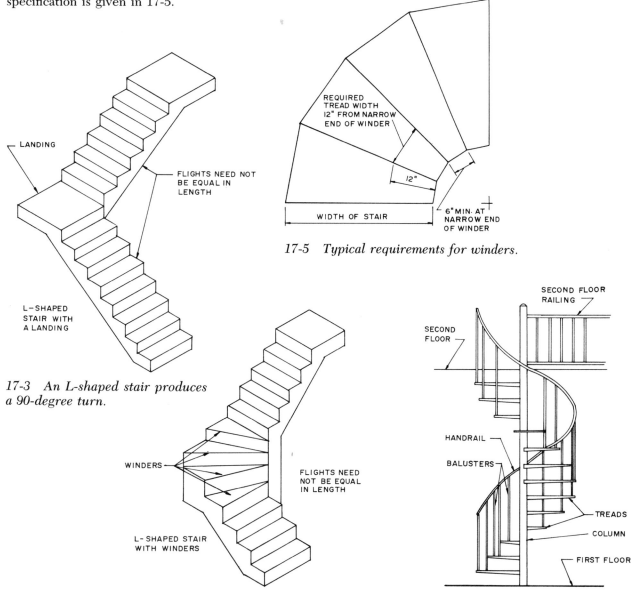

17-5 Typical requirements for winders.

17-3 An L-shaped stair produces a 90-degree turn.

17-4 Winders can be used instead of a landing.

17-6 A typical factory-made spiral stair.

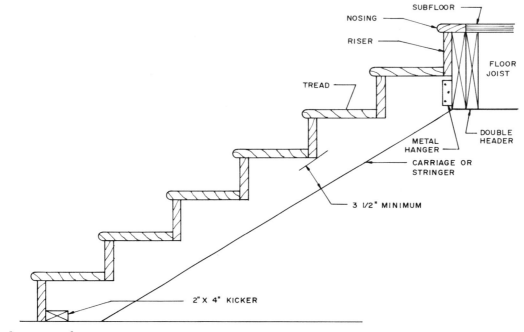

17-7   *The parts of a stair.*

Parts of a Stair

The parts of a typical wood framed stair are shown in 17-7. The load is carried by a notched frame called a **stringer** or **carriage.** This is usually a good-quality 2×12 member and is one continuous piece from floor to floor. The **tread** is the board on which you step. The **riser** is the vertical board that butts the tread.

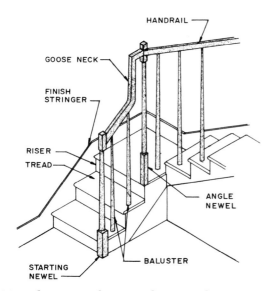

17-8   *The parts of a typical stair railing.*

The **unit run** is the width of the tread, and the **unit rise** is the height of the riser. The rounded edge of the tread that overhangs the riser is the **nosing.**

The parts of a railing are shown in 17-8. All of these parts are available from stair manufacturers. A wide variety of designs are available.

Stair Specifications

The specifications for a stair should be given on the architectural working drawings. They must meet the requirements of the local building codes. The following examples are typical.

Handrails are required on each side of enclosed stairs. Private stairs 30 inches or less in width can have a handrail on just one side. They meet requirements such as those shown in 17-9.

Residential stairs must have a minimum width of 30 to 32 inches and headroom of 6'8". The maximum rise is 8 inches and the minimum tread is 9 inches. Open sides of stairs require some form of a handrail. Required heights range from 30 to 34 inches.

Stair Design

When the floor is framed, the rough opening for the stair is constructed. Its size depends on the design

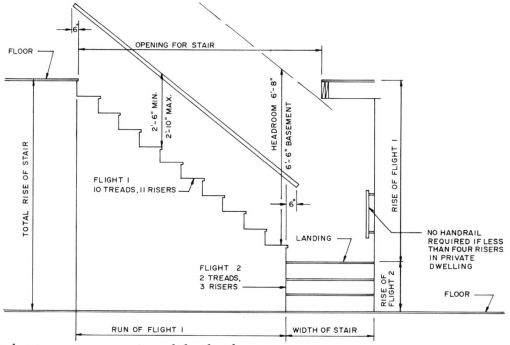

17-9 *Typical stair requirements. Consult local codes.*

of the stair. Usually the stair dimensions are specified on the architectural working drawings (see 17-10). If they are not, the framer must design the stair. One of the first things to do is find the tread and riser sizes, keeping in mind the requirements of the building code.

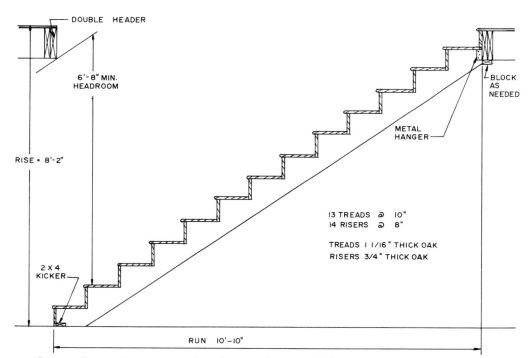

17-10 *A typical stair design drawing, as found on architectural drawings.*

Finding the Number of Steps

Find the total rise. Typically this would be found on a section drawing. A distance of 105⅛ inches is common for a house with an 8-foot ceiling, 2 × 8 ceiling joists, and ¾-inch plywood subfloor on the second level. A 7-inch rise is comfortable and is chosen for the first calculations. Dividing the total rise by 7 gives the number of risers, which is 15. Since the floor at the top of the stair serves as a tread, there is *one less* tread than riser. Therefore this stair has 15 risers of 7 inches and 14 treads. Now select a tread size. The narrower the tread, the steeper the stair, and the less floor are required. The wider the tread, the easier it is to use the stair, but the riser must be reduced. For comfortable use, the tread-to-riser proportion can be ascertained by the formula: two times the riser plus the tread equals 24 to 25. For example, two times an 8-inch riser plus 9-inch tread equals 25. If this stair uses a 9-inch tread, it will have a run of 14 treads times 9 inches, or 126 inches—or 10 feet 6 inches (see 17-11).

If the number of risers comes out uneven, such as 15.8 risers divide the total rise by an even number of risers, such as 16 in this case. This will give the size of the riser to be used.

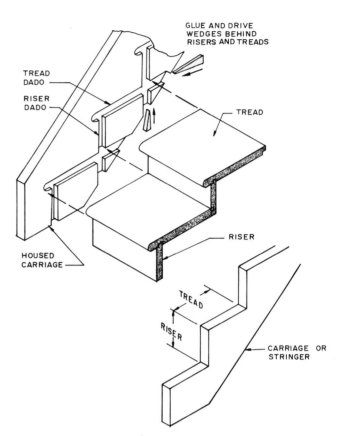

17-12   *Two types of stair carriages.*

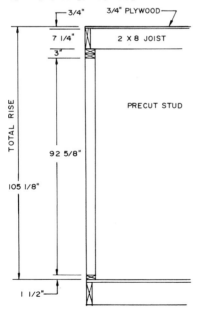

TO FIND THE NUMBER OF RISERS DIVIDE THE TOTAL RISE BY THE DESIRED RISER SIZE. IF THIS COMES OUT UNEVEN, AS 15.8 RISERS, DIVIDE THE TOTAL RISE BY 15 OR 16 TO GET THE ADJUSTED RISER SIZE.

17-11   *Finding the number of treads and risers.*

Stair Construction

Generally, the first thing to do is to lay out and cut the carriage boards. Two types are in use. One is 2-inch stock with the tread and risers cut out. The other has the carriage board dadoed to receive the risers and treads (see 17-12). This last type is often purchased from a stair manufacturer. However, a framer can rout the grooves on the job.

Lay Out the Carriage Board

The tread and riser sizes are set on the framing square with stair gauges. A stair gauge is a small metal clamp placed on the square locating each of the needed dimensions. Lay out each notch as shown in 17-13. Repeat this layout until all the steps are located. Then mark the thickness of the tread board on the first riser. This is the line of cut that makes the first step plus the tread to be the same height as the other risers with treads. The distance between the notch and the bottom of the carriage should be at least 3½ inches.

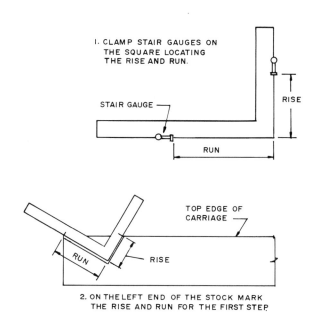

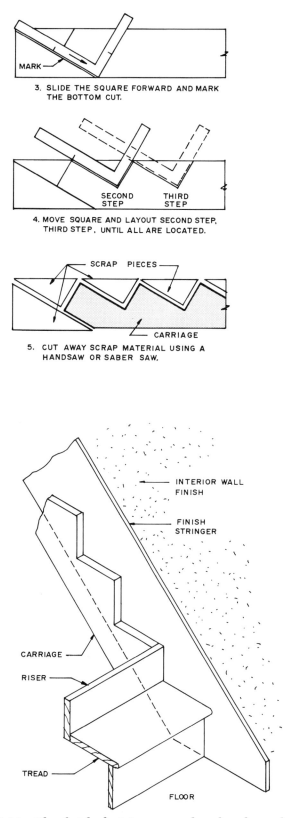

1. CLAMP STAIR GAUGES ON THE SQUARE LOCATING THE RISE AND RUN.

STAIR GAUGE

RISE

RUN

TOP EDGE OF CARRIAGE

RUN

RISE

2. ON THE LEFT END OF THE STOCK MARK THE RISE AND RUN FOR THE FIRST STEP

MARK

3. SLIDE THE SQUARE FORWARD AND MARK THE BOTTOM CUT.

SECOND STEP

THIRD STEP

4. MOVE SQUARE AND LAYOUT SECOND STEP, THIRD STEP, UNTIL ALL ARE LOCATED.

SCRAP PIECES

CARRIAGE

5. CUT AWAY SCRAP MATERIAL USING A HANDSAW OR SABER SAW.

17-13   Laying out a stair carriage.

Cut the carriage using a handsaw or sabre saw. Do not use a circular saw, because it undercuts the mark and weakens the carriage.

Two carriage boards are used on stairs under 3 feet in width and three or more on wider stairs. A third carriage on 3-feet or narrower stairs is a good practice to follow and increases the stiffness of the tread.

Preparing the Rough Opening

Framing an opening in a floor is explained in Chapter 6. It shows that double headers are used on each end, and, in some cases, the floor joists on each side of the opening are doubled when the opening runs parallel with the joists. If the opening runs perpendicular to the joists, a series of tail joists are fastened to double joists along each side of the opening.

Installing the Stair Carriage

The kicker is nailed to the floor, and a ledger, if used, is nailed to the double header as shown in 17-7. Next, a one-inch-thick finished stringer is nailed through the finished wall covering, such as gypsum board, to the wall studs. It gives a finished wood surface to the sides of the stair (see 17-14). Then the carriage board is nailed to the ledger, kicker, and studs. It may be secured to the header with metal hangers instead of a ledger.

INTERIOR WALL FINISH

FINISH STRINGER

CARRIAGE

RISER

TREAD

FLOOR

17-14   The finished stringer can be placed on the wall behind the carriage.

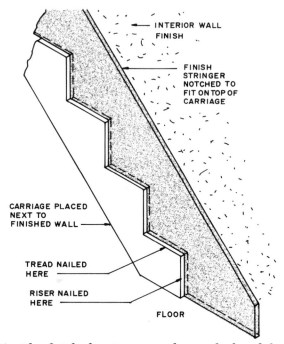

17-15   *The finished stringer can be notched and fit over the carriage tread and riser notches.*

An alternate method is to install the carriage next to the finished wall, and nail a notched finished stringer over it as shown in 17-15. The stringer is usually a 1 × 12 good-quality board. Nail the finish stringer with finishing nails, and set the heads.

Next install the risers. After several have been nailed to the carriage board, install the treads against them. Cut the finished tread boards to width. Remember to allow the specified nosing, which is usually 1 to 1½ inches. Cut away material on the back side of the tread. Nail the treads to the carriage board using finish nails. Drill the nail holes in the tread, if there is a danger of splitting or if the wood is very hard. Set the heads of the nails. Continue working up the stair, installing riser and tread boards.

Installing Housed Carriages

The housed carriage boards are nailed to the header and supported by a ledger or metal hangers. The carriage board supports the treads and risers and serves as the finished stringer. The risers are installed next, starting at the bottom step. Working from behind the stair, the riser is set in the dado and secured lightly with a wood wedge. Then the tread is set in place. The tread wedge is coated with glue and tapped firmly in place. The riser wedge is removed, coated with glue and tapped firmly in place (see 17-16).

Installing Railings

Various types of **railing** are available, and manufacturer's instructions should be followed. Basically, the **ballusters** are evenly spaced, and holes are drilled in the treads and **handrail.** The **newel post** is attached to the floor or carriage as specified by the manufac-

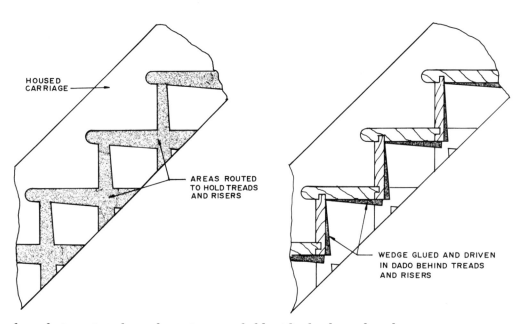

17-16   *Treads and risers in a housed carriage are held with glued-wood wedges.*

turer. The bottom dowel of the balluster is coated with glue and set in the holes in the treads. The top end of the balluster is coated with glue, and the handrail holes are lined up and set upon this end. Any end joints in the handrail are made and glued before installing ballusters. A typical installation is shown in 17-7.

Framing a Landing

Landings are framed much like a floor. The actual support depends on the circumstances, but that shown in 17-17 is typical.

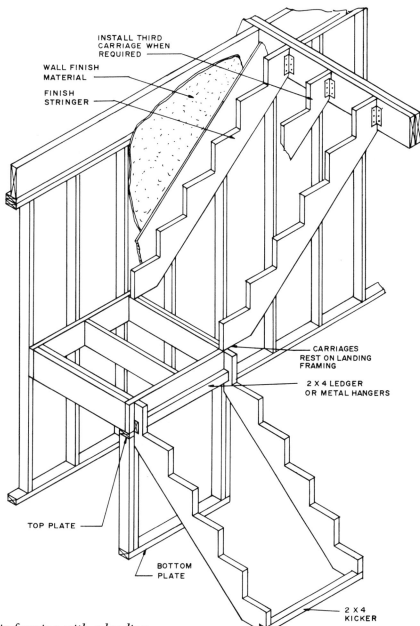

INSTALL THIRD
CARRIAGE WHEN
REQUIRED

WALL FINISH
MATERIAL

FINISH
STRINGER

CARRIAGES
REST ON LANDING
FRAMING

2 X 4 LEDGER
OR METAL HANGERS

TOP PLATE

BOTTOM
PLATE

2 X 4
KICKER

17-17   *Typical stair framing with a landing.*

18

Installing Interior Trim

Various types of mouldings are used to trim the interior of a building. Typical examples are shown in 18-1. Mouldings are available in hardwoods, softwoods, and plastic. They are available unfinished and prefinished.

Casing moulding is used to frame door and window openings and conceals the joint between the finish wall material and the frame. Typical widths range from 1⅝ to 4½ inches.

Base mouldings are used to conceal the joint between the finish wall material and the floor. Typical sizes range from 1¾ to 7¼ inches.

Base shoe moulding is used with the base moulding to conceal the joint between hardwood, softwood, vinyl, or ceramic tile floors and the base moulding. A commonly available size is ½ × ¾ inch. Base shoe moulding is omitted if the floor is to be carpeted.

Quarter round is a general-purpose moulding used wherever an inside corner joint needs to be con-

cealed. Typical sizes are ¼, ½, ¾ and 1¹⁄₁₆ inches.

Panel moulding is used to cover the top edge of panelling when used for wainscotting and to cover other panel joints as needed.

Crown mouldings are used on interiors where the ceiling and partition meet. They can be combined with other mouldings to produce detailed trim (see 18-2). Crown mouldings are available in sizes from 1¾ to 7⅜ inches.

Cove mouldings serve much the same purpose as crown mouldings.

Brick mouldings are nailed to the exterior side of door and window frames. The brick veneer or other siding butt against the moulding.

Drip caps are placed above door and window openings and direct rain out beyond the surface of the door or window.

Corner guards are used to protect the corners of interior partitions that may be damaged by passing traffic.

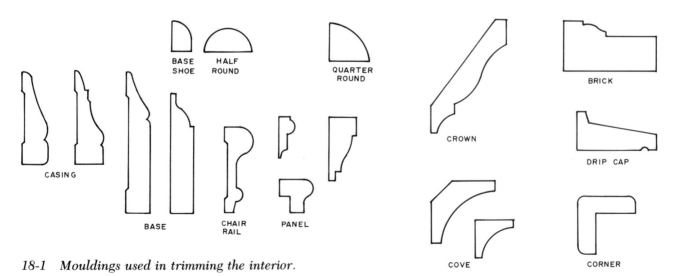

18-1   Mouldings used in trimming the interior.

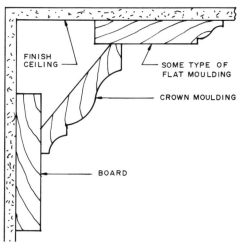

18-2 *Mouldings can be combined to form detailed trim.*

Trimming Wood Framed Windows

Casing around windows may use a **wide stool** and an **apron** or a **narrow stool** and **casing** on all four sides as shown in 18-3 and 18-4. Specific details of window construction vary according to the manufacturer, but the installation of casing is similar for all.

Notice that in 18-3 the casing is installed on all four sides with the corners mitred. It is set back from the window frame 3/16 to 1/4 inch. This is probably the most commonly used method. Another method involves installing a wide window stool along the bottom of the opening as shown in 18-4. The stool extends beyond the sides of the window so that the side casing can butt against it. The casing installed below the stool is called the apron.

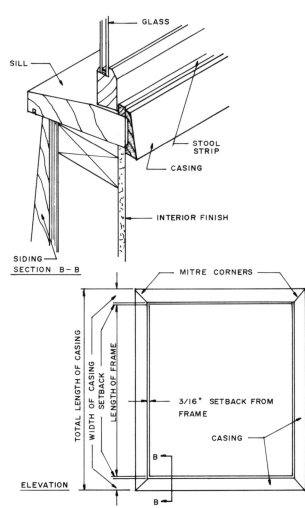

18-3 *The narrow stool is used when the casing is run on all sides of the window opening.*

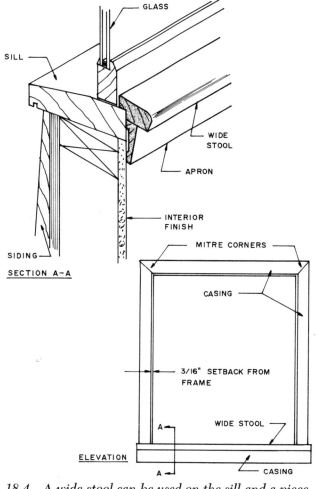

18-4 *A wide stool can be used on the sill and a piece of casing is installed below it. The side casing butts on top of the stool.*

257

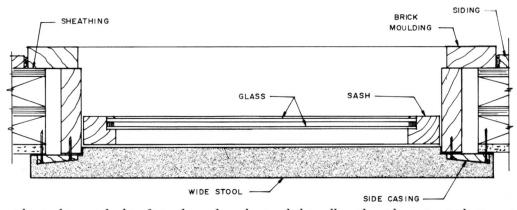

18-5   *The wide stool is notched to fit to the sash and extended to allow the side casing to butt against it.*

If a wide stool is to be used, it is installed first. It is cut to length and notched on each end to permit it to come within ⅛ of an inch of the window sash. It is nailed to the sill. If the stool is to be painted, it can be face-nailed, with nails set and the holes filled. If it is to have a natural finish, it can be toenailed on the edge facing the sash (see 18-5).

When cutting casing, the length is equal to the size of the window frame, plus two times the size of the setback, plus two times the width of the casing. It is nailed using finishing nails, and the heads are set (refer to 18-3).

Bay and bow windows have very wide head and seat boards. These units are cased on all sides as described in 18-3. A typical detail is shown in 18-6. (See Chapter 16 for additional details.)

Casing is nailed at the thin edge into the window frame with 4d or 5d brads. Since there is a danger of splitting the casing, some prefer to drill small holes before nailing. The thicker edge of the casing is nailed through the finish wall material into the studs with 6d or 7d finish or casing nails. They are located in pairs about every 16 inches. The mitre joint has a nail driven into it from the top to attempt to keep if from opening. A glued spline joint in the mitre will be more likely to reduce joint opening. Some plans call for a butt joint at the corners of the casing. Mitre and butt joints are nailed as shown in 18-7.

Door casing is applied much the same as described for window casing. The casing is set in about ³⁄₁₆ of an inch from the edge of the door frame. The length of the side casing is equal to the distance from the surface of the floor to the inside of the door frame plus the setback and the width of the moulding. The length of the top piece is equal to the distance inside the door frame plus twice the setback and twice the width of the moulding. The thin edge of the casing is nailed to the door frame with 4d or 5d brads, and the thicker edge to the stud with 6d or 7d finishing or casing

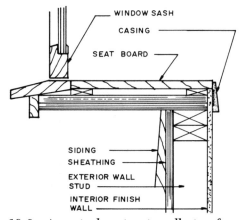

18-6   *A typical casing installation for bow and bay window units.*

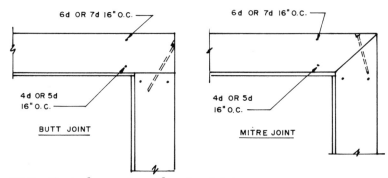

18-7   *Typical ways to nail casing joints.*

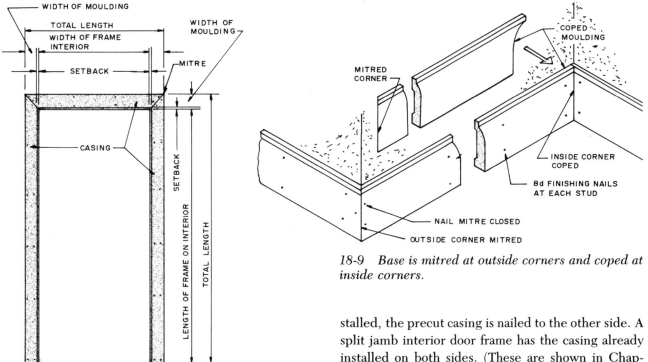

18-8   A typical cased interior door opening.

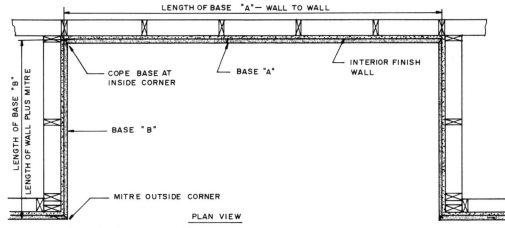

18-9   Base is mitred at outside corners and coped at inside corners.

nails. They are spaced every 16 inches, and the heads are set (see 18-8).

If the floor is to be carpeted, the side casing is run to the subfloor. If it is to have hardwood flooring, the finished flooring is installed before the door openings are cased.

Some interior door frames arrive on the site with the casing nailed to one side. After the unit is in-stalled, the precut casing is nailed to the other side. A split jamb interior door frame has the casing already installed on both sides. (These are shown in Chapter 16.)

Installing Base Moulding

Base moulding is installed with a mitre joint at outside corners and a coped joint at inside corners (see 18-9). The following discussion is related to the layout shown in 18-10. Begin by measuring very carefully the length of wall "A." Cut the ends square and the base to the required length, and nail in place. Do not cut too long, because the base will begin to bow as temperature and moisture changes occur. Nail the

18-10   Measuring the length of sections of base.

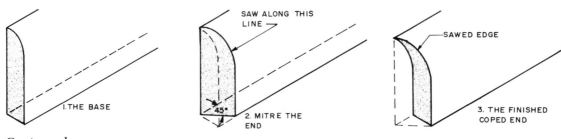

SAW ALONG THIS
LINE →

SAWED EDGE

1.THE BASE

45°

2. MITRE THE
END

3. THE FINISHED
COPED END

18-11   Coping a base.

base to each stud with two 8d finishing nails. Measure the length of base "B." The length is equal to the length of the wall plus the thickness of the base needed for the mitre at the outside corner. The interior corner must be coped. A coped joint hides any crackage that occurs due to shrinkage. To cope the base, cut on a 45-degree mitre. Then, using a coping or sabre saw, cut the shape of the moulding formed by the mitre cut (see 18-11).

The coped base will fit against the abutting base as shown in 18-12. If a base shoe is to be installed, measure, cut, mitre, and cope in the same manner as described for the base. It is nailed into the floor so that if shrinkage occurs, there will be no crack between the base shoe and the floor.

Another type of base is a square-edge board with a moulding, such as a small cove moulding, nailed on top. In this case the inside corner is formed as a simple butt joint, and the moulding is coped and nailed on top. The outside corner is mitred (see 18-13).

If the base material is not long enough to reach without joining two pieces, they may be joined with a scarf joint (see 18-14).

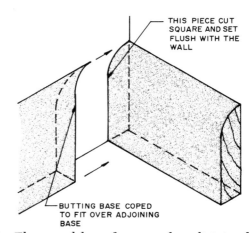

THIS PIECE CUT
SQUARE AND SET
FLUSH WITH THE
WALL

BUTTING BASE COPED
TO FIT OVER ADJOINING
BASE

18-12   The coped base fits over the adjoining base, forming the corner.

Installing Ceiling Moulding

Ceiling moulding uses crown moulding to cover the intersection of the ceiling and wall, as shown in 18-15. A single crown moulding can be used, or a more elaborate installation can be made by combining several mouldings. Outside corners are mitred, and

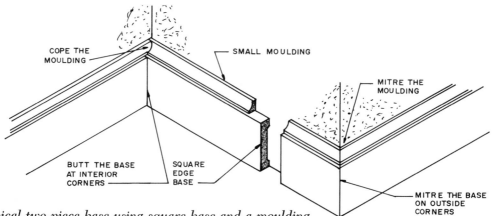

COPE THE
MOULDING

SMALL MOULDING

MITRE THE
MOULDING

BUTT THE BASE
AT INTERIOR
CORNERS

SQUARE
EDGE
BASE

MITRE THE BASE
ON OUTSIDE
CORNERS

18-13   A typical two-piece base using square base and a moulding.

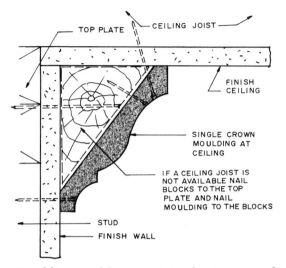

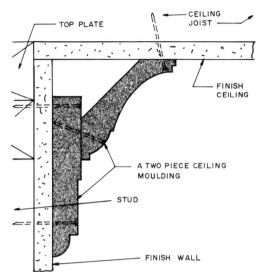

18-14   Mouldings and base are joined using a scarf joint.

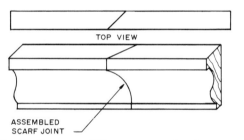

18-15   Ceiling moulding covers the intersection of the wall and ceiling.

inside corners are coped as described for the installation of the base.

The crown moulding is nailed at the bottom into the top plate or a stud in the wall and at the top into a ceiling joist. If a ceiling joist is not available, nail triangular blocks 8 to 10 inches long to the top plate and nail the top edge of the crown moulding to them as shown in 18-15.

Often the moulding is not long enough to reach from one wall to the next. The moulding is joined using a scarf joint cut on a 45-degree angle (refer to 18-14).

The first piece of moulding is cut square on the end that will butt against the wall in the corner. If it is long enough to reach the entire length, it is cut square on both ends. If it is not long enough, one piece will be cut square on one end, and mitred on the other to form the scarf joint. The matching piece will be cut the same way, but on opposite ends as shown in 18-16. The pieces to butt this moulding will be mitred so that the end can be coped.

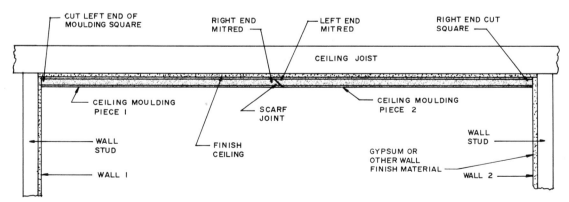

18-16   Long runs of moulding and base often must be spliced with a scarf joint.

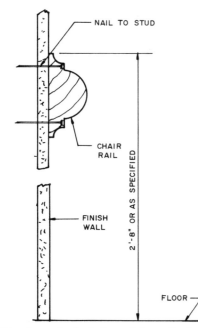

18-17 *A typical chair rail installation.*

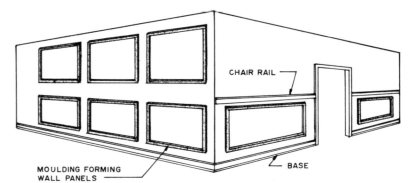

18-18 *Wall moulding can be used to form decorative panels.*

Installing Chair Rail

Chair rail is installed flat on the wall, usually 2′8″ above the floor. Begin by snapping a chalk line on each wall at the desired distance above the floor. The first piece has a square end and butts a wall in a corner. If it is not long enough to reach the entire distance, mitre the end to form a scarf joint as described for ceiling moulding. Place the moulding on the chalk line, and nail it to the studs with 6d finishing nails. It can also be checked with a level. Inside corners are coped and outside corners are mitred (see 18-17).

Installing Wall Moulding

Wall moulding is used to introduce decorative features to otherwise plain wall surfaces. Any of the many flat mouldings can be used. The panels can be various sizes and shapes, and curved moulding sections are also available. The ends of the moulding are mitred to form the corners (see 18-18).

The complete moulding assembly is usually built much like a picture frame. The pieces are cut to length and assembled, before nailing them to the wall. The most accurate way to measure the length is using the inside corner (see 18-19). After the pieces are cut to length, hold each corner together with a corner clamp. Some prefer to put some glue on each surface before closing the mitre. Drive a brad into the joint from each corner (see 18-20). Set the brad below the surface, and fill the holes as required by the type of finish to be used.

Secure the assembled moulding unit to the wall with 6d finishing nails driven into wall studs. Use a level or chalk line, and also mark vertical lines.

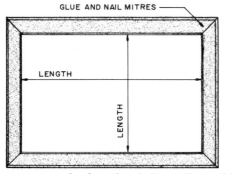

18-19 *Measure the length of the wall moulding to the inside corners.*

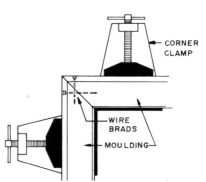

18-20 *Glue and nail each corner using a corner clamp.*

19

Finishing the Exterior

The framer must examine the architectural drawings of the building elevations and wall sections to ascertain the specified exterior finish material. Among these are solid wood, hardboard, plywood, wood shingles, aluminum, steel, vinyl, and masonry products.

Wood Siding

Quality wood siding is easy to work, relatively free from warp, and holds paint well. Best-quality wood siding should be free from knots and pitch pockets, because they will tend to bleed through the paint. It should have a moisture content of 10 to 12 percent, except in dry areas, where the moisture content could be as low as 8 percent. Wood siding should be stored flat and protected from the weather. It should be primed as soon as it has been installed.

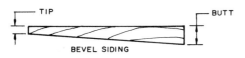

19-1 Bevel siding. (See table for sizes.)

The architectural drawings should specify the specie of wood. Some species hold up better, and others are more expensive. The best species include cypress, redwood, cedars, eastern white pine, sugar pine, and western white pine. Yellow poplar, spruce, Ponderosa pine, and western hemlock are also good. Southern pine, western larch, and Douglas fir are rated as fair.

Horizontal Wood Siding

Horizontal wood siding is available in three types—**bevel**, **drop**, and **boards**. They are manufactured in a variety of patterns, from solid wood, hardboard, and plywood.

Wood Bevel Siding

Typical sizes for **bevel siding** are given in illustration 19-1 and table 19-1. These will vary some with the different lumber manufacturing associations in various parts of the United States or Canada. Usually one side has a rough-sawn surface and the other a smooth planed surface. The rough surface is often exposed when a stain is to be used.

Table 19–1 Bevel siding sizes.

Nominal (inches)		Dressed dry (inches)	
Thickness	Width	Thickness	Width
½	4	all	3½
	5	15/32 butt	4½
	6	3/16 tip	5½
¾	8	all	7¼
	10	¾ butt	9¼
	12	3/16 tip	11¼

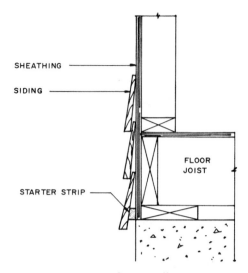

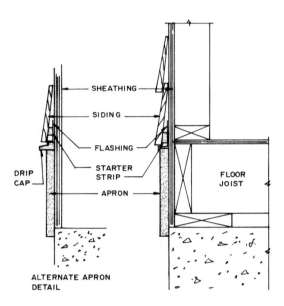

19-2 Two ways to start the installation of bevel siding.

Installing Solid Wood Bevel Siding

Bevel siding begins with the bottom course at the sill. There are several ways to start the bottom course (see 19-2). One uses a wood **starting strip** that holds the bottom of the first course out from the foundation. Another uses an **apron board,** sometimes called **fascia,** around the sill and has a **drip cap** of some kind on top. The choice depends on the decision of the architect and will appear on the elevations and wall section.

Bevel siding should overlap at least one inch. The exact overlap and exposed surface depend on the width of siding required and the need to space around windows. If possible the top edge of the siding should butt up against the bottom of the window sill. To see if this is possible, measure the distance from the window sill to the top of the foundation, allowing some overlap of the foundation. If this distance can be divided to give one inch overlap or more and have a course end at the bottom of the window, then this is the measurement used. If not, then the course at the window will have to be notched around the window. This should be carefully done so that a minimum of space is left.

The size of nail to use depends on the type of sheathing and the thickness of the siding. The nail must penetrate the stud 1½ inches (see table 19-2).

When nailing the siding, the nail should be placed so that it misses the bottom edge of the course below (see 19-3). This is necessary to allow for expansion and contraction of the siding.

Table 19–2 Wood siding nailing recommendations.

Siding thickness	With plywood sheathing	With nonnail-bearing sheathing
½″	7d	2″ plus thickness of sheathing
¾″	8d	2¼″ plus thickness of sheathing

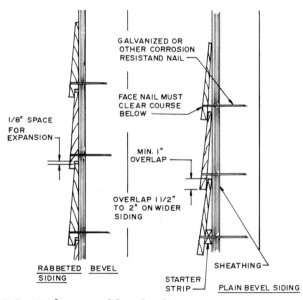

19-3 Nailing wood bevel siding.

There are several ways to frame external corners when installing bevel siding (see 19-4). One mitres the siding and the other butts it against corner boards. A 1-inch nominal square strip is used to form an internal corner. Metal corner strips are also used for inside and outside corners.

Whenever possible avoid having to butt wood siding to complete a course. If this is necessary, be certain the butt joint is made with clean, square cuts. Some dip the cut end in a water-repellent preservative to protect it from rot.

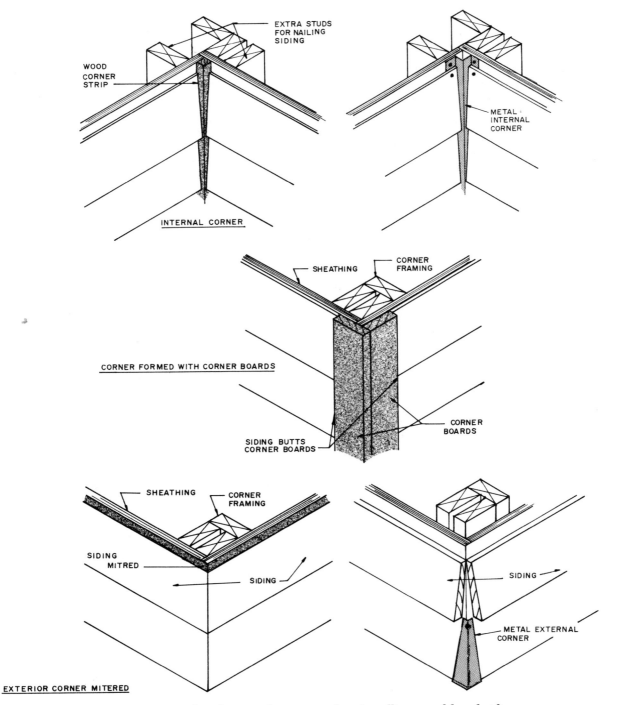

19-4 Ways to construct internal and external corners when installing wood bevel siding.

Other Solid Wood Siding Profiles

There are many patterns of **drop siding** manufactured. Some of these are shown in 19-5. While the sizes of drop siding available vary, those given in table 19-3 are typical.

Installing Other Wood Siding Profiles

These siding materials are installed in the same manner as bevel siding, except they are placed flat against the sheathing. The tongue on each piece is inserted in a groove or rabbet in the adjoining piece. A space is left between each to allow for expansion and contraction (see 19-6). The siding is face-nailed with galvanized nails. Six-inch-wide siding is nailed through the siding into a stud with only one nail. Wider stock requires two nails. Details for starting the first course are shown in 19-6. Internal and external corners are formed in the same way as described for bevel siding.

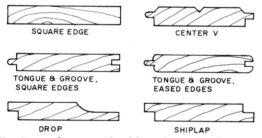

19-5   *Several types of rabbeted wood siding.*

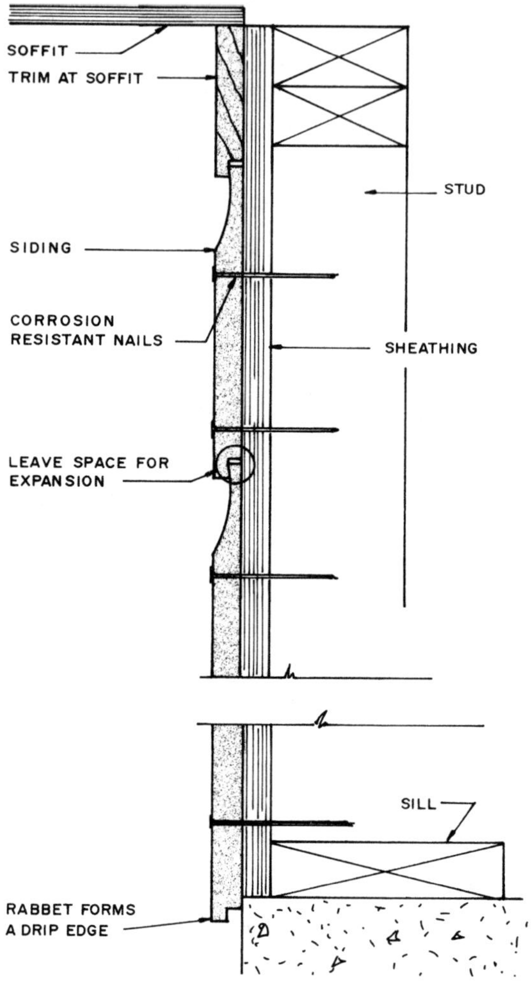

19-6   *Installing rabbeted profile wood siding.*

Table 19–3 Wood siding sizes.

Nominal (inches)		Actual (inches)		
		Shiplap	Tongue-and-groove	Drop siding
1 × 4	Overall	——	3⅜	——
	Face	——	3⅛	——
1 × 6	Overall	5½	5⅜	5⅜
	Face	5⅛	5⅛	5
1 × 8	Overall	7¼	7⅛	7⅛
	Face	6⅞	6⅞	6¾
1 × 10	Overall	9¼	9⅛	9⅛
	Face	8⅞	8⅞	8¾
1 × 12	Overall	11¼	11¼	11⅛
	Face	10⅞	10⅞	10¾

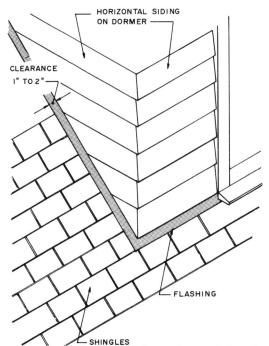

19-7 *Keep the siding away from the roof shingles.*

Other Applications

Dormers usually have wood siding in a horizontal application. The siding is applied as just described, except it is cut 1 to 2 inches short of meeting the roof. This cut end must be coated with water-repellent material and carefully painted to keep moisture out of the wood (see 19-7).

Another frequently occurring situation is when the siding changes to another pattern. A typical example is the use of horizontal siding on the end wall and then vertical siding or panel siding on the gable end. One way to handle this is to install a drip cap and flashing on top of the horizontal siding (see 19-8). This provides a means of drainage for water coming down the gable end. Another technique is to set out the gable end framing, and cut the ends of the vertical siding on an angle, providing a drip edge (see 19-9).

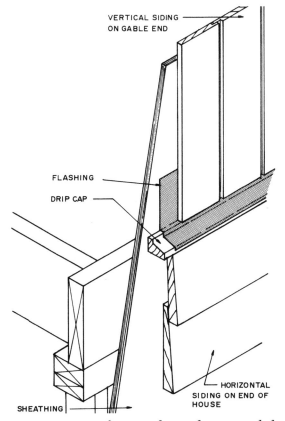

19-8 *A transition of materials can be accomplished with a flashed drip cap.*

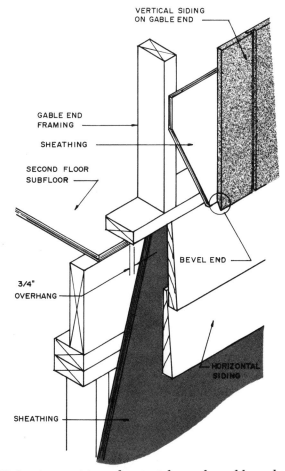

19-9 *A transition of materials on the gable end can be made by setting out the gable-end framing.*

267

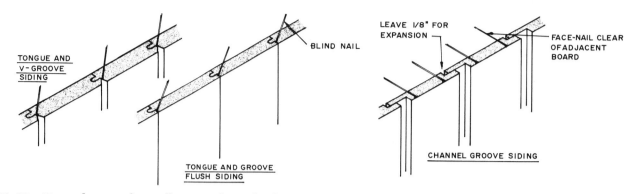

19-10   Typical vertical installations of wood siding.

Vertical Solid Wood Siding

Vertical solid wood siding includes **tongue-and-groove** and **rabbeted siding** and some form of **board-and-batten.** The tongue-and-groove and rabbeted siding fits flat against the sheathing, and is one board thick (see 19-10). The board-and-batten uses square-edge boards flat against the sheathing and to cover the space between the boards (see 19-11).

Recommended nailing patterns are shown in 19-10 and 19-11. The nails are placed to allow for expansion and contraction.

Whereas horizontal siding can be nailed to the studs, vertical siding requires other preparation. Solid 2 × 4 blocking 24 inches O.C. between the studs provides good nailing. If nonnailable sheathing is used, 1 × 4 furring strips can be nailed 24 inches O.C. across the wall and the siding nailed to them. If ⅝-inch or thicker plywood sheathing is used, the siding can be nailed into the sheathing. Place a layer of permeable building paper that allows water vapor trapped in the wall to escape over the sheathing.

Installation at the sill and soffit and forming inside and exterior corners are shown in 19-12.

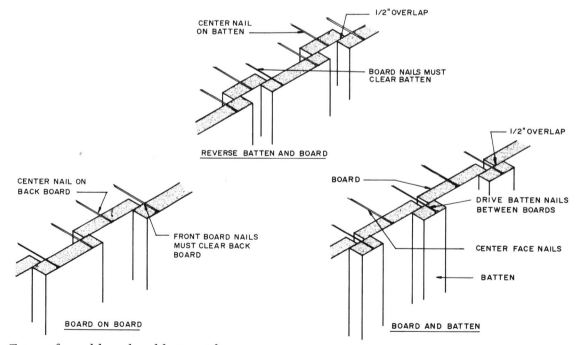

19-11   Types of wood board-and-batten siding.

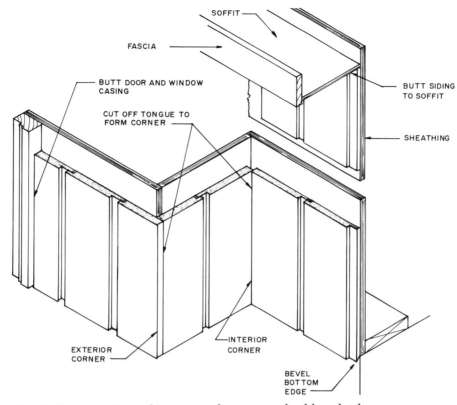

19-12   Installation details for vertical wood tongue-and-groove and rabbeted siding.

Nails Used with Wood Siding

Nails commonly used to install wood siding are shown in 19-13. They should be galvanized steel or a corrosion-resistant material. Ring-threaded or spiral-threaded nails have the greatest holding power. Smooth-shank nails may loosen over a period of years.

There are three types of points available. The blunt point reduces splitting. The diamond point is possibly the most commonly used point. The needle point has good holding power but is more likely to split the siding than the other two.

Wood Shingles and Shakes

Wood shingles and shakes are made from cedar, redwood, and cypress, and they are available in a variety of sizes and patterns. **Shingles** are sawed flat on both sides and are available in *random widths* as well as uniform widths of 4, 5, and 6 inches (also called **dimension shingles**). They are available in four grades and at lengths of 16, 18, and 24 inches. Examples of some of the patterned dimension shingles are shown in 19-14. **Shakes** are available as **straight split, tapersplit,** and **handsplit-and-resawn.** They are available in 18-, 24-, and 32-inch lengths and random

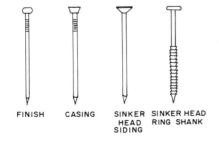

19-13   Nails used to install wood siding.

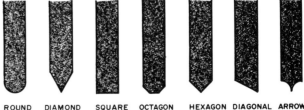

19-14   Standard decorative sawn-wood shingles.

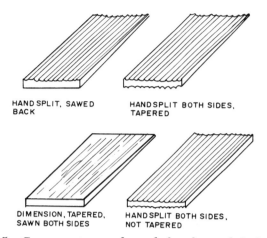

19-15 *Common types of wood shingles and shakes.*

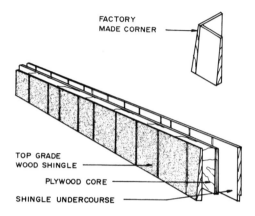

19-16 *A typical factory-made wood shingle panel for use as exterior siding.*

widths. The surface is very rough because it is formed by splitting the log (see 19-15).

Grading of shingles and shakes varies with the species of wood. Western red cedar grades are No. 1, No. 2, and No. 3; redwood grades are No. 1 and No. 2; and bald cypress grades are No. 1, Bests, Primas, Economy, and Clippers. The No. 1 grade in each case is the best.

Random-width shingles are packed by the **square** (100 square feet) while dimension widths are packed 1000 shingles per **bundle.**

Another wood shingle product is a **panel** product having wood shingles bonded to a plywood backer board. Panels are usually one shingle wide and 8 feet long (see 19-16). Prefabricated corner boards are available.

Installing Wood Shingles and Shakes as Siding

The wall to receive the shingles must have a sheathing, such as plywood, that will hold nails. If soft sheathing, such as foam plastic, is used, 1 × 4 furring

strips must be nailed over the sheathing and into the studs. The spacing between the furring strips equals the shingle exposure (see 19-17). The sheathing must be covered with a building paper that permits the passage of water vapor from inside the building.

The shingles are laid in uniform courses, similar to bevel siding. The amount exposed to the weather can be varied to help meet the heads and sills of windows in a proper manner. Recommended shingle exposures are given in table 19-4.

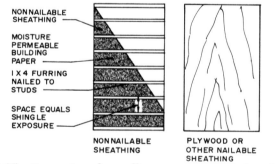

19-17 *Preparing the wall to receive wood shingles.*

Table 19-4 Wood shingle and shake siding exposure length recommendations.

(inches)	Shingles			Shakes		
Length	16	18	24	18	24	32
Single course	6–7½	6–8½	8–11½	8½	11½	15
Double course	8–12	9–14	12–16	14	20	——

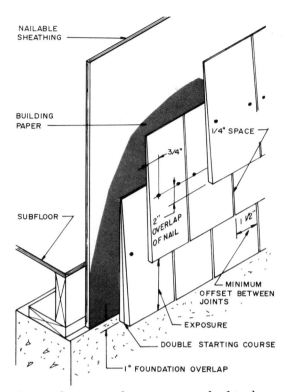

19-18 *Applying single-course wood shingles and shakes.*

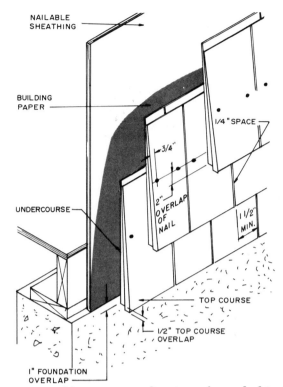

19-19 *Double-course application of wood shingles and shakes.*

Wood shingles are applied as a single or double course. Single-course application is shown in 19-18. The first course is doubled, providing a drip edge on the outside shingle. It should overlap the foundation by one inch. Each course is nailed over the one below, leaving the calculated exposure. It is nailed so that the shingle above overlaps the line of nails by 2 inches. A ¼-inch space is left between shingles and the space should be offset at least 1½ inches from a

joint above or below it.

The double-course application is shown in 19-19. Each course is doubled. The top shingle in each course overhangs the undershingle by ½ inch. In both cases lower-grade shingles are used on the under layers.

When the shingles are laid, they can have the bottom edge staggered to form a "random" pattern (see 19-20).

19-20 *The butt end of wood shingles and shakes can be staggered to produce a rougher, textured appearance.*

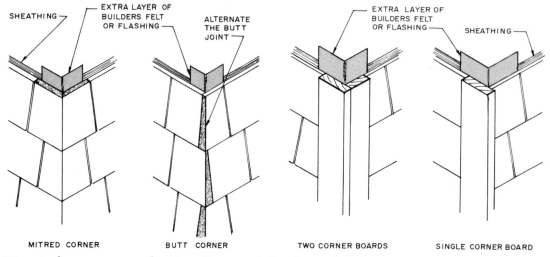

19-21   *Ways to frame corners when installing wood shingles and shakes.*

Interior and exterior corners can be formed using corner boards or by cutting and fitting the shingles (see 19-21).

The long shingle panels available are installed by applying building felt over the sheathing and nailing the panel directly into the studs. If nail-holding sheathing is used, they can be nailed to it (see 19-22).

Factory-assembled corner units are available for interior and exterior corners (see 19-23).

Nails Used with Wood Shingles

Rust-resistant nails are required. The screw type are recommended. Normally, 3d nails are used on the undercourse and 5d on the overcourse. Longer nails can be used, if needed. The nails are placed about ¾ of an inch from each edge of the shingle. Shingles

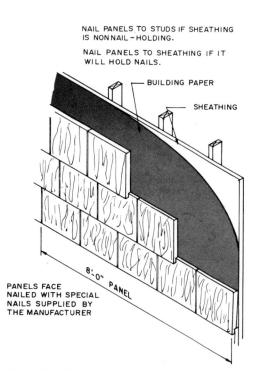

19-22   *Wood shingle panels cover large areas rapidly.*

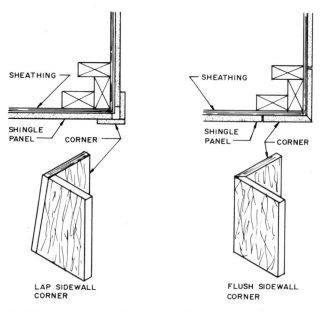

19-23   *Factory-made lap and flush wood shingle corners are available.*

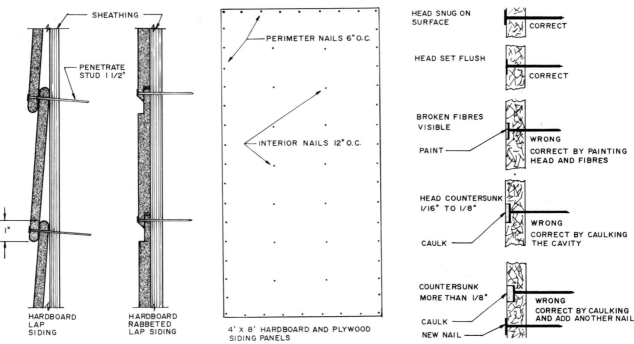

19-24 *Nailing hardboard siding.*

19-25 *Nailing pattern for hardboard and plywood siding panels.*

19-26 *Recommended nailing head placement for hardboard siding.*

narrower than 8 inches require two nails. Those wider require three nails. The nails should be driven flush with the surface of the shingle but should not crush the wood below the head.

Hardboard Siding

Hardboard siding is manufactured in a variety of patterns and is available as **lap siding** and **panel siding.** The lap siding is applied as described for wood lap siding, except that the nail penetrates both pieces, whereas rabbeted siding is face-nailed (see 19-24). Typical siding widths and recommended minimum exposures are given in table 19-5. Panel sizes and thicknesses are given in table 19-6.

The spacing of studs required for various hardboard products is specified by the manufacturer.

Nails should penetrate the studs 1½ inches. For most hardboard lap siding, 8d galvanized box nails are used, spaced a maximum of 16 inches O.C. Hardboard panel siding uses 8d galvanized box nails, spaced 6 inches O.C. around the perimeter and 12 inches O.C. at stud locations inside the panel (see 19-25). The nail must be snug or flush with the surface of the siding. If it breaks the surface and is recessed, it must be painted or caulked. Nailing recommendations of the American Hardboard Association are shown in 19-26. Hardboard siding joints are handled the same as plywood siding (refer to 19-32 following under *Installing Plywood Panel Siding*).

Table 19–5 Typical sizes of hardboard lap siding.

Siding width (inches)	Maximum exposure (inches)
12	11
8	7
6	5

Table 19–6 Typical sizes of hardboard panels.

Panel sizes (feet)	Thickness (inches)
4 × 8	7/16
4 × 9	7/16

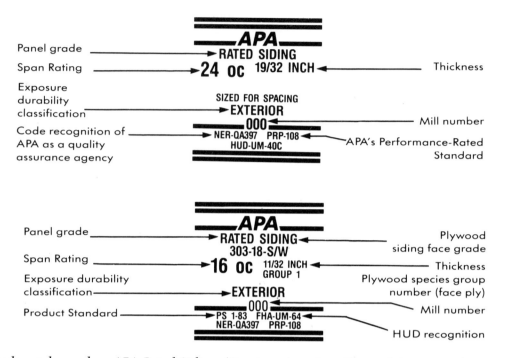

19-27   *Grade marks used on APA-Rated Siding.* (Courtesy American Plywood Association)

Plywood Siding

Plywood siding is also available as lap siding and panel siding. Plywood siding is made by bonding wood veneers with a waterproof adhesive. It is available in a variety of wood species and textures. The most common texture is a rough-sawn top veneer. Another type, Medium Density Overlaid (MDO), has a resin-treated fibre overlay sheet bonded to it. This provides a smooth, tough, check-free surface that holds paint well.

Siding manufactured to the standards of the American Plywood Association is identified by a grade mark on each panel. Several such grade marks are shown in 19-27.

Plywood siding panels are available in a variety of surface patterns. Some are shown in 19-28. Panels most frequently used are 4 × 8 feet, but panels 9 and 10 feet long are available.

Installing Plywood Lap Siding

Plywood lap siding is available in a range of widths up to 12 inches. It requires a minimum overlap of 1 inch and ⅛ of an inch clearance between butted siding ends and unions with casings on doors and windows and other trim. This clearance must be caulked.

Plywood lap siding can be nailed directly to studs or to nailable sheathing if it has a Span Rating on its grade mark. The Span Rating is the allowable maximum spacing of the studs. The studs must be braced with diagonal bracing or a structural sheathing. Building paper is stapled to the studs before installing the siding.

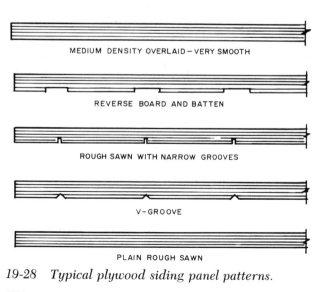

MEDIUM DENSITY OVERLAID – VERY SMOOTH

REVERSE BOARD AND BATTEN

ROUGH SAWN WITH NARROW GROOVES

V-GROOVE

PLAIN ROUGH SAWN

19-28   *Typical plywood siding panel patterns.*

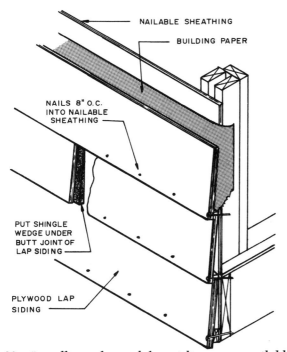

19-29 *Installing plywood lap siding over nailable sheathing.*

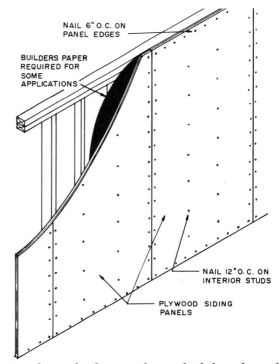

19-30 *Plywood siding can be applied directly to the studs. This is a vertical panel application.*

Plywood lap siding when applied over nailable sheathing is nailed to 8 inches O.C. along the bottom edge of the siding with the nails driven to penetrate the top edge of the lower course (see 19-29). Use 6d nonstaining box, casing, or siding nails for siding ¾ inch or thicker. If nailed directly to the studs or over nonnail-holding sheathing, nail the lap siding at the bottom edge at each stud.

Installing Plywood Panel Siding

American Plywood Association Rated Siding has four basic classes identified by the series number 303. Each of the series 303 classes is subdivided into categories depending on appearance standards.

APA-Rated Siding panels can be applied directly to the studs, and no diagonal bracing is needed, if the stud spacing does not exceed that shown on the grade mark (see 19-30). Building paper can be omitted, if the panel joints are battened or shiplapped. Square-edge joints require backing with building paper. Plywood siding panels can also be applied over any type of sheathing.

APA-Rated Siding panels can be applied horizontally, if the horizontal joints are backed with 2 × 4 blocking (see 19-31).

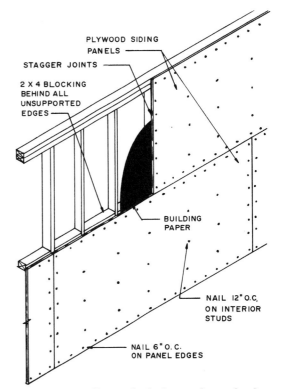

19-31 *Horizontally applied plywood panel siding requires blocking at all unsupported edges.*

275

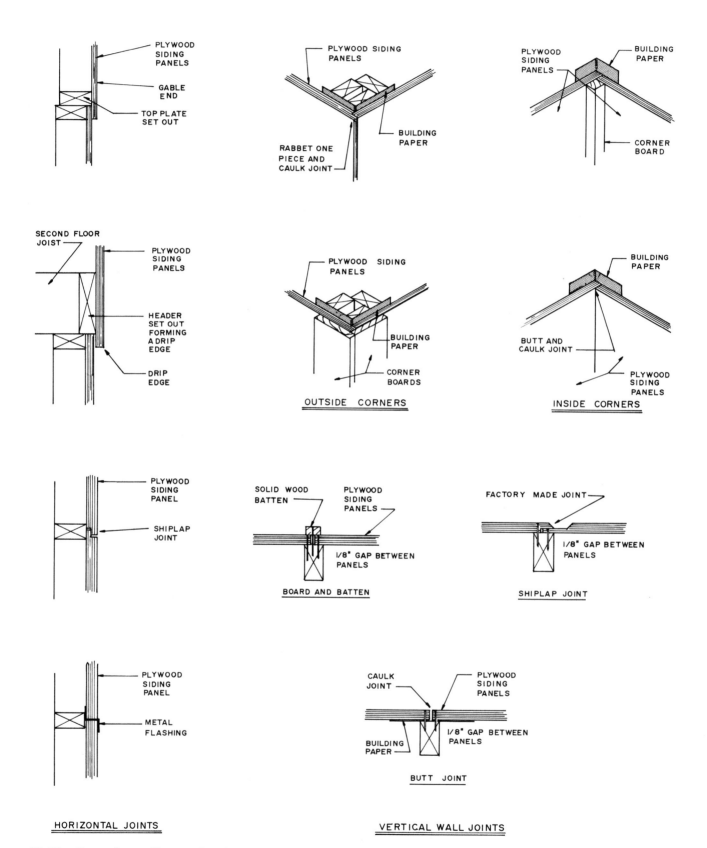

19-32 *Typical installation details for plywood siding panels. Hardboard siding joints are handled in the same manner.*

A ⅛-inch clearance between panels and door and window casings is required. The panel should be nailed at 6 inches O.C. on the edges and 12 inches O.C. at interior studs. Some typical installation details are shown in 19-32.

Vinyl and Aluminum Siding

Vinyl and **aluminum siding** are available in a variety of patterns, surface textures, and colors. The factory-applied finish requires no additional coatings after installation. These materials are generally not installed by the framing crew but by contractors specializing in their installation. Typical installation details are shown in 19-33 and 19-34.

Vinyl siding has no structural strength and must be nailed to nailable sheathing. Corrosion-resistant nails are supplied by the siding manufacturer. Aluminum siding is installed much the same as vinyl siding. Some types use a fibre backing panel behind each piece. Manufacturers of these products supply detailed installation manuals.

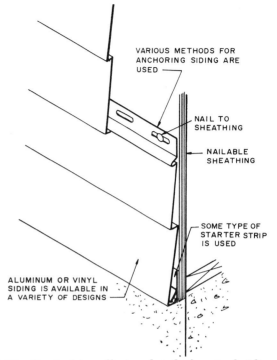

19-33 Typical installation details for vinyl siding.

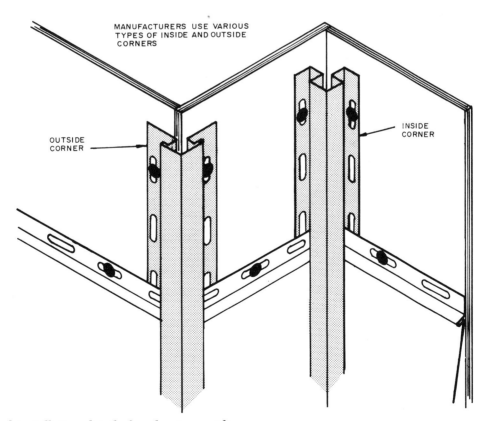

19-34 Typical installation details for aluminum siding.

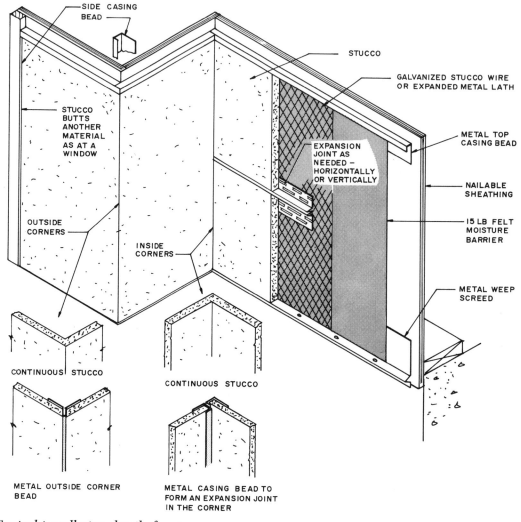

19-35   Typical installation details for stucco.

Stucco Wall System

Another exterior wall finish material is **stucco**. It is usually not installed by the framing crew, but rather, by craftsmen who specialize in this work. Typical installation details are shown in 19-35. Traditional stucco is made of cement, sand, and lime. Generally, it is applied in three coats, producing a thickness of ¾ of an inch or more.

The sheathing is covered with 15-pound builder's felt to protect if from the moisture in the stucco. A layer of **stucco wire** or **metal lath** is nailed over the builder's felt. It is nailed directly to nailable sheathing or to the studs when nonnailable sheathing is used. A good sheathing to use is ⅝-inch plywood or oriented strand board.

The first coat, called the **scratch coat**, has a rough raked finish. The second coat, called the **brown coat**, has a smoother floated finish. The final coat, called the **color coat**, is tinted the desired color and can have any of a number of finished textures.

A new and increasingly popular form of stucco is sometimes referred to as **synthetic stucco** or **synthetic plaster**. One type uses a glass fibre-reinforced portland cement plaster mixed with a special bonding adhesive. It is applied over a woven wire fabric lath as shown in 19-36.

Another material is made using an acrylic polymer formula for the adhesives and coatings. All materials making up the wall finish are supplied, forming a com-

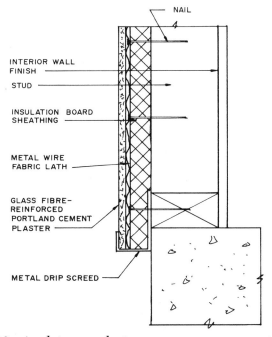

19-36 *Applying synthetic stucco over woven wire fabric lath.*

plete system that has four components. These are detailed in 19-37.

Building the Cornice

A **cornice** is the exterior trim on a structure where the wall and roof meet. It usually consists of the **soffit**, **fascia**, **vents**, and various **mouldings**. The design of the cornice is shown on the working drawings in the wall section drawing. This details each part and shows the amount that the roof is to overhang the exterior

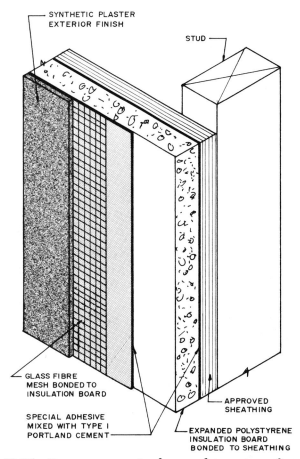

19-37 *Four components of a complete system of synthetic stucco.*

wall. The framer uses this drawing to build the cornice. (A variety of cornice designs is shown in Chapter 11.)

20

Porches and Decks

Wood-framed porches are an important part of the design of some styles of traditional homes and find wide use. They usually have some form of a roof. They typically provide access to the entrances into a house. Decks are usually larger, generally on the rear of the house, and provide a private area for relaxation. Both have similar construction requirements. A most important consideration is that they are exposed to the elements and therefore must resist rot, decay, expansion, contraction, and checking (see 20-1).

Materials

Post, joists, and decking or flooring should be either pressure-treated wood or a specie, such as redwood or cypress, that naturally resists decay when exposed to the elements. Porch floors may be tongue-and-groove boards, providing a closed floor, or square-edge boards with a space between, allowing for drainage. Tongue-and-grooved boards trap water in the grooves and tend to deteriorate faster than open floor material. Tongue-and-groove porch floors require frequent painting or other waterproofing. Porch floors, such as those used on a second-floor porch or balcony, are often waterproofed to keep the water from dripping on the area below. They are built, flashed, and waterproofed much like a flat roof. The decking can be waterproof plywood.

Decks are usually floored with 2-inch planks, spaced ¼ to ⅜ of an inch apart to permit drainage and allow the floor to have air circulation, thus drying the planks.

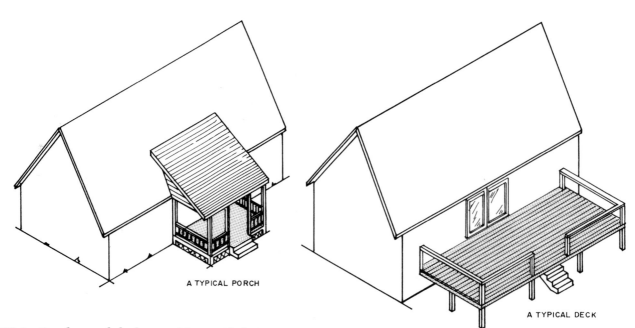

A TYPICAL PORCH

A TYPICAL DECK

20-1 Porches and decks provide outside living space.

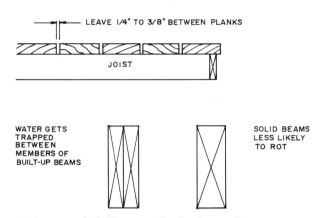

20-2 Wood decks must be built to allow air to circulate so that they can dry after exposure to rain or snow.

Air Circulation

Porch and deck materials must be installed so that air can circulate between adjacent members and promote drying. Some framers prefer to use solid beams below decks and porches rather than built-up beams, because moisture tends to get between the built-up members and could possibly produce rot and damage due to freezing (see 20-2).

Connectors

Metal connectors, such as joist hangers and angles, must be heavily galvanized and designed for exterior use. Nails must be galvanized or aluminum. Since the wood is exposed to the weather, it is subject to expansion and contraction. This tends to loosen nails and weaken joints. Bolts or screws provide more permanent connection. These must be weather-resistant. Wood ledger strips can also be used. (Refer to Chapter 6 for detailed information.)

Preservation

Wood porches are frequently painted, because this blends them in with the color scheme of the house. There are porch and deck paints available for this use. Decks are usually left natural and need a yearly coat of a clear weatherproofing sealer that protects the fibres of the pressure-treated wood. There are products available that will bleach the wood deck back to the natural wood color.

Foundations

Porches and decks are often built using wood posts. These must be pressure-treated. The footing used depends somewhat on the local soil conditions, but those shown in 20-3 are typical. The use of concrete footings extending above grade keeps the post above the soil. Use some form of metal post anchor to attach to the footing. Many installations insert the post into the soil and rest it on a concrete pad or gravel bed in the bottom of the hole.

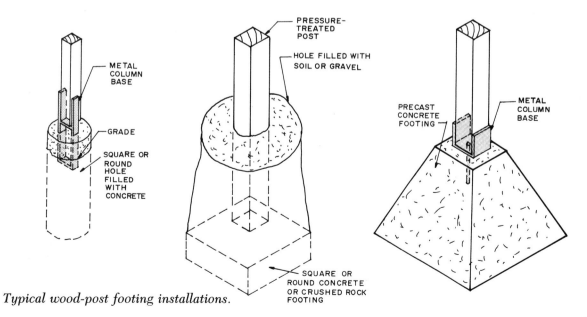

20-3 Typical wood-post footing installations.

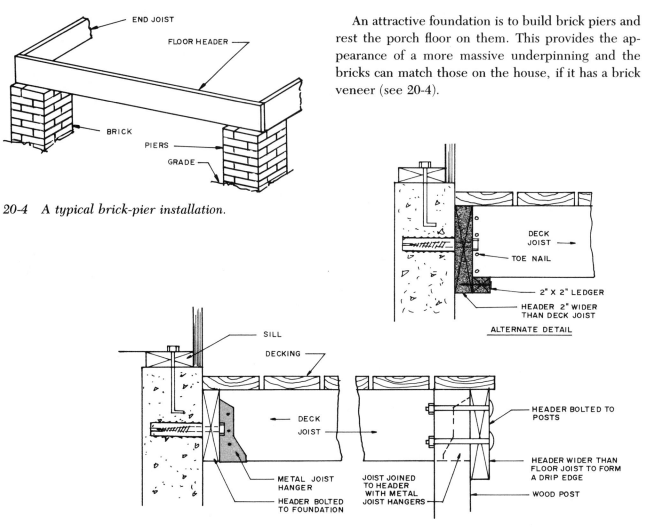

An attractive foundation is to build brick piers and rest the porch floor on them. This provides the appearance of a more massive underpinning and the bricks can match those on the house, if it has a brick veneer (see 20-4).

20-4   *A typical brick-pier installation.*

20-5   *One way to frame an open deck that joins the house at the foundation.*

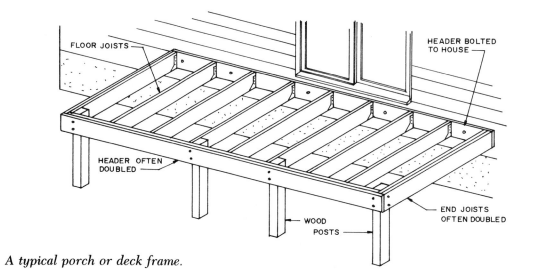

20-6   *A typical porch or deck frame.*

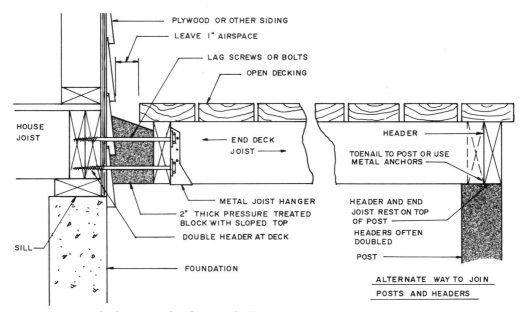

20-7   *One way to join a deck to wood siding and allow for air circulation.*

Building Wood-Framed Porches and Decks

There are many ways to frame a porch or deck. The problems to be faced are how it is to be secured to the foundation or wall of the building and whether the deck is to be open or waterproofed. The following details show some commonly used solutions.

In 20-5 are typical details for an open deck that joins the house at the foundation. A wood pressure-treated header is bolted to the foundation. The deck joists are secured to this with metal joist hangers or ledgers in the same manner as used in floor construction. The wood posts are bolted to a header on the outer side of the deck, and the joists are joined to it with metal joist hangers or ledger strips. The floor of the deck can be placed level with the floor of the house or dropped below it. In areas of heavy snow it is important to drop the floor of the deck somewhat, so that the floor can be opened after a snow. The posts can be extended above the deck to form a support for a railing (refer to 20-14 for an example of this). A typical framed installation is shown in 20-6.

Typical details for an open deck that joins the house against horizontal wood or plywood siding are shown in 20-7. It sets out the edge of the decking from the wall to allow rain to pass down below the deck.

An alternate method of construction is shown in 20-8. Here the deck header is bolted to a doubled house floor header. The open decking is set out about one inch from the sheathing and the corner is flashed. This same type of construction can be used for an open deck or balcony at the second-floor level.

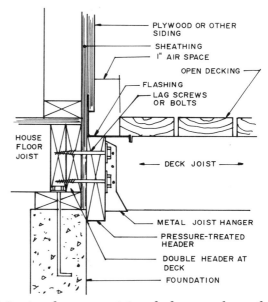

20-8   *Another way to join a deck or porch to a frame wall at the floor header. Notice the flashing at the joint.*

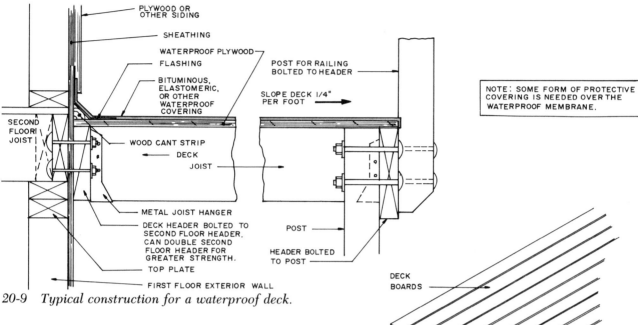

20-9   *Typical construction for a waterproof deck.*

A detail for a waterproof deck is shown in 20-9. This is often used when a balcony is built on the second-floor level. The structure is built as described earlier, and a deck of waterproof plywood is used. This is covered with some form of waterproof membrane, which could be bituminous, elastomeric, or metal. The deck must slope to the outer edge. To protect the membrane, some type of protective surface is required. Most commonly a wood grating is built and laid loose over the membrane (see 20-10).

Decks can be cantilevered beyond the row of posts or piers. A beam is placed on the posts, and the joists rest on top of it. The size of the beam and joists depends on the span. Careful planning should occur so that the cantilever does not exceed safe distances. A typical detail is shown in 20-11.

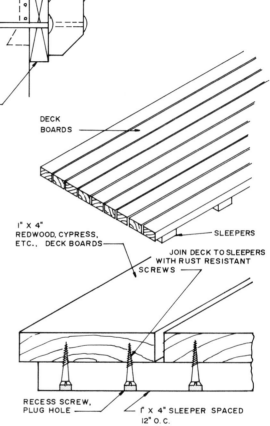

20-10   *A wood grating can be used to protect the waterproof deck membrane.*

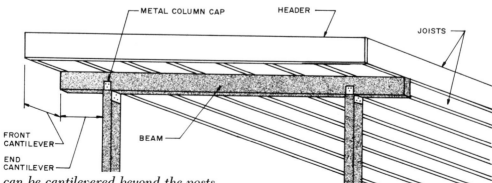

20-11   *Decks can be cantilevered beyond the posts.*

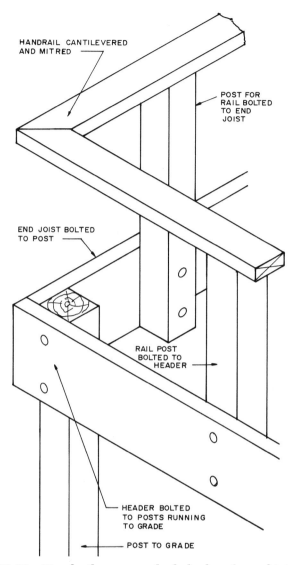

20-12 *Handrail posts can be bolted to the end joists and header.*

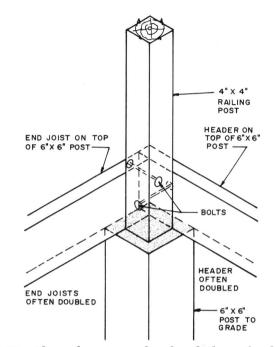

20-13 *The rail posts can be placed above the deck posts when the floor framing rests on top of the posts.*

Railings are built in many ways. The height of the railing is specified by the building code. Railings are required for porches and decks with the floor above the ground a specified distance, such as 30 inches. The minimum height of the railing is specified, such as 36 inches. It is necessary for the railing to be rigid and strong. Railing posts can be bolted to the floor header and a joist as shown in 20-12 and 20-13. The floor decking is cut to fit around the post. The posts could extend above the floor and form the vertical rail support as shown in 20-14. The railing posts could be bolted to the outside of the header and end joists as shown in 20-15 on the following page.

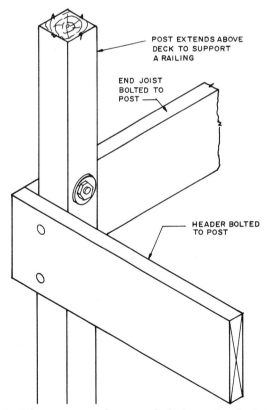

20-14 *The posts can be extended above the deck for use when building the railing.*

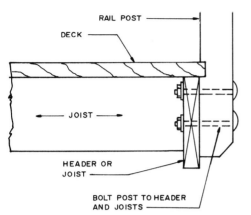

20-15 *The rail post can be bolted to the outside of the end joists and header.*

The design of the railing can vary considerably. Only a few of the many possibilities are shown in 20-16 and 20-17. If the deck or porch is close to the ground and does not require a railing, some people like to build some form of seat around the edge (see 20-18).

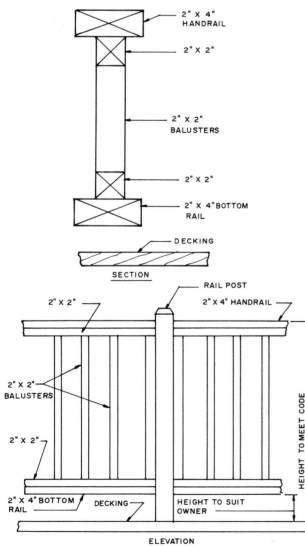

20-16 *A typical porch or deck railing.*

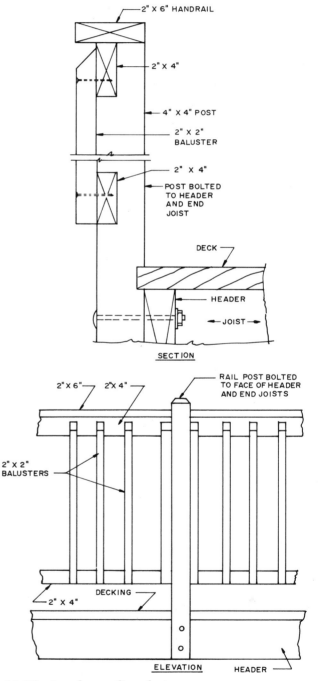

20-17 *Another railing design.*

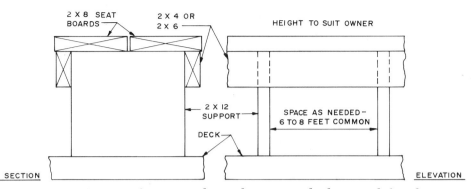

20-18　*Decks and porches with floors close to grade can have a seat built around the edge instead of a railing.*

Steps

Some type of wood steps is required to get from the porch or deck to grade. (These are built as described in Chapter 17.) Pressure-treated lumber should be used. The design of the stair must meet local building codes. The following is typical of such codes. Stairs with four treads or less do not require a handrail. Handrails must be 30 to 40 inches above the stair tread. The stair rise must be at least 4 inches and not more than 8 inches. The minimum tread width is 9 inches, and the minimum stair width is 30 inches.

The stair stringers can be nailed to the header and rest on a 2×2 ledger or joined with a metal joist hanger. The end of the stringers on the ground can rest on 4-inch concrete blocks set into the soil (see 20-19). The handrail posts can be bolted to the stringer, and the handrail design can be the same as the railing (see 20-20).

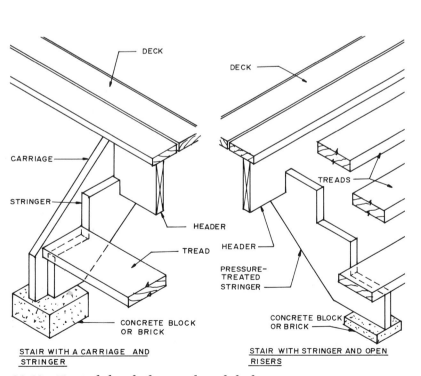

20-19　*Typical details for porch and deck stairs.*

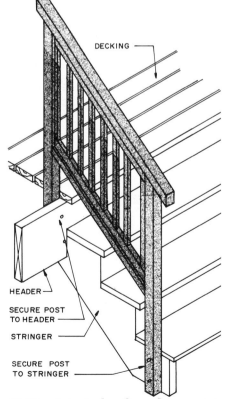

20-20　*A typical railing along a stair.*

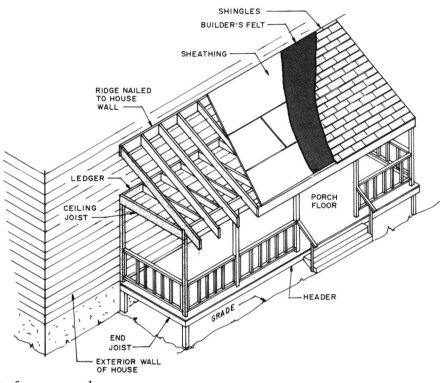

20-21   *One way to frame a porch.*

Porch Roof Construction

The porch roof is framed in the same manner as discussed for roof construction (refer to Chapters 11, 12, and 14). Most often it has a single sloped surface, although a gable roof can be used. The posts extend up to the headers, which carry the rafters. The size of these members must be selected so that they carry the required loads. The ridge is secured to the wall of the house. As the shingles are put on, flashing must close the joint between the roof and the wall. Typical detail drawings are in shown in 20-21 and 20-22.

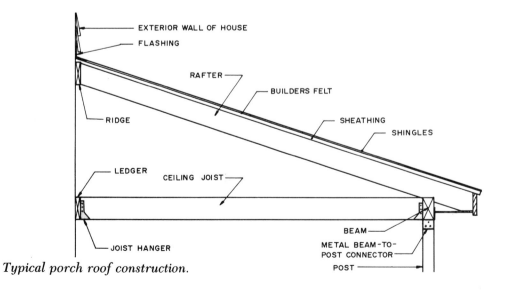

20-22   *Typical porch roof construction.*

APPENDICES

Appendix A

Structural Framing and Wood Floor Nailing Requirements

Structural Floor Framing Nailing Requirements

Type of Connection	Nailing Method	Number of Nails	Nail Size	Comments
Joist to sill or girder	toenail	3	8d	
Header to joist	end-nail	3	12d/16d	
Header or stringer joist to sill	toenail	——	8d	24 inches O.C.
Built-up beams and girders	face-nail	——	12d	12 inches O.C. on top and bottom, two 12d at each end
Wood bridging	toenail	2	8d	

Structural Wall Framing Nailing Requirements

Type of Connection	Nailing Method	Number of Nails	Nail Size	Comments
Bottom plate to stud	end-nail	2	12d/16d	or four 8d toenail
Top plate to stud	end-nail	2	12d/16d	
Bottom plate to joist	face-nail	——	12d/16d	16 inches O.C.
Double studs	face-nail	——	12d/16d	24 inches O.C., stagger
Double top plates	face-nail	——	12d/16d	16 inches O.C.
Top plate overlaps and intersections	face-nail	2	12d/16d	
Header, two pieces	face-nail	——	12d/16d	16 inches O.C., stagger on each edge
One-inch diagonal bracing	face-nail	2	8d	to each stud and plate

Structural Ceiling Framing Nailing Requirements

Type of Connection	Nailing Method	Number of Nails	Nail Size	Comments
Ceiling joists to top plate	toenail	3	8d	
Ceiling joist laps at partition	face-nail	3	12d/16d	

Structural Roof Framing Nailing Requirements

Type of Connection	Nailing Method	Number of Nails	Nail Size	Comments
Rafter to top plate	toenail	3	8d	
Rafter to parallel ceiling joist	face-nail	3	12d/16d	
Rafter to hip or valley rafter	toenail	3	8d	
Rafter to ridgeboard	toenail	3	12d	
One-inch collar beams to rafter	face-nail	3	8d	
Two-inch collar beams to rafter	face-nail	2	12d	

Wood Flooring Nailing Requirements

Tongue-and-Groove over Subfloor	Nailing Method	Number of Nails	Nail Size	Comments
3/8″			6d	
1/2″	all blind-nailed		7d	all spaced 10 to 12 inches apart
5/8″			8d	
1″			8d	
1¼″			8d	
1½″			9d	
2″ planks		2	16d	at each bearing or as recommended by manufacturer

Appendix B

Subfloor, Roof, and Wall Sheathing Nailing Requirements

(Common or box nails may be used unless otherwise specified.)

Solid Wood	
1″ x 8″ or less	Face-nail with two 8d
Wider than 1″ × 8″	Face-nail with three 8d
2″ planks	Face-nail with two 16d
Plywood Sheathing Fasteners spaced 6 inches on center at edges and 12 inches on center on interior bearings except for floors, where 10 inches on center is required.	
½″ or less	6d comon or deformed shank
⅝″ to ¾″	8d common or 6d deformed shank
⅞″ to 1″	8d common or deformed shank
1⅛″ to 1¼″	10d common or 8d deformed shank
Plywood Combined Subfloor Underlayment	
¾″ or less	6d deformed shank
⅞″ to 1″	8d deformed shank
1⅛″ to 1¼″	10d common or 8d deformed shank
Particleboard Wall Sheathing Nails spaced 6 inches on center at edges, 12 inches on center on interior bearings except floors, where 10 inches on center is required.	
⅜″ to ½″	6d common
⅝″ to ¾″	8d common
Fibreboard Sheathing Fasteners spaced 7 inches on center at exterior edges and 6 inches on center at intermediate supports.	
½″	6d common or 11-gauge corrosion-resistant roofing nails with ⁷⁄₁₆″-diameter head and 1½″ long
25/32″	8d common or 11-gauge corrosion-resistant roofing nails with ⁷⁄₁₆″-diameter head and 1¾″ long
Panel-Type Siding to Framing	
½″ or less	6d corrosion-resistant siding or casing nails
⅝″	8d corrosion-resistant siding or casing nails

Appendix C

Canadian Lumber Floor Joist Spans, Feet and Inches

Span data for Canadian lumber in Appendices C through I have been determined on the same basis as those published by the National Forest Products Association. Spans are based on the use of lumber in *dry service* conditions and the use of base values for *strength* and *stiffness* that have been modified for *repetitive member use, size factor,* and *load duration.*

Appendix D includes a table that gives a slope factor that must be used to determine the sloping distance. The horizontal span in the table is multiplied by the slope factor to get acceptable sloping distances. For example, if a slope is 4 in 12 and the horizontal rafter span is 12'6", the sloping distance is 12.5 × 1.054 = 13.175 feet or 13'2".

(Spruce-Pine-Fir)

(Sleeping Rooms and Attics)											
Maximum Allowable Spans (feet-inches)											
	2 × 6			**2 × 8**			**2 × 10**			**2 × 12**		
Spacing (inches)	**Grade** Sel. Str.	No.1/ No.2	No.3	Sel. Str.	No.1/ No.2	No.3	Sel. Str.	No.1/ No.2	No.3	Sel. Str.	No.1/ No.2	No.3
12	11-7	11-3	9-8	15-3	14-11	12-4	19-5	19-0	15-0	23-7	23-0	17-5
16	10-6	10-3	8-5	13-10	13-6	10-8	17-8	17-2	13-0	21-6	19-11	15-1
19.2	9-10	9-8	7-8	13-0	12-9	9-9	16-7	15-8	11-10	20-2	18-3	13-9
24	9-2	8-11	6-10	12-1	11-6	8-8	15-5	14-1	10-7	18-9	16-3	12-4

(Courtesy Canadian Wood Council)

(Spruce-Pine-Fir)

(All Rooms Except Sleeping Rooms and Attics)											
Maximum Allowable Spans (feet-inches)											
	2 × 6			**2 × 8**			**2 × 10**			**2 × 12**		
Spacing (inches)	**Grade** Sel. Str.	No.1/ No.2	No.3	Sel. Str.	No.1/ No.2	No.3	Sel. Str.	No.1/ No.2	No.3	Sel. Str.	No.1/ No.2	No.3
12	10-6	10-3	8-8	13-10	13-6	11-0	17-8	17-3	13-5	21-6	20-7	15-7
16	9-6	9-4	7-6	12-7	12-3	9-6	16-0	15-5	11-8	19-6	17-10	13-6
19.2	9-0	8-9	6-10	11-10	11-6	8-8	15-1	14-1	10-7	18-4	16-3	12-4
24	8-4	8-1	6-2	11-0	10-3	7-9	14-0	12-7	9-6	17-0	14-7	11-0

(Courtesy Canadian Wood Council)

Appendix D

Canadian Lumber Rafter Spans, Feet and Inches

(Spruce-Pine-Fir)

(Flat or Low Slope,* No Ceiling Load, Live Load—20 psf)											
Maximum Allowable Spans (feet-inches)											
	2 × 6			2 × 8			2 × 10			2 × 12		
Spacing (inches)	**Grade** Sel. Str.	No.1/ No.2	No.3	Sel. Str.	No.1/ No.2	No.3	Sel. Str.	No.1/ No.2	No.3	Sel. Str.	No.1/ No.2	No.3
12	15-2	14-9	12-0	19-11	19-6	15-3	25-5	24-7	18-7	30-11	28-6	21-7
16	13-9	13-5	10-5	18-2	17-5	13-2	23-2	21-4	16-1	28-2	24-8	18-8
19.2	12-11	12-7	9-6	17-1	15-11	12-0	21-9	19-5	14-8	26-6	22-7	17-1
24	12-0	11-3	8-6	15-10	14-3	10-9	20-2	17-5	13-2	24-1	20-2	15-3

* Slope not over 3 in 12
(*Courtesy Canadian Wood Council*)

(Spruce-Pine-Fir)

(Flat or Low Slope,* No Ceiling Load, Live Load—30 psf)											
Maximum Allowable Spans (feet-inches)											
	2 × 6			2 × 8			2 × 10			2 × 12		
Spacing (inches)	**Grade** Sel. Str.	No.1/ No.2	No.3	Sel. Str.	No.1/ No.2	No.3	Sel. Str.	No.1/ No.2	No.3	Sel. Str.	No.1/ No.2	No.3
12	13-3	12-11	10-5	17-5	17-0	13-2	22-3	21-4	16-1	27-1	24-8	18-8
16	12-0	11-9	9-0	15-10	15-1	11-5	20-2	18-5	13-11	24-7	21-5	16-2
19.2	11-4	10-11	8-3	14-11	13-9	10-5	19-0	16-10	12-9	23-1	19-6	14-9
24	10-6	9-9	7-4	13-10	12-4	9-4	17-8	15-1	11-5	20-11	17-6	13-2

* Slope not over 3 in 12
(*Courtesy Canadian Wood Council*)

Rafter Slope Factor

Slope (in 12)	3	4	5	6	7	8	9	10	11	12	13	14	15	16	17	18	19	20
Slope Factor	1.031	1.054	1.083	1.118	1.158	1.202	1.25	1.302	1.357	1.414	1.474	1.537	1.601	1.667	1.734	1.803	1.873	1.944

Note: Sloping Distance = Rafter Span multiplied by Slope Factor

(Spruce-Pine-Fir)

(Medium or High Slope,* No Ceiling Load, Heavy Roofing, Live Load—20 psf)

	Maximum Allowable Spans (feet-inches)											
	2 × 4			2 × 6			2 × 8			2 × 10		
	Grade											
Spacing	Sel.	No.1/		Sel.	No.1/		Sel.	No.1/		Sel.	No.1/	
(inches)	Str.	No.2	No.3	Str.	No.2	No.3	Str.	No.2	No.3	Str.	No.2	No.3
12	10-7	10-1	7-7	16-8	14-9	11-2	21-11	18-8	14-1	27-3	22-9	17-3
16	9-8	8-9	6-7	15-2	12-9	9-8	19-4	16-2	12-2	23-7	19-9	14-11
19.2	9-1	7-11	6-0	13-11	11-8	8-10	17-7	14-9	11-2	21-6	18-0	13-7
24	8-5	7-1	5-5	12-5	10-5	7-10	15-9	13-2	10-0	19-3	16-1	12-2

* Slope not over 3 in 12
(*Courtesy Canadian Wood Council*)

(Spruce-Pine-Fir)

(Medium or High Slope,* No Ceiling Load, Heavy Roofing, Live Load—30 psf)

	Maximum Allowable Spans (feet-inches)											
	2 × 4			2 × 6			2 × 8			2 × 10		
	Grade											
Spacing	Sel.	No.1/		Sel.	No.1/		Sel.	No.1/		Sel.	No.1/	
(inches)	Str.	No.2	No.3	Str.	No.2	No.3	Str.	No.2	No.3	Str.	No.2	No.3
12	9-3	8-10	6-8	14-7	13-0	9-10	19-2	16-5	12-5	24-0	20-1	15-2
16	8-5	7-8	5-10	13-3	11-3	8-6	17-0	14-3	10-9	20-9	17-5	13-2
19.2	7-11	7-0	5-4	12-3	10-3	7-9	15-6	13-0	9-10	19-0	15-11	12-0
24	7-4	6-3	4-9	11-0	9-2	6-11	13-11	11-8	8-9	17-0	14-2	10-9

* Slope not over 3 in 12
(*Courtesy Canadian Wood Council*)

(Spruce-Pine-Fir)

(Medium or High Slope,* No Ceiling Load, Light Roofing, Live Load—20 psf)

	Maximum Allowable Spans (feet-inches)											
	2 × 4			2 × 6			2 × 8			2 × 10		
	Grade											
Spacing	Sel.	No.1/		Sel.	No.1/		Sel.	No.1/		Sel.	No.1/	
(inches)	Str.	No.2	No.3	Str.	No.2	No.3	Str.	No.2	No.3	Str.	No.2	No.3
12	10-7	10-4	8-8	16-8	16-3	12-8	21-11	21-3	16-1	28-0	25-11	19-7
16	9-8	9-5	7-6	15-2	14-6	11-0	19-11	18-5	13-11	25-5	22-5	17-0
19.2	9-1	8-10	6-10	14-3	13-3	10-0	18-9	16-9	12-8	23-11	20-6	15-6
24	8-5	8-1	6-1	13-3	11-10	9-0	17-5	15-0	11-4	21-11	18-4	13-10

* Slope over 3 in 12
(*Courtesy Canadian Wood Council*)

Appendix E

Canadian Lumber Ceiling Joist Spans, Feet and Inches

(Spruce-Pine-Fir)

	(Drywall Finish, No Future Sleeping Rooms and No Attic Storage)											
	Maximum Allowable Spans (feet-inches)											
	2 × 4			**2 × 6**			**2 × 8**			**2 × 10**		
	Grade											
Spacing	Sel.	No.1/		Sel.	No.1/		Sel.	No.1/		Sel.	No.1/	
(inches)	Str.	No.2	No.3	Str.	No.2	No.3	Str.	No.2	No.3	Str.	No.2	No.3
12	12-2	11-10	10-10	19-1	18-8	15-10	25-2	24-7	20-1	32-1	31-4	24-6
16	11-0	10-9	9-5	17-4	16-11	13-9	22-10	22-4	17-5	29-2	28-1	21-3
19.2	10-4	10-2	8-7	16-4	15-11	12-6	21-6	21-0	15-10	27-5	25-8	19-5
24	9-8	9-5	7-8	15-2	14-9	11-2	19-11	18-9	14-2	25-5	22-11	17-4

(Courtesy Canadian Wood Council)

(Spruce-Pine-Fir)

	(Drywall Finish, No Future Sleeping Rooms and Limited Attic Storage Available)											
	Maximum Allowable Spans (feet-inches)											
	2 × 4			**2 × 6**			**2 × 8**			**2 × 10**		
	Grade											
Spacing	Sel.	No.1/		Sel.	No.1/		Sel.	No.1/		Sel.	No.1/	
(inches)	Str.	No.2	No.3	Str.	No.2	No.3	Str.	No.2	No.3	Str.	No.2	No.3
12	9-8	9-5	7-8	15-2	14-9	11-2	19-11	18-9	14-2	25-5	22-11	17-4
16	8-9	8-7	6-8	13-9	12-10	9-8	18-2	16-3	12-4	23-2	19-10	15-0
19.2	8-3	8-0	6-1	12-11	11-9	8-10	17-1	14-10	11-3	21-8	18-2	13-8
24	7-8	7-2	5-5	12-0	10-6	7-11	15-10	13-3	10-0	19-5	16-3	12-3

(Courtesy Canadian Wood Council)

Appendix F

Canadian Lumber Floor and Ceiling Joist Spans, Metric

Floor Joist Spans: Living Quarters (Spruce-Pine-Fir)   Maximum spans (m)

Grade		38 × 140			38 × 184			38 × 235			38 × 286		
Nailed & glued subfloor thickness (mm)		Bridging & strapping joist spacing (mm)											
		300	400	600	300	400	600	300	400	600	300	400	600
15.5	SS	3.24	2.95	2.57	4.26	3.87	3.38	5.26	4.91	4.32	5.90	5.51	5.13
	No. 1&2	3.14	2.85	2.49	4.12	3.75	3.27	5.09	4.74	4.18	5.71	5.32	4.96
	No. 3	3.08	2.80	2.43	4.05	3.61	2.95	5.00	4.42	3.61	5.61	5.13	4.19
18.5	SS	3.24	2.95	2.57	4.26	3.87	3.38	5.45	4.95	4.32	6.42	5.90	5.26
	No. 1&2	3.14	2.85	2.49	4.12	3.75	3.27	5.27	4.79	4.18	6.21	5.71	5.09
	No. 3	3.08	2.80	2.43	4.05	3.61	2.95	5.10	4.42	3.61	5.92	5.13	4.19

(Courtesy Canadian Wood Council)

Floor Joist Spans: Bedrooms & Attics (Spruce-Pine-Fir)   Maximum spans (m)

Grade		38 × 140			38 × 184			38 × 235			38 × 286		
Nailed & glued subfloor thickness (mm)		Bridging & strapping joist spacing (mm)											
		300	400	600	300	400	600	300	400	600	300	400	600
15.5	SS	3.59	3.26	2.85	4.56	4.25	3.75	5.26	4.91	4.57	5.90	5.51	5.13
	No. 1&2	3.47	3.16	2.76	4.41	4.11	3.62	5.09	4.74	4.42	5.71	5.32	4.96
	No. 3	3.41	3.10	2.71	4.33	4.04	3.37	5.00	4.66	4.12	5.61	5.23	4.78
18.5	SS	3.59	3.26	2.85	4.72	4.29	3.75	5.72	5.26	4.79	6.42	5.90	5.43
	No. 1&2	3.47	3.16	2.76	4.57	4.15	3.62	5.53	5.09	4.63	6.21	5.71	5.25
	No. 3	3.41	3.10	2.71	4.48	4.07	3.37	5.44	5.00	4.12	6.10	5.61	4.78

(Courtesy Canadian Wood Council)

Ceiling Joist Spans (Spruce-Pine-Fir)   Maximum spans (m)

Grade	38 × 89			38 × 140			38 × 184			38 × 235		
	Joist spacing (mm)											
	300	400	600	300	400	600	300	400	600	300	400	600
SS	3.22	2.92	2.55	5.06	4.60	4.02	6.65	6.05	5.28	8.50	7.72	6.74
No. 1&2	3.11	2.83	2.47	4.90	4.45	3.89	6.44	5.85	5.11	8.22	7.47	6.52
No. 3	3.06	2.78	2.43	4.81	4.37	3.82	6.32	5.74	5.02	8.07	7.33	6.34

(Courtesy Canadian Wood Council)

Appendix G

Canadian Lumber Roof Rafter, Solid 89-mm Floor Beam, and Subflooring Spans, Metric

Roof Rafter Spans (Spruce-Pine-Fir)

Roof Snow Load—1.5 kPa Maximum spans (m)

Grade	38 × 89			38 × 140			38 × 184			38 × 235		
	Rafter Spacing (mm)											
	300	400	600	300	400	600	300	400	600	300	400	600
SS	2.81	2.55	2.23	4.42	4.02	3.51	5.81	5.28	4.61	7.42	6.74	5.89
No. 1&2	2.72	2.47	2.16	4.28	3.89	3.40	5.62	5.11	4.41	7.18	6.52	5.39
No. 3	2.67	2.39	1.95	3.95	3.42	2.79	4.80	4.16	3.40	5.87	5.08	4.15

(Courtesy Canadian Wood Council)

Solid 89-mm Floor Beam Spans (Spruce-Pine-Fir)

Maximum spans (m)

Grade	Supported length (m)	Supporting one floor in houses				Supporting two floors in houses			
		89 × 235	89 × 286	89 × 337	89 × 387	89 × 235	89 × 286	89 × 337	89 × 387
SS	2.4	4.13	4.81	5.41	5.89	3.01	3.40	3.70	3.91
	3.0	3.70	4.31	4.84	5.12	2.50	2.83	3.10	3.28
	3.6	3.37	3.85	4.18	4.40	2.16	2.46	2.69	2.86
	4.2	2.99	3.38	3.68	3.88	1.92	2.19	2.41	2.56
	4.8	2.67	3.03	3.30	3.49	1.74	1.99	2.19	2.34
No. 1&2	2.4	3.49	4.07	4.57	4.98	2.65	3.09	3.47	3.78
	3.0	3.13	3.64	4.09	4.46	2.37	2.76	3.10	3.28
	3.6	2.85	3.32	3.73	4.07	2.16	2.46	2.69	2.86
	4.2	2.64	3.08	3.46	3.77	1.92	2.19	2.41	2.56
	4.8	2.47	2.88	3.23	3.49	1.74	1.99	2.19	2.34

(Courtesy Canadian Wood Council)

Subflooring, Thickness (mm)

Maximum spacing of supports (mm)	Plywood	Waferboard and strand board		Lumber
		R-1, 0-1 grades	0-2 grade	
400	15.5	15.9	15.5	17.0
500	15.5	15.9	15.5	19.0
600	18.5	19.0	18.5	19.0

(Courtesy Canadian Wood Council)

Appendix H

Canadian Lumber Built-Up Floor Beam Spans, Metric

Built-Up Floor Beam Spans (Spruce-Pine-Fir)   Maximum spans (m)

Grade	Supported length (m)	Supporting One Floor in Houses Size of beam (mm)					
		3-38 × 184	4-38 × 184	3-38 × 235	4-38 × 235	3-38 × 286	4-38 × 286
SS	2.4	3.84	4.43	4.70	5.42	5.45	6.29
	3.0	3.43	3.97	4.20	4.85	4.87	5.63
	3.6	3.14	3.62	3.79	4.43	4.19	5.14
	4.2	2.78	3.35	3.25	4.10	3.60	4.76
	4.8	2.43	3.14	2.84	3.79	3.15	4.19
No. 1&2	2.4	3.25	3.75	3.97	4.59	4.61	5.32
	3.0	2.90	3.35	3.55	4.10	4.12	4.76
	3.6	2.65	3.06	3.24	3.74	3.76	4.34
	4.2	2.45	2.83	3.00	3.47	3.48	4.02
	4.8	2.30	2.65	2.81	3.24	3.15	3.76

(Courtesy Canadian Wood Council)

Built-Up Floor Beam Spans (Spruce-Pine-Fir)   Maximum spans (m)

Grade	Supported length (m)	Supporting Two Floors in Houses Size of beam (mm)					
		3-38 × 184	4-38 × 184	3-38 × 235	4-38 × 235	3-38 × 286	4-38 × 286
SS	2.4	2.80	3.36	3.27	4.11	3.62	4.77
	3.0	2.24	2.98	2.62	3.49	2.90	3.86
	3.6	1.86	2.49	2.18	2.91	2.42	3.22
	4.2	1.60	2.13	1.87	2.49	2.07	2.76
	4.8	1.40	1.86	1.64	2.18	1.81	2.42
No. 1&2	2.4	2.46	2.85	3.01	3.48	3.50	4.04
	3.0	2.20	2.55	2.62	3.11	2.90	3.61
	3.6	1.86	2.32	2.18	2.84	2.42	3.22
	4.2	1.60	2.13	1.87	2.49	2.07	2.76
	4.8	1.40	1.86	1.64	2.18	1.81	2.42

(Courtesy Canadian Wood Council)

Appendix I

Canadian Lumber Glued-Laminated Floor Beams, Metric

Glued-Laminated Floor Beam Spans

Maximum spans (m)

Stress grade designation	Beam width (mm)	Supported length (m)	Supporting One Floor in Houses Beam depth (mm)						
			228	266	304	342	380	412	456
20f-E	80	2.4	4.32	5.04	5.76	6.48	7.20	7.92	8.64
		3.0	3.87	4.51	5.15	5.80	6.44	7.09	7.73
		3.6	3.53	4.12	4.70	5.29	5.88	6.47	7.06
		4.2	3.27	3.81	4.36	4.90	5.44	5.99	6.53
		4.8	3.06	3.57	4.07	4.58	5.09	5.60	6.11
	130	2.4	5.51	6.43	7.35	8.26	9.18	10.10	11.02
		3.0	4.93	5.75	6.57	7.39	8.21	9.03	9.86
		3.6	4.50	5.25	6.00	6.75	7.50	8.25	9.00
		4.2	4.16	4.86	5.55	6.25	6.94	7.64	8.33
		4.8	3.90	4.54	5.19	5.84	6.49	7.14	7.79

(Courtesy Canadian Wood Council)

Glued-Laminated Floor Beam Spans

Maximum spans (m)

Stress grade designation	Beam width (mm)	Supported length (m)	Supporting Two Floor in Houses Beam depth (mm)						
			228	266	304	342	380	412	456
20f-E	80	2.4	3.28	3.83	4.37	4.92	5.47	6.01	6.56
		3.0	2.93	3.42	3.91	4.40	4.89	5.38	5.87
		3.6	2.68	3.12	3.57	4.02	4.46	4.91	5.36
		4.2	2.48	2.89	3.31	3.72	4.13	4.54	4.96
		4.8	2.32	2.71	3.09	3.48	3.86	4.25	4.64
	130	2.4	4.18	4.88	5.57	6.27	6.97	7.66	8.36
		3.0	3.74	4.36	4.99	5.61	6.23	6.85	7.48
		3.6	3.41	3.98	4.55	5.12	5.69	6.26	6.83
		4.2	3.16	3.69	4.21	4.74	5.27	5.79	6.32
		4.8	2.96	3.45	3.94	4.43	4.93	5.42	5.91

(Courtesy Canadian Wood Council)

Notes: Supported length means ½ the sum of the joist spans on both sides of the beam. Straight interpolation may be used for other supported lengths. Spans are clear spans between supports. For total span, add two bearing lengths.

Appendix J

Southern Pine Floor Joist Spans, Feet and Inches

Floor Joists—Sleeping Rooms and Attic Floors (Empirical Design Values), 30 psf Live Load, 10 psf Dead Load, *l*/360

Size (inches)	Spacing (inches on center)	Grade			
		Select Structural	No. 1	No. 2	No. 3
2 × 6	12	12-3	12-0	11-10	10-5
	16	11-2	10-11	10-9	9-1
	24	9-9	9-7	9-4	7-5
2 × 8	12	16-2	15-10	15-7	13-3
	16	14-8	14-5	14-2	11-6
	24	12-10	12-7	12-4	9-5
2 × 10	12	20-8	20-3	19-10	15-8
	16	18-9	18-5	18-0	13-7
	24	16-5	16-1	14-8	11-1
2 × 12	12	25-1	24-8	24-2	18-8
	16	22-10	22-5	21-1	16-2
	24	19-11	19-6	17-2	13-2

(Courtesy Southern Pine Marketing Council)

Floor Joists—All Rooms Except Sleeping Rooms and Attic Floors (Empirical Design Values), 40 psf Live Load, 10 psf Dead Load, *l*/360

Size (inches)	Spacing (inches on center)	Grade			
		Select Structural	No. 1	No. 2	No. 3
2 x 6	12	11-2	10-11	10-9	9-4
	16	10-2	9-11	9-9	8-1
	24	8-10	8-8	8-6	6-7
2 x 8	12	14-8	14-5	14-2	11-11
	16	13-4	13-1	12-10	10-3
	24	11-8	11-5	11-0	8-5
2 x 10	12	18-9	18-5	18-0	14-0
	16	17-0	16-9	16-1	12-2
	24	14-11	14-7	13-2	9-11
2 x 12	12	22-10	22-5	21-9	16-8
	16	20-9	20-4	18-10	14-5
	24	18-1	17-5	15-4	11-10

These spans are based on the 1993 AFPA (formerly NFPA) Span Tables for Joists and Rafters and the 1991 SPIB Grading Rules. They are intended for use in covered structures or where the moisture content in use does not exceed 19 percent for an extended period of time. Loading conditions are expressed in psf (pounds per square foot). Deflection is limited to span in inches divided by 360 and is based on live load only. Check sources of supply for availability of lumber in lengths greater than 20′0″.

(Courtesy Southern Pine Marketing Council)

301

Appendix K

Southern Pine Ceiling Joist Spans, Feet and Inches

Ceiling Joists—Drywall Ceiling, No Attic Storage (Empirical Design Values), 10 psf Live Load, 5 psf Dead Load, *l*/240

Size (inches)	Spacing (inches on center)	Grade Select Structural	No. 1	No. 2	No. 3
2 × 4	12	12-11	12-8	12-5	11-7
	16	11-9	11-6	11-3	10-9
	24	10-3	10-0	9-10	8-2
2 × 6	12	20-3	19-11	19-6	17-1
	16	18-5	18-1	17-8	14-9
	24	16-1	15-9	15-6	12-1
2 × 8	12	26-0	26-0	25-8	21-8
	16	24-3	23-10	23-4	18-9
	24	21-2	20-10	20-1	15-4
2 × 10	12	26-0	26-0	26-0	25-7
	16	26-0	26-0	26-0	22-2
	24	26-0	26-0	24-0	18-1

(Courtesy Southern Pine Marketing Council)

Ceiling Joists—Drywall Ceiling, No Future Sleeping Rooms, but Limited Storage Available (Empirical Design Values), 20 psf Live Load, 10 psf Dead Load, *l*/240

Size (inches)	Spacing (inches on center)	Grade Select Structural	No. 1	No. 2	No. 3
2 × 4	12	10-3	10-0	9-10	8-2
	16	9-4	9-1	8-11	7-1
	24	8-1	8-0	7-8	5-9
2 × 6	12	16-1	15-9	15-6	12-1
	16	14-7	14-4	13-6	10-5
	24	12-9	12-6	11-0	8-6
2 × 8	12	21-2	20-10	20-1	15-4
	16	19-3	18-11	17-5	13-3
	24	16-10	15-11	14-2	10-10
2 × 10	12	26-0	26-0	24-0	18-1
	16	24-7	23-2	20-9	15-8
	24	21-6	18-11	17-0	12-10

These spans are based on the 1993 AFPA (formerly NFPA) Span Tables for Joists and Rafters and the 1991 SPIB Grading Rules. They are intended for use in covered structures or where the moisture content in use does not exceed 19 percent for an extended period of time. Loading conditions are expressed in psf (pounds per square foot). Deflection is limited to span in inches divided by 240 and is based on live load only. Check sources of supply for availability of lumber in lengths greater than 20′0″.

(Courtesy Southern Pine Marketing Council)

Appendix L

Southern Pine Rafter Spans, Feet and Inches

Rafters—Light Roofing; No Finished Ceiling; Snow Load (Empirical Design Values), 20 psf Live Load, 10 psf Dead Load, $l/180$, $C_D = 1.15$

Size (inches)	Spacing (inches on center)	Grade			
		Select Structural	No. 1	No. 2	No. 3
2 × 4	12	11-3	11-1	10-10	8-9
	16	10-3	10-0	9-10	7-7
	24	8-11	8-9	8-3	6-2
2 × 6	12	17-8	17-4	16-8	12-11
	16	16-1	15-9	14-5	11-2
	24	14-1	13-6	11-9	9-1
2 × 8	12	23-4	22-11	21-7	16-5
	16	21-2	20-10	18-8	14-3
	24	18-6	17-0	15-3	11-7
2 × 10	12	26-0	26-0	25-8	19-5
	16	26-0	24-9	22-3	16-10
	24	23-8	20-3	18-2	13-9

(Courtesy Southern Pine Marketing Council)

Rafters—Light Roofing; No Finished Ceiling; Snow Load (Empirical Design Values), 30 psf Live Load, 10 psf Dead Load, $l/180$, $C_D = 1.15$

Size (inches)	Spacing (inches on center)	Grade			
		Select Structural	No. 1	No. 2	No. 3
2 × 4	12	9-10	9-8	9-6	7-7
	16	8-11	8-9	8-7	6-7
	24	7-10	7-8	7-1	5-4
2 × 6	12	15-6	15-2	14-5	11-2
	16	14-1	13-9	12-6	9-8
	24	12-3	11-9	10-2	7-11
2 × 8	12	20-5	20-0	18-8	14-3
	16	18-6	18-0	16-2	12-4
	24	16-2	14-9	13-2	10-1
2 × 10	12	26-0	24-9	22-3	16-10
	16	23-8	21-5	19-3	14-7
	24	20-8	17-6	15-9	11-11

These spans are based on the 1993 AFPA (formerly NFPA) Span Tables for Joists and Rafters and the 1991 SPIB Grading Rules. They are intended for use in covered structures or where the moisture content in use does not exceed 19 percent for an extended period of time. Loading conditions are expressed in psf (pounds per square foot). Deflection is limited to span in inches divided by 180 and is based on live load only. The load duration factor, C_D, is 1.15 for snow loads. Check sources of supply for availability of lumber in lengths greater than 20'0".

(Courtesy Southern Pine Marketing Council)

303

Rafters—Medium Roofing; No Finished Ceiling; Snow Load (Empirical Design Values), 20 psf Live Load, 15 psf Dead Load, $l/180$, $C_D = 1.15$

Size (inches)	Spacing (inches on center)	Grade			
		Select Structural	No. 1	No. 2	No. 3
2 × 4	12	11-3	11-1	10-9	8-1
	16	10-3	10-0	9-4	7-0
	24	8-11	8-5	7-7	5-9
2 × 6	12	17-8	17-4	15-5	11-11
	16	16-1	15-4	13-4	10-4
	24	14-1	12-6	10-11	8-5
2 × 8	12	23-4	22-3	19-11	15-3
	16	21-2	19-3	17-3	13-2
	24	18-6	15-9	14-1	10-9
2 × 10	12	26-0	26-0	23-10	18-0
	16	26-0	22-11	20-7	15-7
	24	23-6	18-9	16-10	12-9

(Courtesy Southern Pine Marketing Council)

Rafters—Medium Roofing; No Finished Ceiling; Snow Load (Empirical Design Values), 30 psf Live Load, 15 psf Dead Load, $l/180$, $C_D = 1.15$

Size (inches)	Spacing (inches on center)	Grade			
		Select Structural	No. 1	No. 2	No. 3
2 × 4	12	9-10	9-8	9-6	7-2
	16	8-11	8-9	8-3	6-2
	24	7-10	7-5	6-8	5-0
2 × 6	12	15-6	15-2	13-7	10-6
	16	14-1	13-6	11-9	9-1
	24	12-3	11-1	9-7	7-5
2 × 8	12	20-5	19-8	17-7	13-5
	16	18-6	17-0	15-3	11-7
	24	16-2	13-11	12-5	9-6
2 × 10	12	26-0	23-4	21-0	15-10
	16	23-8	20-3	18-2	13-9
	24	20-8	16-6	14-10	11-3

(Courtesy Southern Pine Marketing Council)

These spans are based on the 1993 AFPA (formerly NFPA) Span Tables for Joists and Rafters and the 1991 SPIB Grading Rules. They are intended for use in covered structures or where the moisture content in use does not exceed 19 percent for an extended period of time. Loading conditions are expressed in psf (pounds per square foot). Deflection is limited to span in inches divided by 180 and is based on live load only. The load duration factor, C_D, is 1.15 for snow loads. Check sources of supply for availability of lumber in lengths greater than 20'0".

Rafters—Heavy Roofing; No Finished Ceiling; Snow Load (Empirical Design Values), 20 psf Live Load, 20 psf Dead Load, *l*/180, $C_D = 1.15$

Size (inches)	Spacing (inches on center)	Grade			
		Select Structural	No. 1	No. 2	No. 3
2 × 4	12	11-3	11-1	10-1	7-7
	16	10-3	9-8	8-8	6-7
	24	8-11	7-11	7-1	5-4
2 × 6	12	17-8	16-7	14-5	11-2
	16	16-1	14-4	12-6	9-8
	24	14-1	11-9	10-2	7-11
2 × 8	12	23-4	20-10	18-8	14-3
	16	21-2	18-0	16-2	12-4
	24	18-3	14-9	13-2	10-1
2 × 10	12	26-0	24-9	22-3	16-10
	16	26-0	21-5	19-3	14-7
	24	22-0	17-6	15-9	11-11

(Courtesy Southern Pine Marketing Council)

Rafters—Heavy Roofing; No Finished Ceiling; Snow Load (Empirical Design Values), 30 psf Live Load, 20 psf Dead Load, *l*/180, $C_D = 1.15$

Size (inches)	Spacing (inches on center)	Grade			
		Select Structural	No. 1	No. 2	No. 3
2 × 4	12	9-10	9-8	9-0	6-9
	16	8-11	8-8	7-9	5-10
	24	7-10	7-1	6-4	4-9
2 × 6	12	15-6	14-10	12-11	10-0
	16	14-1	12-10	11-2	8-8
	24	12-3	10-6	9-1	7-1
2 × 8	12	20-5	18-8	16-8	12-9
	16	18-6	16-2	14-5	11-0
	24	16-2	13-2	11-10	9-0
2 × 10	12	26-0	22-2	19-11	15-1
	16	23-8	19-2	17-3	13-0
	24	19-8	15-8	14-1	10-8

(Courtesy Southern Pine Marketing Council)

These spans are based on the 1993 AFPA (formerly NFPA) Span Tables for Joists and Rafters and the 1991 SPIB Grading Rules. They are intended for use in covered structures or where the moisture content in use does not exceed 19 percent for an extended period of time. Loading conditions are expressed in psf (pounds per square foot). Deflection is limited to span in inches divided by 180 and is based on live load only. The load duration factor, C_D, is 1.15 for snow loads. Check sources of supply for availability of lumber in lengths greater than 20′0″.

Appendix M

Western Lumber Floor Joist Spans, Feet and Inches

Floor Joists—(Empirical Design Values) 30 psf Live Load, 10 psf Dead Load, *l*/360

Species or Group	Grade	2 × 6			2 × 8			2 × 10			2 × 12		
Span →		12″ oc	16″ oc	24″ oc	12″ oc	16″ oc	24″ oc	12″ oc	16″ oc	24″ oc	12″ oc	16″ oc	24″ oc
Douglas Fir-Larch	Sel. Struc.	12-6	11-4	9-11	16-6	15-0	13-1	21-0	19-1	16-8	25-7	23-3	20-3
	No. 1 & Btr.	12-3	11-2	9-9	16-2	14-8	12-10	20-8	18-9	16-1	25-1	22-10	18-8
	No. 1	12-0	10-11	9-7	15-10	14-5	12-4	20-3	18-5	15-0	21-8	21-4	17-5
	No. 2	11-10	10-9	9-1	15-7	14-1	11-6	19-10	17-2	14-1	23-0	19-11	16-3
	No. 3	9-8	8-5	6-10	12-4	10-8	8-8	15-0	13-0	10-7	17-5	15-1	12-4
Douglas Fir-South	Sel. Struc.	11-3	10-3	8-11	14-11	13-6	11-10	19-0	17-3	15-1	23-1	21-0	18-4
	No. 1	11-0	10-0	8-9	14-6	13-2	11-6	18-6	16-10	14-3	22-6	20-3	16-6
	No. 2	10-9	9-9	8-6	14-2	12-10	11-2	18-0	16-5	13-8	21-11	19-4	15-10
	No. 3	9-6	8-2	6-8	12-0	10-5	8-6	14-8	12-8	10-4	17-0	14-8	12-0
Hem-Fir	Sel. Struc.	11-10	10-9	9-4	15-7	14-2	12-4	19-10	18-0	15-9	24-2	21-11	19-2
	No. 1 & Btr.	11-7	10-6	9-2	15-3	13-10	12-1	19-5	17-8	15-5	23-7	21-6	17-10
	No. 1	11-7	10-6	9-2	15-3	13-10	12-0	19-5	17-8	14-8	23-7	20-9	17-0
	No. 2	11-0	10-0	8-9	14-6	13-2	11-4	18-6	16-10	13-10	22-6	19-8	16-1
	No. 3	9-8	8-5	6-10	12-4	10-8	8-8	15-0	13-0	10-7	17-5	15-1	12-4

Residential occupancy sleeping rooms (BOCA only). Attics with storage under the Standard Code. Does not apply in UBC areas.
(*Courtesy Western Wood Products Association*)

Floor Joists—(Empirical Design Values) 40 psf Live Load, 10 psf Dead Load, *l*/360

Species or Group	Grade	2 × 6			2 × 8			2 × 10			2 × 12		
Span →		12″ oc	16″ oc	24″ oc	12″ oc	16″ oc	24″ oc	12″ oc	16″ oc	24″ oc	12″ oc	16″ oc	24″ oc
Douglas Fir-Larch	Sel. Struc.	11-4	10-4	9-0	15-0	13-7	11-11	19-1	17-4	15-2	23-3	21-1	18-5
	No. 1 & Btr.	11-2	10-2	8-10	14-8	13-4	11-8	18-9	17-0	14-5	22-10	20-5	16-8
	No. 1	10-11	9-11	8-8	14-5	11-1	11-0	18-5	16-5	13-5	22-0	19-1	15-7
	No. 2	10-9	9-9	8-1	14-2	12-7	10-3	17-9	15-5	12-7	20-7	17-10	14-7
	No. 3	8-8	7-6	6-2	11-0	9-6	7-9	13-5	11-8	9-6	15-7	13-6	11-0
Douglas Fir-South	Sel. Struc.	10-3	9-4	8-2	13-6	12-3	10-9	17-3	15-8	13-8	21-0	19-1	16-8
	No. 1	10-0	9-1	7-11	13-2	12-0	10-5	16-10	15-3	12-9	20-6	18-1	14-9
	No. 2	9-9	8-10	7-9	12-10	11-8	10-0	16-5	14-11	12-2	19-11	17-4	14-2
	No. 3	8-6	7-4	6-0	10-9	9-3	7-7	13-1	11-4	9-3	15-2	13-2	10-9
Hem-Fir	Sel. Struc.	10-9	9-9	8-6	14-2	12-10	11-3	18-0	16-5	14-4	21-11	19-11	17-5
	No. 1 & Btr.	10-6	9-6	8-4	13-10	12-7	11-0	17-8	16-0	13-9	21-6	19-6	16-0
	No. 1	10-6	9-6	8-4	13-10	12-7	10-9	17-8	16-0	13-1	21-6	18-7	15-2
	No. 2	10-0	9-1	7-11	13-2	12-0	10-2	16-10	15-2	12-5	20-4	17-7	14-4
	No. 3	8-8	7-6	6-2	11-0	9-6	7-9	13-5	11-8	9-6	15-7	13-6	11-0

Residential occupancies include private dwelling, private apartment, and hotel guest rooms. Deck under CABO and Standard Codes.
(*Courtesy Western Wood Products Association*)

Appendix N

Western Lumber Ceiling Joist Spans, Feet and Inches

Ceiling Joists—(Empirical Design Values) 20 psf Live Load, 10 psf Dead Load, l/240

Species or Group	Grade	2 × 4			2 × 6			2 × 8			2 × 10		
		12″ oc	16″ oc	24″ oc	12″ oc	16″ oc	24″ oc	12″ oc	16″ oc	24″ oc	12″ oc	16″ oc	24″ oc
Douglas Fir-Larch	Sel. Struc.	10-5	9-6	8-3	16-4	14-11	13-0	21-7	19-7	17-1	27-6	25-0	20-11
	No. 1 & Btr.	10-3	9-4	8-1	16-1	14-7	12-0	21-2	18-8	15-3	26-4	22-9	18-7
	No. 1	10-0	9-1	7-8	15-9	13-9	11-2	20-1	17-5	14-2	24-6	21-3	17-4
	No. 2	9-10	8-9	7-2	14-10	12-10	10-6	18-9	16-3	13-3	22-11	19-10	16-3
	No. 3	7-8	6-8	5-5	11-2	9-8	7-11	14-2	12-4	10-0	17-4	15-0	12-3
Douglas Fir-South	Sel. Struc.	9-5	8-7	7-6	14-9	13-5	11-9	19-6	17-9	15-6	24-10	22-7	19-9
	No. 1	9-2	8-4	7-3	14-5	13-0	10-8	19-0	16-6	13-6	23-3	20-2	16-5
	No. 2	8-11	8-1	7-0	14-1	12-6	10-2	18-3	15-9	12-11	22-3	19-3	15-9
	No. 3	7-6	6-6	5-3	10-11	9-6	7-9	13-10	12-0	9-9	16-11	14-8	11-11
Hem-Fir	Sel. Struc.	9-10	8-11	7-10	15-6	14-1	12-3	20-5	18-6	16-2	26-0	23-8	20-6
	No. 1 & Btr.	9-8	8-9	7-8	15-2	13-9	11-6	19-11	17-10	14-7	25-2	21-9	17-9
	No. 1	9-8	8-9	7-6	15-2	13-5	10-11	19-7	16-11	13-10	23-11	20-8	16-11
	No. 2	9-2	8-4	7-1	14-5	12-8	10-4	18-6	16-0	13-1	22-7	19-7	16-0
	No. 3	7-8	6-8	5-5	11-2	9-8	7-11	14-2	12-4	10-0	17-4	15-0	12-3

Use these loading conditions for the following: Limited attic storage where development of future rooms is not possible. Ceilings where the roof pitch is steeper than 3 in 12. Where the clear height in the attic is greater than 30 inches. Drywall ceilings.
(*Courtesy Western Word Products Association*)

Appendix O

Western Lumber Rafter Spans, Feet and Inches

Roof Rafters—(Empirical Design Values) 20 psf Live Load, 15 psf Dead Load, *l*/180

Species or Group	Span Grade	2 × 6			2 × 8			2 × 10			2 × 12		
		12″ oc	16″ oc	24″ oc	12″ oc	16″ oc	24″ oc	12″ oc	16″ oc	24″ oc	12″ oc	16″ oc	24″ oc
Douglas Fir-Larch	Sel. Struc.	18-0	16-4	14-0	23-9	21-7	17-8	30-4	26-6	21-7	35-5	30-8	25-1
	No. 1 & Btr.	17-7	15-3	12-5	22-3	19-4	15-9	27-3	23-7	19-3	31-7	27-4	22-4
	No. 1	16-5	14-3	11-7	20-9	18-0	14-8	25-5	22-0	17-11	29-5	25-6	20-10
	No. 2	15-4	13-3	10-10	19-5	16-10	13-9	23-9	20-7	16-9	27-6	23-10	19-6
	No. 3	11-7	10-1	8-2	14-8	12-9	10-5	17-11	15-7	12-8	20-10	18-0	14-9
Douglas Fir-South	Sel. Struc.	16-3	14-9	12-11	21-5	19-6	16-9	27-5	24-10	20-6	33-4	29-1	23-9
	No. 1	15-7	13-6	11-0	19-9	17-1	13-11	24-1	20-10	17-0	27-11	24-2	19-9
	No. 2	14-11	12-11	10-6	18-10	16-4	13-4	23-1	20-0	16-4	26-9	23-2	18-11
	No. 3	11-4	9-10	8-0	14-4	12-5	10-2	17-6	15-2	12-4	20-3	17-7	14-4
Hem-Fir	Sel. Struc.	17-0	15-6	13-6	22-5	20-5	17-5	28-7	26-0	21-3	34-10	30-2	24-8
	No. 1 & Btr.	16-8	14-7	11-11	21-4	18-5	15-1	26-0	22-6	18-5	30-2	26-1	21-4
	No. 1	16-0	13-10	11-4	20-3	17-6	14-4	24-9	21-5	17-6	28-8	24-10	20-3
	No. 2	15-2	13-1	10-8	19-2	16-7	13-7	23-5	20-3	16-7	27-2	23-6	19-2
	No. 3	11-7	10-1	8-2	14-8	12-9	10-5	17-11	15-7	12-8	20-10	18-0	14-9

No snow load. Roof slope greater than 3 in 12. Heavy roof covering. No ceiling finish. (*Courtesy Western Wood Products Association*)

Roof Rafters—(Empirical Design Values) 30 psf Snow Load, 15 psf Dead Load, *l*/180

Species or Group	Span Grade	2 × 6			2 × 8			2 × 10			2 × 12		
		12″ oc	16″ oc	24″ oc	12″ oc	16″ oc	24″ oc	12″ oc	16″ oc	24″ oc	12″ oc	16″ oc	24″ oc
Douglas Fir-Larch	Sel. Struc.	15-9	14-4	11-10	20-9	18-4	15-0	25-10	22-5	18-3	30-0	26-0	21-2
	No. 1 & Btr.	14-11	12-11	10-6	18-10	16-4	13-4	23-0	19-11	16-3	26-8	23-1	18-11
	No. 1	13-11	12-0	9-10	17-7	15-3	12-5	21-6	18-7	15-2	24-11	21-7	17-7
	No. 2	13-0	11-3	9-2	16-5	14-3	11-8	20-1	17-5	14-2	23-3	20-2	16-6
	No. 3	9-10	8-6	6-11	12-5	10-9	8-9	15-2	13-2	10-9	17-7	15-3	12-5
Douglas Fir-South	Sel. Struc.	14-3	12-11	11-2	18-9	17-0	14-2	23-11	21-2	17-4	28-5	24-7	20-1
	No. 1	13-2	11-5	9-4	16-8	14-5	11-9	20-4	17-8	14-5	23-7	20-5	16-8
	No. 2	12-7	10-11	8-11	16-0	13-10	11-3	19-6	16-11	13-9	22-7	19-7	16-0
	No. 3	9-7	8-3	6-9	12-1	10-6	8-7	14-10	12-10	10-6	17-2	14-10	12-2
Hem-Fir	Sel. Struc.	14-10	13-6	11-7	19-7	17-10	14-8	25-0	22-0	18-0	29-6	25-6	20-10
	No. 1 & Btr.	14-3	12-4	10-1	18-0	15-7	12-9	22-0	19-1	15-7	25-6	22-1	18-0
	No. 1	13-6	11-9	9-7	17-2	14-10	12-1	20-11	18-1	14-10	24-3	21-0	17-2
	No. 2	12-10	11-1	9-1	16-2	14-0	11-6	19-10	17-2	14-0	22-11	19-11	16-3
	No. 3	9-10	8-6	6-11	12-5	10-9	8-9	15-2	13-2	10-9	17-7	15-3	12-5

Roof slope greater than 3 in 12. Heavy roof covering. No ceiling finish. (*Courtesy Western Wood Products Association*)

Appendix P

Typical Loads for Glulam Beams

Typical Loads* for Glulam Roof Beams**

Span in feet	Roof Beam 3″ ×			
	6	9	12	15
10	272	745	1104	1380
14	———	335	676	986
16	———	224	518	789
20	———	115	272	505

Typical Loads* for Glulam Floor Beams**

Span in feet	Floor Beam 3″ ×			
	6	9	12	15
8	266	896	1200	1500
14	———	167	397	774
16	———	112	266	519
20	———	———	136	266

* Loads shown are pounds per lineal foot including weight of beam.
** Applicable for straight, simply supported beams.
(Consult the manufacturer for specific load data.)

Appendix Q

Metric Conversion

Feet and Inch Conversions

1 inch	=	25.4mm
1 foot	=	304.8mm
1 psi	=	6.89kPa
1 psf	=	0.048kPa

mm	=	millimetre
m	=	metre
kPa	=	kilopascal
psi	=	pounds per square inch
psf	=	pounds per square foot

Metric Conversions

1 mm	=	0.039 inches
1 m	=	3.28 feet
1 kPa	=	20.88 psf

Inches to Millimetres and Centimetres
MM—millimetres   CM—centimetres

Inches	MM	CM	Inches	CM	Inches	CM
⅛	3	0.3	9	22.9	30	76.2
¼	6	0.6	10	25.4	31	78.7
⅜	10	1.0	11	27.9	32	81.3
½	13	1.3	12	30.5	33	83.8
⅝	16	1.6	13	33.0	34	86.4
¾	19	1.9	14	35.6	35	88.9
⅞	22	2.2	15	38.1	36	91.4
1	25	2.5	16	40.6	37	94.0
1¼	32	3.2	17	43.2	38	96.5
1½	38	3.8	18	45.7	39	99.1
1¾	44	4.4	19	48.3	40	101.6
2	51	5.1	20	50.8	41	104.1
2½	64	6.4	21	53.3	42	106.7
3	76	7.6	22	55.9	43	109.2
3½	89	8.9	23	58.4	44	111.8
4	102	10.2	24	61.0	45	114.3
4½	114	11.4	25	63.5	46	116.8
5	127	12.7	26	66.0	47	119.4
6	152	15.2	27	68.6	48	121.9
7	178	17.8	28	71.1	49	124.5
8	203	20.3	29	73.7	50	127.0

Appendix R

Associations Involved in the Grading, Manufacturing, and Promotion of Wood and Related Products

United States

American Lumber Standards Committee
P O Box 210
Germantown, MD 20875-0210

American Plywood Association
P O Box 11700
Tacoma, WA 98411-1700

California Lumber Inspection Service
1885 The Alameda
P O Box 6989
San Jose, CA 95150

California Redwood Association
405 Enfrente Drive, Suite 200
Novato, CA 94949

National Forest Products Association
1250 Connecticut Ave, NW
Washington, DC 20036

Northeastern Lumber Manufacturers Association
272 Tuttle Road
P O Box 87A
Cumberland Center, ME 04021

Northern Softwood Lumber Bureau
P O Box 87A
Cumberland Center, ME 04021

Pacific Lumber Inspection Bureau, Inc.
P O Box 7235
Bellevue, WA 98000-1235

Redwood Inspection Service
405 Enfrente Drive, Suite 200
Novato, CA 94949

Southern Forest Products Association
P O Box 64170
Kenner, LA 70064

Southern Pine Inspection Bureau
4709 Scenic Highway
Pensacola, FL 32504-9094

Timber Products Inspection
P O Box 919
Conyers, GA 30207

West Coast Lumber Inspection Bureau
P O Box 23145
Portland, OR 97223

Western Wood Products Association
Yeon Building
522 S.W. Fifth Ave.
Portland, OR 97204-2122

Canada

Alberta Forest Products Association
11710 Kingsway Ave., Suite 104
Edmonton, Alberta, Canada T5G 0X5

Canadian Lumberman's Association
27 Goulbourn Ave.
Ottawa, Ontario, Canada K1N 8C7

Canadian Wood Council
1730 St. Laurent Blvd., Suite 350
Ottawa, Ontario, Canada K1G 5L1

Cariboo Lumber Manufacturers Assocation
197 Second Ave. North, Suite 301
Williams Lake, British Columbia, Canada V2G 1Z5

Central Forest Products Association, Inc.
P O Box 1169
Hudson Bay, Saskatchewan, Canada S0E 0Y0

Council of Forest Industries of British Columbia
555 Burrard St., Suite 1200
Vancouver, British Columbia, Canada V7X 1S7

Interior Lumber Manufacturers Association
1855 Kirschner Road, Suite 350
Kelowna, British Columbia, Canada V1Y 4N7

MacDonald Inspection
211 School House Street
Coquitlam, British Columbia, Canada V3K 4X9

Maritime Lumber Bureau
P O Box 459
Amherst, Nova Scotia, Canada B4H 4A1

National Lumber Grades Authority
260-1055 West Hastings St.
Vancouver, British Columbia, Canada V6E 2E9

Ontario Lumber Manufacturers Association
55 University Ave., Suite 325
P O Box 8
Toronto, Ontario, Canada M5J 2H7

Pacific Lumber Inspection Bureau
1110-355 Burrard St.
Vancouver, British Columbia, Canada V6C 2G8

Quebec Lumber Manufacturers Association
5055 Boulevard Hamel West, Suite 200
Quebec, Quebec, Canada G2E 2G6

Western Red Cedar Lumber Association
1200-555 Burrard St.
Vancouver, British Columbia, Canada V7X 1S7

Index